Scattershot

Scattershot

LIFE, MUSIC, ELTON AND ME

BERNIE TAUPIN

monoray

First published in Great Britain in 2023 by Monoray, an imprint of
Octopus Publishing Group Ltd
Carmelite House
50 Victoria Embankment
London EC4Y 0DZ
www.octopusbooks.co.uk

An Hachette UK Company
www.hachette.co.uk

Published in the United States by Hachette Books, an imprint of Perseus Books, LLC,
a subsidiary of Hachette Book Group, Inc.
1290 Avenue of the Americas
New York, NY 10104

ISBN 978-1-80096-075-6 (hardback)
ISBN 978-1-80096-078-7 (trade paperback)

A CIP catalogue record for this book is available from the British Library.

Cover design by Mel Four
Print book interior design by Jeff Williams

Printed in Great Britain

10 9 8 7 6 5 4 3 2 1

Portions of "Bernie Taupin's Visual Anthem" by Richard Bailey, MA, are reprinted
by permission of the author. The essay originally appeared in the 2020
exhibition catalog *Bernie Taupin: American Anthem*.

Song credits appear on page 399.

This FSC® label means that materials used for the product have been responsibly sourced

MIX
Paper | Supporting
responsible forestry
FSC
www.fsc.org   FSC® C104740

For Heather, Charley & Georgey, obviously.
Elton, naturally.

I was looking for America in a western movie /
Saw a young gunslinger with something to prove

—BERNIE TAUPIN
"Last Stand in Open Country"

In repentance and rest is your salvation,
in quietness and trust is your strength.

—ISAIAH 30:15

Contents

Author's Note

I never intended this to be a conventional autobiography. My brain doesn't work that way. I have no sense of specific timelines, and recollections and dates are as bad as my sense of direction. Simple detail eludes me. In the same way, I'm characteristically immune to manuals, mathematics, and legalese. My attention span is terrible, especially when it involves subject matter that doesn't interest me. It all comes from an overloaded brain that's incapable of shutting down. If there is anyone who could use the part of it that lays dormant, it's me. Alright, I know that's a myth, but my point is it never goes to sleep. At night it simply switches over to dream mode and I dream concurrently nonstop. If I wander off on a separate tangent during a particular narrative in this book, blame it on this affliction. There's just too much going on in that compartment to ply myself with established restrictions. At the same time don't confuse this disorder with any sort of hyperintelligence; I'm by no means Mr. Big Brain. I just like stuff, and when stuff interests me I seem to be incapable of dispersing it accordingly. It just stays front and center, bouncing about, refusing to settle down and let one thing come after another. Damn this *me, me, me* brain.

Lou Reed said, "Just because I wrote it doesn't mean I know what it's about." Lou was right. What people want isn't always what I can provide. Information on lyrical composition isn't always forthcoming, certainly not when the keys to recall are lost. Who, and why, and what they're about is ponderable, but never definitive. In my catalog I've got as many of those as I've got the painfully obvious, and an equal number that are esoteric and inspired by some specific source. Bennie, as in the Jets, was based on the Maschinenmensch in Fritz Lang's *Metropolis*, and "All the Girls Love Alice" was inspired by the 1968 black comedy *The Killing of Sister George*. That's if you're interested, and a great deal of our fan base are. That's fine, and I'm happy to oblige if I can remember. The thing is, what's important isn't so much trivia as pleasurable emersion into reverie. Songs should be treated not only as escapism but as thought-provoking in the same way as motion pictures or modern art. Take a ride and invest yourself in letting your ears create visuals that are your own invention. Don't rely on me—I'm liable to make things up.

Once Upon a Time in the West End

Mighty oaks from tiny acorns grow.

—HENRY FORD

L ondon, late 1967. What am I doing? Keeping my mouth shut and trying to remain as inconspicuous as possible. Where am I? In a tiny recording studio tucked in the rear of Dick James's palatial music publishing offices on New Oxford Street. Why am I here? To meet a certain piano player called Reg Dwight, who I've been informed will be somewhere hereabouts.

Along with the sound engineer and the tape op (words I will only become acquainted with in the months to come), there are half a dozen sartorially well-heeled and impressively coiffed young men in the room. The one lounging to my left, skinny, tall, and criminally good-looking, turns and eyes me laconically, telling me, "I dig your shades." I present him with an appreciative nod, having absolutely no idea what he's referring to other than the fact that I'm thrilled that there indeed may be something about me that he "digs."

Understand that back then I was what decades later would be considered "tragically unhip." In my peacoat and bland pants, I was merely nondescript, a product of the medieval North. Where once I was Jack the Lad in my backyard, I am now a floundering Dick Whittington. But chance is an angel, and I have in my simple wisdom answered an ad placed by Liberty Records in the *New Musical Express* seeking talent.

I'm not sure if I have any—it remains to be determined—but I'm giving it a shot, and according to my Liberty contact, Reg Dwight might be the answer.

Alright . . . back to the studio. Anonymity temporarily secure, I glance up and notice a TV on the wall above the recording console. On the grainy black-and-white screen, I make out the blurry image of someone sitting and playing the piano. I'm made aware by the conversation around me that this individual is actually only several strides down the hall in the connecting studio, where he is, according to my laconic friend, "laying down an overdub."

I'm swimming upstream against a strong current of groovy terminology and surrounded by severe trendiness, but I throw caution to the wind and inquire of my Byronesque acquaintance, "Could that blur on the screen be a certain Reg Dwight?"

As he concurs, things get ugly. The engineer swivels around in his chair and demands to know if I'm supposed to be there. All eyes on me, I turn the color of Beelzebub's ass and attempt to explain just as the door opens.

Heads swivel theatrically. Enter Reg Dwight, asking if there might be a Bernie Taupin in the room. I don't know Reg, but I love him already. He's refreshingly square, chunky with Buddy Holly glasses and a kind face. More so, imperative to my dignity, he is unadorned by embroidery and crushed velvet.

Introductions wait until we have repaired to the street and I have commenced breathing. Apparently, Reg plays in a band backing the six-foot-seven blues belter Long John Baldry while making some extra cash performing on demos. We adjourn to the Lancaster Grill around the corner on Charing Cross Road, a block from the legendary Denmark Street, London's Tin Pan Alley. Incidentally, an urban myth will later circulate that I wrote the lyrics to "Your Song" sitting on the roof of a building on this street, but, hey, that's another story.

We talk: the conversation is easy. We eat: eggs, sausage, and baked beans. We bond on music: a connection that will never be broken. I'm a country kid, still wet behind the ears; he's shy like me but experienced in the local music territory. He wants to write songs; so do I, and best of all, he likes what I've written so far . . . "Do I have more?" I do indeed. It's fanciful stuff, whimsical and somewhat pretentious, but in keeping with the trends of psychedelia and Hobbitism.

I like him tremendously because he's not condescending. I sense a kindred spirit: we're outsiders looking for a way in, and I'm willing to play along, Sancho Panza to his Don Quixote. We agree to give it a shot . . . let's go tilt some windmills. There's nervous energy in the air, a feeling of possibility. I leave the café invigorated and head for the Underground.

Hell, what have I got to lose? I'll give it a month and see what happens.

What's It All About, BT?

But his dreams were as gigantic as
his surroundings were small.
—THOMAS HARDY
Jude the Obscure

There's a small boy in a summer field. His games ride the wind, he has an army of thousands at his back and his knees are brown and bruised from battle. The sun, high and warm in the waking hours of the day, spreads across his theater setting the stage for adventure propelled by the written word. A short, small, gray concrete bridge over a trickling stream is only so in a reality that is currently uninhabited. In the child's mind it is the Pons Sublicius across the Tiber River and he is Horatius. There is no absolute quiet, no dragonfly whir, no birdsong along the hedgerows, only the cacophony of the Etruscan horde as he makes his stand and slays the great Lord of Luna.

Deeds of heroism torn from the pages of classical poetic narrative ignite his imagination. They are the fuel of his backstory, pumped into his mental treasury by literary disciples and loving hands. Played out in the medieval landscapes of a wild and thorny East Midlands, under blue skies of buffeting cumulus clouds on spacious verdant terrain, he is Lancelot today and Lochinvar tomorrow. He is inventive, solitary in his pursuits, and unattached to others of his age who are confused and unfamiliar with the identities he assumes. Solitary is a trait that will follow him through his life, a characteristic that will enable his artistic goals while empowering him with solace in troubled times.

4

In due course, his penchant for acting out the heroic deeds of fictionalized characters from ancient times will be replaced with a roistering fervor for a more contemporary, but tarnished, antihero. One who lived and breathed in the real world. Bad to the bone or just deeply flawed, either way, he was complex and individualistic before being hijacked and neutered by Hollywood. The Samaritan they created from the blueprint bore no resemblance to the prototype. Scrubbed clean of trail dirt and shorn of bad intent he inhabits an embroidered shirt resplendent with fringe and sequins. His boots are shined, his hat is white, his palomino impossibly perfect. He sports a brace of pearl-handled silver pistols and carries a guitar. With a song on his lips, he rides regularly into the sunset, as the rising coda of his theme swells to a crescendo. One day, in a contrary mood, the boy will recollect him more fondly, but for now, this is not the cowboy he wants to be.

I WAS BORN in the county of Lincolnshire, England, and learned nothing in school. My education came through my mother, her father, and in the grooves of vinyl albums. My memories of secondary school are of fog and damp, soggy leaden soccer balls, and hulking provincial thugs in donkey jackets and Wellington boots. Blousy teenage girls, already pining for the plastic factory, twittered collectively and dreamed of teddy boy boyfriends and Babycham. Idealism in short supply, theirs was to marry young and to fade into domesticity. It was a time of simple aspirations, repetition stifling any air of expectancy. I watched my teachers coexist with the ideology of "like father, like son" and the low value of female worth. Their skills in the classroom bordered on brute force and questionable ethics to get the job done. They taught only the basics, never venturing to indoctrinate any hint of modernity. It was a mystifying contemptuousness that did a disservice to their calling, a mothballed logic that reeked of apathy. It was abundantly clear we weren't worth it, a fact that had me believe that daring to be different was tantamount to treason.

After the war, my father resumed his employment in a comparatively changed world. Pre-conflict, he had abandoned any citified pursuits in favor of country living. Rather than suffer the indignity of life as a low-level drone, he chose to forge his own path in a part of the country steeped in Roman history and predominantly agrarian activity. My mother, because she loved him, had forsaken the artistic and cultural benefits of cosmopolitan life to be his rock. I believe that swapping the gratifications of urbanity for a different aesthetic was one of the bravest things she ever did in her life. For a woman as idiosyncratic and completely in the thrall of every facet of the arts, it was a choice that could not have been made easily. Together my parents were a contrast in diversity. My father, a man of old-fashioned sensibilities, used his words sparingly. Gruff on the exterior, his love for his sons was as big as the county he chose to call home. I would, in due course, acquire their individual proclivities, inheriting my mother's artistic panorama and my father's emotional reticence while adopting his ability to see through everyone else's bullshit.

The inconsistency of our homes from the year of my birth in 1950 to the banner year of my big adventure in 1967 was of distinct variance. Within the space of a few odd years, we had moved from the primitive and isolated semidetached farmhouse where I was born into a spacious limestone manor house built in the eighteenth century. It was a significant bump, a generous perk of the large local agricultural and livestock estate where my father was employed as farm manager. Our relocation to this inexplicably fancy upgrade was a boon for us all, and it was there that the presence of my grandfather was most keenly felt. We called him Poppy, and his knee was a learning chair. He dispensed wisdom with a warm uncomplicated joy, a love for the subject matter validated by the twinkle in his eyes. His gentle coaxing facilitated a quest for creative expression and instilled in me innumerable passions, most notably caring for the quality of words and the stimulation of verse. A master of arts and educator by profession, he was the teacher I was never going to encounter in the classroom. I was only eleven years old when he died, but he remains an indelible memory. The day he passed away is the only time I ever saw my mother cry.

My father's desire to strike out on his own was eventually understandable. I can't honestly recall us complaining too much, even though the prospect of duplicating our current accommodations was seriously doubtful. The day we left, my mother and I sat together on a window seat in the empty dining room. Between us on a large linen napkin was a yellow sponge cake. On the napkin were printed images of idyllic green pastures and horses frolicking behind rustic fence lines. I remember it clearly as if it were yesterday. I recollect being enchanted by these depictions. They looked foreign and unrelated to any kind of farming I'd ever seen and appeared to be of another world far away. Pointing at the pictures on the napkin, I looked up at my mother and said, "I want to live there."

Whatever pipe dreams I may have embraced temporarily, it couldn't have prepared me for the harsh reality of self-employment. What my father had sprung for was the mother of all fixer-uppers. A dilapidated two-story stone farmhouse fronting an expansive run-down, overgrown yard containing a broken-down barn and a long, grubby brick battery house. Chickens! So that was it; he was staking his claim on eggs. For a guy who knew his livestock, it seemed a strange alternative and not one I expected. However, in a world where God's hand deals the cards, it's chickens that would ultimately play a major role in designating my future.

The house had serious antiquated flair. It was an enumeration of code violations and infractions that would see it condemned by contemporary standards. The electricity was iffy, the plumbing antiquated, and the floors uneven. Upstairs the boards creaked and swelled, and in winter the only warmth was emitted by paltry two-bar heaters and a fireplace in the living room. Our one toilet was a green metal portable potty in the cellar. Ventilated by a couple of yards of corrugated piping that snaked haphazardly out a small upper window, it was a garish contraption. Looking like a bad science experiment, it was equally as uncomfortable as it was intimidating. In the dead of winter, descending the stairs to utilize it gave literal meaning to the term "freezing your ass off."

All this being said, the front room was frequently cheerful, especially on Sunday afternoons when the family was sequestered together after church and lunch. It was all very Thomas Hardy, the quintessential hearth and home, the coal fire glow countering the combative window rattling of the north wind.

There was a comforting drowsiness, a protective blanket of intimacy that imbued the room with a natural warmth. In the muted light of the gray afternoon, I remember the hypnotic glow of embers, a bath in a tin tub by the fire, and the radio.

The big boxy wireless sitting in the window brought into our home a curious blend of entertainment. I can't remember liking it that much, but it's all we had. It was all about familiarity that brought some anachronistic frivolity to what would otherwise be a quiet Sunday afternoon. It had become a ritual, a roster of eclectic fare that began at noon with the boisterous cockney bandleader Billy Cotton bellowing out his trademark cry, "Wakey-Wakey." This heralded an inexhaustible fifty minutes of variety-style musical merriment and straitlaced crooning. The *Billy Cotton Band Show* was followed by *The Clitheroe Kid*, a show featuring the numbskull escapades of a four-foot-two-inch, forty-year-old man playing an eleven-year-old schoolboy. In an era when Archie Andrews (a ventriloquist dummy) was on the radio, I suppose this premise wasn't that odd.

The village we'd settled in was Owmby-by-Spital. Quaintly named but not unusual in the British countryside, and completely indicative of Lincolnshire where the customary "by" indicated it was once a settlement of the Danes. At the time of our arrival there were roughly three hundred inhabitants, one small general store, a gas station, and an electrician—that was it. It dated back to the reign of William the Conqueror, the first Norman monarch of England. At night, unless the moon made an exception, it was black as ink and as still as the grave. By day it wasn't a whole lot livelier, tranquility being the omnipresent climate. Outside of the occasional tractor or car, human traffic was sparse. When the snows came in winter, the village disappeared.

It was the countryside surrounding the village that I owned. An expansive acreage of abundant locations on which to roam and propagate my quests. Before my burgeoning teenage years brought down the curtain on these productions, I lived my days long and lost in an independent state of innovation. I was selfish with my time, paying little heed to the industrious purpose of my father. I collected a few eggs but felt no compulsion to do much else. The battery was loud and unpleasant, hundreds of individual cramped cages full of squawking birds with little to do but be angry. Outside of producing eggs, they filled the air with a film of oily feather residue and crapped incessantly. Deposits of the latter accumulated in pyramid mounds beneath their cages where it was bulldozed into pits at either end of the building by a rotating plough. Yes, pits of shit, and thankfully not a job for a small boy. Shoveling out these trenches was about as bad as it could get, but Lord love him, my father got down in there and got it done. If there's one thing it proved to me, it was the ingenuity and resolve of my father, because in a short space of time he'd tidied up the place and started building a new home for us. With little help other than his own two hands, in under a year he built a very practical red brick bungalow. It might not have won any architectural prizes, but it wasn't going to fall down around our ears.

It was in this home that I spent the remainder of my time before fate played a winning hand six years later. I was eleven when we transferred from "the old house," as it became known from then on. Along with our move to a more reliable structure came a significant change in my interests. I buried my nose in books, made friends with some locals, and fell under the spell of music. Pre-Beatles, what was generally listened to north of London was American rock and roll. Interestingly enough, Elvis wasn't that big a deal in and around our area. Whether or not it had something to do with his refusal to tour outside the States, thus creating a lack of familiarity, I couldn't say. It was a fact, though, that the artists who had played regionally were those in favor. The Everly Brothers, Buddy Holly, Roy Orbison, Gene Vincent, and in particular Eddie Cochran were certainly the flames that burned brightest.

At the same time that music was seducing me, so was a thirst for a deeper understanding of the American West. Never having succumbed to the sterilized cowboy, pious do-gooders were regarded with a smattering of contempt. I'd seen a couple of John Ford movies and had loved Fred Zinnemann's *High Noon* starring Gary Cooper, all of which had helped in dispelling the image of a sanitized culture. I'd also gotten ahold of books, namely Stuart Lake's *Wyatt Earp*, Walter Lord's Alamo account *A Time to Stand*, and eventually Ramon F. Adams's *Six-Guns and Saddle Leather.* The first two would in time be debunked by historical reappraisal, but the latter was a meticulously compiled reference and guidebook to everything written about law keepers and the lawless. Years later, of course, Sergio Leone, Clint Eastwood, and most indelibly Sam Peckinpah would restore realism to the genre and eradicate clichés. For now it was hunt and peck on my part to find fragments of the truth, and as I did, the more I learned the more I felt an affiliation with something not part of my upbringing. This cross-pollination of visuals and a certain kind of music would ultimately create a gravitational pull not easily ignored.

By the time I'd failed my eleven-plus (the basic exam to determine if you were worth an academic education or not), I was deeply under the spell of country music, or at least as much of it that existed on the airwaves. Johnny Horton was the first artist who had cut through the pabulum churned out on the BBC. Songs like "North to Alaska," "The Battle of New Orleans," and "Sink the Bismarck" were narratives that stood out among the bland pop dreck that made up the majority of the typical playlists. The life changer, though, was Marty Robbins's bittersweet cowboy ballad "El Paso." This was the blue touch paper and led to his 1959 album *Gunfighter Ballads and Trail Songs,* which became the first album I ever owned. It remains to this day the single most influential record of my early years before The Band's *Music from Big Pink* encouraged me to follow my instincts in 1968. When it came to the crunch, I knew I wanted to write stories.

My musical epiphanies were popping up all over the place, but little did I know that a history lesson was waiting just down the road. But first, a detour.

HAVING SURVIVED THE customary servitude at the secondary modern school in Market Rasen, a bus ride of seven miles from our village, an appointment had been made for me to meet with the local youth employment officer. It was a perfunctory ordeal conducted by a bland, tweedy civil servant sucking on a pipe. In a cubicle the color of sick, one could only imagine how many rejects spat out of the secondary school system had been given few options by someone with so little enthusiasm. Girls were encouraged to take up factory jobs, and the boys farmwork or an apprenticeship of some sort. For the most part, these options were expected and desirous for the majority, and any inquiries as to a creative or nonmanual career was treated like Oliver Twist asking for more.

I was fifteen years old, the dismissal age for the working class equivalent of cannon fodder. In our educational holding pen we were herded in for a few paltry years and tossed out unceremoniously to pad out the rank and file. Somewhat intimidated by my apathetic drone, I attempted to hedge around the employment officer's suggestions of ditch digging in favor of something more cosmopolitan. He seemed thrown by this, and like a monkey with an abacus he attempted to assimilate this solicitation, resetting his usual shtick for a more devious way to stifle my request. While I was thinking journalism, a Jimmy Olsen cub reporter sort of thing, he second bested me with a job printing the paper rather than writing for it. I folded and agreed. What was I to do? I needed a job. Palpable smugness brightening his face, he rubber-stamped "position filled," and shooed me out, hopes dashed, mission accomplished.

When your former classmates are composed of boys nicknamed Bonehead, Wiggy, and Grunter, it's pretty much preordained that novelist and playwright aren't in the cards. Still, exceptions should have been made, giving an inch of possibility to those who might have envisioned a stepping stone to something better. I really don't recall how deep my disappointment ran, I can only remember turning up for my first day of work with not much enthusiasm and a sense of grim resolve. Perhaps it wasn't going to be all that bad; maybe, just maybe, I'd fold into the fabric of blue-collar life. After all, it was honest work, union benefits, and decent prospects. Agh, but that was it; the prospects bit. The finality of this outcome set in when at my interview I was informed that after six years on the floor and enrollment in night school I'd receive my diploma when I was twenty-one.

Six years! I hadn't even thought about it in those terms. It seemed like a lifetime, like entering a dark airless chamber and having the door disappear. Once I saw where I'd be working, this assessment seemed even more like a reality.

On my arrival, I was introduced to the foreman, Frank, a grubby little man in brown overalls and a pockmarked face full of blackheads. After a pep talk about workplace protocol, including a no tolerance rule for smoking and profanity, contradictory in nature given that Frank smoked like a chimney, I was ushered into what was to be my lot in life.

The shop floor of the Lincolnshire Standard Group was a massive Dickensian space full of thundering machinery and ink-stained men in leather aprons. Of course, everyone smoked and swore profusely, shouting and cussing above the roar of the presses.

It was all downhill from day one. I never attended one class of night school, I had little or no enthusiasm for the work at hand, and while my fellow workers were affable enough, the overall barrage of conformity was stifling. Frank was always hovering around, getting in my ear about his socialist agenda and the horrors of pop music.

I began to undermine the principles that Frank so openly embraced. Besides being a total Bolshevik, he was also horribly racist, which seemed curious given the fact that I don't think there was a single Black person in the entire county of Lincolnshire.

So with slacking on my part very much in evidence, and the prominent installation of record albums like Otis Redding's *Otis Blue* and Brownie McGhee and Sonny Terry's *At The Bunkhouse* on display by my lunchbox, Frank's apoplexy upon his realization was palatable. I also started smoking, even challenging Frank on the hypocrisy of his edict, pointing out that I appeared to be the only one on the floor not lighting up. Gratifyingly, these breaches of authority seemed to confuse him and he began to distance himself from any confrontation with me, obviously preferring not to break in a new hand. Why didn't I just resign? Eventually I did, well not quite. I just didn't show up one day, and that was it.

ON THE WEEKENDS, my friends and I would ride our thumbs around the surrounding villages and towns. Pubs back then paid little heed to the rules and regulations of the law, for while the legal age to drink was eighteen, we were bellying up to the bar at fifteen years old. From early adolescence, when I was hoisted onto a stool to sing a few verses of "Barbara Allen," pubs radiated a special invitational magic. Back then we played a lot of snooker, ate in cheap transport dives, and slept in barns, empty buildings, and cricket pavilions. We kept warm with cheap whisky, wore army surplus, and probably smelled pretty bad. We also thought we were all that and a bag of chips, hitchhiking rebels mirroring the exploits of the great American itinerants. Hardly. In reality, we were in fact just transient beatniks with a penchant for petty thievery and an aversion to soap and water.

What happened next was completely ironic. I got a job working on a poultry farm. Instability assured without money and embarrassed at the thought of becoming completely indolent at home, I grasped at the first straw to come along. This was a broiler chicken operation located on isolated acreage a couple of miles west of the neighboring village. Generally frowned upon these days, broiler chickens are raised specifically for meat production. Of course, the cruelty of it all was lost to me in those days, drudgery being my only complaint. My job? A complete dogsbody, hired to toil under a manipulative and solitary regime.

The dictator in question was the operational manager, Mike. Mike was a clever bastard. Masquerading under the guise of benevolent big brother, he decided to take me under his wing while ingratiating himself by way of a hip repartee. He had me at first with his admiration for American jazz drummer Louie Bellson, not something you'd expect from someone running a chicken farm in Lincolnshire.

Mike's strategy was to make it look like he was doing all the work when he was doing none at all. He'd start something, show me the ropes, pretend he was needed elsewhere, and leave me to do the lion's share. I was there at 6 a.m. while he'd show up at 10, professing to have been up since 5. Mike was the kind of guy who if you were drowning in quicksand, he'd charge you for the rope to pull you out.

It was tough, strenuously hard work that made my days on the factory floor pale by comparison. Also Frank, while being a complete dick, was at least upfront in being a dick, unlike Mike who was devious, a liar, secretly imperious, and lazy to boot.

I worked grinding hours, either toiling in the stuffy broiler sheds, with little ventilation and under narcoleptic fluorescence, or outside where the bitter wind blew hard and cold across the flat farmland from the North Sea. There was, however, a raw beauty in the hardscrabble landscape, a sort of witchy primitive amalgamation of fertility and brittle expiration. Things were certainly better when Mike wasn't around, which was often, and having spent so much of my young life in solitary pursuits for hours on end was no problem. This was by no means the soft cradle of summer greenery and prodigious secrecy that had enchanted me in my formative years. No, this was blissfully barbaric.

Somewhere in the Bible it says, "You will do well to pay attention as to a lamp shining in a dark place." Cryptic perhaps, but very soon a series of incidents made sense of this statement in symbolic ways. One Saturday morning after my feeding stint was complete and Mike had run out of things for me to do, I hopped on my clapped out BSA Gold Star and took off for RAF Faldingworth. The RAF base was the home of an old school friend and had a furtive backstory in Cold War history. In the late 1950s, the site had become a nuclear weapons store for the RAF's V-bomber force. In times of crisis, missiles from the base would be distributed to nearby V-bomber airfields, a fact that gave rise to all manner of doom-laden schoolboy scenarios.

Although it was in the process of winding down, the base still housed air force personal and civilian employees northeast of the airfield. My friend had been one of the only people I'd really bonded with at secondary school, in as much as we shared a similar fatalistic overview of its "failure to communicate." We were on the front lawn, most likely recounting the horrors of our educational gulag and shooting the breeze in general, when I heard it.

The window of the house next door was open and from inside came a familiar sound. It was country music alright, but nothing like anything I'd heard before. Let me assure you, in Lincolnshire in 1966 you did not hear any kind of classic country music, anywhere. Certainly not like this, and certainly not wafting out a neighbor's window. Oh, there were country hits in England, but what was on hand was not the real McCoy. For every rarity like Johnny Horton or Marty Robbins, there was an abundance of Slim Whitman, Jim Reeves, Eddy Arnold, and the quirky tunes of Roger Miller. What I was hearing presently was manna from Heaven, something so pure, so undiluted, so completely mesmerizing.

"Sorry about that racket, he's a Yank" came the apology by way of my friend. Snapped out of my trance, it was all for me to do but hold myself back from collaring him and demanding an introduction. I guess my friend had never tapped into my musical proclivities and figured if it wasn't the Beatles, it was "shite."

Apparently, Vince (the Yank in question) was one of several US military personnel assigned to advise their UK counterparts on whatever it is those sort of people did. Vince had a fantastic accent. Hailing from Kentucky, he chewed gum, actually said "shucks," and called me "buddy." He was entirely different from any English person I'd ever known.

When I inquired as to what was playing he answered by saying, "You like the Everly Brothers?"

"Yup," I replied, trying to sound like Gary Cooper.

"Well, buddy, them's the original Everly Brothers."

Them's was Alabama's own Ira and Charlie Louvin, and the album was their 1956 classic *Tragic Songs of Life*. He was right, the genus of the Everly's sound could be linked directly to the Louvins.

I read the album cover like a book, imploring Vince to play the record repeatedly. So much so that in the end he gave it to me, shrugging his shoulders and saying he'd pick up another stateside. Stateside! How magical did that sound?

Ira, an exceptional mandolin player, sang in an achingly high tenor while Charlie played guitar and handled the bottom register. What was extraordinary was how they traded harmonies, with Ira swooping down while Charlie went up. At times it was impossible to tell when the change was made, a weird and magical blend of Appalachian alchemy that caused one writer to later state, "This was more than close-harmony singing; each instance was an act of transubstantiation." It didn't end there. By afternoon's close, I'd tapped into Vince's complete record collection. The man didn't have a whole lot, but what he had was golden.

The other album that he gave me (that I still have to this day!) was Lefty Frizzell's *Saginaw Michigan*. Frizzell, arguably one of country music's all-time greatest singers, was another winning discovery. The album's title track, a perfect bookend to Johnny Horton's like-minded tale of gold rush fever across the Yukon River in "North to Alaska," was another visual feast for the ears. The album also featured wonderful examples of Frizzell's unique voice and honky-tonk style including "What Good Did You Get (Out of Breaking My Heart)" and "I Was Coming Home to You," tracks that when I first heard Merle Haggard I knew immediately where he'd found his voice. Vince also informed me that Roy Orbison revered Lefty Frizzell, a fact that was corroborated in the 1980s when the Big O chose Lefty as his Traveling Wilburys name.

Another classic I heard that day was Hank Snow's "Ninety Miles an Hour (Down a Dead End Street)" along with his 1959 doom and death album *When Tragedy Struck*. I heard Kitty Wells's gospel disc *Dust on the Bible* and recordings by traditional guitarists Merle Travis and Doc Watson. Watson's music, in particular, had a profound effect. Blind from a young age, the North Carolina native shifted gears in styles moving among bluegrass, folk, blues, and country. It was authentic mountain music that brought to mind ethereal hollers and backcountry life tucked away in places where time moved slowly and the echo of rustic music bounced off the hills. It's hard to emphasize just how much all this music meant to me. It was the shot I needed at the right time. It wasn't just the discovery factor that picked me up; it was how it commandeered my enthusiasm.

Don't misunderstand me, I enjoyed and reveled in what was currently making waves in a general sense, but the most popular bands of the day were clearly drawing their influences from a deeper well. The Beatles and the Stones weren't just covering Chuck Berry, the Marvelettes, and Bo Diddley. Their instincts had far more investigative flare. Ringo was singing Buck Owens, and Mick was interpreting Slim Harpo and Arthur Alexander, a lot of these originators making their way to British seaports by way of merchant seaman as well as armed forces personnel like Vince. So while I was happy to enjoy these discoveries via the toppermost of the poppermost, it wasn't enough. I had in me a deeper desire to search for something different, a wider range of what was out there, not exactly hiding in plain sight, but evidently existing off the radar somewhere. It was my crusade, an archeological adventure, that became a lifelong quest.

After this euphoric weekend, the cold hard truth of Monday morning dragged me into the frozen dawn with an icy hand. Mike's charm offensive was no longer in evidence, which proved that while you can put a crochet cover on a toilet roll it's still an asswipe underneath. The days felt longer, the tasks more menial, and Mike's dictatorial agenda more and more demanding.

It all came to a head with an outbreak of fowl pest, a fatal, viral disease that can spread like a plague. The chickens started dying by the dozens. In fact, they were dying so rapidly that the backlog of bodies was building up at an alarming rate. The mandatory method of disposal was incineration, and this is where it got ugly. On a windswept patch of desolate ground at the rear of the property, a large incinerator had been set up and guess who was designated to feed the fire?

Anything that had preceded this event, any unpleasant job I might have been handed that caused me to question the requirements of servile employment, had not set me up for my descent into this avian Hades. For days on end, while Mike manning a forklift ferried the dead to my station at the furnace, I did nothing but shovel carcasses into the flames.

With a bone-soaking drizzle setting in and a wet wind whipping across the open ground, I took stock of the situation at hand. As black, rancid smoke billowed from the metal extractors and maggots crawled in the burst cavities of putrid birds, I prayed for delivery from bondage. Even with a scarf tied around my face, the noxious immolation of flesh and feathers permeated my nose, clothes, and quickened my sagging mental stability. I implored of a God I knew only casually to please install in me some directive. Obviously, the Lord and I were like-minded because the following Sunday, I quit. I couldn't look at a chicken, let alone eat one, for the next two years.

A MONTH LATER on June 17, unemployed but expectant, I thumbed through a music weekly and noticed an advertisement.

I think the accompanying letter I sent in response to the ad, along with the mythology attached to its mailing, has a little more quirkiness about it than has previously been divulged. Sure, I popped in a few abstract inconsistent verses constituting what I imagined to be au courant imagery, but it was my pitch that was fantastic codswallop. Unsure as to what songwriting consisted of, I covered my incompetence by way of flowery purple prose. It was something about my work having some probability in being the basis for a new kind of beat poetry. How it wasn't tossed in the bin after a good chuckle is anyone's guess.

If I didn't know what a songwriter was back then, I'm not sure that I know what one is now. When I think of songwriters, I instinctively think of George and Ira Gershwin, Lerner and Loewe, Cole Porter, and the rest of the architects of the Great American Songbook. That was a proper job where you get up and go to work, sweating it out around the piano, loosened ties, shirt sleeves rolled up, and lots of coffee. Then came the Brill Building era. Same set of circumstances, different participants: Goffin and King, Barry Mann and Cynthia Weil, Doc Pomus and Mort Shuman, and so on. Separate rooms, different floors, all slogging it out over a hot keyboard creating hits for fledgling acts and established hitmakers. The only place this sort of collective exists anymore is Nashville. The art of songwriting in certain areas can be an assembly line of alternating individuals sitting across from each other with guitars trying to find different ways of saying the same thing. On one of my first trips to Nashville, I was cajoled into investigating the prospect of joining in this compositional conglomerate. Apprehensive to say the least, I walked into a publisher's office on Music Row and had all my worst fears confirmed. The place was a warren of cubicles filled with jobbing songwriters playing musical chairs. I've no doubt that among them they were coming up with the goods, but it was clearly not anything I felt comfortable sitting in on.

Contrast this to the singer-songwriter. The world is inundated with them, good, bad, and mediocre, legendary, immensely popular, and criminally obscure. For the most part they work alone, crafting in their own personal space, hunched over their instrument searching for chord changes and words. They snatch inspiration from the world as they perceive it, mining from despair and joy, heartbreak, and their own personal, social, and political agenda.

I've never felt aligned to any of these scenarios. Being referred to as a songwriter is kind of weird. Maybe that's because I'm not actually writing a song, I'm just contributing to a melody. I work alone, and only occasionally. It's not even close to an everyday thing; in fact, outside of jotting down a few notes here and there, for most of our careers I've put all my effort into contributing only in the months prior to an album being made. Sure, when we started out it was a little different, a closer collaboration, more constant perhaps, but still separate creative nerve centers. Not so much "two rooms at the end of the world," but more like two rooms in the same apartment! We loved it, we put our all into it, but I'm still questioning if I wasn't just a messenger delivering whimsical propositions. Any concrete evidence that I wasn't doing anything other than flying by the seat of my pants has yet to be presented.

I imagined that a professional songwriter was someone who does that work solely for a living and not on the side while pumping gas during the day. Back then I was so desperate to be thought of as the embodiment of a worldly versifier I didn't question the quaintness of what I really contributed. Elton is most certainly a singer-songwriter. I'm just the writer bit, a writer who, on occasion, has sung.

What I became was, and always has been, an enigma to me. Everything I'd ever invested in since the day I was born collided in one mother of all pileups the moment I left home, all the complexities of youth ricocheting off each other. Fantasy and poetry, mythology, the American West, and a cornucopia of music, music, and more music. Arriving in London, I had little time to invent myself; I was imageless and complete in my naivety. I'd like to have projected a more stellar representation, idealistic country bard, moody poet, or hobo rebel, anything to wash away what I knew to be the truth. Funnily enough, out of my reserved nature all those former attributes were assigned to me without any work on my part. Perhaps there was some truth to these assumptions, and as much as I would come to loathe being referred to as a "poet," that moniker at the starting gate jelled nicely with the idealism of the era.

I'm a rock and roll anomaly who has functioned unintentionally as a rock star. Never wanted to be one, but have played one on and off on occasion. When Elton and I first met with producer Gus Dudgeon, Dudgeon directed the bulk of the conversation to me thinking I was the singer and Elton was the other guy. My visage on our 1970s albums was not the norm for a collaborator, creating for me a higher profile and the illusion that I was an accepted extension of the band. This afforded me a degree of recognition on the streets, especially in the States where I actually was for a time treated with an uncomfortable degree of reverential treatment. But no matter how much illogical behavior I have indulged in, no matter how much celebrity entwinement I have encountered, I have always attempted to inhabit a world of normality. The cocoon of fame would kill me. Had it happened, it would have completely rewired my system and I'm not sure I want to imagine the outcome, though it would be a lie to say I've traveled the centerline and encountered madness and fame only on the periphery. I believe it is where I came from that has ultimately always been my saving grace.

I'M JUST A country kid who got lucky. I got the best friend the world had to offer and a world that offered us everything; the parental backbone that never wavered in its support, a mother who invested me with her dreams and through whom I have lived vicariously; and a God who allowed me to make mistakes and redeem myself. In Carol Reed's movie of Graham Greene's *The Third Man*, Holly Martins declares, "I'm just a hack writer who drinks too much and falls in love with girls." Slightly over-self-deprecating perhaps, but for a time I might have imagined this to be a good inscription on my tombstone. There is however another saying: "Those who cannot remember the past are condemned to repeat it." Luckily, while not equipped with razor-sharp recollection, my recall is lucid enough to prevent this from happening.

In a restaurant, I can't sit with my back to the door. Not sure if I'm OCD, but I excel at organizational skills. Slightly claustrophobic, not crazy about heights. Love martinis but one is enough. Tend to be opinionated at times but good at reigning it in. Love long-legged women, clueless about cars, love trucks. I read several dozen books a year, cook every night, and am uncomfortable if music isn't playing. Don't like scat singing or modulation, jazz is my preferred music, and my favorite colors are black and dark blue. Have no problem eating on my own in a restaurant, have to have a dog, and hate clowns and circuses. I'd never heard a Pink Floyd album until 2015, Penderecki's "Polish Requiem" can make me cry, love trains, and am a confirmed sushi snob. I've never wanted to be anyone else, but if I had to choose I'd be Michael Caine. Michael Caine who rides horses like Buster Welch, plays guitar like Kenny Burrell, and sings like Vince Gill. The best bumper sticker I ever saw said, "I Brake for Brian Wilson." Love the smell of liver and onions, love onions hate liver. I think Mick Jagger is unique as a lyricist; *The Wild Bunch* is the greatest American movie ever made; and "Amazing Grace" is the best redemption song ever written.

That's the short version, if you want more feel free to continue.

The Ballad of Reg and Bern

A tinkling piano in the next apartment.

—ERIC MASCHWITZ AND JACK STRACHEY
"These Foolish Things"

Sheila hated my coat. I can't say I blame her. It hung on a hook on the back of our bedroom door like a Neanderthal artifact from the Natural History Museum, its only credentials for hipness being that the members of bands like Cream and Pink Floyd wore ones like them. I'm not sure if theirs stunk the way mine did, but when it rained, which was often, it smelled like an uncured yak hide. Afghan coats were in style, as were kaftan jackets, three button tees, and velvet pants. I'm positive we didn't succumb to the latter, but as for everything else, my new best friend and I did our very utmost to look the part.

Sheila was Reg's mother. Brassy, busy, and at that time stereotypical of the suburban clerical go-getter. Like so many of her social compatriots, she liked a drink, a knee's up (a party), and a quick chorus of "Down at the Old Bull and Bush." With her neighbor, a blousy lovely called Mavis, and her delightfully jovial sister, Win, they would sit in the front room listening to James Last albums, laughing raucously and smoking prodigiously. Still, she didn't like my coat. "Bleedin' smelly, ole thing!" she would exclaim repeatedly.

I was wearing my hair like Steve Marriott of the Small Faces, like long, straight curtains parted in the middle, and shoulder length. Reg, channeling John Lennon circa "All You Need Is Love," was sporting a splendid walrus mustache, untidy brown curls, and in the ultimate tip of the hat to the hippest Beatle, a pair of gold rimmed granny glasses. Lennon, who'd ditched his heavy horn-rimmed Buddy Holly bifocals only recently, had instigated a fashion trend with these tiny specs, and it was only a matter of time until my enterprising amigo coughed up the necessary for his own. On the day of purchase, my friend, feeling decidedly à la mode, was sitting across from me on the train ride home to Northwood Hills testing out his acquisition on the nightly newspaper. Suddenly, the obviously overtightened specs exploded, a shower of small brass screws, lenses, and frames springing from his face into the open pages of the *Evening Standard*, a single temple left swinging limply from one ear. The look on my friend's face was as priceless as the laughter that followed.

Small incidents like this happened frequently in our equally small world, a world of hope, potent optimism, and limited charity. An army of two, we were soaking up the incoming international tsunami of American sound. Every nano fraction of liberal creativity, unstoppable fusion of urban insurrection, and quotidian musical coup d'etats rushed into our embrace and took our breath away.

The streets of this time both in the US and the UK were ringing with raucous protest. War and government were the enemy; idealists and demagogues thrashed out their differences with bullhorns and placards. On soapboxes in the parks, pseudo-revolutionaries in their berets and Che Guevara T-shirts bellowed out flatulent manifestos while in the hallowed mahogany halls of Parliament political dogma fell on the deaf ears of England's youth.

We bought the underground press without understanding it. Did we read it? Never. It just rested under our arms, a trendy talisman, a stamp of approval, a wink of the eye to alert the straight we were hip. Most of it was unreadable anyway, printed on pages of garish psychedelic glossiness; you'd need a magnifying glass and a PhD in boredom prevention to make it through any article. Usually grumbling unintelligible pretense by some contemporary firebrand like Germaine Greer or Tariq Ali, it was all terribly affected, overwritten, and underwhelming. No one appeared to be in sync with any rational concept of the era we'd just escaped. Freedom was fleeting, and the Greatest Generation, like the baby, was being tossed out with the bathwater. The ashram and commune set may have looked groovy in their red Communist pins and Mao Tse-tung merchandise, but outside of fornication and inhalation they were obviously painfully unaware that the man they sported on their T-shirts was responsible for slaughtering more men, women, and children than Hitler and Stalin combined.

We were patently aware that so much of the music we were listening to was politically charged, but to my mind, at least there was some ingenuity and creative variation driving it. Lyric propelled by melody, whether high octane and dangerous or lilting and hypnotic, conveyed in us more awareness of the universal status quo than a slew of interchangeable talking heads ever could.

Music was our godhead, the town crier, plugged in and potent. Songs were everything to us, and we wanted in so badly we could taste it. When Johnny Cash *shot a man in Reno, just to watch him die*, I believed him. I wanted to get to that place, that level of storytelling.

Backtracking to the short but intermediary time before my introduction to Reg's formative home at Frome Court is essential history. It began with a train that brought me south in 1967, at age seventeen, depositing me and one battered leather suitcase at King's Cross station. On arrival and at the invitation of my dad's brother, Henri, and their younger sister, Genevieve, I'd taken up residence at their French family enclave 68 Howards Lane, a large but comfortable house on a leafy, polite street in the distinctly middle class suburb of Putney.

My grandparents crossed the English Channel at the turn of the century settling in Sydenham, a suburb of London, and established a wine importing business in the city. At the same time, they found ample time to get busy and impressively produce five children, four boys and one girl. The offspring were duly shipped back to France to be educated and then left to their own devices. Some remained, some returned, one of which was my dad, who, after serving heroically in North Africa and Burma during WWII, turned his back on city life and embraced his passion for animal husbandry and farming. During my formative years at home, my parents would frequently converse in

French, my mother having mastered the language while being schooled in Switzerland.

GENEVIEVE, WHOSE ANGELIC wing I had always found comfort under, was known to everyone in the family as Tati, a bastardized turn on "tante," the French translation for aunt. Tati was a confirmed spinster and a family treasure. Although she would be the last to admit it and was unfailingly self-effacing, she was that which around everything revolved. The closest thing to a matriarch the current generation possessed, she was quintessentially of a different era and unapologetic of her embrace of nurturing and matronly hobbies. She knitted, sewed, darned, and had the largest cat I'd ever seen. She was simultaneously delighted by my presence and equally enthusiastic about a culture she had absolutely no grasp of.

At one time or another, the house on Howards Lane was a hotbed of youthful testosterone. Uncle Henri, through his wife, Mathe, had sired enough sons to constitute over half a French soccer eleven. Six strapping boys, all of whom occupied space in this large three-story dwelling, each unique in his own way, friendly, familiar, and good-natured. They were a hunky, good-looking brood, boisterous, sporty, and completely bereft of sibling rivalry.

My assigned crib was a tiny cubicle on the second floor to the left of Henri and Mathe's room and across the hall from Tati. It was basically a narrow bed along the wall on one side with a shelf and lamp several feet above the headboard and a bare table on the opposite wall where I laid out my meager belongings. That was it, spartan indeed, but better, I imagined, than the kind of rat-infested and freezing squats many of my struggling contemporaries were inhabiting elsewhere.

Possibly it was my inherent fear of the aforementioned vermin that caused me during my first night's slumber to dream of them. What their significance might have represented is anyone's guess, but they poured out of the cellar bellow, up to my room, and under my sheets. Thrashing frantically in my sleep, I managed to tangle up royally in the dangling chord of the weighty light fixture on the shelf above. Down it came, several pounds of blue porcelain disintegrating on my head and knocking me out cold. Being unconscious, I got a good night's sleep, until I awoke groggily the next morning nestled amid a collection of jagged pottery and shards of glass. Trussed up in electrical wire, my back and arms a welter of cuts and scratches, sheets red with blood, and an egg-sized lump front and center of my forehead, I was lucky not to have severed an artery.

Years earlier, as a small child, this home had seemed enormous. Cavernous and exciting, even years later it had lost none of its allure. It was an exploratory maze, a three-tiered warren of bedrooms, bathrooms, cellars, kitchens, quaint cubbyholes, and attics. It had an antiquated magic that wasn't so much dowdy as mysterious without being scary. The kind of place where the most predisposed imagination could locate a transportive wardrobe or looking glass.

The true oddity was a large living room that seemed to serve no purpose other than to idle in inertia. Like Miss Havisham's unrequited reception room minus the cobwebs, it sat forever dormant. In the entire time I visited or stayed I never saw one person enter or entertain there. I'd sneak in every once in a while to digest the intense silence, my feet making little more than a shuffling swish on the gaudy carpeting, my visuals tracking across this dead room of antiquated quilted armchairs, frumpish overstuffed couches, and plethora of ceramic tchotchkes. Framed photos of indistinguishable ancients, sepia soaked, so distant that it was doubtful any current habitant could name them, vied for space in the overly polite mustiness. It smelled of age and mothballs, talcum powder and stale lavender.

This peculiarity aside, it was a residence of dueling characteristics. Every big house has its secrets, and this one was no different. It was here in one particular room at the age of fourteen that I had made a discovery that was to completely revamp my musical outlook and thrill me in ways that can only be compared to tantric sex and St. Paul's Damascan light.

The cabinet in which this treasure lay was in the dining room, a main artery in the thoroughfare of the household. Accessing it in solitude was not easy. Mealtimes were sacrosanct, especially on the weekends when the tribes gathered and the continentality of Frenchness reached its zenith. At any given time, any number between ten and twenty raucous family members descended on Howards Lane. Massive appetites in tow, and with a devout religiosity to church and food, the soul and stomach were doubly blessed. If you closed your eyes it would be hard not to imagine yourself at a full-on faux alfresco banquet somewhere on the sun-kissed hills of old Provence. In suburban Putney, the escargot soup and cassoulet were flowing.

MY HOLY GRAIL, the cabinet of which I speak, this teak receptacle of questionable vintage, stood thirty inches off the ground and was about four feet in length. It had a wobbly sliding door and an old but serviceable turntable on the right side. Piled high indiscriminately to the left was an absolute jumble of discs stacked with no uniformity or cataloguing whatsoever. This was a cabinet totally forgotten, an artifact of earlier years. Possibly used extensively in the past, it was now the archeological dig of my young life. It was situated by the dining room door, and at some previous time most likely had a virile life given the variation of eclectic music housed within. With the exodus of offspring and interchanging generational tastes, the appreciation of any of the genres that were gathering dust within spoke volumes to me of who might well have dictated the tastes of earlier Taupins.

Back home in Lincolnshire, I had a meager record collection: a few current scratchy pop singles and some hit parade shows taped off the BBC onto our bulky Robuk reel-to-reel recorder. But outside of that, this being 1964 and the distinct musical changes currently taking place, it was still the first generation of rock and rollers who had us strapping on our tennis rackets before the bedroom mirror.

Shuffling through this grab bag of discarded discs, it was easy to access what music had rung out of the family's tinny turntable over the previous decade. The French tastes were to be expected. Some of the old guard by way of Edith Piaf, Georges Brassens, and Charles Trenet, the obvious like Johnny Hallyday and Sylvie Vartan, and the glossy yé-yé EPs by a collective of continental chanteuses such as Frances Gall, Jacqueline Taieb, and Chantal Goya. Most though were by Mireille

Mathieu and Françoise Hardy, two of France's most iconic and prolific stylists. The rest were just some cheesy classics, mundane chamber
music, and awful Gallic opera. It was underneath, deep down at the
very bottom that the real treasure lay: old 78s by the kinetic and robust
skiffle pioneer Lonnie Donegan. Born Anthony James Donegan, he'd
come up through the ranks of British trad jazz, playing with stal-
warts of the genre such as Chris Barber and Ken Colyer. Ultimately,
his ambition, and depending on who's doing the talking, his outward
cockiness, outgrew the confines of his contemporaries. After an opening slot at the Festival Hall supporting blues musician Lonnie Johnson,
he changed his name and in 1955 became England's first major rock star
and premier musical influence. Embracing and inventing it in equal
quantities, skiffle was folk music on amphetamines. Under Donegan's
frantic fanning style and hiccuping vocals, he created a wholly original format that was to be emulated by literally hundreds of British
teenagers. History may have rewritten the parable as "I heard Elvis
and everything changed," but two years before the Mississippi Flash
meant diddly-squat. Instead, a squirrelly little Scottish runt had every
teenager in the UK wanting to be him. Skiffle was cheap and exciting, driven by percussive energy: It was a washboard, a tea-chest bass,
and cheap Spanish guitars playing accelerated versions of traditional
American folk ballads. It spawned a nation of wannabes, including the
formation of John Lennon's Quarrymen. Skiffle brought Lennon and
McCartney together. John may hastily have said, "Before Elvis there
was nothing," but with all due respect, I beg to differ. Lonnie may
not have been in the league of Louis Armstrong, Frank Sinatra, Hank
Williams, and Robert Johnson, but he was undoubtedly the first to
introduce England's fledgling rock gods to some of the greatest grassroots music ever written.

At that point in my musically uneducated adolescence I didn't know
anything about songwriter credits. I never once bothered to study the
labels and consider the small print in parentheses barely legible below
the artist's name. I just presumed whoever was singing it made it up,
those weighty rotating shellacs leading me to believe that this patently
Scottish product, landlocked in a wholly British musical habitat, could

be the purveyor of such mythical tales. "Rock Island Line," "The Grand Coulee Dam," "John Henry," and "My Dixie Darling" staggered me with their storytelling, and who was I to question their authorship?

Eventual curiosity in the performer and associated literature would soon lead me to the true vendors of this Americana magic. It's almost impossible to truly describe how these songs transported me and became the arrow pointing to everything that was to come later. Woody Guthrie, Huddie Ledbetter (aka Lead Belly), A. P. Carter, and the extraordinary work of musical archivist Alan Lomax opened up a door to another world.

Country music was birthed in Bristol, Tennessee, in 1927. Black R & B, bastardized and rebranded as rock and roll, slithered greasily out of Sun Studio in 1954. Charley Patton helped invent Delta blues in 1929, and the Beatles soaked the Cavern Club walls with hormonal sweat in 1961, but for one skinny-assed English kid, the big bang came out of a ramshackle radiogram at 68 Howards Lane, Putney, London, in 1964.

The great American troubadour Ramblin' Jack Elliott once told me that Lonnie Donegan was one of the most unpleasant men he'd ever met, which upset me tremendously. But then again, Ty Cobb wasn't a terribly nice guy either, and he was arguably the greatest baseball all-rounder of all time. Personally, I assure myself that especially in our formative years, we all suffer from momentary lapses of assholedom.

In 2002, Elton and I received the British Music Trust Award at the Grosvenor House in London. In a taped tribute to us, a visibly frail Lonnie Donegan said, "I've not spent enough time with Bernie—so if you see me advertised at your local, do pop around and say hello, I would love that." Ironically, it was not to be, as he passed away the day before the award ceremony. He had been on a late-life UK tour and had suffered a heart attack in Lincolnshire twenty-four miles from where I was born. Prophetic to say the least, it's immeasurable how much I owe him.

I didn't stay at Howards Lane very long, as it just wasn't practical. Reg and I needed to be in closer proximity of each other in order to create effectively and interact more personally. In truth, we were becoming closer and closer as friends with the obvious realization that in order to fight our battles it was best to do so as a united front.

I fully appreciated the effort the southern branch of the Taupin family had made in accommodating me, especially the delightfully matronly and sympathetic ear of Tati. She might not have known Mick Jagger from Michel Legrand, but she could chuckle like a schoolgirl and bring the sun out on a cloudy day. It had been fun during my first week at Howards Lane to accompany her to her clerical job in the City, London's predominately financial area. Tati worked in the offices of Uncle Henri's wine importing business and allowed me to tag along in order to hunt and peck out my virgin verse on one of their fantastic old Olivetti typewriters. The office itself was too beautiful to be termed démodé, but it did have a wonderfully anachronistic feel about it. Pre-Formica, aluminum, and plastic, it was all wood and smelled of mahogany and pipe smoke. It's leather-covered desks and tall burnished oak filing cabinets with brass handles brought to mind government war rooms and Kenneth More movies. There were inkwells, blotting paper, and items that scratched, rattled, and thumped rather than things that hummed and whirred with agitated clinical ISO noise.

It was here that I hammered out so many of the lyrics to what would become some of the very first songs Reg and I ever collaborated on. Fanciful, flowery, and naive, yet too innocent and childlike to be tainted by pretension, they mirrored the times without being derivative. After years of hesitancy regarding their worth, I've come to the conclusion that I'm no longer ashamed of their pedigree. They can be set alongside the work of contemporaries such as Cream collaborator Pete Brown, Floyd architect Syd Barrett, and the likes of Donovan and Procol Harum's Keith Reid, all of whom were relishing the fame we aspired to achieve, as we were all, in fact, picking fruit off the same tree.

Retrospectively, it's odd to think that these guileless paeans to a bright new tomorrow were conceived in an inherently buttoned-up bastion of the Old World. In many ways, this area of London was the very antithesis of the counterculture, an ultraconservative army of like-minded autocrats retaining a death grip on tradition. Like René Magritte's surrealist painting *Golconda* come to life, they poured out of the suburbs every morning, aligning parts of a precision machine, identical in every way. Bowlers, brollies, and briefcases, gray pinstripe pants, and neatly folded copies of the *Times* snapped to attention under their arms. Likewise, they disembarked en masse in the belly of bureaucracy, marching like an army of replicants, cloned civil servants on the hamster wheel of repetition. Sitting on the train surrounded by this homogeneous horde is an indelible memory, the most totally British image of postwar England that I can recollect. My presence among them can only have been a sad reminder of what they had fought the war for. Peering over their papers they looked down their noses, sneered visibly, and tutted with disdain. In my proto-hobo garb and shoulder-length hair, I was an eyesore, an unnatural blemish on their uniformity, as conspicuous as Boxcar Willie at the Carlton Club.

My noxious coat in tow, I moved in with Reg: 3A Frome Court, Pinner Road, Middlesex, to be exact, and a step in the right direction for all concerned. Here, we were able to really knuckle down to the business at hand. Conveniently, Sheila's job kept her absent during the day so that in the tranquility of the apartment, we could fire up the conveyor belt on our creative engine. The apartment was small but had a sympathetic vibe conducive to our nascent songwriting.

It was situated on the second floor with two sets of stairs on each side: an interior set that led up from the front door and a stone set on the exterior that led up to the rear entrance and into the kitchen. It was a small kitchen that led to the hallway, which ran the length of the apartment. Immediately outside the kitchen to the right was a relatively spacious living room that housed Reg's upright piano. Turning left, the hallway ended with the bathroom at the left, Sheila's bedroom in the middle, and our room next to it on the right.

Sheila was handling things solo until her husband, Reg's stepfather, Derf (Fred in reverse), came home from working a contracting job in Nigeria. So from the get-go, Frome Court had enough elasticity in the air to accommodate the ebb and flow of camaraderie and good humor. Although Sheila's personality would morph into something different over time, back in those fledgling days it was on an even keel of encouragement and bawdy affability. I worked in our bedroom at the back of the apartment, and Reg hammered away in the living room at the front. It was either me heading down the hall with a "Hey, try this," or him heading in the opposite direction with a "Come take a listen." Heady times indeed, both exciting and thrilling. The obvious reward of cohabitating manifested itself in a more immediate form of gratification. The work may not have been what it would become, but it was where we began in earnest.

It was like embarking on an exotic adventure, standing on the jetty gazing into the open mouth of an uncharted river. We didn't know what lay ahead, but we were ready for anything. Disappointment might lay around any given bend, and our confidence was occasionally rattled, but we knew we were improving every day, and driven by sheer love of what we were doing, the possibilities limitless in our exuberant minds.

We still, however, had to sweat the small stuff. Over the years, my progression in all things culinary is something I'm immensely proud of. It's something I excel at, something I am passionate about, and something that I invest a great deal of time in. I cook every day, I do my own marketing. It's cerebral and satisfying in the same way I'm nurtured by music, literature, and art. The preparation, the purpose, the aromas, and the subtle fragrance and muted rainbow of spices. In 1968, I couldn't fry an egg.

There was a particular evening back then when in the absence of Sheila and with hunger driving the bus, we decided to go it alone. Armed with a packet of Wall's pork sausages and a box of strawberry Instant Whip, we approached the utensils and appliances as if offering sacrifice, the mocking hiss of gas and snickering yowl of electricity thrumming in time with our hapless trepidation. How hard could it be? Oil in the pan, sausages in the pan, whack the heat up, no problem. Strawberry powder in the bowl, milk in the bowl, whisk in the bowl, easy peasy. Not so hard.

Small tongues of flame began to form in the pan, cooking oil spat viciously, and the bangers turned black as the flames danced higher. My attention drawn from mixing duty to sausage inferno, I inadvertently raised the whisk from the bowl. Like spackle catapulted from a trowel, a perfect spray of pink goop jettisoned around the kitchen walls. Lots of smoke, fire, and panic ensued. Managing to extinguish our disaster without burning down Frome Court, the cleanup left us famished. "You get the cornflakes, I'll get the milk!"

It was pretty early on that Reg tested the waters. We were inseparable, joined at the hip, and completely the inhabitants of our own world. So it was only natural that he would add to the confusion that must have been raging in his psyche by placing his hand on my thigh. This was done almost clinically as if he felt it necessary, but at the same time wanting to get it over with. Elton was still a long way from coming out, and even further from understanding it, the consummation of his chosen path being several years from this point. This innocent approach was done with zero aggression and lacked anything of a predatory nature. If anything, I think it made me laugh. It was easily deflected and immediately understood. Of course, if I had reciprocated, it would have spelled disaster. One of the tried-and-true components of our lasting relationship has been those parts of our personalities that have always remained polar opposites. If we'd have been sexually like-minded, it would have undoubtedly, eventually crashed and burned. Would our friendship have endured? Would our working relationship be fractured? Not to mention the songs themselves, just imagine how the lyrical input of our compositions would have deviated in an alternate universe. Had this been the case, some of our most enduring classics would certainly have never come to pass.

Interestingly enough, I don't recall being remotely disturbed by this action or the knowledge that my best friend harbored homosexual tendencies. I imagine that perhaps I wasn't altogether convinced initially that gay Reg was a reality, and perhaps in my naivety thought that his proximity to a charismatic homosexual, like his former employer, the singer Long John Baldry, had rubbed off on him. Considering where I came from, you'd imagine my machismo might have been inflamed by this affront to my manhood, but, once again, I bow to the roots of my raising to have steered me away from pigeonholing my friend as a flaming queer. The other glaring omission in this assessment was that my friend wasn't in the slightest bit camp. In an era where grating stereotypes were the product of puerile comedy, and effeminate composites made any gay man a lisping rouged Nancy boy, Reg was everything that screamed "not gay." A hardcore soccer fan, eclectic musical tastes, tough as old boots, hell, Reg was my very own Ronnie Kray, the gay half of the Kray brothers, the East End's notorious twin gangsters.

We may have built our mutual affinity for each other on a bedrock of music and contemporary culture, but we came from decidedly different backgrounds that would eventually define our carbon footprint in the world. Happy childhood, unhappy childhood, it's easy to understand how Reg, an only child under the thumb of an emotionally remote and domineering father would find solace in the friendship of me, the product of a carefree and affectionate adolescence. I was the imaginary brother who became a reality, and I can only imagine that Reg realized, and was relieved, that what he had wished for was a real friend rather than a temporary lover.

As much as some people might think, we have never been a beast with two heads. Outside of those burgeoning years, we have never lived in each other's pockets or clung to each other's coattails. From the moment we made our mark, we severed our umbilical cord and went our own way. Our devotion to each other has never wavered, and our friendship grew substantially just as our lifestyles took radically different paths. We grew up fast; we had no choice. We may not have matured in the conventional sense, but as far as our camaraderie is concerned, it attained loftier heights. Cerebral. Telepathic. Call it what you want. Geography may perpetually separate us, and outside pursuits and alternate careers may hamper our social interplay, but nothing can sever the bond we forged at Frome Court. It was a secret society with two members still totally in tune, respect and love being our singular constant.

In the beginning, we had each other's backs, but with me being the newbie in town and still a little wet behind the ears, he was the major contributor when it came to a protective and nonjudgmental attitude. From certain parties I encountered a relative level of condescension in our small but urban enclave of workhorses. I was either deemed too introspective, bumpkinesque, or ignored completely due to my lack of hands-on musicality. Reg saw my capabilities, understood my worth, and guarded it. I learned fast, didn't need to make a spectacle of myself, soaked in my surroundings, and eventually had the last laugh.

Oh, we did get out, of course; we weren't chained to our suburban sweatshop. Since our initial deal with Dick James Music as could be/might be songwriters, in-the-trenches purveyors of bland pop, we had made a habit of spending several days a week "hanging out" at his offices situated above the Midland Bank at 71-75 New Oxford Street just off Charing Cross Road. We'd gravitated here in the shadow of the newly erected Centre Point building by way of our much-recorded and recounted introduction through Ray Williams, the boyish wunderkind of the emerging Liberty Records. Having responded to Ray's initial ad, Reg and I had both separately visited his plush and intimidating offices in Mayfair. For my part, an invitation to "pop by sometime" to discuss my submissions was drolly improbable considering I inhabited a fanciful world, countrified and over five hours away from his groovy fiefdom.

Time out. Let's bypass all the baloney and dispel myths here. Legend has it that I was reticent to answer the ad and my mother ultimately mailed my submission (I just forgot, OK?), and Ray randomly pulled my package of lyrics from a pile of contenders and handed them to Reg. How many lyricists do you honestly think responded to the advertisement? Er, me, that's how many!

Our reason for making DJM a pit stop was twofold. It's here that we'd make demos of our songs, and it's here that we'd socialize with the studio staff, all of whom had become partisans to our cause. We were still creating work that, on one hand, was our contribution to Dick James's desire for MOR ballads (that is, middle-of-the-road) suitable for the Engelbert Humpderdinck– and Cilla Black–styled performers who relied on outside material while keeping our chops honed by knocking out our hippy renderings. For this we were being payed the princely sum of £5 a week for me, and £10 for Reg, given that he did the singing. Not a lot to live on even back then, but we divested it frugally and managed to scrape by.

The four-track studio where we worked was located in the rear while the rest of the floor was made up of offices inhabited by employees of varying degrees of importance. On one hand, the airless cubicles squir-reled away in back were occupied by the old guard, Dick's cronies from the past retained benevolently, no doubt out of a sense of loyalty, aging music publishing veterans whose time had come and gone and who were still clinging on to an almost vaudevillian past. Artifacts of the radio's dustier days, they did their best to look relevant in their shabby suits and shuffling gaits. Clipboards in hand, they would puff on their pipes and talk earnestly of old school affairs and Matt Monro covers.

The larger offices occupied the cooler real estate up front adjacent to Dick's expansive domain. This is where the young guns resided, the record pluggers whose job it was to wine and dine the tastemakers and radio programmers. They were a flashy lot in their double-breasted suits, kipper ties, and good haircuts. Laddish and good-humored, they added color and a degree of trendy virility to the place. They were joc-ular and friendly even while being on a faster track than we smaller fry. These guys operated in a zone of accepted chauvinism, a principality of sexist quips, and expense accounts.

The hub of everything was undoubtedly the reception area. When not working in the back or kibitzing in the cutting room, we would hang out here and watch the traffic. There was a coterie of songwriters vying for studio time back then, some like us waiting for a break and others who had a foothold on the ladder. All, though, would inter-act and hang casually talking shop around the expansive Naugahyde couch fronting Dick's office. Being that Dick had been blessed with the good fortune to secure the Beatles publishing in 1963, the occa-sional mop-top might on occasion swing by to use the facility. We were years away from proving that, in Dick's case at least, lightning does indeed strike twice.

If we were cutting demos, or inclined to dine in, we'd send out for sandwiches. These were picked up by the office errand boy or as we referred to them back then "runners." The young lad currently employed in this role was an eager to please South Londoner full of youthful bustle and barrow boyish charm. The fact that he would go on to become one of England's greatest living actors is a placeholder of no short measure. His name, Gary Oldman!

Out of the office we ate cheaply, we had no choice. Indian food was as exotic as we got, which is no surprise considering it was then, and remains to this day, as British as fish and chips. To put a healthy edge in our diet and to placate discerning friends, we often frequented Cranks vegetarian restaurant in Soho. Personally, this was never to my taste. It seemed like a cuisine still not yet perfected, everything tasting like cardboard and nuts. More often than not, though, we took lunch at the Lancaster Grill around the corner from Dick's on Charing Cross Road. Here in the spot where Reg and I first discussed collaborating. The food was as basic as it gets, and as cheap as you'd want. That greasy spoon is still a pivotal compass point in our history, the spot where we both said, "I do." Whatever it is today, and if anything in our narrative merits one of those blue oval plaques, it's that emporium of weak tea and beans on toast that gets my vote.

We'd pour over the music press here, which at the time consisted of a quartet of weeklies. *Melody Maker*, *Disc*, *Record Mirror*, and the *NME*, the latter being the one to carry the infamous ad introducing Liberty Records in June 1967. The ad that both Reg and I had responded to and, ultimately, brought us to this very spot. These periodicals served as our town crier alerting us to new releases of interest, who was playing the clubs, and info on incoming American artists gigging in the UK. We may not have been terribly interested as to whether Edgar Broughton had changed his lineup or that the Groundhogs were playing the University of Leeds, but they were instrumental in alerting us to major happenings, seismic shifts in the current scene that had all manner of emerging bands carving out notable introductory releases while vying for quality time on the stages of London's hippest clubs and the developing festival culture. Beating us to the punch and making waves were groups like the fantastic folk rock band Fairport Convention, the inventive psych swirls of Family and Traffic, and the doom-laden crunch of the soon-to-be metal behemoth Black Sabbath.

IT WAS SOMEWHERE around this time that it was suggested that my friend jump ship from jobbing songwriter and become Elton John, erstwhile recording artist. Our first stab at notoriety being an appallingly heavy-handed piece of maudlin junk entitled "I've Been Loving You." Reg's name change had come sometime earlier due to necessity and a little brainstorming. In an age when normality in branding had become de rigueur, it was sensible on our part to adopt something in the middle. Elvis, Buddy, Marty, Daryl, and Dion were names of another era. Mick and Keith, John and Paul, Ray, Roger, Pete, Eric, Jimi, George, and Ringo! All these had a routine coolness and modernity compared to Reg and Bernie, which in comparison sounded like a combined company of plumbing and accountancy.

The fact that we allowed ourselves to be saddled with this dreck shows a desperation on our part to achieve success. It was even made more so by my noninvolvement in its composition. Along with its B side, Elton had composed both. Melodically stagnant and lyrically bland, it was a sad submission to everything we aspired not to be. We were allowing our dreams to become hijacked in order to acquire even the most abhorrent degree of fame.

I'm happy it tanked, of course. Had this withering piece of wax charted, the whole gambit of our desired path would have temporarily been harnessed to a rotisserie of working men's clubs and end of the pier reviews before oblivion.

It was to prove a prodigious wake-up call for us, an unsubtle kick in the pants that ultimately led to a serious reset and unforeseen intervention. Directly before this took place, though, things got weird. Elton got engaged, and a humongous wrench got thrown in the works.

I'm not going to pretend to remember how this astonishing occurrence happened, but sometime during Elton's stint backing Long John Baldry he'd met a young woman called Linda Woodrow. They became friends and Elton had been persuaded to believe that there was more to it than an amicable relationship. At a time when he was still unsure of his own sexual orientation and how to distribute his pent-up love, it was extraordinary to watch him approach a traditional heterosexual dance. I truly don't think he knew what hit him and was just swept up in the accepted normality of it all. Perhaps it was a hangover from his background and a subconscious attempt to eradicate his true feelings and fall into the footsteps of traditionalist values.

The consequences of all this was that we moved out of Frome Court and into a gloomy basement apartment on Furlong Road in Islington, a decidedly iffy area that is now one of London's most expensive boroughs. I was extremely intimidated by Elton's fiancée, who had a commanding presence that wasn't to be trifled with. Like a big scary bird she dominated our acreage, ruling with impunity under the guise of benevolent monarch. Tall and fixated on her appearance, she reminded me of a skinny Mrs. Potato Head with all her applications exaggerated to comical effect. Towering wigs and exaggerated lashes plugged in and applied along with powder and paint in a daily ritual that ceased only when she felt she had escaped what lay beneath. I don't think she liked me very much, but then again I can't say I blame her. I'm sure she viewed me as subversive, deviantly attempting to drive a wedge between them to thwart her quest to transform her beau from Bob Dylan into Buddy Greco, or at worst a respectable accountant. I certainly never felt that I in anyway tried to rock the boat or sabotage her marital expectancy. I found out much later on that she thought I was a stoner, which in retrospect impresses me immensely considering my proximity to the drug culture at the time was a blip on the horizon. For the most part, I just tried to steer clear of any acrimony and hope for the best.

Her fixation with cleanliness, while bordering on obsession, came with serious double standards. If she was Lady Tremaine and we were a couple of Cinderellas, then her precious dog was the ugly sisters combined. For while we vacuumed and dusted, her scraggly hound would crap and piss with impunity. "Here a turd, there a turd, everywhere a turd, turd" was our mantra, and while we hopscotched around the defecation, it was hard not to smell rebellion along with urine on the wind.

The interesting thing is that I can't recall writing anything at Furlong Road, I don't even know if we had a piano. It just wasn't a creative environment, our number one daily objective being to get the hell out of there. It didn't help that it was a basement flat, perennially dark, any joie de vivre sucked out of it by the overwhelming vacuum of apprehension. Emerging from it was like coming up for air, the diminishing returns of what it had to offer harnessing us with all number of questions. Most crippled by these questions was my friend, who was undoubtedly agonizing over how to handle his impending wedding vows. They were shallow times and a low in both self-confidence and compositional improvement, both digging us deeper into a quagmire of self-doubt.

It all changed with an intervention after Elton, in a staged cry for help, opened all the windows, stuck his head in the gas oven, and awaited a dramatic response. Perhaps due to the unorthodox nature of his attempt, gas on low and an embroidered pillow to rest his head on, sympathy was not forthcoming. Obviously not the reaction he craved, I laughed out loud while Linda merely looked down at him, rolled her eyes, and walked out. Little was left but to take the bull by the horns and forcibly convince my buddy of his sexual proclivity. It needed a much more experienced and explosive personality than myself, not to mention a real honest-to-gosh queer to tear down the walls of heartache. Enter Long John Baldry and the night of a thousand cuts.

The details of our retreat from Furlong Road has been chronicled in great detail both in book and song, and in unauthorized biographies along with Elton's tremendous account. Our song "Someone Saved My Life Tonight" illuminates a slightly fictional and fantastical account of the event and the participants. In reality it was just a drunken evening that changed everything.

The gas oven episode, ludicrous as it appeared on the surface, was indeed a call to arms. It might have been an amusing hiccup in our story, but the consequences and the conclusion of that particular night out cannot be overemphasized. At the culmination of the evening, after several stops, we staggered into the Bag O'Nails, a rock star habitat in the heart of Soho. It was here that Baldry delivered the gay equivalent of the Gettysburg Address. Perhaps not quite so eloquent and fueled by brandy rather than political zeal, it nonetheless stirred its directee into his great awakening.

With Dutch courage driving the bus, we somehow managed to wend our incredibly inebriated way home. It was lucky for the locals that this was an era before car alarms, because in our attempt to navigate our collision course we slumped over dozens of automobiles and crashed into numerous garbage cans before hurtling through the front door and into the angry arms of the abyss. Immediately, I ducked for cover while Elton, fueled by alcohol yet slapped sober by the reality of it all, sallied forth to administer Linda's Waterloo. It was, of course, ugly. With Elton's ultimatum delivered, he fled to the sanctuary of my room, passing out on a threadbare stretch of protective carpeting.

The next day, Elton's stepfather arrived early to assist us in abandoning ship while Linda lobbed several threatening bombs. She was pregnant, would inject air bubbles into her veins, and I'm sure blamed the entire debacle on me. Of course, it was all fabricated as they'd never had sex, we weren't junkies, and I was blameless, just sitting on the curb watching the whole train wreck happen.

Revitalized by our retreat to Frome Court, 1969 hove into view with a smile. Things started to change for the better. It was as if a refreshing breeze had blown away the cobwebs of our grim, fugacious months, and sun and light had replaced the gray film tarnishing our outlook.

One of the key factors to the tide turning and a renewed vigor in our songwriting was the arrival of Steve Brown at Dick James's offices. Steve was tall and hippieish and had obviously been retained in order to bring some musical expertise and modishness to the company. He was a lovely man, gentle and soft-spoken, and he completely evoked the current climate of peace and love. I'm not sure what his exact title was, but I imagine it was an invented moniker that embraced all elements of the creative while cutting out the deadwood. Troubleshooting I guess you could call it, but one thing's for sure: he hated formulaic middle-of-the-road shit.

This was initially disturbing, and, although we were having absolutely no success with it, it was the devil that was paying our meager wage. Luckily, and to our great relief, it wasn't our heads he wanted but our hearts. Guaranteed, he loathed the puerile pop we were writing to keep bread on the table, but the man had done some sniffing around and heard a couple of the off-the-clock trippy pastiches we were knocking out. In no uncertain terms he suggested we forget trying to compete with straitlaced pop songwriters like Tony McCauley and Don Black and simply be ourselves. This of course was music to our ears, but "What about Dick?"

To give Dick his due, he succumbed without a fight. I imagine he was smart enough to realize we weren't capable of pub sing-a-longs and might be better off dipping our toes into experimental waters. He even green lit another single that, with our new untethered status and burying the memory of our initial debacle, we were able to create with relative ease.

If "I've Been Loving You" had sounded like a Kathy Kirby reject, "Lady Samantha" was a solid slice of gothic pop rock. Sort of "Long Black Veil" meets "Cold Blows the Wind," it had a nice screaming guitar courtesy of Caleb Quaye and solid drum fills by Roger Pope. Produced by Steve, it wound up being what was referred to back then as a *turntable hit*. Joe Public weren't turning out in droves to purchase it, but it caused a ripple and was our first stab in the direction we wanted to travel.

With this uptick and our confidence boosted, my writing took a slight change of direction. Outside the commercialized pap that we'd been commissioned to produce, so many of our songs lyrically had been completely esoteric and deficient of any real meaning. Once again, it was all about imagery, full of gaudy word painting, and its hallucinatory nonsense was becoming repetitive.

Around the time we'd come up with "Lady Samantha," we'd written a song called "Skyline Pigeon" that actually had us feeling like we'd turned a corner. Although still slightly ethereal, it had a distinct sense of open space and a nice metaphor for freedom. Steve loved it, and it became our first song to elicit two cover versions right out of the gate.

With the likes of "Velvet Fountain," "The Year of the Teddy Bear," and "A Dandelion Dies in the Wind" relegated to the archives, I was now mining for ideas between the pages of what I was currently reading.

Outside of food and travel and a small contribution rent-wise, my only vices were music and books. Musicland on Berwick Street in Soho and Foyles on Charing Cross Road were our go-to havens for ear and eye recreation, respectively. The former was run by two tremendously hip gay guys called John and Ian who, at the end of every week, would receive all the coolest imports from the US, sometimes a month ahead of their UK release. The music we discovered in the countless hours we spent in that cozy vinyl grotto, propping up the counter and fanning through the bins, is overwhelming. It was if we were sonically possessed, a landslide of classics raining down on us in a time so incredibly prolific and innovative it was all we could do to not steal in order to feed our habit. These fertile months that rolled into the climax of the '60s had us grappling for a cornucopia of sublime recordings. Leonard Cohen's first two records, Love's *Forever Changes*, Miles's *Bitches Brew*, Cash's *At Folsom Prison*, Dylan's *John Wesley Harding* and *Nashville Skyline*, Hendrix's *Electric Ladyland*, Neil Young's first solo albums, and Leon Russell's stunning eponymous album. It was also where I was baptized in the rolling tom-tom drums of Levon Helm ushering in "Tears of Rage" from *Music from Big Pink*, The Band's extraordinary debut album and still to this day my favorite rock record ever. Oh, then of course, there was the emerging Joni Mitchell, the Byrds's groundbreaking *Sweetheart of the Rodeo*, and be still my heart, Laura Nyro's *Eli and the Thirteenth Confession*, perfumed lyric sheet and all.

I'm just skimming the surface, of course, and while England was certainly contributing with many emerging bands and artists with interesting ideas and worthwhile things to say, it was hard for me to shake the pull of a fabled America. It had tugged at me constantly since my Putney epiphany, the revelatory record collection of an American ex-serviceman and the tale of a West Texas town called El Paso. Obviously, I would have to wait years to instigate this type of vintage collage and be brave enough to tap into these genres, but inspired by The Band's sepia-infused and atmospheric timelessness, I would eventually play my hand.

For now, it was all too much in the best way possible, and we imbibed at the well, absorbing this miraculous landslide of innovation. There was something exotic about these releases winging their way across the waves like intoxicating sirens whispering in our ears and luring us onto a different kind of rock.

Foyles, of course, was a more sedate and traditional English environment, books being a little more secretive in their allure, but no less exciting than their rotating counterparts in what they harbored between their covers. Financially, I worked it out that if I made my choice wisely, I could purchase one book and by the time I'd read it my coffers would be replenished enough to buy another, and so on. Browsing was a ritual, and I would spend a good amount of meditative downtime cruising the shelves. *The Lord of the Rings* revival was in full swing, and I, like hundreds of my contemporaries, was drawn to this staggeringly original epic.

I had latched on to the phantasmagorical with messianic zeal, and anything that took me out of the realm of reality and into strange, twisted worlds and heathen universes was likely to have me nose-down between the pages. Given the introspective nature that I was prone to adopt, it's hardly surprising that literature of this nature was bound to affect and eventually find its way into my writing. Velvet fountains and tartan-colored ladies would soon be replaced by tales of Valhalla and sea dogs sailing their ships into the docks of dawn. Our new work would ultimately lend from authors as varied as Mervyn Peake, whose dark foreboding trilogy of the decaying Castle Gormenghast would leave their imprint on songs like "The Cage" from the *Elton John* album. A little more earthbound, but no less heroic in nature, were Mary Renault's historical novels based on the life of Alexander the Great. The "King Must Die" in particular is a direct lift from the title of one of those books.

Back at Frome Court, we set about writing copious amounts of songs, some of which would eventually find their way onto our first album. Steve had once again come through and assured Dick that this was the right thing to do in order to further spread the word and put a spotlight on the emerging talent of my best friend. Steve had proved to be our absolute champion, taking not just a shine to our songwriting but also to us as individuals. We became fast friends and it was soon obvious that we had struck gold as he became our mentor, confidant, and emotional sounding board. Sharing the same musical tastes, we would often spend weekends at his apartment in Croydon lying on the floor between his speakers, soaking in the sounds, and getting impossibly drunk on Merrydown cider, the contact high from his potent hashish joints elevating the music into sonic improbability.

Our 1975 concept album *Captain Fantastic and the Brown Dirt Cowboy* chronicles much of what I'd written about up to this point, but the song "Better Off Dead" from that recording is certainly the most evocative of how London felt to us in the late '60s after our *Empty Sky* album sessions were done for the night. Once again produced by Steve and completed in April 1969, recording our first official long player left us heady and euphoric by evening's end, the adrenalin of owning our souls heightened by the kinetic energy of the West End. We were doing what we wanted to do, not what someone was telling us to, and that in itself made creating the project a jubilant and thrilling experience. It's been described as everything from psychedelic rock to progressive pop and folk rock, and while it may not be Van Morrison's *Astral Weeks*, it has a genuine sense of optimism in its energy. We would record late, and if the trains had stopped running, we'd bunk up in town with the Salvation Army. Let me clarify. Steve's dad, Major Fred Brown, ran the Salvation Army's center at Regent Hall, at a church on Oxford Street. It was there in the major's apartment above the hall that, after consuming something greasy and mentally filming the disenfranchised denizens of the night, we'd crash when our pounding hearts were finally stabilized.

Empty Sky was the rumbling before the storm. A little bit of everything, it's not hard to understand why people struggled to put their finger on what it was exactly. I won't capitulate to knowing myself, but I can say in all honesty that we were attempting to emulate our heroes and put our own stamp on the proceedings. A Stones-like title track, a nod to Leonard Cohen and Bob Dylan, certainly a stab at Procol Harum, and some wistful British traditionalism make it hard to pigeonhole. Aside from the cryptic abomination that is "Hymn 2000," it's an acceptable debut but more importantly, a harbinger of growth and improvement.

The album was released in June 1969, and while we basked in its not wholly indifferent reception, we took time out in the following months to attend two historical musical happenings. On July 3, Rolling Stones guitarist Brian Jones, recently dismissed from the very band he founded, died in his swimming pool, and two days later the Stones played a free concert in Hyde Park. Elton and I strolled in with 500,000 punters and with relative ease secured a nice spot on the green not more than a few hundred yards from the stage. It was a glorious day with a harmonious spirit in the air and good vibes on the ground below. With plenty of wiggle room and the cool green grass to stretch out on, we felt lucky not only to be there but to be an actuality at last, if only at the starting gate. Hell, we'd made an album!

We may not have been opening for the Stones yet, but King Crimson were. Obviously, they had the edge on us. After a fierce bidding war, Island Records had signed them and just released their debut album *In the Court of the Crimson King*, a bombastic bit of prog rock whose title track was full of mystical imagery and fantastical references. *Well, I thought to myself, I guess someone else is reading the same stuff as me.* That someone happened to be a guy named Pete Sinfield, and I was a tad jealous. What was worse, I secretly liked it. Not something that was normally my cup of tea, but since he was obviously mining the same inspirational source, I couldn't help but admire the fact that his grandiose verses made mine a little bit eighth grade.

Finally, the Stones came on pretending like they were sorry Brian Jones was dead, and proceeded to rush through a half-hearted tribute that included some flowery verse by Shelley coupled with the release of three thousand white butterflies, the majority of which plummeted senselessly to the stage. Releasing winged things at a live event is not always a good idea. We attempted the same thing at the Hollywood Bowl in 1973. I should know, because I was under one of five pianos spelling out Elton's name and housing hundreds of white doves. When the lids were raised not a bird stirred. Terrified by the blazing lights, they refused to fly and remained stunned and immobile. Even when they were scooped up and fed to the air by hand, they simply fluttered apathetically to the ground.

Given that the Stones hadn't performed in a couple of years, and that Mick appeared to be wearing a dress, it wasn't bad. A bit rusty, but it was obvious that in Mick Taylor, Brian Jones's replacement, they had found a remarkable guitarist of great finesse. Someone who could more than adequately fill their deceased founder's shoes. Whatever the consensus, it was a grand day and a good time was had by all.

Outdoor gigs back then were an iffy affair, staging and sound not being as polished as they would become decades later. The elements could play havoc with the dispersion of sound, a fact that we were about to be a party to not more than a month later.

The decision to make the pilgrimage to the Isle of Wight was an easy one. Bob Dylan, who hadn't played live in over three years and had been in semiretirement since his motorcycle accident in 1966, was returning to the stage. Hidden away in Upstate New York, he'd rarely been seen, and rumors of his health and welfare were rife on the musical grapevine. His country-tinged album *Nashville Skyline* had been released several months earlier, confusing some and charming others. Reimagining himself as a hillbilly troubadour, he looked happy and healthy on the cover, his scruffy persona inhabiting the potent, airy music inside.

Equally as enticing was that The Band would be backing him, as well as playing their own set. Being that their debut album, *Music from Big Pink*, had affected me so radically, it was a no-brainer that I would want to check out this coterie of remarkable musicians and singers. Their eponymous sophomore classic would not be released for another month, further cementing their grasp on an antique America and spawning a whole new genre of music while inspiring me to create the lyrical content for the album that would become *Tumbleweed Connection*.

There was a group of us that traveled by train to Portsmouth, then by hovercraft across the choppy waters of the English Channel. It's a practical, but none too glamorous, form of transportation, especially when at capacity and your fellow travelers, fueled by ale and burgers, are retching in close proximity. Being young and vigilant though, we bore all this in our stride, and it was an adventure from which Elton and I along with Steve and a couple of boys from Dick's office expected great things.

The comparisons to the sunny day in the park with the Stones should be noted. Along with the significant geographical difference (about four hours to get there all told), the weather was overcast and gloomy, the ground scrubby and damp, and the vistas bleak. We were also out of luck in our proximity from the stage, the equivalent of several city blocks seemingly standing between Bob and us. Still we settled in and waited and waited.

In between opening acts, Jeff Dexter, the impish scenester who spun discs at the London club Middle Earth, relentlessly pounded the crowd with the Stones recently released "Honky Tonk Women." It sounded really good, loud, aggressive, and raw. That is, for the first few times. After that, Charlie Watts's introductory cowbell elicited a collective groan from many of the 150,000 in attendance.

Finally, two hours late and with the wind picking up and the sun already set, The Band ambled onto the stage. Were they good? They were very, very good. However, the sound, while not terrible, was hindered by a PA that couldn't compete with the velocity of the wind. This caused an uncomfortable drifting of sound that set the music and vocals into a wavelike pattern that lost them momentarily one second only to bring them back the next. Disappointing? Of course, not to mention disconcerting. We were cold and uncomfortable enough as it was without being subjected to the meddling of the elements.

It was pretty much the same when Dylan, dressed in a white suit, sauntered on unannounced around 11 p.m. Let's face it: it's hard when you're older to assume the persona of your younger self. The idea of sitting close to fourteen hours in a damp field hemmed in by thousands of disgruntled hippies, a portable toilet a speck in the distance, and not a crumb to be had is so incongruous to the current me, someone who doesn't like restaurants that don't take reservations—it's as foreign as Bali is from Birmingham.

I might have pretended it was worth the wait back then, and if I did, I was a complete idiot. Our migratory trek, even viewed through rose-colored glasses and factoring in romantic reflection, still left a lot to be desired. Dylan played for a miserly hour, and it was OK but far from inspiring. His tardiness was disrespectful to an adoring crowd that was prepared to be volcanic in its appreciation. After so long away it could have been a triumph of magnanimous proportions. Then again it was Dylan, a man who has never concerned himself with losing out in order to remain contrary. At least at the Isle of Wight show you could actually discern what song he was singing, unlike in later years when he turned it into a guessing game.

Taking the pulse of what was percolating was easily accessible. Places like the Marquee on Wardour Street and Klooks Kleek in West Hampstead were cheap enough that we could go multiple times without breaking the bank. One of the very first shows we took in at the latter was Brian Auger and the Trinity featuring Julie Driscoll. Driscoll, who remains woefully underrated and unappreciated in the annals of British rock, was a mesmerizing performer. Willowy, stylish, and beautiful, her serpentine hand gestures and trancelike stare set her apart from her contemporaries. An interesting fact is that Driscoll and Auger were one of the very few to ever cover a song by songwriter David Ackles. Ackles would loom large in Elton's and my personal history at a later date when he would open for us at the Troubadour in West Hollywood and I would produce his album *American Gothic*. Currently, we were simply huge fans of his work and blind to what the future held.

If I were to have to cite one musical event in those heady days of Elton's and my incubation that was a complete game changer it would have to be the Charles Lloyd Quartet and Rahsaan Roland Kirk performance at the Hammersmith Odeon. The reasons why are several. Up to this point, jazz had been uncharted waters for me. I was hip enough to certain elements of instrumental experimentation from listening to the likes of Paul Horn, Gary McFarland, and Moondog, the eccentric Viking of Fifth Avenue. But true jazz, per se, was not on my shopping list.

That performance was a completely heterogeneous experience. Creeping up on me with stealth and sophistication, it overwhelmed me with its complexity while at the same time introduced me to improvisation and tonal abstraction. I recall being totally infatuated by these powerful African American musicians who seemed to be operating on a different wavelength to what I was used to. It wasn't just their intensity and obvious dedication, but the powerful interconnection that was entirely divergent from the interplay between rock bands. Where rock musicians dominated their own space and commanded a singular spotlight, these guys hunkered in on each other, a scrum of solidarity riding the groove and reading each other by some kind of fluid telepathy.

Looking back on it today, just the fact that I witnessed Charles Lloyd, Keith Jarrett, and Jack DeJohnette (who tuned his kit while soloing) together on the same stage is right up there among my heavenly musical highlights.

After we put Furlong Road in our rearview mirror, we were welcomed at Frome Court. Derf was back full time from abroad, making things a little snugger but no less amiable. By this time I was certainly a fixture there, and to this day, no matter the eventual outcomes and how acrimonious it all became, I'm still indebted to the generosity both Elton's mother and stepfather afforded me back when I was still in my teens.

Elton and I certainly made the most of our limited space at the apartment. If Dick James's offices were our destination to divest ourselves of the products of our labor and a place to record and store our ammunition, then Frome Court was where we squirreled away our modest acquisitions and maintained our regime of compositional trade-off.

Our room may have been small, but it was orchestrated to our needs. Cheap black spring-loaded metal bunkbeds were pressed against the wall (I occupied the top) where Elton would hang his beads and bangles at night, causing an irritating jingle when you were trying to get a decent night's sleep. There was a "his side" and a "my side," and both sides were incredibly well-organized (something we have in common to this day). Elton was obsessed with collecting those weekly historical magazines chronicling world wars and art and science. He would purchase these periodicals and then invest in binders to pull them all together into a complete encyclopedia. I was more about books, so my side was a little thinner due to the fact that our meager retainer didn't allow me many luxuries. Of course, pride of place was given to our albums. Again, because of limited funds, I had to pick and choose wisely. My ultimate choices were branded with my initials in tiny print on the rear lower right side of the jacket, so as not to confuse mine with his. I recall Elton found this strange in so much as he probably couldn't envision a time when we wouldn't be sharing a room in the suburbs of London.

On Monday morning, October 27, 1969, Sheila fried up a couple of eggs slotted in some toast and brewed three cups of tea while I wrote something called "Your Song." I don't think it took me more than ten minutes, but it's eventual melodic accompaniment and release would traverse decades, becoming our signature song and, in the minds of many, our first bona fide classic. It might sound like an oxymoron, but there was a simple complexity to it that completely mirrored my own adolescent turmoil. In retrospect, what I'm proudest of is the song's honesty. I was seven months shy of my twentieth birthday, a virginal crusader, idealistic in my concept of innocence and love. The protagonist in the song is untarnished and unsophisticated. Like ourselves (and I include Elton in this because of his own simple untapped desires), we were uninitiated in sexual deceit and the crueler machinations of seasoned deception. That would all come later, but as for now, this simple ode to a fictional infatuation was the best autobiography I possessed. Without Elton's melody, it never would have flown. It melds the two components perfectly. The opening chords usher in a haunting embrace so in sync with the lyric, it's no wonder we realized that the last two and a half years hadn't been for nothing.

With "Your Song" we turned a corner, setting us on a path to a heightened awareness of our capabilities and a more mature approach that eventually morphed into a style that was completely our own. It concluded our first phase, a time of incalculable memories, a growth spurt that plucked me out of unthinkable probabilities in the anonymity of the barren north.

Turning Left at Greenland

This scepter'd isle, this other Eden, demi-paradise,
this blessed plot, this earth, this realty, this Los Angeles.
—SHAKESPEARE / STEVE MARTIN
Richard II / *L.A. Story*

E ven the smog couldn't curb my enthusiasm. Though the earth below was not yet visible, I was fully aware that in a matter of minutes we would penetrate this vast carpet of putrid orange and touch down in Los Angeles. It floated like a contaminated alien spaceship, an immense decomposing cloud trapped between the San Gabriel and Santa Monica Mountain ranges. Although the Clean Air Act had just been passed, it would be several years until its stipulations would begin to eradicate the extensive pollution. Like London's fog, the smog was so debilitating at times that in addition to the obvious health issues, it caused multiple freeway pileups and pedestrian casualties. In the early hours it lay low, hugging the ground and forcing the sun to remain dormant until it did its damage and retreated into the sky. With a sickly yellow pallor, it swirled through the streets like a wafting plague, choking the morning. Undoubtedly, it was a problem, but one that wasn't about to infringe upon my expectations.

LA had been a long time coming, and in all honesty, there were times when I imagined I might never make it here. I'd often wonder: Had circumstances played their hand differently and I'd chartered a different course than the one I was on, would I have grown tired of the farm, taken the bull by the horns, and emigrated? There was no doubt this is where I wanted to be, but if it had been in any other capacity, would I have had the nerve? Music and American culture had driven me here ever since the quirky Englishness of my adolescence had been replaced by the holy grail of a mythic America.

Our transition to the West Coast experience came to a skidding halt once we left the terminal building. Sitting at the curb was a red double decker London bus emblazoned along the side with a banner reading *"ELTON JOHN HAS ARRIVED!"* Not terribly subtle, but then nothing was in the hands of our PR representative, Norman Winter. Norman, fleshy of face with a razor-cut pageboy haircut and high-waisted polyester pants, was a complete caricature of the motor-mouthed showbiz huckster. Like something Mel Brooks might invent, he was in every way so stereotypical that it was hard not to be slightly amused by his overwhelming presence.

After the obligatory photos were taken in front of the bus—shots, I might add, in which we all look significantly bemused—we boarded our transport and commenced to circumvent the freeway and rumble through the backstreets. This route was due to the fact that the top speed of the bus eliminated it from access to the 405 freeway. As Cadillacs, Mustangs, and all manner of flashy automobiles roared past us, we couldn't help but wonder why we weren't enjoying the luxury of a limo instead of feeling like we were back home on the 183 to Golders Green.

Humiliation aside, once we made it onto Sunset Boulevard, excitement replaced disappointment. This was fabled territory, and for this group it was thrilling to be actually beholding familiar sights previously only seen in the movies and on TV.

Outside of Elton, myself, bassist Dee Murray, drummer Nigel Olsson, and equipment manager Bob Stacey, additional fellow travelers included our original mentor Steve Brown, graphic designer David Larkham, and manager Ray Williams. Ray was the only member of our party who had actually been stateside before and the only one with some knowledge as to the lay of the land.

Disembarking in front of our hotel, the notorious Continental Hyatt House, we scrambled as quickly as possible into the foyer rather than draw attention to our mode of transport. The Hyatt House, known to its multitude of musical patrons as the "Riot House," was an institution and the first real hotel I'd ever stayed in. I'd only recently turned twenty and was not terribly grown-up. It was an exhilarating thrill to have my own room with a TV, a bed bigger than a coffin, and an altogether foreign appliance called a shower. Bear in mind we were products of the British '50s. As a child I'd grown up in houses without electricity and bathed in a tin tub in front of the fireplace. Even in the advent of our sojourn to the States, we were still hitting the tub only once or twice a week. At Elton's mother's apartment, where we were currently still residing, hot water had to be rationed out, and with four bodies to cleanse it was necessary to deal it out democratically.

Many will tell you that the 1960s idealistic bent and hippy dream died alongside Meredith Hunter in the toxic atmosphere of the Altamont Speedway. The Stones' free concert that ended in violence and murder is often cited as the final nail in the coffin of a decade both turbulent and artistically innovative. The decennium was over anyway, and being that this concert took place in Northern California at the tail end of the decade in December 1969, all the Hells Angels, who had been hired as security, did, along with their acts of transgression and subjugation, was simply hasten the inevitable.

But in Los Angeles, California, in August 1970, it just seemed like more '60s to me. I can't say I noticed any change. If there was a border line between the decades, it was blurred and unconvincing. It was two years after Robert Kennedy was gunned down in the Ambassador Hotel, the war was still raging in Vietnam, Nixon was still in the White House, and Charlie Manson and company were on trial downtown. On the street and in the stores and restaurants, things were still pretty trippy, and the overall aura was most definitely of a laid-back and harmonious nature. Being British still elicited excitement and much appreciated attention from the girls. Brian Wilson was right, by the way. Not only were they *the cutest girls in the world*, they were also infused with a confidence and vitality that we limeys were completely unaccustomed to.

We touched down in LA on Friday, August 21, and had a few days to kill before we were scheduled to open at the Troubadour on August 25. Naturally, we hit the road running and dove into the discovery pool right away. On the night of our arrival, David Rosner, who was our US publishing connection, and his wife, Margo, took a group of us to investigate the sight of what was to be our introduction to the American Stage. The Troubadour was a club with a legendary pedigree. The owner, Doug Weston, was an imposing six foot six. Rangy and vaguely anomalous with Colonel Custer–length locks and a sizable knife strapped to his hip, he exuded a sort of retro pioneer persona when in an earlier time he might have been trapping beaver on the banks of the Colorado River. He'd turned his venue into one of the most prestigious springboards for talent in the United States, a veritable oasis for the emerging singer-songwriter movement of the 1970s. All the major players had either graced its stage or would in the following months. James Taylor, Carol King, Joni Mitchell, Cat Stevens, and Jackson Browne had all benefited from initial exposure here, as had other burgeoning acts like Linda Ronstadt, Van Morrison, and various Eagles.

The club, located in West Hollywood on Santa Monica Boulevard just east of Doheny Drive, was a funky looking building of mismatched components that had changed little in its decor or design since opening in the late 1950s. This gregarious institution attracted not just the patrons, but it also acted as the official clubhouse for all manner of transient musicians' networking and plotting strategy. At its bar, bands were formed, songs were swapped, and deals were made.

On that first night when I stepped through the door, I lucked out. The headliner was the progressive bluegrass band the Dillards. I'd been introduced to the group through their wonderfully exuberant 1968 album *Wheatstraw Suite* and had been a fan ever since. Elton and I were so enamored with them that we would ultimately take them out with us as an opening act three years later. The opening act that night, however, was not quite as impressive but would in the fullness of time divest themselves of each other to become serious players. The duo in question, Longbranch Pennywhistle, was a pairing of J. D. Souther and

Glenn Frey, both regulars in the Troubadour's storied bar. They would soon part ways, with J. D. excelling as a writer of superior quality songs, and Glenn going on to be one of the founding members of a little old band called the Eagles.

The following day there was only one thing on our minds. When Elton had initially suffered some momentary doubt about making the trip, I swear that the clincher in persuading him otherwise was the opportunity to experience Tower Records. The temptation had proved too great and paid off in spades. Now we were here and in need of binoculars to see the other end of the store. Tower Records was an institution that had begun in Sacramento in the early '60s before expanding to San Francisco and eventually Los Angeles. Ultimately, it would cover the world, but for now one was all we needed. Kids in a candy store is putting it mildly. Miles of aisles, it was stocked to the gills with every genre imaginable in every format possible. As much as we thought we knew, and as hip as we imagined we were to all manner of obscurities, Tower Records opened up a whole new world. While hot new releases were heavily touted at the forefront of the store, stacked several feet high and embraced heavily by promotional materials, the exploratory treasures, rarities, and other unknowns lay in the deeper recesses of the acreage. I can't even begin to recount how much music I discovered here.

To this day, I can still recall my very first purchase in LA. It was a pair of Stars and Stripes emblazoned tennis shoes that I bought from Zeidler & Zeidler, a hip clothing store at the corner of Sunset and Laurel Canyon Boulevard. It had the distinction of being located directly around the corner from the legendary Schwab's Pharmacy. The lunch counter at Schwab's had been a popular Hollywood hang from the 1930s through the 1950s, and was said to be where the director Mervyn LeRoy discovered Lana Turner. In all honesty, old Hollywood was still very much alive, and when I say alive, I mean that so many of the stars that reigned during the golden era were still significantly visible not only at the old established restaurants and watering holes but cruising the Strip and standing in line for ice cream at Baskin-Robbins. Yeah, that was indeed Jack Lemmon and Gene Kelly behind me waiting on a cone. I also caught Lauren Bacall hopping out of her convertible to pick up cookies at Famous Amos, and Rock Hudson gassing up at the Chevron station. In due course, I would often see Alfred Hitchcock and Jimmy Stewart in their respective booths at Chasen's, Phyllis Diller singing standards with the piano player at Perino's, and on one occasion I made change for Barbara Stanwyck at the Santa Palm Car Wash. Well into the '70s it was not unusual to still spot the old guard out and about. I often sat at a table adjacent to Orson Welles at Ma Maison on Melrose while Gregory Peck and Fred Astaire could often be seen wandering around Rod Stewart's house parties. Gary Grant got around also, and he spent the day with us at one of our Dodger Stadium gigs in 1975. I also have a great photo of me and Mae West taken at a party Elton threw for his former manager John Reid. In the shot, she looks as stuffed as Trigger, but she was in fact still sharp as a tack. Elton and a couple of guys visited her at her home a couple of days later. She swanned into the room, took one look at her guests, and declared, "Agh, just what I love, wall to wall men."

What I found interesting was that these two generational factions were colliding with tremendous ease. After all, the older generation had existed in a period of time that, while follically and sartorially different, was no less unhinged on a recreational level. Ever since the Jazz Age, there had been hellions stoking the fires of musical insurrection and prodigious debauchery, alcohol, and drugs. The likes of jazz cornetist Bix Beiderbecke, old-time banjo player Charlie Poole, and a host of silent movie stars were the blueprint of things to come, and they lived life to such extremes that the first generation of classic rock paled by comparison.

The fact that rock and roll was met with such animosity and derision is puzzling. It shouldn't have been anything new to anyone. Change comes in waves, and in the first instance what was branded as a flash in the pan by the purveyors of the Great American Songbook was in all likelihood viewed as a threat to their standing in the hierarchy of popular music. They were seeing the writing on the wall, and initially, although they were loath to admit it in their heart of hearts, they most likely knew it spelled out their demotion to antiquity. They were still in step with a certain demographic, but to the young in general relegated to be curios of a fading era.

Dean Martin may have rolled his eyes when the Stones debuted on his TV show in 1964, and Frank Sinatra famously dismissed Elvis's music as a "rancid smelling aphrodisiac," but in their defense, I imagine there was some underlying fear involved. After all the grumbling and snide asides, Martin and Sinatra eventually changed their tune and realized there was gold in them thar hills.

If only they'd experienced some precognition, these two, especially, would have seen that there was room on the playground for everyone. Once their initial attitudes melted, they shared the charts simultaneously along with those they'd derided. Dean Martin, for example, knocked the Beatles out of the number one spot on the charts in 1964, while Frank Sinatra achieved the same position in 1966. Hurdling the likes of the Monkees and the Mamas and the Papas, Frank was back again three years later doing it his way in the company of Creedence Clearwater Revival and Sly & the Family Stone. Times certainly changed along with attitudes. Dean would ultimately sire a rock musician, have a Beach Boy as a son-in-law, and be regarded as the consummate icon of cool. Meanwhile, Frank wound up in a kaftan and beads singing Laura Nyro songs with The 5th Dimension.

My one and only interaction with Sinatra came at the Universal Amphitheater in 1978. He'd been known to perform "Sorry Seems to Be the Hardest Word" in concert, but he was now trying out a brand-new number we'd recently penned for him specifically. This, of course, was aces in our book as there are secret lists stored in the minds of all songwriters that contain the names of those we dream of singing our songs. The song in question, "September," was tailor-made for Frank's inimitable style, and while it probably wasn't a classic by any means it had a weary world-worn resolve that fit what was by that time his slightly faltering baritone.

What made this concert so special outside the inclusion of our song was that, as always, Sinatra went out of his way to credit the songwriter and arranger of whatever song he was performing. When it came to the introduction of our number, Frank became the only person ever in the entertainment business to say my name using the French pronunciation. It was an indelible moment, the personalization of it taking me completely by surprise. Almost at the same time a hand fell on my shoulder. A rather large hand, I might add, that was connected to the equally imposing personage of Jilly Rizzo, Frank's longtime consigliere and chief aide. After determining that I was indeed me, he leaned in and said, "Frank wans ta sees ya." This didn't sound like a request, but then I didn't need to be persuaded. Along with my friend, Alice Cooper, who was my date that evening, we trundled along in the wake of Jilly's formidable gait. Sinatra, who was not known to perform encores, was concluding his set and taking a bow as we were ushered into what I imagined to be a holding area for guests. To my surprise, it wasn't more than ten minutes before we were invited in to take tea with the Chairman.

Frank Sinatra in the flesh; was I impressed? Let me tell you while I've always appreciated meeting fellow artists and musical heroes, I'm rarely impressed to the point of giddy fandom. I've always been of the belief that no matter their background, we're all equal in God's eyes, the blood in our veins comparable and the pants we wear put on the same way. Well, that theory lasted for about as long as it took to write that last line. Sure, he'd filled out a little and the lines in his face were slightly more pronounced, but it suited him. Interestingly enough, he wasn't wearing his toupee and while his hair was certainly thinning it didn't appear to be radically receding. His tuxedo was immaculate and his handshake firm and sincere. My presence wasn't initially so much in the moment as it was reviewing the movie that was unspooling in my head. An instantaneous journey from his Hoboken roots to here and now. It was a life I knew back to front, and for all my criteria as to the rules of engagement, I'll admit I was awestruck. The history contained in this one individual exceeded the norm. Arguably the greatest song stylist of the twentieth century, his was a life comparable to a great American novel crafted by the combined authorship of Runyon, Hammett, and Hemingway. The singular embodiment of a career lived to the fullest, synonymous with everything vibrant, provocative, and galvanizing in the decades since he'd had bobby-soxers peeing their pants at the Paramount Theatre in 1944.

He couldn't have been more personable, and when he placed his hand on my shoulder and expressed an admiration for our songs, it felt more like a benediction than a compliment. A photo exists of the moment and in it the look on my face is a combined blend of glazed adulation and obsequious terror. The fact that the integrated legacy of his music and personal style is still emulated and revered today is a testament to the far-reaching appeal of his timeless panache and undiminished hipness. In my book, he's still the king.

The two days preceding our opening night at the Troubadour were a whirlwind blend of the obvious and the exploratory. Our record company sent us to Disneyland. Thankfully, this was done via limousine rather than a continuation of the London bus theme. This being 1970, Disneyland was still controlled by a serious dress code and had a negative attitude toward long hair. In other words: no hippies allowed. The only member of our party they seemed to find less than desirable was photographer Ed Caraeff. We'd been introduced to Ed via Danny Hutton, one of the three lead singers in the popular band Three Dog Night. We'd befriended Danny's band after they'd been the first American act to become familiar with our material prior to our initial visit. They'd covered our song "Lady Samantha" on their second studio album, 1969's *Suitable for Framing*. Ed had shot the cover photo and in turn became an associate, and that ultimately led to us. Ed's pedigree was impressive. Just the fact that he'd snapped the infamous shot of Hendrix setting his guitar on fire at the Monterey Pop Festival was enough to give him serious cultural status. Ed would go on to be intertwined with our designer, David Larkham, on many of our best known '70s album covers. For now though, it was his impressive Afro that seemed to be causing derision with the fresh-faced guardians of the gate. After a certain amount of haggling and assurances that Ed was not in fact part of the Weather Underground, we were allowed access to the Magic Kingdom.

Amusement parks of this magnitude were an unknown entity to us. What we knew as fun fairs were a depressing oddity, either rickety transient affairs that set up shop on the local village green for a couple of days, or permanently situated installations along the blustery piers of seedy seaside towns. Reeking of cotton candy and rancid chip fat, they more often than not revolved around the bumper cars where tinny '50s pop blasted out while the ticket takers, perennial chancers hung louchely onto the back of the cars, flirting with teenage girls. It was all horribly depressing and socially demoralizing, especially for horny young schoolboys who were outplayed by enviable carneys. Still, I was at Disneyland and they weren't. Chaperoned by a perfectly coiffed and delightful guide, we spent the day doing Disney as it was then. Up the Matterhorn, through the Haunted Mansion, and across a Frontier that didn't particularly align with my sense of realism but was kitsch enough to be amusing in a sanitized coonskin cap and historically whitewashed sort of way. Pioneering women spotlessly turned out and effervescent, interacting with equally jolly Native Americans portrayed by white high school summer jobbers in raven-colored wigs. The Jungle Cruise and Pirates of the Caribbean were still in their infancy and operating in their original format, this being several decades before they were altered by political correctness in the 2000s.

So much has been written about Elton's debut at the Troubadour that I'm loath to repeat the obvious. The celebrity turnout has been touted, but in all honesty I can't recall it being excessive. Aside from Neil Diamond doing the introductory honors and Quincy Jones and Leon Russell front and center, that's about it. I'm told there were a couple of Beach Boys in attendance (who have, to the best of my knowledge, never been identified), and I did meet the drummer of Buffalo Springfield. In the years following, if everyone who claims to have been present during that week was actually there, we could have played Dodger Stadium instead of waiting until 1975.

I've always wondered how many people in the crowd that opening night had actually heard our album. I'm of the opinion that it was more about word of mouth than indoctrinated ears. I think it was established through the grapevine that it was the place to be. A bit like the Devils Tower in *Close Encounters of the Third Kind*, a certain element of enlightened individuals were fine-tuned into perceiving that something special was about to happen, hence the atmosphere of reserved expectancy in the room as Elton took the stage. It was a relatively short set, nine songs in total. Five from our current album, two from *Tumbleweed Connection*, which was yet to be released, one B side, and one cover. No marathon, but enough to solidify Elton's onstage presence and our writing chops. I don't recall sitting, just pacing, watching from all vantage points as the crowd reaction, like a ripple, gathered momentum into a wave of genuine acclamation. Undoubtedly, the crowd had no preconceived idea as to what to expect from his performance. All they'd seen were a couple of moody promotional shots that gave no clue to what this supposedly introspective bespectacled Englishman had to offer performance-wise. There's more reason to believe that they were expecting Randy Newman rather than Jerry Lee Lewis channeling Randy Newman, but it was certainly Elton's incendiary acrobatics and vocal sincerity that closed the deal. As if charged by a sort of galvanization, the room exploded, all components of affected composure temporarily unspooling. Many years later, Leon Russell admitted to me that he turned to Shelter Records boss Denny Cordell at the conclusion of the show and exclaimed, "Well, that's me done!"

LA Times critic Robert Hilburn's review of the show in the following day's paper didn't hurt either. It was glowing and succinctly declared the show "magnificent," our music "staggeringly original," and my lyrics as "capturing the same timeless, objective spirit of the Band's Robbie Robertson." He concluded by stating, "He's going to be one of rock's biggest and most important stars." Pretty potent stuff that I imagine was hard not to let go to our heads. This being said, the aftershock of this musical eruption was by no means immediate, and it was necessary to put things into perspective in order to let the penny drop. It was as obvious as the nose on your face that it had been a successful gig, but after all, it was just one gig and it would be premature to get overly excited.

What Hilburn's review did do was create a buzz locally that certainly helped in filling the club for the remainder of the week. It also most likely reverberated up north to San Francisco where we were due to travel after concluding our LA run. This was to be at the Troubadour's sister location on Bush Street between Union Square and Nob Hill. It should be duly noted that the *Chronicle*'s review of our first show in the Bay Area was snotty at best while our reception was once again rapturous. Perhaps the notice was structured to slap us back down after the *Times*'s critical acclamation. San Francisco had a reputation for tough crowds and a cynical press corps, but given the choice, conquering the former as opposed to impressing the latter seemed like the better deal. I'm not sure this first whiff of negativity soured us in any way as our record company was already making good use of all that was positive. While we were wrapping up our West Coast commitments, they were strategizing our forward propulsion. Up next, New York and the irrepressible Norman Winter was relentless in making damn sure that Elton John's name was echoing down the Eastern Seaboard. The wave was gathering momentum and Norman was surfing the crest, spreading the word in the only way he knew how, loud and unfiltered, his fervid personality soaking the arbiters of influence with an ocean of stunt publicity and laudatory hype. Eventually, it would trickle down into the Southern states and on into the heartland. If there is one major misconception in all this, it's that the opening night at the Troubadour made us overnight sensations. It may have changed our lives, but it didn't buy the game. We had work to do, a lot of work.

In mulling it over, it also occurred to me that another component that added to the night's triumph was the other two guys. Some of the crowd's initial skepticism (if pockets of it existed) might have griped that our band wasn't comprised of a conventional lineup. Some may have conceded that the absence of a guitarist at a time when six-string virtuosos were as necessary as mashed potatoes and gravy was, in our case, tantamount to insanity. The originality of a trio consisting of only piano, bass, and drums didn't sound so good on paper, but what people didn't take into consideration, if they were indeed questioning our logic, was that the bass player and drummer in question were Dee Murray and Nigel Olsson, respectively. These were no ordinary side-men, as proved spectacularly on our opening night. Their playing was fearless, almost symphonic in its clarity, and they managed to create a melodic tsunami. Dee's chromatic fills and momentary accents played into the melody as innovative as the achievements of any lead guitar while Nigel's drumming was almost classically creative, rolling thunder and gentle rain in equal measures, his deft timing and touch blending with Dee's bottom end to formulate a rhythm section of orchestral pro-portions. It was all totally original, and quite honestly, I don't think the crowd had ever seen anything like it.

ONE DAY I ran into Kris Kristofferson in the lobby of the Hyatt House. Kris's debut album had been released several months prior to our first visit and he was already being hailed as a major new force in songwriting. I'd been hugely impressed by his work and was equally as enthusiastic about the material on his sophomore record *The Silver Tongued Devil and I*. The best of his songs (and there were many) were destined to become country standards and were achingly magnificent in their poignancy and intellect. We exchanged pleasantries, compli-mented each other on our burgeoning success, and hoped we'd run into each other again somewhere down the road.

As it happens, somewhere down the road was the bar of the Speak-easy Club, in 1972. The Speak was a rock star hang on Margaret Street in London that, since the '60s, had seen its tiny stage attract a wealth of musical aristocracy. Its restaurant and horseshoe bar catered to the same crowd, and is still talked about in reverential terms today as ground zero for many legendary musical firsts.

Kris was at the bar with a fresh-faced young Midwesterner called John Prine. Prine, a former mail carrier from Illinois who, like Kristof-ferson before him, was making waves and creating a significant buzz with his first two releases. In the country-folk vein, his material con-veyed a wonderful sense of melancholy, social commentary, and ruminations on the common man. Like Kris, he was destined for great things, and quite rightly so. John was an impossibly sweet man, wise beyond his years, and funny as hell.

John was, however, currently feeling no pain due to rather too much of whatever it was he was drinking. This was fine, he was young, in London for the first time, and enjoying a night out. The only problem was that he was due to appear on *The Old Grey Whistle Test*, the late-night live studio TV show hosted by Bob Harris.

The fact that this performance was becoming increasingly more imminent was of the utmost concern to Kris. After all, John was Kris's discovery and it was thanks to him that John had been signed to Atlantic Records. So, in a way, he felt responsible, and with no record company minders availing themselves I was enlisted to aid in manhandling the intoxicated troubadour to his date with the mic.

There are possibly those who were there that night that might recall it with more clarity than I, but to my recall, we managed to get him through it without any major disasters. There is no footage, or none that I can find, of his performance that night. All that is available is his appearance on the same show the following year where he's singing "Dear Abby" looking sparkly eyed and in no need of support.

The way I remember it was that there was black coffee and a great deal of keeping him sandwiched upright between the two of us. Kris tuned his guitar, stuck it in his hands, and we maneuvered him into the studio. By this time he'd regained a little more confidence in his equilibrium, and providing he remained stationary, there was less likelihood of him pitching forward. It was the falling backward that concerned us. If he closed his eyes and rolled his head back at an emotive moment, chances were he might lose his balance. In an effort to avert this, it was decided we should remain with him in the studio. Crouched out of camera sight, like Elvis on Ed Sullivan, he was shot from the waist up as we, at intervals, placed reassuring hands on his ass to keep him vertical. He made it through surprisingly well, and with business conducted we repaired to the Speakeasy where any further recollection of the evening ends.

Record companies were an altogether different animal back then. Long before they began consuming each other and elevating themselves into corporate juggernauts, they operated on a looser and less buttoned-up hierarchy. There was more air circulating between individuals, less watching your back, and undoubtedly more of an invitational nature where artists were concerned. Our label, UNI (short for Universal City Records and owned by MCA), was the perfect example. Originally housed along with Norman's publicity crib in the two-story Sol Hurok Building on Sunset, they had soon after our arrival moved to MCA's headquarters in the more imposing Black Tower over the hill on Lankershim Boulevard in the San Fernando Valley. The structure might have been monolithic and modern in design, but the offices remained untainted by administrative oppression. Situated on the ninth floor, it had an open-plan feel that allowed everyone to interact visually. Unlike today, where executive offices encircle a tightly packed nest of impersonal cubicles continuously lit by a twenty-four hour barrage of florescent strips, back then in UNI's headquarters the light poured in generously through a glass wall of windows that illuminated an overall atmosphere of interactive conviviality.

We enjoyed visiting and were always made welcome by everyone involved in the job of selling what we had to say. They genuinely believed in us, and it was obvious from the start that getting us seen and heard with the optimum results was of primary order. While MCA was run by the more conservative and straitlaced Mike Maitland, UNI's ship was steered by the irrepressible and gregarious personality of Russ Regan. Russ, whose hearty phrases and expansive gestures became much mimicked by the band, was a character of enormous likability. His mantra of "I love you guys," and a much-repeated declaration that due to my affiliation with a rustic past I'd "been here before," remained in his vocabulary until he passed away in 2018.

This comical element aside, Russ's smarts were undeniable. It was his ears that had picked up on our album and seen the potential in it even after five other major companies had turned it down. Even Larry Uttal of Bell, who had a licensing deal with Dick James, our publisher, and head of our British record label said, "No, thank you." Like Dick Rowe, the Decca record head of A&R who passed on the Beatles, Uttal spent the rest of his career kicking himself in the pants.

Equally as industrious were Russ's executive team. The two main guys were national sales manager Rick Frio (a dead ringer for comedian Bud Abbott) and promo head Pat Pipolo, who was tenacious and savvy and was responsible for the increasing auditory presence of our records on radios across the country. It was Pat's insistence, after escalating airplay on Black radio, that we released "Bennie and the Jets" as a single in 1973. In the face of stiff resistance from us, he made it happen, and due to its phenomenal popularity, we were duly repentant of questioning his better judgment.

They all dressed like narcs, of course, like undercover cops trying to infiltrate the youth culture. It was sweetly obvious that they (not unlike Sinatra) had ditched their corporate clothing overnight for loud prints, flared pants, and Nehru jackets. Muttonchop sideburns and mustaches were in evidence while their hair, which I imagine had once been conservatively cropped, was now regulation mop-top.

Russ on the road was always fun. Joining us on many occasions as we crisscrossed the country, he would invariably find the most spacious room available in the Holiday Inns we constantly camped out in. I'm not sure that they offered suites back then because he'd always reserve two adjoining rooms, turning one into his own personal entertainment center. Making good use of his expense account, there would always be an abundance of club sandwiches, hamburgers, and fries available during the afternoon prior to our shows. While we took full advantage of these liberal feasts, Russ, like some benevolent potentate, would expound on his world vision, one that I might add revolved around the global microcosm of Elton John and his unquestionable and impending universal dominance.

Headliners invariably grew wary of us as an opening act, and although we supported some legends both current and classic it didn't take a crystal ball to foresee we'd soon be switching roles and bringing in our own choices. We'd entertained the crowds warming up for the likes of Derek and the Dominos, Leon Russell, The Kinks, and the Byrds, but once the tables had turned, things got way more interesting. At the Santa Monica Civic, our first LA auditorium show in November of 1970, our opening acts were the firebrand folk queen Odetta and an emerging slide guitar player called Ry Cooder.

Without a doubt my favorite opening act ever was at the Boston Tea Party, a psychedelic rock venue in Kenmore Square across the road from Fenway Park. The inclusion of the Reverend Gary Davis (*or* Blind Gary Davis) on the bill just goes to prove how diverse rock shows were at the time. Some noteworthy pairings included the Staple Singers and the MC5, The Who and Tony Williams Lifetime, Tim Hardin and Fleetwood Mac, Ten Years After and Big Mama Thornton, and Miles Davis opening for Laura Nyro.

Gary Davis, an ordained minister and fingerpicking genius in the blues gospel style, was an almost mythological entity. Born in North Carolina, he'd relocated to New York in the 1940s, performing on street corners and teaching guitar to an array of future notables such as Stefan Grossman, David Bromberg, Dave Van Ronk, and Bob Weir. At the point of his inclusion on our bill, I'm at pains to say that I was not familiar with this seventy-four-year-old genius, yet the epiphany of his performance and its long-reaching legacy still resonates today. Bob Dylan sang *No one can sing the blues like Blind Willie McTell*, which is as may be, but for my money, while I too admire McTell, no one, simply no one, played like Gary Davis. His style: alternating thumbed bass and high string melody, both parts picked simultaneously, materialized like ragtime piano on guitar. The guitar in question, a Gibson J-200, was his preferred instrument and featured on the majority of his recordings. His 1960 album *Harlem Street Singer*, one of the few blues records to be recorded by legendary jazz engineer Rudy Van Gelder, is regarded as one of the most pristine and breathtaking records of the folk era. It's lost none of its intimacy over the years and still constantly spins on my turntable, remaining an inspirational document of an extraordinary voice and feral instrumentalism. If I have one regret it's that I never got to shake his hand and thank him, prematurely, for what I would ultimately derive from his otherworldly talent.

It was at the same time that we were initially frequenting UNI's offices that I started to notice an individual cut from distinctly different cloth. He conducted himself at a discreet distance from everyone else and was in total contrast to the modish dress and grooming of his hyperactive colleagues. Ramrod straight and tall with distinct military bearing, his shirts were tailor fitted and western in design, his jeans straight legged and pressed with perfect creases. Wearing yellow aviators, he sported an impressive tan and wore his hair slicked back rather than combed forward. Most impressively of all, though, were his highly polished, snip toe cowboy boots.

In due course, curiosity got the better of me and I inquired as to his position in the company. It turned out that David Skepner was MCA's West Coast liaison with Nashville, a conduit to mainstream country music and obviously someone I needed to know.

While country's influence had been gradually seeping into the repertoire of some of rock's most notable musicians, it was still a fringe genre scoffed at and maligned by a younger generation of record buyers who mistrusted it and viewed it as a mawkish and clichéd bastion of conservatism. The Byrds's magnificent country rock classic *Sweetheart of the Rodeo* had been ridiculed by their fans while influential practitioners of the art form such as Gram Parsons, Chris Hillman, and Michael Nesmith of the Monkees would struggle to push it into the mainstream with groundbreaking albums like the Flying Burrito Brothers' *The Gilded Palace of Sin* and Nesmith's *Magnetic South*. Even the Dillards with their intoxicating blend of country, bluegrass, and rock were little known outside a hard-core but limited fan base. It would take time, but in the coming years with the advent of Linda Ronstadt and the Eagles, the lines defining the old and new would dissolve into a cohabitating alliance. Different elements interacting led to something new, and everyone it seemed was returning to the well. Even the Grateful Dead with their acid-infused jams and trippy psychedelia would in due course see their music forged on the crucible of Americana.

As for now, David Skepner seemed to be the first real bridge to the kind of music I had accidentally been initiated into so many years ago. Back then, the source material had seemed unobtainable, the tenants of my turntable like fictional characters from some sprawling saga of colonial history. Now with my traversing of the Atlantic and a possible introduction to someone with his hand in the flame, the distance didn't seem nearly as unimaginable.

I think David was impressed by the audible sigh I let out when shuffling through a stack of albums in his office and discovered that both Bill Monroe and Kitty Wells were MCA artists. Bill Monroe, the undisputed father of bluegrass, and Kitty Wells, the original "Queen of Country Music," not to mention the first female country singer to top the US country charts, were revered in a way only the exalted are.

Aside from being an excellent source of conversation, David was also responsible for kick-starting a casual recreation that would escalate over years into a grand passion and all-consuming aspect of my life. He took me riding.

When the invitation had first arisen I'd assumed we'd be heading out of town to some suburban stables or local equestrian center, not saddling up within walking distance of his office.

Because of its affiliation with Universal Studios, the MCA Tower that housed our record company sat handily at the entrance to Universal's extensive and historic film lot. In 1970, it was still a modest and bare-bones tourist attraction, a bit rinky-dink in comparison to the Goliath it's become. Throughout the day, half a dozen or so tram cars would trundle at intervals down designated routes that wound around a warren of mammoth sound stages and along paths that bypassed a limited number of set pieces and cheesy attractions.

The most colorful and effective structure on the lot was Six Points Texas, the faux western town that had been in use effectively in one configuration or another since the silent era. It was pretty damn authentic, and it was impressive to ruminate on its history. Some famous boots had strode along these streets, and iconic westerns both film and TV had been shot here. This is where we saddled up and would on several occasions leisurely amble around, circumventing this make-believe world in a unique take on the Universal Studio Tour experience. Of course, I'd always wanted to get on a horse. What red-blooded Anglo infant didn't? Galloping across the western plains was a required visual of our childhood dreams, and while this wasn't exactly the Chisholm Trail, it was still a great starting point, even though given the surroundings as they were, I was, in a way, still playacting.

David was not an LA guy. It wasn't just in the way he carried himself and the way he dressed, but it was in his no-nonsense manner and political outlook. It wasn't that he was rabidly conservative, it was that his values were more countrified, simpler, and uncluttered by new age hocus-pocus. He admired plenty of contemporary music, including ours. It's just that he was a traditionalist at heart and yearned to be free from the yoke of citified expectancy. I found him completely refreshing, not just for our shared musical proclivity, but in his straightforward appraisal of a divided nation. For someone who'd always been determined to weigh up both sides of an argument, the clarity of his logic went a long way to enable me to see things through corrective lenses rather than rose-colored glasses. He made it perfectly clear he no longer wanted to be the token cowboy in the LA office; he was hankering to fly the coop and be cinching up his horse in Tennessee.

The other two major country stars on MCA were the unparalleled and innovational Loretta Lynn and Conway Twitty, the unmistakable baritone from Helena, Arkansas, whose songs of pain-ridden guilt and steamy sexuality put an added edge to country's already domestically turbulent song content. Loretta Lynn then and up to her passing in 2022 was always the best female country star there ever was. I can hear her songs over and over and they still sound fresh and valid, perfect picture postcards, each one depicting indelible vignettes of hardscrabble life. Her language was unique, colloquial without being hackneyed, economic and visual, the songs sing like short stories. Her records sparkle and her melodies dance. You can almost smell the content of her songs, the washing on the line, biscuits baking, and the whiskey breath of her troubled men. Her melodies are so economically simple they become indelible, ingraining themselves in your head and refusing to leave.

David had developed a close personal relationship with Loretta, which in late 1972 led to him leaving MCA and accepting the role of her personal manager. He'd got what he dreamed of, and I was thrilled for him. It was a position he fulfilled with tremendous success until their parting of ways in 1986.

The last time I saw David was when he invited me to an awards show he was attending with Loretta. The most memorable moment of the event being the entrance of Doolittle Lynn, also known as Mooney, Loretta's rakish husband and unpredictable inspiration for so many of her most personal and reflective songs. If there was ever a poster child for a good ole boy, it was Mooney Lynn. Obviously late, and obviously drunk, he barged into the room, a case of beer under his arm and a beaten-up straw Stetson tipped back on his head. That this was done during a particularly tender performance by Dottie West didn't deter him from tossing beer cans to various tuxedoed guests while inquiring loudly, "Y'all OK?" and "Who wants a cold one?" Perfect material for another song, perhaps.

There's a coda to my episode with MCA's country roster. Several years later the label also signed Merle Haggard, which would have been literally too much for me to assimilate. Loretta Lynn *and* Merle Haggard? To say I like Merle Haggard is an enormous understatement. Haggard is, without a doubt, not only my favorite male country artist of all time, but one of my favorite artists—period. He was the entire package. Johnny Cash had charisma and wrote good songs, George Jones had the voice and had sung other people's good songs, but Merle sang like Lefty Frizzell and wrote unbelievably good songs. He also played a mean guitar and lived his life like the most riveting and all-encompassing country song you've ever heard. I'll defer to Emmylou Harris, my absolute Americana heroine, who succinctly said, "If you tried to introduce someone from Mars to country music, you'd play them one of Merle's records."

Around the time that Haggard's piss and vinegar songs like "Okie From Muskogee" and "The Fightin' Side of Me" were irritating hippies and incensing liberals, I'd met a a young talent manager with some loose connection to Merle's people. In the course of a dinner conversation one night, and perhaps with a little too much happy juice on board, I posed a completely hubristic suggestion. Fresh from my well-received production on David Ackles's *American Gothic*, I proposed we approach the Bakersfield badass with the idea of me getting in the studio with him and maybe creating something that could cross over and give an even better understanding of his music to the Woodstock generation.

Presumptuous? No kidding. Impetuous? Completely. What was I thinking? Instead of telling me I'd have a better chance getting Robert Goulet to record with Frank Zappa, my dinner companion totally concurred, deeming the idea "far out" and "trippy."

I don't think I have to tell you what the response from Kern County was. I'm just glad I wasn't in the room when the offer was presented. If they laughed, it was understandable. If they were perplexed, that was acceptable also. Although I'm not sure the latter, in all honesty, would have been a conceivable reaction. Merle and his posse were hard-living country boys, totally alienated from rock music and the musicians who made it. Suspicious and at times antagonistic, even violent toward nonconformists of the long-haired variety, it would be years before the outlaw movement broke down the barriers between the genres and ushered in mutual respect. For now, though, what did some twenty-two-year-old tea bag pinko know about the subgenre and strongly defined backbeat of the Bakersfield Sound?

Anyone who might imagine that the initial reverence afforded us at the Troubadour spelled out immediate rewards would be sorely mistaken. Cash was scarce and any residuals from our embryonic sales were still in the pipeline and only beginning to trickle out. If I wanted to reside here, off the clock as it were, I wasn't going to be able to afford hotel prices. Determined to acquire a foothold in LA even if it meant scraping by, then so be it. Enlisting our colorful PR agent Norman to assist in finding something suitable might not have been the wisest choice, but under the circumstances he was the only one available, being that my contacts were severely limited.

What Norman found was a dirt cheap apartment in a small cinder block complex on the corner of North Bronson and Franklin Avenue. Devoid of any character, it was a drab three room rental with a few sticks of furniture and a distinct tenor of "hiding out." Like one of those anonymous backwater motels in the movies where some on-the-run character holes up to escape the law or vengeful pursuer.

While not labeling it an altogether dangerous neighborhood, it was still a little sketchy due to the twenty-four-hour market directly across the road. The parking lot was a magnet for transients, drug dealers, and all manner of unsavory individuals. Back then, both hookers and hustlers operated openly along Sunset and Hollywood Boulevards east of Laurel Avenue. At night they would retreat to the alley adjacent to the market as if it was their own personal green room. It was a time-out between tricks, and they'd mill around sassing the cops and sparring with each other in a lewd, alien banter. They obviously had each other's backs but were at pains to admit anything that might be misread as a sign of weakness. Bathed in pools of artificial light, the garishness of their composition was painfully accentuated, the withering nature of their calling exposed in the bilious fluorescence. Within due course, as if almost on cue, they would respond to some unified clarion call and dissolve back into the night.

I wasn't exactly existing on Spam sandwiches and Tab, but any invitation to dine out on someone else's dime was hard to refuse. It was also a great way to get to know the city and learn from a select few of trusted Angelenos where all the hidden hot spots were. Russ Regan had proved to be a tappable source when it came to suggestions, his fondness for food being easily assessed by the ample dimensions of his girth. It was Russ who'd feted us on our first night in LA. Before visiting the Troubadour he'd taken us all to dinner at a popular Italian restaurant at Sunset and Roxbury called Martoni Marquis. It was a pretty big time for us and naturally we were impressed, even more so when we had our first celebrity sighting in LA and saw Sonny Bono eating clams at a table in the corner. We also found out that George, the dad of Micky Dolenz of the Monkees, had died from a heart attack on the roof of the restaurant in 1963. A bit of trivia that was completely de rigueur of LA's storied subculture.

I'd like to think I wasn't completely naive, but at times my inability to rationalize things could be suspect, especially when trying to comprehend aspects of a culture with which I was completely unfamiliar. A perfect example of this is when I was duped into believing something that, had I weighed its possibility logically, I might not have so easily believed. It was the perfect instance of innocence abroad. I was aware that the musical singing group the Osmonds were Mormons, but since it was at the time a predominately American religion, I wasn't terribly familiar with its fundamentals. I was also aware that these teen sensations donated a hefty portion of their income to the LDS church, which undoubtedly contributed to the organization's considerable wealth. Why, then, would they not repay the group's generosity with some sort of laudatory edifice? So it was that some wag, I can't remember who, told me that the bugle-blowing golden figurine atop the majestic Mormon temple between Selby Avenue and Temple Way on Santa Monica Boulevard was in fact Donny Osmond. In actuality, it was the Mormon angel, Moroni, the catalytic avatar of the church's backstory. Expecting me to know this would be like asking me to name the members of Supertramp. I was no theologian of Mormonism, so a figurine of Donny Osmond it was.

I wouldn't say LA changed overnight, but all vestige, with the exception of a few holdouts of its vivid late '60s vintage so prominent on my arrival, was dissolving into nostalgic trivia. I'm gratified that I got to see how the Strip and its surrounding neighborhoods looked before a systematic metamorphosis replaced its characteristic charm and chaotic funkiness with a more modern branding.

By 1973, Ed Pearl's Ash Grove on Melrose Avenue was gone. Once called the West Coast University of Folk Music, it was arguably the most important music venue in California. Its pedigree can't be contested; even the Troubadour, which still continues today mainly as a launch pad for fledging acts, couldn't match the Ash Grove for its historical roster of legendary performers. Primarily a folk, blues, and bluegrass club, its stage at one time or another was graced by a wealth of history so expansive and impressive it's almost overwhelming to conceptualize. Son House, Bukka White, Muddy Waters, Howlin' Wolf, Joan Baez, Pete Seeger, the New Lost City Ramblers, Bill Monroe, Chuck Berry, Johnny Cash, Lightnin' Hopkins, and Ravi Shankar to mention just a handful out of hundreds. The Improv, a stand-up comedy joint, now inhabits the space where the Ash Grove used to stand.

Ciro's, where the Byrds cut their teeth and Jimi Hendrix played guitar in Ike and Tina Turner's band, after several name changes, including Art Laboe's operated by the eponymous DJ, disappeared in 1972 and became The Comedy Store. Filthy McNasty's, a pint-size biker bar with its ramshackle sign and stockaded exterior, hung in for a while like a roadside dive from the middle of nowhere. P.J.'s, the fashionable jazz and pop club on Santa Monica Boulevard that was so popular with TV and film personalities in the mid-'60s, was on its last legs at the onset of the '70s and was soon The Starwood, a starting point for many of the decade's hair metal, punk, and new wave bands. Likewise was Gazzarri's, a rock institution at Sunset and Doheny that had book-ended decades by having both the Doors and Van Halen as house bands. Owned by Bill Gazzarri, a gregarious man with a penchant for dressing like a Chicago-style gangster, it remained a huge draw for kids from the mid-'60s up until the early '90s. Like the Troubadour, the Whisky a Go Go (or simply the Whisky) at Sunset and Clark has seen its glory days long passed. Its presence has become sadly faceless, a drastic fall from grace from the time it ruled the hood with celebrated sets from Buffalo Springfield and Love, to incendiary performances by the Stooges, Alice Cooper, and Led Zeppelin.

The best jazz club, Shelly's Manne Hole on Cahuenga Boulevard, ran out of money and closed in '72. Co-owned by its namesake jazz drummer Shelly Mann, it had showcased the very best of the very best. With its ramshackle facade looking like a set piece from Harry Potter's quirky Diagon Alley, the club had hosted from its inception in the early '60s the likes of Miles, Monk, Blakey, and Evans. As eras progressed so did the acts, ushering in the experimental hard bop and more contemporary sounds of folks like Sonny Rollins, Herbie Hancock, and the Milt Jackson–Ray Brown Quintet. The two shows I caught there were certainly memorable. At one, the avant-garde saxophonist Archie Shepp tested the audience's mettle with forty-five minutes of discordant shrieks and squawks until some wag at the back stood up and yelled, "We can take it as long as you can." A similar situation took place when I saw Rahsaan Roland Kirk. I'd first seen Kirk some years earlier with Elton at the Royal Albert Hall in London and he'd been sublime. Not so much this time. Not unlike Miles in his later years, he played inter-mittently while smashing up chairs on the bandstand and claiming it was part of his act.

Along with the Manne Hole, I'd frequented most all of these venues either in their final days or on into their lingering demise.

I've seen many great artists who have since passed on, among them Albert King, Guy Clark, McCoy Tyner, Doc Watson, Little Richard, and Jimmy Scott. I also saw a great many acts in their infancy. In the months following my initial disembarkation, I caught club performances by the Eagles, Linda Ronstadt, Jackson Browne, Bill Withers, and comedian Steve Martin. In years to come, and I mean years to come, quashing any idea of regarding them as contemporaries, I caught the first LA shows by The Police (I received a little red Police whistle at the door), R.E.M., Bruce Springsteen, and the Pretenders. The fact that they are looked back on now as legacy acts is quite disturbing considering we were well into career phase two when they were just getting started.

The gradual change started early on. In the advent of my arrival, another restaurant I'd fallen into in terms of convenience was a joint next to Gazzarri's. The Windjammer had formerly been Villa Nova; it was owned by Vincente Minnelli and reportedly where Marilyn Monroe hooked up with Joe DiMaggio on a blind date.

Overdue for its rendezvous with the wrecking ball, it would very soon become a rock and roll institution called The Rainbow Bar and Grill. The building adjacent to it would be transformed into the Roxy, a music venue with On The Rox, a private club located on the upper level. Interestingly enough, the Rainbow's opening night on April 16, 1972, was actually a private party celebrating our *Honky Château* album, which became our first US number one long player.

The Rainbow's legacy looms large, its origins in the '70s far out-weighing its later history. Not that it hasn't remained the axis around which the ever-changing climate of musical groups alternate. Every decade has seen a different hierarchy commandeering the premier booths; a hodgepodge of changing players, it graduated from the club-house of my contemporaries into a home away from home for hair bands and heavy metal heroes from the '80s on.

In the early to mid-'70s, a small loft located up a short set of wooden stairs in the Rainbow led to the lair of the Hollywood Vampires. In short, the Vampires were a celebrity drinking club. Formed by my friend Alice Cooper, it consisted of a rotating cast of characters depending on who was in town at any given time. The principles were, aside from Alice and myself, Ringo Starr, Micky Dolenz, Harry Nilsson, Keith Moon, and on occasion, John Lennon.

Outside of these gatherings I didn't spend a whole lot of time in the Rainbow; it just wasn't my sort of place. I favored The Palomino Club over the hill in North Hollywood on Lankershim, just down the road from Universal. This is another story and we'll get to that in due course. The Rainbow was all a little too formulaic for my taste: the same faces, the same posturing, and in general a generic type that didn't deviate much from the obvious. Along with the rock elite in residence, there'd be an inordinate amount of coked-up record company guys in satin tour jackets and bad pants kowtowing to the star contingent. There also could at times be an ominous negative energy in the place. Boorish patrons like the Sunset Strip hustler Kim Fowley peddling his particular brand of excessive hucksterism and reiterating his mantra with relentless repetition. Then there were the aggressive drunks, none more unpleasant than Led Zeppelin drummer John Bonham. Along with the band's manager, Peter Grant, a completely horrible man, the two made for a pair of ogreish bullies who could suck the air out of the room with their intimidating presence. Years later, Bonham was so despicably brutish to a dear friend of mine that cutting him any slack has never been forthcoming. Bad behavior comes in many forms, and in rock and roll it's de rigueur, but there's a distinct difference between juvenile poor taste and habitual cruelty. I'm a committed Zeppelin fan and love Page, Plant, and Jones. Bonham was a phenomenal drummer, shame he couldn't have inhabited his skin with the same positive energy to that which he applied to his sticks, too.

In total contrast, the most comical evening I spent in the Rainbow was at a table with someone you'd fully expect to be a complete misery guts. Guaranteed, he'd polished off the best part of a bottle of scotch, but Van Morrison was a laugh riot. Yes, that Van Morrison,

Mr. Grumpy Pants himself, Ireland's answer to Ebenezer Scrooge. I don't recall the circumstances of being at the table, but whatever they were gave me insight into what tickled his fancy. He basically ignored any other conversation that was taking place and seemed to be amusing himself by indulging in impersonations of *The Goon Show*, a '50s British radio show of character-driven absurdist humor voiced by Peter Sellers, Spike Milligan, and Harry Secombe. Watching the gnomic bard of Celtic soul chuckling at his own impressions of Bluebottle, Neddie Seagoon, and Eccles was almost as entertaining as the real thing.

The Roxy was a great place to catch acts; it was intimate, comfortable, and easy to access without any unnecessary preamble. Being that I was one of a limited number of people initially given a key to On The Rox, it was simply a matter of descending the stairs and entering a private side door into the club to access your table.

Why I'd been granted this key privilege is anyone's guess. Initially, there couldn't have been more than thirty members and it was proclaimed that it wasn't about who you were or what you were worth, it was all about "whether or not you fit the vibe of the bar." I'm gratified I was deemed cool enough, as it really was a comfortable and relaxing environment, a large, warmly lit living room with an incredibly attractive group of girls tending bar.

My earliest recollections of the Sunset Strip between Crescent Heights and North Doheny Drive are abundantly clear. For starters, the level of architecture was lower, making the neighborhood less formal and allowing, air quality permitting, a clearer view of LAX somewhere off in the distance. High rises were nonexistent, the tallest buildings being hotels, which outside of the Hyatt House were rare. The emerging Sunset Marquis around the corner on Alta Loma was tucked away and unobtrusive. In due course, it would become the new home for hot bands in town once the legend of the Riot House began to tarnish. Most of the other lodging choices were cheap motels scattered on and off the Strip, usually with a drive-in forecourt and a handful of deteriorated cottages or two tiers of interconnected rooms. Offering the bare essentials, their funkiness and pulp fiction vibe offered a defiant appeal to wannabe bohemians. Janis Joplin succumbed to a lethal dose of heroin in the Landmark Motor Hotel on Franklin. Jim Morrison lived in room 32 of the Alta Cienega Motel, and the band Spirit were photographed for the cover of their 1968 album *The Family That Plays Together* descending the steps of the Sunset Motel. On Sunset at Highland this popular dive was the cheap alternative to the Hyatt House for struggling road dogs strapped for cash in 1970.

So much of what was familiar then has no place in the world as it is now. The rustic merchandising cobbled together in the two blocks across from Tower Records is the perfect example of hippie commerce frozen in time. From Holloway Drive heading west a couple of blocks, it was an indelible montage of that which was totally indicative of the time period.

Head shops were a quaint staple of the era. Back then, when a lid of marijuana could get you a life sentence, establishments that catered to the consumption of it were rampant. Heady with the smell of incense, their merchandise was colorful, plentiful, and creative. Naturally with my knowledge of all things narcotic being next to zilch at the time, a grand imagination was required.

An extensive variation of paraphernalia including hash pipes, bongs, and water pipes were in abundance, the latter coming in alternating sizes from modest to elaborately sculptured mazes of bulbous glass direct from Castle Frankenstein. There were roach clips, rolling papers, and other drug-related accessories all constituting what I imagined to be a legal gray area. The cocaine age wasn't particularly represented at that time, grinders, spoons, and scales waiting in the wings for the blizzard of marching powder that would become preeminent several years later. To coincide with their status as emporiums of the counterculture, the *Los Angeles Free Press* and other underground periodicals were stacked up in racks on the floor, and psychedelic art and R. Crumb comics lined the walls. In relationship to the merchandise peddled, the artwork was geared to the obvious, as in lots of Grateful Dead.

Interspersed within the same alternative enclave and cut from similar cloth were stores like Propinquity. Reeking of patchouli oil and haunted by subliminal new age Muzak, it sold a mixed bag of overpriced nostalgia: mechanical money boxes, vintage Coca-Cola signs, and I LIKE IKE campaign buttons. Long before racial stereotypes were reassessed, it also offered lawn jockeys, Aunt Jemima cookie jars, and other uncomfortably insensitive tchotchkes. With my own interior decorative tastes hovering somewhere between Sgt. Pepper and Edward Gorey, I purchased a couple of lava lamps and way too many sand candles. These I shipped back to England and distributed throughout my minuscule country cottage while simultaneously painting all the walls black.

A few doors down from the Hyatt House was another iconic hub relative to the time period. Popular with some of our party, not so much me, The Source, a vegan restaurant blessed with a distinctly in-your-face karmic overload, was frequented by an unfathomable number of devotees. Our own in-house hippie, Steve Brown, aside from being a sensible barometer of career advice, was at the same time a fully paid-up member of anything overtly transcendental. He loved it. Owned by Father Yod, formally an ex-marine called Jim, The Source doubled as a clubhouse for his relatively harmless cult called the The Source Family (not to be confused with the murderous Manson Family). The benevolent Yod dispensed his cuisine (of acquired taste) with a side order of Utopian ideology. The staff were as blissful as you might imagine, all flowing linen robes and sackcloth belts. The guys all looked like Mike Love circa the *Sunflower* album, and the waitresses all looked like Squeaky Fromme. If I'd been a pasture cow out to graze, I might have enjoyed the food a little more. Every dish came padded with an inordinate amount of alfalfa sprouts, the hidden entree consisting mainly of fermented plant foods and macrobiotic substitutes for anything resembling real food. It was on the sidewalk outside The Source that I first encountered The Children of God, the religious fringe group that had spirited away Fleetwood Mac's Jeremy Spencer and had inspired the line about Jesus freaks handing out tickets for God in "Tiny Dancer."

I was more apt to make the trek west, up the street to the Old World. It sat slightly above traffic level slicing into the intersection where Holloway Drive merged onto Sunset. The food was standard fare for the time, burgers, salads, and sandwiches, unimaginative but a better alternative than the lawn clippings at The Source. It was also immeasurably more of an open window to my surroundings, a place to seclude myself in a corner and ponder this fresh terrain. It was a crow's nest of observation, the first napkin-scribbling establishment in the US to indulge my introspective nature.

It was a gradual ascent up the leasing ladder, but my next rental certainly turned a corner in terms of location. It was a small boxy 1950s-style house that sat a couple of hundred feet north of Santa Monica Boulevard on Doheny Drive. A couple of years later, I would invest in my own first real home on this street. Farther up above Sunset and well-appointed, it would become synonymous with my life in LA from that moment on.

My FIRST THREE years in LA had been a test run, and as the dominos began to fall, gaslighting myself was not an option. In 1973, for the princely sum of $84,000, I bought the first and most significant home I ever owned in LA proper.

First Bite

If the Heart Machine is destroyed,
the entire machine district will end up in ruins!

—GROT, Guardian of the Heart Machine
Fritz Lang's *Metropolis*

The shots were loud and drew me to the window. People always say they sound like firecrackers. I beg to differ. That night they sounded exactly how I imagined gunfire would sound. Explosive and clamorous, the echoing aftermath ricocheting off the wet walls in the boxy confinement of the dimly lit alley.

From four stories above, I looked down. It was after midnight, and on the ground below two NYPD cops stood over what looked like a pile of rags. It was clear that the rags were very dead, and were in fact a crumpled corpse. The cops looked like hulking crows contemplating carrion, frozen shadows, their guns still drawn, the adrenalin most likely still pumping through their veins.

Like time standing still, there was momentary silence. Then the sirens began. Within seconds the whole area was lit up. What only moments ago had been a singular act of violence became a gruesome circus. The rain came down, squad cars screeched in, and the ambulances arrived. The night became a cacophony of radio chatter and yelling, everything blending together in an emulsifying frantic drama. The cross-weaving illumination of the emergency vehicles' flashing lights strobed the downpour, turning everything from a grubby duskiness into a hellish crimson.

Welcome to the Big Apple, November 1970, my very first night in New York.

The next morning I sat down and wrote *And now I know Spanish Harlem are not just pretty words to say / I thought I knew but now I know that rose trees never grow in New York City.* The first two lines to a song that, as of yet, had no title and would remain incomplete for over a year.

It had been culture shock taken to the extreme. A week earlier, I'd been sunning by the pool on the roof of the Continental Hyatt House in LA. Soaking in the whole West Coast vibe, California already had me at "hello." I was feeling positively transcendental, elevated by this kaleidoscopic Eden. In my mind, I'd already made the move. This is where I belonged, and this is where I intended to spend my life, everything preceding it had been a formality, an education preparing me to live my dream.

Now here, I was feeling not quite so confident. Overnight, I'd gone from Hockney's aquamarine Utopia into Dante's Inferno. Every detail, even down to the way people looked, fearful and frigid or edgy and confrontational, was marred with some antithetical replication of serenity. Everything was gray, the sky seemed compartmentalized, and the rushing nature of everything made me anxious and uneasy. Subway trains, grime laden and graffiti covered, rattled violently, reverberating and shrieking beneath the sidewalks. In their wake, squalls of polluted stygian steam rose into the streets, the traffic rolling slowly through it like zombies out of fog. Garbage, like mountainous black snowdrifts, piled up along the sidewalks. Horns blared for no reason, pedestrians screamed at invisible adversaries, and in the shadows verminous creatures emerged from dumpsters. Rats and trash and violence, oh my! My laid-back garden of earthly delights was being contradicted by this grim East Coast counterpart, eradicating my vision of a Technicolor Gotham. This wasn't *Breakfast at Tiffany's*; this was *Midnight Cowboy*. All of which goes to show you just how wrong first impressions can be.

If the Sunset Strip's notorious Hyatt House, the Riot House to those on the rock 'n' roll hamster wheel, was LA's go-to hotel, then Loews Midtown in New York City was its East Coast counterpart. Situated on Eighth Avenue between Forty-Seventh and Forty-Eighth, Lowsey's

Madtown, as our band rechristened it, was the crash pad of choice for UK touring bands at that time. There's a wonderful postcard from the mid-'60s on which the hotel is illustrated as glamorous and sun-lit, a contemporary hipster joint designed by the Jetsons, Manhattan in the background looking like Miami Beach. Well-heeled vacationers exit gleaming Cadillacs, an elaborate three-tiered art deco sign hanging off the right side welcoming one and all to Coolsville. In reality, it was a grubby unattractive cigarette carton–shaped building, weather-beaten and characterless, a combination of coffee-colored grunge and sleet-eviscerated off-white. Inside, however, it was totally palatable, all the usual amenities being perfectly adequate, the camaraderie among the visiting musicians taking the edge off things and softening the harsher exterior climate.

The hotel's interior made for a safe haven, but it was out on the street that a social readjustment was essential. Watch your back, walk fast, act crazy. It was all about attitude. In the safety of our limos, we were able to circumvent any danger. Heading to gigs or radio station PR, we could check out the action without feeling threatened. Like a police lineup behind a one-way mirror, we viewed the suspects while avoiding eye contact. The perfect example being the lurid carnival of Times Square, a mass of humanity seething with iffy elements. On the sidewalk out front of peep shows, pop shops, porn theaters, and greasy spoons, pimps, pushers, and hustlers masqueraded as barkers and car-neys, blending together in a palate of sleazy enterprise. It was a fashion show produced by Loki, the murk of the evening transcended by the clashing creativity of this colorful train wreck. Sartorially uncoordi-nated, it was wardrobe divested of modesty. Both garish and outland-ish, it spotlighted the accosting nature and intimidating jive of bunco and solicitation. Purple flares and angora coats, crochet vests, and gold shirts. Emerald green blouses, red wool slouch hats, and satin, lots of satin. As the pimp hierarchy strutted their stuff in ermine-trimmed regality, their charges, even in the depth of winter, traipsed back and forth wearing next to nothing. Like cinema verité presented as blax-ploitation with cameos by Joe Buck and Ratso Rizzo, it's an indelible scene, as frozen in my memory as the temperature of the time.

These guys weren't clowns; they were entrepreneurial, street savvy, and dangerous. Behind masks of both coercion and harassment was a fringe element living in a dominion of their own design. Dog-eat-dog, it was all they'd ever known, the pecking order maintained by intimidation and violence. It's more than likely that it was one of them, or someone very much like them, who ended up dead below my window in an alley off Eighth Avenue.

Was I scared? I wouldn't say scared, shaken perhaps, but as usual I persuaded my curiosity to counter any fear I might have felt. I didn't see the actual killing, just the result seconds later. Bullets don't wait to be witnessed, and in the aftermath, I became resolute. If I was going to be spending time here and returning due to it being a major musical hub, then I needed to come to terms with it. Eventually, that happened. And while I initially found it unsettling, New York ultimately became my favorite city in the world. Like a love affair, though it was baby steps at first.

How did I turn the tide? Thanks in part goes to a young man by the name of Eric Van Lustbader. Eric wrote for the music industry magazine *Cashbox*. Under the abbreviation EVL, he was the first journalist in the United States to champion our music. On our arrival in New York, he had interviewed Elton and me in the office of David Rosner, who ran the Dick James publishing arm in the US.

Not only did he get our music, but he got me. We fell into easy conversation and realized we had many of the same interests, not just music, but literature also. Not necessarily of a highbrow nature, but science fantasy and, in particular, the work of Michael Moorcock. Moorcock was not only a purveyor of the genre, but a musician who at times moonlighted with the English space rock band Hawkwind. His most fantastical creation was a sword and sorcery antihero, the albino emperor, Elric of Melniboné. Wielding a huge black sword named Stormbringer, Elric carved a path through countless books. It was pulp fiction and a passing phase for me, but for a short time they entertained me and lit up my early bedsit life. While my passion for Americana was of primary importance, it had been writers like Moorcock, Ursula K. Le Guin, and Lord Dunsany who had stimulated the core of my earliest collaborations with Elton. *Empty Sky* and much of what came before it is a tip of the hat to these mercurial authors.

Born and raised in Greenwich Village, Eric was a native New Yorker and a walking GPS. Under his tutelage I found the rhythm of the street and the pulse of the city. Every day he'd head over to the hotel and we'd hit the streets. Eric knowing the lay of the land was beneficial, and before long I'd given up looking over my shoulder and ceased my peripheral assessment of every passerby.

We had particular goals in mind, and at the forefront were rare bookstores and anyplace dealing primarily in science fiction and fantasy. These tended to be small step-down establishments below street level. Dusty and cluttered, they were more often than not run by an equally dusty-looking staff who were both fanatical in their work and encyclopedic in their knowledge of the subject matter. It was also the first time I'd encountered the cult of comic book collecting, and while never submitting to it, I did admire the artwork. Ultimately though, dialogue in bubbles wasn't going to blow my skirt up, and I saw them for what they were, collectables in plastic sleeves, the rarest commanding astronomical prices.

A good representation of New York in the early '70s can be witnessed in a handful of movies. *The French Connection*, *Serpico*, *Taxi Driver*, and in a more sensationalistic but still no lesser accurate depiction, *Death Wish*. All of them emblematic in their portrayal of the city and its inhabitants, especially the police. One of the things that I found curious from day one was how the cops on the West and East Coast were in complete contrast with each other. In California they were immaculately attired, uniforms pressed and pristine. Well-groomed behind their hip Ray-Bans, many were movie-star handsome, especially the CHP officers in their formfitting tan outfits and gold helmets. In New York, most were a rumpled, unkempt mess. Haircuts didn't appear to be on the list of enrollment requirements. Shaving, apparently, was optional, and smoking seemed compulsory. A coalescence of the outer boroughs, they personified their backgrounds, rough and ready and in absolute sync with the landscape. In fact, two tribes in perfect harmony with their habitats.

All the things that had initially unnerved me about New York were totally reversing themselves, and a reappraisal found me seeing everything in a new light. It was all about the energy, inhabiting the pace and changing gear. The solution for being at one with the city meant incorporating the vibe and merging into the fast lane. Show purpose, don't be reticent. You want a cab? Get in the street. Never order from a deli counter unless you know what you want, and never ever look like you don't know where you're going.

Cab culture in itself was not for the faint of heart, but then for those disposed to amassing ammunition for composition, it was completely invigorating. Taxi drivers were an amalgamation of esoteric ethnic complexity. Fueled by coffee and adrenaline, their aggressive and competitive driving habits, not to mention their irreverent social commentary was like stand-up comedy. The only difference being that they were sitting down careening through traffic like a demented Pac-Man channeling Lenny Bruce. In an Uberless era, they were delightfully rude. Unrepentantly uncensored, they were heavy on opinions and even heavier on the horn.

Eric also knew where to eat and was adept in knowing where to find the best for less. I was still months away from kicking my expense account up a notch, so eating on the cheap was essential. Back then it was mostly inexpensive trattorias on the Lower East Side or good pizza joints almost anywhere. My most indelible memory though has to be discovering the hot dogs of Nathan's Famous. When on the run and in need of a quick-fix pick-me-up power lunch, Nathan's was unbeatable. These puppies weren't the limp waterlogged wieners sold in the arcades of English seaside resorts. No sir, these were a revelation, still the best dog in town; long, skinny, and firm on a soft white bun, they snapped deliciously when you bit into them. One hundred percent beef and grilled, they were completely addictive. Lucky for me, because back then I could eat and drink anything and not put on an ounce. I was as wiry as a whippet with a twenty-seven inch waist and a heathy appetite. Some things never change, and to this day whenever I pass under that green and white awning on Fifth Avenue, the garish clutter of yellow signage vying for space above the milling throng never fails to transport me back to that long gone winter when I was oh, so young and forever hungry.

Upon my return to New York the following summer with a little more cash to spread around, Eric introduced me to the Russian Tea Room. With its spacious red leather booths and ornate gold ceiling, the art deco Russo-Continental restaurant on West Fifty-Seventh had been an established institution ever since being founded in 1927 by members of the Russian Imperial Ballet. Being of a tonier nature than my previous haunts, I was swanning it up royally, adopting a nonchalant air and feigning sophistication. That is until an unfortunate incident with some chicken Kiev leveled the playing field. Unaware of the construction of a dish I had never encountered, I plunged my fork into the butter-filled breast, releasing a stream of the scalding contents and scoring a direct hit to the eye. Half blind, my cornea stinging like blazes, I swore profusely, drawing the attention of a good-looking athletic young man in the adjoining booth. My humiliation was only multiplied tenfold when Rudolf Nureyev inquired if I was *khorosho*? OK? I was not, and needless to say my embarrassment kept me clear of the Russian Tea Room for some time.

Eric continued to be a constant source of discovery and direction in all things New York. We pretty much walked everywhere, and up to this day it's still the most liberating aspect of the city. If you've got the energy and the inclination, you can walk from Manhattan to Brooklyn, all destinations are doable. Try doing that in LA or London and see how far that gets you. I'm by nature a geographical Luddite; if I tell you to turn left, then by all means turn right! Simply put: if you want to get where you're going, don't rely on me for directions. I may still take wrong turns in New York, but at least I was schooled early on in the nature of the grid. Not only did I learn that avenues run north and south and that streets go east and west, but I became adept at differentiating neighborhoods, which sealed the deal. By the time we were back playing Carnegie Hall in June 1971, I was a pro. The city, still internally raw, was fashioning itself for a magnanimous makeover. It would be years before it happened, but with entrepreneurial visionaries establishing august architectural and social change, the city was secretly morphing and about to undergo an impressive rebirth. On the south-western tip of Manhattan, near the shore of the Hudson River, the impressive monoliths of the recently erected twin towers of the World Trade Center gave credence to this with their sturdy durability and all-encompassing eye on the future.

On our initial trip, outside of the live album we cut at A&R Studios, we played only three dates in the tristate area, one in Syracuse and two at the concert promoter Bill Graham's Fillmore East on Second Avenue. The latter were as a support act for Leon Russell, who was not only a major star at the time but one of our heroes and a huge inspiration to Elton as a piano player. Leon was like a ringmaster, directing his band with the fervor of a Pentecostal preacher. Indoctrinated in the gospel tradition, the effect of it had never subsided and had infused his music from the get-go. The native Oklahoman had started his career with the legendary LA session band, The Wrecking Crew, playing on hundreds of Top 40 hits from the '60s. So many, in fact, that it would be easier to list what he didn't play on than what he did. Now he had come into his own and was reaping the rewards for his years in the trenches. With his top hat, flowing mane of white hair, and piercing blue eyes, he was the very personification of messianic rock star zeal.

The first night we played the Fillmore, Leon popped his head into Elton's dressing room and asked us if he could introduce us to some-one. Dutifully following him, we were led up a back staircase into a theater box overlooking the right side of the stage. The box was empty, except for a slight individual in a rumpled white suit standing in the shadows with his back to us. Even when he turned to greet us and Leon introduced him as Bob, I was still not sure who this was. Then it dawned on me, "Oh shit, yeah, I know this guy." It was post his motor-cycle wreck, and Bob Dylan looked like the Woodstock and Nashville Dylan, scraggly chin beard, short curly hair, and that smile somewhere between sly knowing and cultivated shyness. He complimented us on the *Tumbleweed Connection* album, and in particular, how much he liked the lyrics to "My Father's Gun." We weren't there more than a few minutes, and whether he stayed for the show I don't know. Naturally, it was gratifying to receive the benediction of someone who had kicked open so many doors and recorded so much music that only a fool would refuse to find groundbreaking. It was my initial encounter with Bob, and over the years I've had several. On each occasion he has always been uncharacteristically conversational and complimentary. The last time was years ago at Elton's fundraising Oscar party in 2001 when an extremely dapper Dylan sporting a cape and ivory handled cane turned up unannounced and requested to sit at my table. Having just scored an Academy Award for "Things Have Changed" from the movie *Wonder Boys*, he was effusive about hoping to repeat the win in 2002 with "Waitin' for You," a song he'd just written for *Divine Secrets of the Ya-Ya Sisterhood*. His enthusiasm was almost childlike, and to see him completely obsessed with winning was a million miles from his image as a shapeshifting contrarian.

Generationally, those of us from that period who played the Fillmore East and West have an opinion of Bill Graham. They range from derogatory to indifferent, complimentary to worshipful. To some he was a bully, to others a guardian angel. While I didn't spend a great deal of time with him, what little I did gave me the impression of a man of great resilience and fortitude. Resolute in nature that many saw as controlling, he did things his way, which in my book isn't necessarily a bad thing if you're carrying the weight. He also had an unquenchable passion for music, creating his venues to spread the gospel rather than augment himself monetarily. If you don't believe me, pick up a copy of his book *Bill Graham Presents*. His descriptions of the acts that played for him are revelatory. His reminiscence of Otis Redding at the Fillmore West is totally in keeping with my own experience of him as a teenager. Redding is without a doubt the greatest performer I've ever witnessed onstage in my life, and to read Bill's two-page description of his performance is goose bump–inducing and completely spot-on. "A panther stalking his prey." "Beautiful and shining, black, sweaty, sensuous and passionate." I can only add one thing to that. When impressionable, sixteen-year-old me saw Redding at the Gliderdrome in Boston, Lincolnshire, he did something I've never seen topped. With

Booker T. and the MGs grinding out the opening riff off "Shake," someone in the wings to the right threw a microphone high into the air at center stage. Redding, immaculate in a dark green suit, strutted from the left side, caught the mic right on the downbeat, and started singing. My jaw dropped and still does today when I think about it.

Bill was always immeasurably kind to us, even when we were a blip in the big picture. He had a respect for musicians that was only tested when they believed their own hype or were blatantly arrogant and cruel. I was truly saddened when I learned of his death in a helicopter crash in 1991.

We played the Fillmore again on our return the following year in 1971, along with some dates in outlying places like Buffalo, Saratoga Springs, and Rochester. No limos here, however. It was a unified front, altogether by bus.

If you're imagining the plush, all mod cons, souped-up super cruisers transporting artists today, think again. These were buses, Greyhound buses, plain and simple. Freezing-ass cold, uncomfortable as hell, and only made acceptable by our sense of humor and complete irreverence to their inhospitable interiors. These last two commodities were of great importance in the early days of touring when perks were in short supply and luxury was pulling off the interstate for a burger, a bathroom, and the cliché of redneck harassment.

Traipsing through local airports to catch regional flights was like herding cats. Shepherded by our lovely, but oh so straight, tour director, Marvin, we would bleat like sheep and generally act like willful adolescents. In the airport gift shop in Normal, Illinois, I found beanie skull caps that had long plastic daisies sticking out of them. The fact that they had NORMAL stitched on the front was too much to resist, and very soon we were all sporting them, including Marvin. I can still see him to this day checking us in at the counter: three piece suit, briefcase, and a twelve-inch daisy sprouting from his head.

There was a tour in '72 when we had "Legs" Larry Smith, drummer of the bygone Bonzo Dog Doo-Dah Band on tour with us. Why? Larry had tap-danced on a track of ours called "I Think I'm Going To

Kill Myself" and Elton being Elton thought it would be fun to have him come on tour and replicate his solo live. An unnecessary expense? Quite possibly, but then again Larry was good value for money and a complete eccentric. For his tap-dancing interlude during the show he performed in a wedding dress and a crash helmet with a wedding cake couple glued to the top. Excellent, indeed, but my reason for recalling his absurdity is slightly more Dadaesque, but no less inventive. In every airport we went through, Larry would purchase one of those black velour squares that had a map of the state embroidered on it in gold stitching. Why? When he'd collected as many as possible he sewed them together and made a suit of them, of course!

A couple of shots of Elton and I taken backstage at the Fillmore by the notable rock photographer Bob Gruen are indicative of that time period. We're both looking at the camera, a couch distance apart, both identical in our demeanor. I wouldn't call it arrogance, but there's a definite nonchalance to our assessment of the lens that speaks volumes about our confidence.

BEING THE NEW kids on the block, Elton and I were expected to either indulge our record company in several promotional prospects, or we were invited (out of curiosity I imagine) to meet a number of music business notables. One of our first ports of call was visiting the legendary FM radio DJ Scott Muni at WNEW-FM. Muni with his low gravelly voice was a New York institution, and at the heart of a time when rock radio was at its very best: varied, vibrant, and exciting. Before the conglomerates neutered it, FM radio was not formatted into sterilized uniformity, and playing hard rock and R & B back-to-back with power pop and the current trend of singer-songwriters was how the classic stations operated. American rock radio had been at the forefront of our baptism into California culture. Even though pirate radio was shaking up the stodgy traits of the BBC back home, there was something inherently edgy and magical about how LA stations, like the fledgling KLOS and KMET, were emblematic of our cultural transformation. Permeating the very fabric of daily life, it played constantly, a soundtrack to the movie of our ascent. Cruising the freeways in our rented Mustangs, top down and bathed in warm wind and sunshine, we'd dial 'em in and crank up the volume.

Who proposed it, I'm not sure, but one day the two of us found ourselves in Atlantic Studios at Broadway and Sixtieth where Roberta Flack and the celebrated record producer Joel Dorn were producing an album for gospel great Marion Williams. Everyone present was delightful and eager to introduce us to Marion, who for some reason couldn't be found. She was finally located hiding in a broom closet behind the consul, too terrified to meet us. Painfully shy, she imagined we were some sort of big deal and fled for cover. Once we convinced her we were nothing of the sort, she relaxed a little but remained unimaginably humble for a woman possessing one of the greatest gospel voices since Mahalia Jackson. Someone else present, who was most definitely not humble or shy in anyway whatsoever, was the preeminent session drummer Bernard "Pretty" Purdie. Whether he was there to work or just passing by is of no consequence, either way he was a fountain of egocentric charm. A sort of musical Muhammad Ali, it was obvious he believed wholeheartedly in his own hype and had never encountered a mirror he could say no to. To this day, he's the only person I've ever met who carried around a briefcase full of 8-by-10s of himself. The album Marion Williams was recording that day, *Standing Here Wondering Which Way to Go*, was released in 1971 and is an unheralded gem.

I FINALLY COMPLETED that lyric that had sprung to mind the morning after my first traumatic night in New York. "Mona Lisas and Mad Hatters" is peppered with references to that rudimentary rough patch. It's not about survival; it's about understanding and coming to terms with the naked truth. My "trash can dream" did come true and "rose trees" do "grow in New York City." The positivity hiding in the lyric emerged in the wake of the first two lines. It's ultimately about searching for the light, and with the help of "people out there like you" it's possible. I often wonder if I'm referencing Eric Van Lustbader in this line.

Eric went on to become a highly successful author, publishing over thirty-five best-selling novels. His character of Nicholas Linnear, introduced in *The Ninja*, a *New York Times* bestseller for twenty-four consecutive weeks, is one of modern fiction's most enduring heroes. In 2003, after the passing of Robert Ludlum and with the blessing of the late author's estate, Lustbader took over *The Bourne Legacy*, writing almost a dozen Jason Bourne novels. To date, he has written over fifty books. As is the way of things, we drifted out of touch. Possibly he was segueing into literary life and our alternate career paths had reached a fork in the road. Maybe it was my own thoughtless abandonment of a fleeting friendship. If it was my doing, I'm truly sorry, things were moving at a breakneck speed. I seemed to be constantly in motion, back and forth from a city he helped me fall in love with. Still, if it was so, there's no excuse. I fall on the sword. They were heady times and it's more likely that the deluge of discovery and the gigantic growth spurt I experienced from that bitter winter of 1970 to the muggy fall of '71 simply washed away a good friend. In little under a year and a half, I had gone from a gunshot to a great awakening.

Close Encounter of the Literary Kind

There is always one moment in childhood when
the door opens and lets the future in.
—GRAHAM GREENE

B ooks are beautiful things. Like vinyl albums, books are both comforting and reassuring. They command respect and cannot be bet-
tered by alternatives. Trying to substitute either one with a flashier form
of technology diminishes the comfort they bring and only leaves you
with a sterile counterfeit representation.

Along with being a voracious reader, I was at one time also a serious collector. By this I mean first editions and, in particular, classic
children's books and twentieth-century fiction. Over the course of
several years, my collection of children's books in particular became
completely comprehensive and extremely valuable. I literally accumulated everything imaginable, the very best of the very best, and in some
cases the rarest of the rare. Not only the usual suspects like Tolkien,
Milne, C. S. Lewis, Kenneth Grahame, Frank Baum, Lewis Carroll,
and J. M. Barrie, but also works by E. Nesbit, Charles Kingsley,
Rudyard Kipling, Hugh Lofting, T. H. White, Roald Dahl, and
Francis Hodgson Burnett. I had first editions of both Hans Christian
Andersen's works and *Grimm's Fairy Tales*, plus a series of original
Arthur Rackham watercolors. Rackham's work was regarded as the fin-
est during the golden age of British book illustration and was featured
in literally dozens of specially printed works from *Aesop's Fables* to *The
Wind in the Willows*.

One of the rarest acquisitions I managed to procure, and later sell, was a copy of Beatrix Potter's privately printed *The Tale of Peter Rabbit*. In 1901, frustrated by her failure to get the book published, Potter used her personal savings to have 250 copies printed. The existence of them has dwindled over the years, and even at the time I found mine they were bordering on extinction. I'm not sure how many still exist today, but I do know that in 2016 one sold in London for £43.400. I've always wondered if it was mine.

My collection of twentieth-century fiction was more specialized; it gravitated to a smaller, though diverse group of authors. These included the likes of Christopher Isherwood, Anthony Burgess, and Gore Vidal, but pride of place was reserved for my two absolute literary heroes: W. Somerset Maugham and Graham Greene. I had everything they had written and had read them all. Maugham's *The Moon and Sixpence* is one of my favorite books. Although he denied it, it is without a doubt based on the life of Paul Gauguin and is magical in its depiction of following your dream even if it means sacrificing everything. I find it unrepentantly romantic, its message of idealism and raw carnal drive toward artistic redemption completely seductive. When I was young it played into all my yearning for something better, a call to arms against toeing the line and taking orders. Similar elements are in several of his other novels, including *The Razor's Edge* and *Of Human Bondage*, both remarkable, but Charles Strickland, the protagonist of *The Moon and Sixpence*, flawed as he is, along with Sydney Carton in Dickens's *A Tale of Two Cities*, is one of the bravest and most inspiring literary characters.

My father worshipped Graham Greene, and so do I. He's a different animal altogether, and his work is inhabited by equally damaged characters. There's a whiff of sweat, whiskey breath, and cheap cigars between the pages of so many of Greene's most indelible novels. The locations are hardscrabble, hot, and populated by conflicted antiheroes in crumpled suits. There is underlying espionage, Catholic symbolism, and a worn-out sense of duty playing out in seedy bars, officers' clubs, and shabby hotels. It's impossible to name a favorite because I've loved them all equally as much. The lighter side of Greene, like *Travels with*

My Aunt, can be charmingly disarming, but it's his gritty colonial narratives that suck you in and have you yearning for lonely wives and tequila.

Greene was as conflicted in life as the characters in his books, which is obviously why he sketched them so realistically. His own story could very well have been his best novel, which is most likely why it took biographer Norman Sherry three volumes to chronicle his extraordinary life. This is a man who'd attend mass, head for a brothel, and wind up in an opium den. A Jesuit priest once said something to the effect that Greene's life was "to show how real holiness can coexist with real imperfection."

I'm no authority, but I think there's a little bit of Greene in each one of his classics. *The Heart of the Matter*, *The Quiet American*, *The Honorary Counsul*, and *The Power and the Glory* contain memorable leading men stranded between retribution and redemption with no hope for either one. Greene was magnificent, almost mythical to me, when he said, "When we are not sure, we are alive." It made perfect sense.

Maugham passed away in 1965, but Greene was still very much alive and living in Antibes, a resort town between Cannes and Nice on the French Riviera. One day I was having lunch with the film director and novelist Bryan Forbes. It just so happened that on this particular occasion I brought up my passion for Graham Greene and Bryan remarked casually, "Oh, Graham, lovely man, had dinner with him last week." You have to understand, Bryan during his storied career had met everybody and knew everybody. Of course, I grilled him mercilessly and he happily recounted several interactions with the celebrated author that had me hanging on every word.

Not long after this, I made an absolutely stunning addition to my collection. Let me give you some background. When Vladimir Nabokov wrote *Lolita*, it had first been published by a Parisian pornographer, and the British publishing houses would have nothing to do with it. Graham Greene, a fan of the book, was determined to see it get a shot in the UK and named it one of the best books of the year in the *Sunday Times*. This was 1955 and the morality police caved in, paving the way for the sensation it became. Indebted to Greene, Nabokov, who was notorious for refusing to inscribe his books, not only dedicated a first edition to his savior, but included along with his signature a beautiful drawing of a green swallowtail butterfly. Mistakenly, the first English edition was in fact not the genuine first edition, the French one was, and it was this version that Nabokov had presented to Greene. When Greene found out a first English edition had gone for a surprisingly large amount, he approached the UK rare book dealer Rick Gekoski and waved his personal copy under his nose. Is everyone following me? Gekoski bit and obtained it for £4,000. The next day I purchased it from him for $16,000 (£9,000). Years later when I sold my complete collection to him he bought back my *Lolita* for $23,000 (£13,000). In 2002, it went up for auction at Christie's and fetched $264,000 (£176,000)! Once bitten, twice shy.

For the time I had it, it was the most treasured book in my library, and I felt a strong need to connect with Greene and assure him it was in good hands. Through Rick, I obtained his address and penned him a short note professing my admiration for him and how I treasured this very unique copy of *Lolita*. I also had the temerity to send him a copy of my 1988 memoir of my childhood, *A Cradle of Halos*. No literary gem, but it wasn't without its charm in describing a vanishing England through the eyes of an impressionistic child growing up in the flat fertile farmlands of postwar Lincolnshire. I duly received a short, but friendly, response wishing me and the book well. That, for the time being, was that.

Soon after all this, I found myself in London working with Elton and trying to stay dry. The weather, I recall, was a beast. Anywhere else you just get wet, but English rain comes with a completely different set of ramifications, and getting caught off guard in it has zero romantic quality. Any English movie where the protagonist (usually Hugh Grant) stands in the middle of the street professing undying love while the heavens unload on him is, in reality, completely stupid. It's not Vietnam, it's Camden Town, and if you're looking to catch pneumonia, you're in the right place. It wraps itself around you like a sodden blanket, seeping into your bones and clawing at your joints like a clammy ghost.

It was on a night like this, with the rain slanting sideways and a serpentine Conan Doyle fog crawling along the Strand, that found me hunkered down and heading for The Savoy Hotel. One of my book dealers had located a pristine first edition of Mary Norton's *The Borrowers* and had arranged for me to pick it up from a courier in the lobby of the hotel. Even with the foul weather, the streets were packed. Commuters in droves poured along the sidewalk, purposeful resolve in their stride, their faces blurred by the rain. Lost in upturned collars and bathed in the clashing luminosity of muted streetlamps and brightly lit shop windows, they moved as one until, individually, they were picked off by their designated destinations. The pubs were crowded, department stores gave sanctuary, and the Tube swallowed the rest. As I ducked into The Savoy, alcohol and luxurious shelter sounded good to me.

Anytime I'm in a hotel, the compass in me points toward the bar. It's like a kitchen in a house, the hub around which everything rotates. A hotel without a bar isn't really a hotel, it's a motel, and a really cheap one at that. I've been in literally dozens of those and they're just boxes in which to sleep when you've only got several hours to do so and you have to be up at 5 a.m. to feed horses. OK, so we're not talking the Days Inn in Turkey Scratch here, we're ruminating on the classics, the hip contemporaries and acceptable chains. They vary from the happy hour lobby variety, a few wire back and Formica stools and a bellman doubling as a bartender who thinks an extra-dry martini is vodka with a jigger of vermouth to the oh-so-hip-you-can't-actually-see-the-bar-at-all. Usually it's a foyer full of distressed couches and hot girls in Alaia dresses who stand around deciding if they want to take your order or not. Then, of course, there are the few, the proud, the irresistible. I've stayed in many hotels with wonderful bars, but then there are the crown jewels: the King Cole Bar in the St. Regis and Bemelmans Bar at the Carlyle in New York, Bar Hemingway at the Ritz in Paris, Coq d'Or at The Drake in Chicago, and The Mansion on Turtle Creek in Dallas.

The American Bar in The Savoy Hotel was legendary and at that particular time, although aware of its status in the hotel bar top ten, I'd not had the pleasure. This being the case, and having bid adieu to my literary mule, I assured myself (with no convincing necessary) that it would be sacrilege not to cross this fabled bar off my list of fabled watering holes.

Reconnecting with memories of the past is sometimes confusing. Similar episodes can occasionally collide and play havoc with the absolute truth. Who cares, right? As long as all these memories exist in and around the time in question. Intimate impressions that come together painting one indelible portrait, it may not have exactly happened this way, but rest assured it definitely happened.

That "maybe," taken into consideration, upon my entrance into the bar I recalled feeling the tug of a prewar clubby time warp. In reality it may have been the '80s, but I was smelling Brown Windsor soup and cigars. Oh yeah, I was stepping back into a misty, swirling renaissance of prewar feminist exclusion, fawning starched-white subservience, and the port and brandy platitude of the Mountbatten set.

Why, you may ask? Well, it started with atmosphere, but then somewhere there was a fireplace and a wingback chair. Given the exterior weather and London's compliance to the cold and damp, my gaze was drawn to a pleasant late afternoon nook in which to play footsie with the buttoned-up past.

It was only then that, in the chair I presumed to procure, I ascertained a presence that, unless I was overwhelmed by antiquated visions of yesteryear was . . . well, could it really be?

The chair itself didn't engulf him completely but did a fairly fine job at securing him from detection. I'm not entirely sure how many patrons in the bar that evening were even aware that, arguably, the greatest novelist of the twentieth century was quietly sipping a cocktail by the fire.

Graham Greene had light emerald eyes, nursed an unidentifiable drink, and seemed deep in thought. He was terribly pale and jowly, which made him look sadder than I imagine he really was. His clothes were loose fitting and slightly worn; you might even have called his tweedy jacket threadbare. He reclined in his clothes as if they were bedfellows from yesteryear, close comfort items that left him attached to his generational counterparts, but still no different than what I imagine he had once inhabited in a more tailored and youthful persona.

What were the odds? So many components could be considered that might be responsible for navigating me to this chance encounter. Even if he dismissed me with a withering look or shooed me away with a contemptuous wave of his hand it mattered not. This was a once in a lifetime opportunity and I was not throwing away my shot.

Perhaps bolstered by the Bryan Forbes connection, his cordial but brief letter, and my ownership of his copy of *Lolita*, I felt I had enough ammunition to make an introduction.

"Mr. Greene?" I inquired.

Still seemingly adrift in his thoughts, he turned his head toward me with no recognizable sense of irritation or mental disruption. His gaze in fact gave little away. There was no smile, just a glimmer of interest I imagine was connected to an internal fuse that switched on automatically in moments like these. I wasn't some nerdy looking academic, neither was I a bookish intellectual in a blazer and slacks. I just looked like who I was, a quasi-stylish, semi-long haired, hard-to-pin-down citizen of the current status quo. I think this interested him, and after confirming my inquiry, he gave me a look that I interpreted as an invite to continue.

Halfway into my prepared spiel, a steward approached. I wasn't sure if he was about to tell me to sod off or take my drink order. Luckily, after no apparent negative direction from Mr. Greene to do the former, I embraced the latter and made a request that could have gummed up things from the get-go. I ordered a vodka martini! Heavens to Betsy, ordering the American bastardization of this Churchillian staple in the presence of someone who not only was notoriously dismissive in his view of the US but whose novels literally reeked of gin was a severely negative shot across the bow.

Outside of a quizzical look that I took to be a combination of disappointment and resignation, he chose to remain mum on the nature of my cocktail choice. I think as a man of extraordinary intellect, he interpreted life at this point in the twentieth century as an interesting diversion and an unavoidable progression that he wasn't going to have to deal with for too much longer. For now, I probably looked like a template for what might or might not be a barometer of things to come.

You may have noted I'm making much of his gesticulations and facial kinesics. That's because I was determined to remember everything. My mental camera was snapping away, recording every detail of this exhilarating happenstance so that it could be processed later and readily available in years to come.

Of course he knew Bryan Forbes and informed me that they had in fact dined recently close to his home in Antibes. More important, he was completely familiar with the fact that his personalized copy of *Lolita* had recently sold. Having absolutely no idea who I was, he was a little slower at connecting the dots in equating its journey to yours truly. Once I'd humbly jogged his memory in regard to my acquisition of the book, and my introductory note and brazen gift, he made some recollective awareness of it by way of a confirming nod. I'm not sure if he was just humoring me, but then I'm not sure that Graham Greene was in the business of bullshitting. He asked after the book, the way a cherished aunt inquires as to the welfare of a beloved nephew. He also pointedly asked if he had responded to my letter, which I was happy to inform him he had. He seemed relieved by this. For a man who'd come from a generation in which letter writing was an integral part of life, this was obviously of great importance.

I'm not going to pretend our conversation was profound or conducted on any stimulating intellectual level. It was informal and polite enough but will forever remain a high point. He was most certainly addressing me in the capacity of a random individual and not someone of celebrity importance, musical, literary, or otherwise.

I was happy with my lot and wasn't about to waste precious seconds providing my credentials. While he may have been familiar with the name Elton John and most likely aware of him as a popular singing star, my identity in the equation was unnecessary grist for the mill. Besides, he conducted himself on such an even keel that my being of any importance would not have altered his temperament. I got the distinct impression this was his nature, and that a fiery and cantankerous Graham Greene didn't exist.

What I drew from this encounter and my observations as to the nature of his personality might be shredded by his biographers.

Perfectly understandable as I had no more than twenty minutes to draw my conclusions, but in this time my own personal summation cannot be stepped upon.

From our brief interlude I learned several things, a couple trivial and one undeniably beneficial. I think, even bolstered by fame, he was inherently shy and uncomfortable with notoriety.

Oh yes, and by way of polite inquiry, I ascertained that he was drinking a classic martini infused with a dash of crème de cassis, a cocktail that I later deduced was named after him and featured in that unequaled bible of bartending, Harry Craddock's *The Savoy Cocktail Book*.

I can't honestly remember how I posed the question, but somehow I managed to make it cryptically ambiguous without sounding pedestrian. I mean, how do you ask a literary colossus from what source he draws his inspiration without sounding like you're trespassing?

He was surprisingly generous in his response, though no less enigmatic. Surreptitiously through sign language, he pointed to a rummy eye with his forefinger, then drew an imaginary line around the room. He followed this with a motion of gathering and concluded with a tap to the side of his temple.

It was the single best thing I drew from our brief interaction; the confirmation that as a writer the scrutiny of life around you was key to all. It was enough verification for me, everything that had preceded our meeting was built on this foundation and his affirmation, no matter how arcane, was sacrosanct.

Not wishing to overstay my welcome and be tripped up by obsequious fawning, I took my leave with as much grace as I thought appropriate. He didn't invite me to drop in on him anytime in Antibes, but he did shake my hand, tender the glimmer of a smile, and mouth a barely audible goodbye.

Nous Avons des Canards dans le Hall

Either this wallpaper goes or I do.
—OSCAR WILDE, on his deathbed

L'Hotel is a twenty-room boutique hotel at 13 rue des Beaux-Arts in the Saint-Germain district on the Left Bank of Paris. Built in 1828 on the location of La Reine Margot's Pavillon d'Amour, the establishment became Hotel d'Allemagne in 1868, changing a few years later to Hotel d'Alsace after the Franco-Prussian War. After a refurbishment in 1967, L'Hotel became a magnet for the well-heeled and romantically inclined. It also has the distinction of being the establishment where Oscar Wilde chose to die.

I'm unsure if this was the main attraction, but it was indeed the former apartment of that fantastic old aesthetic where I decamped with my assistant, Pete, for six weeks in the spring of 1976. Undoubtedly, the room had seen many changes since OW checked out (literally) in 1900, and by the time I moved in it was spaciously intimate and beautifully decorated in deep rich colors and sensual fabrics. Muted lighting accentuated sculpted mahogany dressers and regally appointed recliners while the wallpaper, a lusty print that smacked of bordello chic, was interspersed between cushiony nooks and a giant bed that Oscar could only have dreamed of passing away in. With not even a hint of past ghosts or lingering spookiness, it proffered a luxurious sense of old-world charm inviting its guests to embrace the muse and make good on their literary promises in a way that only Paris can.

Spoiling myself? Yes, I was. Back then (or even now for that matter) I didn't lavish money on homes and cars or any of the other customary rock star acquisitions. I had a rambling spirit and preferred to spend what I had on comfortable travel and imaginative and stimulating locales that might heighten my outlook and rev up the engine of my cinematic observation. I saw myself as a storyteller always, and what better way of obtaining firsthand inspiration than both living it first and recounting it later? I lived my life at times in quotation marks and beset myself with storied adventures, some mundane, some weird and wonderful, but all ultimately cohabitating in the creation of excellent lies and terrible truths.

Pete, my aforementioned sidekick in this Parisian getaway was a farm boy, beefy, ruddy complexioned, and a childhood friend from the time I was barely into my teens. I'd done what, I have since learned, is not a good idea: I'd hired him out of familiarity to be a combination driver, minder, and factotum amigo. He was a brawny lad, not terribly sophisticated, and prone to not understanding the classification of his job ethic, which was to look out for me and not the reverse. Still, he wasn't without a good sense of humor and had an easy unpretentious personality. He also had a highly amusing way of communicating with our foreign hosts. Being that neither of us had much skill with the language, Pete believed that if you spoke English with a French accent you would be understood. I could never convince him otherwise and never really tried since the execution of this endeavor never ceased to amuse me.

L'Hotel had a first rate bar and ducks in the lobby. Two things of immense importance: a great martini and a serious sense of eccentricity. The ducks would waddle around as if they owned the place, investigating luggage and pecking gently at the residents' feet. Duck wranglers not forthcoming, we gingerly stepped around them, allowing them the space they plainly felt was theirs.

Once I got situated in my historic digs and having invited the persona of this fabled city to inhabit my psyche, I was raring to write. As there always is in Paris, there was a timeless and inspiring force. It's in the morning air, the smell of coffee and fresh baguettes. It's in the streets, emanating from the brassieres and sidewalk cafés, garlic and herbs, aiolis, and *les pain au chocolat*.

In the evening, it's in the first warm luminosity of the streetlights, their orange glow reflecting in the wet streets, the sound of laughter and the strains of song invested in the cool evening air. Paris has a natural affinity for composition, as Ernest Hemingway so succinctly put it, *If you are lucky enough to have lived in Paris as a young man, then wherever you go for the rest of your life, it stays with you, for Paris is a moveable feast.* Indeed!

In those days I stayed out late, inhabiting the night in alternate degrees of behavior. However, no matter which way my proclivities played out and whatever hour I hit the pillow, I was always up with the lark. Perhaps it was my country upbringing, I don't know, but whatever it was that snapped my lids open in the a.m. there is no doubting I always loved the morning. In Paris, it was almost ritualistic. To throw open the windows and inhale the intoxicating city air, smell the breakfast aromas wafting up from the courtyard below, and hear the distant sound of bells eradicated sleep and made reparation for the sins of the night.

I avoided bathtubs the way W. C. Fields abstained from water: "Fish fuck in it," he said. Agreed. So who wants to wallow and soak in the previous evenings sweat and smoke when a healthy shower can strip you clean? Besides, French bathtub culture came with a serious streak of bad karma. Five years earlier, Jim Morrison had suffered a massive heart attack in his bathtub only ten minutes from L'Hotel. While not nearly so recently, in the mother of all tub deaths Charlotte Corday had plunged an eight-inch kitchen knife into the chest of revolutionary rabble-rouser Jean-Paul Marat. Not prepared to be next, I left it up to the French pop singer Claude Francois, who in 1978 in a moment of gross stupidity electrocuted himself while trying to fix a broken light bulb while standing in a half-filled tub.

At the time, my work ethic was commendable given the standards I occasionally adhered to. I try not to think back on myself as being lazy, but for me it was always about collecting ideas, drawing from my surroundings, making notes, and most of all, people watching. Paris had some of the best people watching I'd ever encountered outside of airports. So while I made myself commit to the singular activity of writing in my room most mornings, the rest of the day and night I was rigorous in the pursuit of inspiration.

Incidentally, people watching in airports has on occasion caused me to miss flights. Twice in fact, once with Eric Clapton, the second with the actor Richard Harris. On both occasions we were deep in our cups, those times when foolish ideas seem excellent and plans are made with no possibility of fruition. Both times at a characterless bar where over-indulgence erased time and caused us to watch as our flights took to the sky.

It goes without saying that eating was of primary importance here in one of the gastronomical centers of the universe. After an invigorating morning stroll, lunch could last for hours, and the people watching from a terrace table at Les Deux Magots or a likewise location at Brasserie Lipp, both on the Boulevard Saint-Germain, were daily rituals. Both restaurants suffered from tourist activity and reputation by way of connection with the usual suspects. At one time or another the likes of Hemingway, Paul Verlaine, and Simone de Beauvoir had scribbled at these tables while the literary salons that constituted the 1920s whiled away the hours being terribly clever and once again inventing the nostalgia that is Paris.

Other than this, there was one lunch spot that had no connection whatsoever with exclusivity or literary bearing. It was a hole-in-the-wall dive directly across the street from our hotel and without a doubt the best Vietnamese restaurant I've ever eaten at in my life. This restaurant had peculiarities that, other than the food and its bizarre decor, kept us coming back. The staff were as mad as a sack of hammers, which never left me without the notion that we were being filmed. Another was Nina Hagen, the German queen of punk, and *Neue Deutsche Welle*. She was always there, never eating, but talking to a giant green parrot that the proprietors kept chained to a perch by a bandstand that I never once saw used. This odd chanteuse with her multicolored hair and ghoulish makeup would communicate with this bird in weird operatic tones that I'm told she incorporated into her recordings. That such fabulous food could be created in this complete nuthouse only made it all the more appealing. I would return again and again, a slave to its food and lunacy.

And then there were the nights. As always, I divided my time frequenting and sharing equal currency with establishments both tragically hip and seriously suspect. At that time in Paris (and the rest of the world for that matter), Régine Zylberberg was the defining nightclub impresaria. Undisputedly the reigning monarch of exclusivity, she had pretty much invented nightclubbing and was certainly the architect of the discotheque as we have come to know it. Régine was an extraordinary woman, who for some unfathomable reason took a shine to me, and was always beyond generous and welcoming when it came to membership into her impenetrable nighteries. Gaining entry to one of her clubs was like Ted Bundy trying to talk his way into Heaven. Even the membership cards, gold-plated in a custom Cartier case, were the most sought-after accoutrement of the international jet set. Like all the most successful hostesses, she had no vices other than her attraction to handsome and distinguished men. It's said that she once danced the night away with Gene Kelly and then spent the next fifteen days sequestered away with him. Her club, Chez Régine, on rue de Ponthieu, was a mecca for royalty and the mega rich, screen divinity, and only the very coolest of the international rock elite. She once turned away Mick Jagger for wearing sneakers. So what was I doing there? I have absolutely no idea whatsoever.

I had entered Régine's orbit accidentally. I believe it was on an earlier trip to Paris when Elton and I, hosted by the legendary French music producer Eddie Barclay, wound up as his guests at her club. Régine had taken a shine to me not in any romantic sense I assure you, but more in that intuitive way that worldly women bestow patronage on young men unimpressed by celebrity and who are in no way capable of assuming superficiality. I think Régine liked writers and saw me as some contemporary Rimbaud, rough around the edges and on the border of social metamorphosis. Of course, she was completely wrong on all counts, but I guess the simple fact that I harbored a little bit of imagination horribly mistaken as poetry was not lost on her perceptive nature. With her lusty rasp and joie de vivre, I was adopted by this magnetic flaming red-haired queen of the night and integrated into a world of humongous pretension and temporary illusion.

One of the oddest things I ever witnessed at Régine's was the composer and general *enfant terrible* of French pop Serge Gainsbourg emerging from the center of the dance floor playing a piano on a hydraulic lift. Looking like a man who had slept in his clothes for the last month and reeking of Gauloises cigarettes and sour wine, he was not a pleasant presence. Obviously a man with a high opinion of himself, he swaggered around depositing ash onto his lapels and sloshing Bordeaux on his shirt. I don't know if it's some sort of macho Gallic thing, but choosing to smell like the baggage carousel at Orly airport is not, I would imagine, a choice in the best of taste. (I once had to switch apartments in Paris because the housekeeper had such appalling BO that it permeated the entire place.) That a stunning woman like Jane Birkin could crawl into bed at night with a man who looked like he'd been dipped in Crisco and rolled in pubic hair still makes me shudder to this day.

As for now, it was my assistant, Pete, who had to be reined in. Like most high-end nightclubs today, Régine's patrons were only allowed to purchase liquor, wine, and champagne by the bottle. This policy for the "money-is-no-object" members would invariably have guests abandoning half-consumed spirits, magnums of bubbly, and Château Margaux, casting them aside as if they were lukewarm Perriers. Before their seats were cold, Pete, like a mile-high hawk, would zero in on these vacated tables, sweep the leftovers into his jacket, and return triumphantly to our booth presenting the pilfered hootch like a cat depositing a dead mouse.

Pete's favorite mark in these endeavors were Saudi businessmen. Adhering to Islamic law, their abstinence from alcohol didn't prevent them from ordering the most expensive wines available and not touching it. I assumed the reason for this was twofold. They wanted everyone to know they were rich as Croesus, and secondly, sitting there drinking oceans of Coca-Cola all night wasn't going to win them any gold Cartier cards. Pete's eyes would positively light up at the sight of thobes and hijabs making their way into the club, his commando instincts already having robbed them blind.

One night while cruising home in a cab, we passed an establishment so garish it simply screamed, "Gotta see what that's all about." Le Sexy, its unimaginative name aside, was more than you might imagine. Looking like a cross between a strip joint and a Polynesian brothel, it was neither in the true sense of the words. What we discovered was far more intriguing. The exterior, draped haphazardly with Christmas lights and plastic taffeta fronds, was a mesmerizing eyesore. The club's name was spelled out in cracked dull neon, and trembled and flickered above a chalkboard advertising *boissons bon marché*, the tawdry promise of cheap drinks a blatant falsehood given the truth that lay within. After shelling out the entrance fee to a dozing crone in a boxy kiosk not dissimilar to an antiquated fortune-teller booth in a penny arcade, we were directed down a hallway toward an intriguing source of illumination and noise. To the left and right of us were a series of empty rooms, dark and eerily forsaken, like some mise-en-scène abandoned in favor of greener pastures. In this case it turned out to be a large circular bar packed to the gills with jovial patrons in all manner of uninhibited revelry. In total contradiction to its embrace of kitsch and lethargy, everything seemed to revolve around this lively planet suspended in a vacillating solar system. The conviviality was immediately intoxicating, and in no time at all we were drawn in and engulfed into a sea of rollicking frivolity.

Our initial reaction to this out-of-the-way wacko joint was simply one of lowbrow relief. With no disrespect to the grandiose exclusivity of Régine's, the motley ambience of Le Sexy in name alone was refreshingly disarming. It was only on our return visit the next night, a premise instigated by my confirmed belief that this might be the holy grail of people watching, that we learned the true nature of what was what. The process of realization began when we actually started to pay attention to what was going on around us. For the most part, it appeared to be raucous and disheveled businessmen in conversation with not unattractive yet uniformly decorous females seemingly intent on captivating them.

It became clear in a matter of moments: these were escorts working the treadmill of sauerkraut sodden German execs and all manner of wasted European corporate fodder. Genius, but what was the game? It wasn't until the girls worked their way around to us, and quickly realized we weren't typical of their predatory racket, that the climate changed.

Time was money to them, pure and simple, but given that we didn't pose any pimp muscle or undercover threat, they slowly warmed to our lax residency and nonjudgmental nature. We never saw any of them leave with anybody. They just moved in and out of the assembled suits and ties, cajoling and captivating their quarry into buying what seemed like inordinate quantities of champagne. At the end of the evening, they would gravitate tentatively into our consolidated orbit at the bar, intrigued by our nonexclusivity. At this point we had won over the overly protective Slavic barman through both heavy drinking and tipping to the point he'd probably have eighty-sixed anyone even glancing at our stools.

One of the things that had intrigued me from the get-go was why the carpet beneath our feet at the bar always seemed sticky. Gaining traction by orchestrating a repartee with our newfound friends and brokering their trust through broken English, hand gestures, and of course Pete's stylized impersonation of Inspector Clouseau, we got the skinny on the sticky. In order to encourage their quarry to buy them more champagne and not get shit-faced in the process, they would simply empty their glasses under the bar onto the carpet. The more bottles purchased, the more money they made. Anything on top of this was at their own discretion, which, as I pointed out, seemed minimal considering most of these guys were poured into cabs at the night's end, incapable of consummating anything other than their own demise.

They may have fleeced a few rubes in their time . . . who knew? But however they made ends meet, they were a canny set of hustlers.

Getting acquainted with this quirky group was pure gold for someone like me who has always drawn inspiration from alternate lifestyles, and the flotsam navigating its way through a hardscrabble world has filled napkin upon napkin with ideas. They may have been fabricated biographies, embellished adventures, and counterfeit lies, but initially it began with real flesh and blood characters and at least a semblance of the truth.

Eventually, the girls started returning with us to the hotel where we would stay up late communicating in an ever-improving totemistic language. Oddly enough, there was never ever any sexual interaction between any of us. I know, this sounds a lot like buying *Playboy* for the articles, but they were working girls and that meant money changing hands, which, as God is my witness, wasn't going to happen on my watch.

We got to know half a dozen of the women, most of them in their early to late twenties, Gigi being the eldest. Somewhere in her mid-thirties, Gigi was the head honcho, no doubt. It was plain to see that the others looked up to her, totally subordinate, and it was most decidedly what Gigi says goes. Not to sound patronizing or to project stereotypes, but she was a tough cookie with a protective streak that was more Ma Barker than Mother Hen in regard to her girls. She was also sharp as a tack with a fierce thirst for knowledge, which is why I would find her scrutinizing my books as if hoping that they might magically translate themselves. Books were obviously a luxury that were not a priority in her day-to-day quest to keep food on the table and a roof over her head. She would get frustrated when I was unable to explain what she wanted to learn about their contents. They were mostly historical biographies of people I'm pretty certain she was not familiar with. The only person I can recall her recognizing in a photo was Jacqueline Kennedy, which caused her great excitement. Stabbing at the picture with her finger she exclaimed repeatedly, "*C'est Jackie O, c'est Jackie O.*" I gave her the books, it seemed like the least I could do since any sort of monetary handout would only appear condescending, not to mention sending the wrong message.

I did invest in an English to French dictionary, which only proved of minor assistance, but eventually was too time-consuming for a woman who burned as fast as she did and was constantly into the next moment when the present didn't move with her tempo. While I spent my efforts trying to develop some sort of attempted, but ultimately aborted, literary rapport with Gigi, the other girls took advantage of

Pete . . . mercilessly. They had him pegged, and they knew it. You would have thought after watching them in action for about a week he'd have cottoned on, but here he was dancing to their tune and falling face forward into their flirtatious web. They cooed in his ear, flattered his masculinity, and cajoled him into ordering a lot of room service, a convenience they seemed unaware existed until now. All this was on my dime, of course, for which initially I bit the bullet until the lobster became a little too frequent. It was their brutal honesty when it came to my taste in background music however that caused a line in the sand to be drawn!

Ellington: "*Merde.*"

Coltrane: "*Plus de merde.*"

"*Jouez les Beatles, sous-marin jaune.*"

OK, this was one area where they weren't going to get their way. If they were going to chow down on lobster that I was shelling out for (no pun intended), there sure wasn't any way that we were going to be listening to "Yellow Submarine" all night.

In retrospect, I'm not sure Pete's moral standards were in sync with mine, but if he had any hope of copping a freebie, he was sorely dreaming. In their eyes, he was a puppet on a string, an entertaining distraction who performed like a seal and talked funny. He also wasn't addressing the elephant in the room. It would be overly dramatic to say I was saddened, but there was a poignancy to this overall situation. None of us were ever going to be 100 percent comfortable in each other's presence. Not us, not them. No matter how familiar we became, they always seemed to be on their guard. Initially, it was a little like trying to coax a feral deer into trusting you, where you avoid making any sudden moves until eventuality they sense entrapment and run. It was a temporary adventure, a trench truce where two lifestyles meet in the middle and bridge a cultural divide. Sooner than later, both parties exhaust whatever, if any, value from it and move on. It would very soon be evanescent, but not before drawing itself to a rousing and bittersweet conclusion.

I was committed to do a press conference in the lobby of the hotel in a few days to promote a book of recently published lyrics. Our publicist, a charming young woman named Caroline Boucher, was due to come over from the UK to set things up while my dear old friend, the renowned photographer Terry O'Neill, would arrive beforehand to take some candid portraits. Terry's idea was to make the shots as edgy as possible, which is why the resulting photos were pretty close to mirroring my rootless bohemianism at that time. I'll admit, I do look a little weather-worn and grungy in them. Although hardly Serge Gainsbourg, they are decadently Parisian in feel. In one, I'm wrapped in a leather trench coat, crouched in the gutter of a cobbled street, full five-o'clock shadow, cigarette clenched between my teeth. In another taken in my room, I'm shirtless in a cowboy hat. It's all very orchestrated to project a vagabond artist mystique, but being Terry O'Neill he pulled it off and I got to benefit from it.

As an afterthought, one evening I'd communicated to Gigi through an intermediary about the press conference and invited her to check it out if she felt like it, never thinking in a million years she'd either remember or be remotely interested. Besides it was at ten in the morning, a time of day not normally associated with those in Gigi's profession. I forgot all about it and duly turned up with Caroline to face the press. Caroline was a darling, very efficient, but quite conservative in her manner as well as demure, in that very British way. She was also all business, and as soon as everything was orchestrated to her requirements, the press were invited in. They were the usual mix of scrappy and combative foreign journalists along with a smattering of the pandering tabloid vultures from the UK who'd suck up royally for any solicitous tidbit.

The questions had barely begun when there was a commotion at the rear of the room. Heads turned and a hush fell over the assembled journos as Gigi and her crew sauntered into the room looking like the troupe from the Moulin Rouge cabaret. With a blitzkrieg of bonjours and sassy salutations, they plowed through the scruffy hacks with wicked aplomb. I've no doubt those present perceived this as a blatant publicity stunt, although had they focused on the actual publicist they may have come to a different conclusion. Caroline's eyes were as wide as saucers and her reaction was either complete horror or total admiration. Personally, I was leaning to the latter, although I was momentarily thrown and left in a state of shell-shocked bemusement.

With all emphasis temporarily taken off the proceedings and Pete frantically trying to wrangle the *putes folles*, we ducked for cover, our composures to be reset and my apologies to be made.

The press conference resumed swiftly, but it was hard to concentrate. The girls behaved the only way they knew how, which meant feigning interest and stealing the free food. Eventually, the status quo leveled and everything formulated into a feisty Q&A that culminated only when *les filles* took their leave with a brassy *au revoir*.

We never went back to Le Sexy and we never saw them again.

I did write a song about them. Yes, it was slightly embellished, and yes, it was based on the truth:

> *She'd never drop her guard*
> *Under pressure she preferred like all her girls*
> *Who worked the bars*
> *To be a lady in the finest sense*
> *Not your traditional elegance*
> *Of Paris Match and chic expense*
> *But the tough and tardy waiting game*
> *With fat commuters full of cheap champagne*
> *Belching tourists feel no pain*
> *When Gigi takes their wallets*
> *Spends their bodies, keeps the change.*

ELTON AND I made three good albums in France, all of them recorded three hours outside Paris at the Château d'Hérouville, an eighteenth-century bit of chunky nostalgia supposedly once painted by Vincent van Gogh. It was also said that somewhere around the mid-1800s, Fredric Chopin and George Sand made it their own personal love shack and ultimately left their horny spirits to wander the unkempt grounds. As for us, it was a communal living and working operation that proved wholly successful for the time we inhabited it. The living conditions, however, were spartan at best. Sparsely furnished rooms with uncomfortable beds and dodgy plumbing, the distinct impression was that this was designed to be rock and roll boot camp rather than a pampering playpen. Our work ethic was commendable and a certain synchronicity was applied to the way we got things done. I usually came prepared with a little initial ammunition to get things started since my partner had a tendency to dive right in and knock off several songs over breakfast. This frantic pace certainly kept me on my toes and found me crawling out of bed and straight into writing mode. Thankfully, ideas came thick and fast, scribbled down in a fashion that seemed in context with our abstinence from luxury. With no typewriter and years before computers, everything was written longhand in a barely legible script that someone somewhere along the chain of command translated into a decipherable form.

Being France, the food was good, but sometimes not to the taste of all members of our band and crew. A certain element were most definitely of the cornflakes and baked bean persuasion, but luckily a steady rotation of *steak frites* kept any gastronomic mutiny from occurring. There was one dinner, however, where horror of horrors, the kitchen presented the table with six large tureens of fresh oysters. This proved to be a veritable bounty for Elton and myself, who, along with a couple of other ostreophiles, demolished the lot as our appalled comrades looked on with queasy disdain.

The château did come with its oddities, the premier one being George. A caretaker of sorts, or so I believe, George was simple in a harmless, shuffling way. Of course, this didn't prevent some in our party from riffing on his disability and reimagining him as some knife-wielding Quasimodo. Cruel, of course, but in the confines of this setting, it seemed like a necessary attribute. George was intrigued by music and musicians, and his one goal in life was to own a hundred-watt Marshall amp. I'm not sure if he even owned a guitar, but he did own an old stand-up bass that he treated like his wife and referred to as "ma dooooble bazzz." When the moon was full, George would sit on the balcony of his room caressing this instrument, silk stockings hanging from the tuning pegs, and his guttural cooing issuing into the stillness of the night.

Subsequently, I returned to the château to produce an album for a group I had recently signed to Rocket Records, our self-owned label. This proved to be an altogether darker episode. By then the studio had metamorphosed into an even more feudal antiquity; George was gone, and the staff was seriously depleted. There had always been talk of restless spirits and ghosts, strange unexplainable events that had filtered down from client to client. I'm sure much of it was embellished as is the way with such things, but on this visit I can honestly say that things happened that cannot be explained. I'm by nature seriously skeptical about the paranormal and have always believed that rational thinking can eradicate supernatural belief, but put yourself in a spooky-ass château on a stormy night and confidence in practicality flies out the window. The only good thing going for us in this particular instance was that it was consolidated into one night and one night only. It was as if lightning had struck the tower and all the available bad vibes congregated in the same place at the same time. It started with a freaked-out cat and a self-igniting fireplace. I mean the fire literally started on its own and the cat looked like it had been electrocuted. Then the lights went out. Retrieving candles and matches from my bathroom, I noticed that the mirror above the sink had been scratched from the inside out, the cheap reflective adhesive having been mauled as if by internal claws. While thunder rolled and lightning crashed as if on cue, we did what any other group of petrified pals would do in these circumstances and piled into one bedroom and locked the door. This is where things get hazy. With the passing of a fitful night, some were convinced they heard voices and some complained of being tugged or tapped on the shoulder by invisible hands. What is the gospel truth is that when we were playing back tracks in the studio the next day, there were most definitely audible moans and groans on the tape that had disappeared when we replayed them later. The ghosts had obviously given up on a recording career and we were happy to get the hell out of Dodge. The château closed its doors for good in 1985, a year after its owner, plagued by debt, took his own life in a nearby hotel.

Notwithstanding the château haunting, the only unpleasant time I had in France was in Paris, sometime in the early '80s. Almost a decade before Elton entered rehab, he was not doing well. Deep in the stranglehold of addiction, he had rented a large dark and gloomy apartment with the intention of writing some songs for our next album. In the City of Light, this place was an anachronism. He had asked me to come over and work with him, which I did, also making the very sensible decision of renting my own place. After a couple of inadequate options, I settled into a flat smack-dab in front of the Eiffel Tower.

The biggest problem I had, outside the depressing atmosphere permeating Elton's accommodations, were his hours of cognizance. For me, drugs had not yet become a cross to bear. I could dabble, yet do without, and this made for an unbalanced work schedule. Simply put, Elton slept most of the day and worked late into the night, or until the cocaine got the best of him. What made things even worse was how he was composing. He had a workroom set up with a bank of electronic keyboards and rudimentary recording equipment. He would sit there for what seemed like hours cranking out melodies, most of them forgettable, but to someone as high as he was they were brilliant. It was torture for me on several levels: one being that he expected me to go against the grain and come up with lyrics for these unremarkable tunes; the other was much more upsetting: to see your very best friend so disconnected and raw to the bone was heartbreaking. This man who was talented beyond belief and one of the finest musicians and melodists in the musical firmament in the thrall of crash and burn was positively crippling. Once I could make my escape, I'd return to my apartment thoroughly depressed and emotionally drained.

During my stay I had no real social life, as I was flying solo those days, and besides, I was really too distressed to have any fun. For the most part, I'd walk in the mornings, try to pen something applicable to what I could remember from the night before, and wander over to Elton's sometime in the late afternoon. I'd sit in the murky half-light of the kitchen and attempt conversation with whoever was hanging around. There was a young woman serving as a combination housekeeper and Girl Friday who was pleasant enough but seemed fully aware of the lethargy permeating everything. Also present was Adrian, Elton's longtime recording tech who always was, and remains, a beacon of efficiency. However, even he seemed in some sort of hallucinatory state most of the time, his boffin persona working overtime as he gazed at the ceiling and mumbled about floating apparitions. At times, I'd see unsavory characters lurking around in the shadows. Naturally, it didn't take a rocket scientist to imagine what profession these guys were in. Drug dealers always have that nervy energy about them that's partly ingratiating and partly dangerous, like a cornered fox looking every which way at once.

Not much came out of these writing sessions and what did was nothing to be proud of. Eventually, two or three of them ended up on the *Jump Up!* album, but like everything else written between our amicable split in the late 1970s until our return to form with *Too Low for Zero* in '83, these tracks were most definitely subpar by our standards. There were too many cooks in the kitchen, an ever-increasing amount of drugs, and a severe lack of communication between the two of us. The cohesiveness of what had made our partnership work was now fractured, and with various different lyricists in the mix it made for an uneven whole. This is not to belittle his other collaborators, but the universal familiarity with our signature style seemed uneven when interspersed with completely different variants of words and music. In all honesty, I probably should have bowed out of those records that contained songs by multiple writers. If, like on his *A Single Man* album, Elton had worked with just one partner on his three subsequent releases, good, bad, or indifferent, things may have flowed a little more smoothly. Then again there wouldn't have been songs like "Empty Garden."

Yes, there were a few exceptions. It may sound contradictory to say, but when we had decided to test the waters again it wasn't unpleasant. On the contrary, when Elton invited me out to his rented home in the coastal town of Saint-Tropez on the French Riviera, I was thrilled. This was a couple of years prior to the dark cloud that was Paris, and while still using, it was not debilitating, he was more himself, more accessible, but still not 100 percent committed to a monogamous reunion. Placing myself squarely back into that moment in time, all the preceding reflections mean nothing. The best thing to come out of this trip was a song called "Two Rooms at the End of the World," which documents our separation and our eventual reunion. Subsequently in 1991, an abbreviation of this song title was used for a very good documentary and its accompanying album of covers by contemporary artists. Unlike what would transpire later, at least the songs we were writing were written in the way it worked best.

The avalanche of cocaine that was to come later, aside this earlier reset in our reunion, wasn't without its peripheral distractions. As creatively uneven as this time period was, there were interesting occasions and comedic interludes. To start with, the house was bright and cheery, the weather delightful, and a succession of visiting friends kept the whole thing on an even keel.

We spent one long and languid afternoon dining alfresco at the home of French producer Eddie Barclay. It was Eddie who had been my and Elton's chaperone the night at Régine's when Serge Gainsbourg emerged from the dance floor. Eddie's work with the likes of Jacques Brel, Charles Aznavour, and Juliette Gréco had made him hugely respected in his homeland. His Barclay record company and label was at one time the top music production company in France. Along with his varied musical achievements, he'd also gained a reputation as an extravagant and hospitable host. In his trademark white suit, his Saint-Tropez parties were huge media events. Nicknamed Bluebeard by the press, he'd been married and divorced a gazillion times, yet still managed to afford this stunning setting we found ourselves in for lunch.

And what a lunch! It went on for hours. It felt like being in a James Bond movie directed by Roger Vadim. It was so cool, it was almost a parody. All the women looked like either Françoise Hardy or Sylvie Vartan and all the men looked like . . . well, I actually didn't pay that much attention to the men except for Charles Aznavour. Aznavour was simply delightful, humble, and charming. He lived up to his outstanding reputation as a consummate gentleman and humanitarian. Born Shahnour Vaghinag Aznavourian, it's hardly surprising he changed his name. He was, indeed, as one music critic dubbed him "a French pop deity," and one of the best-selling music artists of all time. His voice was a jewel, his songs were romantic, deep, and at times, incredibly profound. Jean Cocteau once said, "Before Aznavour, despair was unpopular," and Bob Dylan called him one of the greatest live performers he'd ever seen. Serenity simply permeated the air around him, and for one of only several times in my life I truly felt I was in the presence of genius. I was lucky to meet him on several other occasions preceding this, and I swear, as God is my witness, he did not disappoint.

I VISITED ELTON twice in Saint-Tropez, and both times were equally enjoyable. As we departed for the airport on our final day, Elton remembered there were a couple of guys in the guesthouse he'd promised a ride back to the UK. Musicians on the rise, they were a nice couple of boys who were feeling no pain from a night out on the town. George Michael and Andrew Ridgeley would go on to make quite a name for themselves in the next decade.

Straight Time

I was asked if my first sexual experience was homosexual
or heterosexual. I said I was too polite to ask.

—GORE VIDAL

I was unquestionably a child of naivety, bright enough in the ways of
make-believe and raw invention but sorely lacking in what constituted reality. The reality in question being not a scholastic view of the
world but the subversive kaleidoscope that churned away beneath the
veneer of polite society no more than a 120 miles from my back door.

This thornier bramble bush of life that I was yet to engage careened
through all manner of subterranean labyrinths in the early 1960s. Rock
and roll and drugs were in the basement, but the kingdom of the queens
congregated in the basement below the basement.

Homosexuality didn't have any refined or contemporary moniker
in the badlands of Lincolnshire. "Poof" I guess was the best we could
muster. As for "queer," it hadn't transitioned and was still reserved for a
peculiar aunt or how you felt after too much cough medicine.

Quixotic youth? Quite possibly. Immature provincial paisano? Most
definitely. In packs, youth can be callous, and impressions back then in
our parochial bubble were easily swayed. I was certainly convinced for
a time that different was not to be trusted, and for someone who was
to blossom into the quintessential loner, the tardy nature of labeling at
a prepubescent age was an ironic fit.

Deprived of a village idiot on whom to bestow our infantile scorn,
it was the seedy oddity who cycled back and forth in front of the

schoolyard and lived in the toolshed behind the local butcher for whom we amassed our stockpile of lies.

I don't recall his real name, but we called him Jasper. And for that I apologize, for while we thought it had a certain predatory ring to it we were sorely ignorant to the countless celebrated chaps currently christened likewise. Our Jasper however didn't disappoint, in his grubby overcoat and overly brilliantined hair, he was in our estimation a poster child for deviant behavior and most certainly a trouser invader of the worst kind. And so it was that the quadrangle echoed with the collective cry of "Jasper is a homo!"

Homo it was for homo was all we had, just an abbreviation, half of a complete word that would only have confused us more than we already were. Homo sounded dirty, and dirty was all we wanted. Homo had an infantile cadence of nursery rhyme simplicity, two syllables creating a conspiratorial war cry.

In all honesty, looking back he was a tad creepy, but guilt by bicycle clips alone was hardly a smoking gun. I can only imagine that he was nothing more than a fringe character alone in the world and seemingly happy with his lot. However, to an impressionable eight-year-old peering from a safe distance into his overheated outhouse, it's not hard to understand why we earmarked him for what he most likely wasn't. In a kerosene glow, he'd sit warming cans of soup on a small green Primus, an ever present dog-end teetering on the edge of his lip. We'd listen as, like some provincial Ben Gunn, he'd question the air in a wheezing dialect, then cackle quietly in response to his own mumbled soliloquies.

This recollection I suppose is an attempt to explain how my very first encounter with anything pertaining to homosexuality, real or imagined, was dealt with on the very basest of levels. We didn't view it as an alternate lifestyle or counterculture, it was simply just another puerile distraction. The age of enlightenment and my lifelong affiliation with kindred spirits of a different persuasion was still almost a decade away.

I don't know if it was my mother's bohemian roots that eventually inoculated me with a sense of open-mindedness, but considering she had been marinated in Weimar culture, basted in the decadent hangover of post-czarist Russia, and slow roasted in the underground rumblings of Swiss neutrality, it was hardly surprising. Too genteel for complete Sturm und Drang, let's just say she was Maria von Trapp with an edge. In a nutshell, she didn't give a rat's ass if you were homo, schmo-mo, lesbo, or anyway the wind blows, and though I failed to comprehend it at the time, it's easy to imagine how her impartial outlook aided and abetted me in the years to come.

When I did make it to London and hooked up with my song-writing soul mate, he was a jobbing musician in the employ of Long John Baldry, a six-foot-seven ex-blues belter currently enjoying chart success as a MOR crooner. Baldry was also unrepentantly gay, not in a flamboyant sense so much as possessing a raspy clandestine bawdiness full of innuendo.

Baldry was the first real gay man I'd ever encountered, and while I was initially intimidated, I was also intrigued. I didn't have a lot to say back in those days as I was still reeling from culture shock. People in London acted and spoke differently, and while my parents' backgrounds afforded me immunity from any sort of dialect that might make me the target of ridicule, I preferred to remain an alien sponge.

It was, to paraphrase the current vernacular, all down to "getting my head around it." I had the capacity to absorb the revolutionary energy at hand, but London was a city of layers with a myriad of avenues, each one beckoning me to experience something new.

NATURALLY, WITH BALDRY'S immense personality directing traffic, one of those avenues became abundantly clear. An evening out in his company might begin with a couple of pints at La Chasse, Jack Barrie's tiny drinking club above the sweaty throb of the Marquee on Wardour Street, but it was sure to end descending countless stairs into one of Soho's surreptitious gay enclaves.

One has to bear in mind that this was at a time when homosexuality had only recently been decriminalized and that the word *gay* was not altogether prominent in referring to "the love that dare not speak its name." Gay caballeros and divorcees still meant something altogether different.

By the same token, there was no radicalization, no organized or unified front. In these dimly lit gin joints, the call to arms was yet to come and the serious nature of individual preference and pride in it was currently under wraps. Fear of being outed was prominent, and for the most part queer culture at that point was still campy at an almost music hall level. In these subterranean haunts over-rouged middle-aged men vied for the attention of seasoned street hustlers while conversing in stereotypical gay slang. The lisping sibilance would fairly ricochet off the walls as "Get her," "Bona drag dear," and "What a naff palone" became the first foreign language I was able to understand.

It's interesting to note that for all its hidden subculture, girly men were a huge hit with the British public. Camp, it appeared, was full of whimsy and gut busting guffaws, providing the sex bit wasn't included. On the radio of the day, the weekend funfest that was *Round the Horne* featured the ultra-thinly veiled gay escapades of Julian and Sandy, two radically swish theatrical types.

IRONY ASIDE, THERE was ultimately something sad and harrowing about all this. For individuals to exist in the shadows, embracing a covert language and existing in sort of a threadbare Victorian nether-world seemed humiliating.

Witnessing this firsthand at a young age, I can't say I was quite so cerebral in my overview of this lifestyle. Sure, I was getting thrown in at the deep end fairly early on, but for as much as I can recall, I might as well have been invisible. Baldry, I imagine, assumed I was fine with it, and he never once made reference to the fact that this was the kind of place that might unnerve a slightly naive teenage transplant. In fact, I imagine he may have pegged me for trade-in-training, an apprentice in the care of my melodic mate. In these situations, Elton most certainly served his virginal wordsmith well. My friend was obviously struggling with his own identity at the time and, while possibly enamored with my innocent allure, was quick to pick up on the fact that I was straighter than a honeymoon dick. For my own part with Reg, I was happy to allow our budding friendship to be interpreted by any interested parties as "hands off; he's mine."

There were times however when my beard was not present to run interference, and my educational agenda was left to fend for itself. In the chilly winter months or on a warm summer evening, I would sometimes find myself cruised or on occasion propositioned on the quiet streets of some of London's swankier areas. This was more often than not done by well-dressed businessmen in big shiny cars looking for some quick relief before motoring home to the wife and kids. It really didn't faze me too much, as by then I was pretty much city savvy to the unwarranted attention of closeted stockbrokers who, let's face it, had far more to lose than me. My intimidation level had flatlined so that in circumstances like this all it took to be rid of any solicitation was a couple of fingers perspicuously presented. As the '60s were careening and skidding to their conclusion, so was my relationship with the past. I was growing up and growing up fast, and along with that came a sense of fearlessness and resolve that exhibited itself in different ways. Simply put, from the get-go I never had any traumatic gay incidents that gave me cause to be cagey or cautious. From here on out, the whole thing became second nature and pretty much a peripheral part of my life. Over the years, my interaction and association with all things gay, including my closest friends and countless contemporaries, has been as much a part of my world as getting up and going to bed.

Ralphie and the Dalí

"Curiouser and Curiouser!" cried Alice.

—LEWIS CARROLL
Alice's Adventures in Wonderland

Let me tell you about Ralphie. For about four years in the mid-'70s, he drove me everywhere in New York. Ralphie wasn't one of those slick silver-tongued limo drivers, the ones with the leather driving gloves and a black wool overcoat—the guys who felt that dropping names was a passport to impressing the clients. Even if you cared that they drove Barbra Streisand to the Met, or hung out backstage at the Apollo with Rick James, the very nature of their audacity seemed more suited to an impressionable wealthy tourist rather than a contemplative rock star. Apparently though, it worked for some, and many of my contemporaries embraced and dug that kind of solicitous familiarity.

Ralphie was a little old guy in a rumpled suit from Jersey with liver spots and the pallor of jaundiced parchment. He was also the salt of the earth, stoic, and nondiscriminatory. If you were driving parallel to him in the left lane and looked over, you'd see no more than a forehead above which a few sparse rows of brilliantined hair were plastered back across his scalp. Short? Yes he was, but this was only accentuated by his tendency to lay back in his seat like an astronaut in a capsule. He was a great driver though, had the patience of Job, a parental disposition to yours truly, and loved the Yankees.

A typical night. We were parked outside Patsy's restaurant on West Fifty-Sixth listening to a ball game. Not just any ball game but the final game of the World Series, October 18, 1977. This particular game had us at odds due to the fact that it was the LA Dodgers going head-to-head with the Yankees. I was a rabid Dodgers fan, baseball being a passion, and this current team, in particular, was golden. It was Tommy Lasorda's first full season as manager, and things had started well for the Big Blue when Steve Garvey put the Dodgers on the board with a two-run triple down the right field line off Mike Torrez, scoring Reggie Smith and Ron Cey. I missed the Yankees tying it up in the second, as I had to run back in the restaurant and placate my date. By the time I made it back out, we'd pulled ahead in the third with a home run by Reggie Smith. With the game going into the fourth and the Dodgers up 3–2, it was time to consign myself to a charm offensive back inside. By the time I returned to the limo, neither myself nor my team were faring well. The Yankees were up 7–3 at the top of the eighth, and I'd pretty much struck out inside. Resigned to the fact that my dinner guest was done appeasing me, I remained sacked out in the back seat as Reggie Jackson became Mr. October and I became LA's other big loser.

Final score: 8–4 Yankees. At least Ralphie was happy.

The elevation from our first tentative steps into New York had progressed at a brisk pace, and very soon our touring party had graduated from Loews Midtown to the City Squire at Seventh and Fifty-First to the Warwick on West Fifty-Fourth. It was at the Warwick where in a fit of rock star chutzpah I had hurled a room service tray out a hallway window. Playing the stupidity card, I'd become irritated by my constant requests for its removal going unheeded. Of course, the vat of Bordeaux knocked back at lunch had nothing to do with it, and the launched projectile had landed in the awning over the front entrance where it remained for several days before detection.

Moving on, I'd tried both The Sherry Netherlands and The Pierre at Fifth and Sixty-First, respectively. I liked them, but it was the Drake on Fifty-Sixth in Midtown that got me from the outset and where you could find Ralphie staked out for the duration of my stays in New York. The staff were a delight, and the manager, Raymond, was a jolly and hospitable soul who seemed genuinely happy whenever I checked in. Oh yeah! It also had a stellar little bar off the lobby that played into my criteria for lodgings of the first order. A great hotel, I still believe, is made only better by two things: a great bar and a good bed. I always imagined that the discoveries in one could benefit the comfort of the other. Of course, this crass way of thinking is possibly idle reflection and wishful thinking from a time I was somewhat of a different animal. If I could jettison a room service tray from a fourth floor window, there is no unearthly reason why I couldn't lust with the same disproportionate antediluvian ethic.

While Ralphie was happy chauffeuring me around the city, he made no bones about retirement. He was no spring chicken after all, and like everyone he had a dream. His was to open a pizza joint in Asbury Park, basic and unfussy, just good pie in a traditional family setting. In truth, I think Ralphie just wanted a place where he could hang with his *paisano* and watch the world go by. Knowing how he viewed things, I could imagine it in my mind's eye. Ultimately, a simple man desires simple things. His, I'll bet you a buck on a blue-assed fly, were Neapolitan colors, checked tablecloths, and candles in Chianti bottles. A string of Christmas lights would be over the bar, a pile of biscotti tins behind it, and Dean, most definitely Dean, softly crooning on the speakers. Ralphie's Pizza.

In the entire time he drove me, nothing seemed to faze him. He operated on a completely even keel. In a city built on the premise that to drive there you must adopt a code of "if there's an opening, take it," that lane appropriation (if there was one) was the territory of the aggressor, and to the loudest voice go the spoils, he was an anomaly. He drove in his own universe, in a hermetically sealed bubble mute to the madness, a code of navigational omertà binding him to a tempered resolve. Ralphie owned the city; the city did not own him.

Let me give you an example of what a class act Ralphie was. Sometime around the fall of 1977, as a favor to a friend, I helped out an aspiring ingenue. She wasn't without talent and appeared at the outset to be a convivial, but driven, young artist desperate to succeed. I took the time out to sift through material with her, produce a series of sessions, and arrange an elaborate showcase. Throughout the project, she maintained a manner of respectfulness, yet it was etched with what to me seemed like a thinly veiled presumptive air. I took it all in stride, and while somewhat captivated by her ballsiness and obvious street smarts, there was on my part an uneasiness that viewed the project with an underlying air of trepidatious caution. My instincts proved to be correct when at the conclusion of our endeavors we all attended a dinner hosted by her two very respectable and personable financial backers. Unleashing her inner beast and flaunting her true colors, she went from a mettlesome but grateful fledgling into an egocentric termagant. With unbridled venom, she tore into her benefactors like Madonna without a fresh toilet seat in her dressing room. To her obviously uneducated palate, their choice of cuisine and restaurant were not to her liking, not lavish enough, and without accommodation for her questionable hangers-on. It was an ugly, ungraceful, and completely unacceptable display. The concept of divadom appeared to have inhabited her before she had earned the right to act like a hellacious asshole. This outburst sealed her fate with me and, after making my feelings known in no uncertain terms, left her scrambling to make amends in the wake of my departure.

After this debacle, I needed air and decided to walk. As a last act of charity, but more likely as a prompt way of eradicating her from my sight, I told her to have Ralphie drive her home, and off I went. I should have known better! When I turned the corner, she piled her cronies into the back of the car and kept Ralphie out until 6 a.m. the following morning. Unaware of the brouhaha that had transpired inside, Ralphie just assumed she had my authority to commandeer him and acquiesced to her demands. This hijacking left me apoplectic and on the verge of first degree murder, a crime from which any sane jury would fully exonerate me given the circumstances. I couldn't imagine what Ralphie had had to endure, but with his usual shrug of the shoulders he took it in stride, even refusing to put the charges on my account and taking the heat for what he deemed his mistake. Karma's a bitch as they say, and her career went nowhere.

Now let me tell you about Dalí. Salvador that is, or The Dalí, as he referred to himself. First though, it might help to elaborate on the nature of coincidence and how in New York during this time period there existed a tendency toward a bizarre form of cultural cross-pollination. The allure of the night and the abundance of hotspots, both stylish and modish, countered with funky dives, derelict rock clubs, and sexually ambiguous bars, all exuded a similar magnetic appeal to an in-crowd of hipsters and fashionistas. Uptown elitism and regal slumming was grist for the mill. It's how the whole thing operated. Go high, go low, West Side, East Side, any way the wind blows. The same faces appeared at the same doors. Whether they were policed by velvet rope and clipboard pretension, or a six-foot Samoan drag queen, the same crowd made it into the same places. The usual suspects recalibrate with the times, but the tribes back then blended in closer proximity of each other than in our current climate. Couturier revelers and rock star posses shared equal ground with actors, artists, authors, and politicians. Each and every one were sucked up into the vortex of a unified tornado. Like anointed lemmings, we tumbled happily from one precipice to another if it was the place to be. At some point it was inevitable that polar opposites would collide. There was always the off chance of an invitation, a nocturnal predisposition to hop into an alien vessel and row yourself to a stranger shore.

I have a vague idea as to how I ended up sitting in the King Cole Bar of the St. Regis on East Fifty-Fifth alongside a slightly familiar group of overly precious lovelies and delicate scenesters, but in the off chance of mistaken identity, I'll refrain from assigning any responsibility. The conduit to this glamorous occasion aside, it was all terribly arty, the cooing and sibilance resonating like an aviary of exotic birds.

The motivation for this coterie of fabulousness was an audience with the surrealist legend, Salvador Dalí. Was I impressed? Intrigued, more likely. By this time, we were all a little blasé, having already hooked up with our fair share of notable luminaries and ignominious rouges. Mind you, though, considering this big fish apparently inhabited a little bit of all the aforementioned traits, it wasn't without a degree of curiosity that I found myself sitting there.

There was a sudden disturbance in the hall outside, and the fluttering at the table reached fever pitch. Standing center stage in the entrance and dressed impeccably in a man's tuxedo was Gala, Dalí's wife, or to be emphatically correct Gala, Marchioness of Dalí de Púbol. Taking in the room with a steely eye and haughty perusal, she beckoned to her rear, eliciting the appearance of about half a dozen aesthetically beautiful young men. Even with her acknowledged appetite for this sort of thing, this outré antic was only the beginning of what would turn out to be an evening totally in keeping with the adjective describing her husband's artistic style.

This phalanx of hunks was dressed in immaculate white suits. They looked like members of some sartorial messianic cult, the kind that might knock on your door with a patronizing smile and a book to change your life. They didn't sit but fanned out along the wall, standing to attention and ignoring the uneasy shifting of chairs as nervous bar patrons edged away from their ivory sterility. "The Dalí is here," Gala announced, and so he was. He appeared beside her and they entered the room together causing a kerfuffle among the adoring throng. They parted like the Red Sea to accommodate the grand couple, and much air kissing was proffered tentatively as we settled into a percipient huddle. Perfunctory introductions were made but quite honestly I didn't think Dalí cared who was there as long as they looked the part and understood that he was the center of attention.

I immediately read him. He was a narcissist of course. He had to be, as no one could live life in this framework and not be. That said, he was an interesting cat. Not in the bebop hipster sense, but in that it was patently obvious the wily old Catalonian had a feline sensibility. An alley cat for sure, smart and alert, his eyes darted left and right reading his peripheral, the accentuation of his waxed whiskers extenuating my appraisal. Like a pantomime villain he twirled them dramatically with his fingers, leaving no room for doubt he was Macavity all the way, a force of feline malevolence.

He was dressed as you might imagine. Not like you or I, but in the guise of a conjurer, theatrically flamboyant enough to bring attention to himself, but not risible in that someone might take him for unhinged. He wore a voluminous cape and purple satin pants with velvet brocaded slippers. His hair was long, a mixture of gray and black, pomaded and straggly, and it hung limply and curled up around his collar.

Having already ordered our drinks, he grazed the table with his eyes as if to ascertain the cocktail with the imbiber. He requested a cup of hot water. Not unusual; he probably brought his own preferred brand. I'm correct. He removed a singular tea bag from inside his cape and dropped it with a flourish into his cup. Pivoting his head slowly he took in the table. Were we paying attention? I wondered if this action was a trick, a way to be sure all eyes were upon him? With his tea bag steeping sufficiently, he removed it delicately with a spoon between his thumb and forefinger. Dipping once more into his cape he extracted a plastic honey bear dispenser and began to pour it effectually into his cup, moving it up and down, shortening and elongating the stream with a hypnotic flourish. With his free hand he reached back into his cape and procured an enormous pair of scissors with which he severed the stream of honey. OK, it was weird! Weird, but cool. There was an audible gasp as he concluded with a sort of ta-da motion, returning both articles to the nether regions of his cloak like a cross draw gunfighter.

It was pure theater, of course, and if you think about it, it's exactly what you might expect from someone conceived by Dadaism. With a propensity for exhibitionism and artwork steeped in subconscious imagery, think *The Persistence of Memory*, we're lucky he didn't melt our watches with a blowtorch. In the end, though, where he probably saw it as performance art, it was ultimately just a party trick. A few years later, my pal Alice Cooper told me that when he hooked up with Dalí back in 1972, he pulled the exact same stunt in the very same location. What does that tell you? It may have been a consistently effective ruse, and while he may get an A for originality, the overall grade is reduced for repetition.

Anyway, that wasn't the end of it. Then we went to dinner!

I jumped in with Ralphie and we headed where instructed. Ralphie had never heard of Salvador Dalí, but seemed amused by the sight of the anomalous artist bustling into the appointed restaurant with Gala and the homogeneous stud club in tow.

The restaurant was a nice place, opulent but not sterile. The clientele, a mixture of well-heeled Manhattanites and bohemian chic, appeared unfazed by Dalí's entrance. If he was a regular, like his party piece, they were probably used to it by now. The staff were sufficiently fawning, much to the old boy's liking, the level of their toadying registering high on the sycophantic Richter scale.

Gala sat at a separate table surrounded by her Mormonesque glee club. They appeared to have lightened up, and I swear I saw lips moving and the flicker of a smile. The Dalí was cool with all this. Being a practitioner of candaulism, their marriage was one of certain arrangements. It was all weirdly esoteric, but in complete compliance to the batshit craziness that engulfed them. They lived separately in adjoining homes. In order to visit her, he had to make a formal request in writing. To his credit he was devoted to her and loved her unconditionally. Even that night, he gazed over at her surreptitiously at one point, announcing to no one in particular, "*Agh, mi musa.*"

Things were loosening up a bit with my companions, who, through the warm afterglow of several glasses of Chianti, lost much of their avant-garde prissiness in favor of a combined louche free fall.

Food was ordered, food was consumed, many bottles came and went. Things were getting pretty woozy all around, and at one point I found myself sitting next to the main man. He was drinking something with brandy in it called a Casanova. It looked syrupy and sweet, the color of diluted blood; I was thankful he didn't order them for the table, which he was apparently in the habit of doing. In due course, he turned to me and in serviceable English inquired,

"You are a poet, yes?"

"Er, no," I answered. I loathe being referred to as a poet. I didn't think he was listening.

"You are like Paul Éluard?"

"Er, no," I responded emphatically, Éluard being the preeminent poet of the surrealist movement and former husband of Gala. He also wrote "*Liberté, j'écris ton nom*" ("Liberty, I Write Your Name"), considered the greatest poem in the French language. So, no, I don't think so.

It's at this point that I noticed he was doodling on a large table napkin. No, not doodling, he was methodically *creating* while conversing with me or anyone in earshot. The conversation part was frustrating as he had an infuriating habit of starting off in English and concluding in Spanish so that the punch line, if there was one, was lost on me. The drawing, though, was spectacular, totally organic, created with whatever was at hand, lipstick, a burnt cork, some cigarette ash and wine. Not a pen or pencil in sight, it was wild, freehand stuff that he was scratching, staining, and rubbing while barely looking down to see what he was doing. I was impressed—it was really good. I know that's dumb, it was Salvador Dalí after all, but I'm sitting next to him and just watching those hands make up for all the hocus-pocus earlier on. The napkin was full of individual fragments and images, unrecognizable constructions and vaguely discernible forms. It was pure Dalí: dramatic, impressionable, and full of humor and light. I was drinking it in when he pushed away from the table. "The Dalí must leave," he pronounced.

Managers and servers rushed over, and the white tribe hovered. Gala circled the table fanning the air in a gesture of farewell as the guests genuflected, and I, too, volunteered gratitude. I eyeballed my dinner companions suspiciously while alternately zeroing in on the napkin. I imagined he was going to fold it up and commit it to his cloak along with the scissors and honey. Nope, as he rose from the table he indeed folded it, but instead of sequestering it away he tossed it into my lap.

"For you, poet," he said and walked away.

I'm not sure what I did that warranted this, but I was ecstatic. Funnily enough, no one in our party appeared to have copped onto our interaction or even witnessed this creation. They suggested moving on to some currently groovy watering hole. I demurred. I wanted to get that puppy home and away from any potential thievery.

I returned to my hotel, laid my prize on the bed, and fell asleep. The next morning I woke to see it there, not a dream, but a solid reality, still tethered together by surrealistic genius, still fabulous. Sighing with contentment, I patted it gently, took a shower, and headed out for breakfast and a good long walk. Returning several hours later it was still there, still at the end of the bed, only now it was neatly folded and freshly laundered. There was absolutely nothing on the napkin!

ONE MORNING NOT long after this, I walked out of the hotel and Ralphie wasn't there. In his place was a hip-looking Black guy in a camel hair coat and driving gloves. I asked where Ralphie was and he didn't know. He also didn't know who Ralphie was, and when I called the company they played dumb. You could almost comprehend the shrugging of shoulders at the end of the line. They were vague and elusive, and information, if they possessed it, was not forthcoming. It was as if Ralphie never existed.

My frustration was palpable. Did he die? Had he retired on a whim? As much I didn't want to admit it, I was ashamed and embarrassed that my knowledge of all things Ralphie was limited. Aside from superficial chitchat, I knew so little about him. I didn't know his surname or the names of his wife and children. Hell, I didn't even know if he had a wife and children. I couldn't call him, I didn't have his number. He lived in Jersey; that's it, that was the extent of my familiarity with his life. He turned up on time and went home when I was done. We just shot the daily breeze, my own selfish pursuits and idle banter keeping things at surface level. I relied on him completely, assuming dependability without throwing a hook in the water to catch something deeper.

I knew all about Dalí because I took the time to learn and was drawn to his art. I know the parallels are questionable and arguments can be made that it's not exactly rational thinking, but in my humble opinion there's a code of common decency that implies that any life that makes an impression is worth investigating.

Dalí was a legend, perhaps more so in his own mind than in that of the general aesthetician. He inhabited an alternate universe, a spoiled man-child catered to and sequestered from the real world by acolytes and sycophants. He was a shameless self-promoter, an artistic carney, but simultaneously a brilliant draftsman and unique artist with a fantastical and grandiose mind. Ralphie was just another working stiff, seemingly happy with his lot—a decent man anonymous among the hubbub and rushing masses of pedestrian flotsam and grinding traffic. Some people pass away and at length no one knows they ever lived. Dalí is revered still, but he was all rhinestones. Ralphie was a diamond.

The Bajan Chronicles

But on the tenth we set foot on the land of the Lotus-eaters.

—HOMER

The Odyssey

I think if you're British-born and of a certain vintage, chances are there will come a time when you will dress as a woman. It's in the blood; it's in the deliriously trippy tradition of pantomime, Monty Python, and the drag attired advertising of the Rolling Stones promoting their 1966 single "Have You Seen Your Mother, Baby, Standing in the Shadow."

I've done it only once (I think), but somewhere a snapshot exists of me in a fully starched maid's outfit complete with a lacy headband and a five-o'clock shadow. I recall looking fatigued in the photo, if not a little piqued. But don't get me wrong, I was in on the joke and OK with the charade, just worn out at the end of a long but not terribly successful idea.

But let me backtrack.

It was December 1975, and Elton and I decided to fly south for the Christmas season. Our tropical destination was to be the balmy dreamscape of Barbados, that lyrical island nestled in the southeastern Caribbean Sea.

It was most likely my idea to settle on this locale having first visited three years earlier whence it solidified and designated a magnetic appeal to my sense of wanderlust. I was to spend much of the remaining decade making this island my home away from home while charting an uneven trajectory but drawing much from the genteel hospitality of both its populace and geography.

With little knowledge at the time of this cozy dominion's status in the history of England's Raj complex (the Queen being a sort of facto-tum ruler), we rented adjacent houses next to the Sandy Lane Hotel, a swank resort in Saint James and a habitat favored by old money and celebrities, both mothballed and brightly shining.

We dragged along with us friends and associates who were duly dis-tributed between the two homes, most of whom were excellent enter-tainment value. Some, however, were of declining emotional worth, their shelf life having expired and their obstruction soon to be purged leaving me a fresh playing field on which to embark anew.

The staff, overseen by a magnificent gentleman by the name of Joseph, were pure gold. Charming and hospitable, they made our stay exquisite with their soulful and accommodating island charm.

Which brings me to the nature of the aforementioned drag act. Because we were so enamored with our staff's desire to make us as com-fortable as possible, some bright spark suggested we return the favor and make them the beneficiary of our waiting on them. We invited them to bring their families and we planned to prepare and serve them dinner. What we failed to communicate was that this dinner would be served by grown men (I use this term lightly) in all manner of female garb.

They duly arrived dressed to the nines, but obviously somewhat uncomfortable to be on the reverse end of what they felt was their duty and calling. Our cooking was mediocre and remains best forgotten, but the barely restrained bewilderment on their faces does not, the sight of their charges looking like a bunch of Nordic barmaids remaining indel-ible. These were family folk, and while they no doubt were nonjudg-mental they just didn't get it, which is why I was left leaning against the stove nonplussed, brandy in hand, and wondering if my skirt was too short.

With staffing duties reset and a sense of order back in place, our seasonal vacation unfolded at a leisurely and relatively tranquil pace. For Christmas dinner Joseph cooked a turkey the size of a small house,

Elton played disco hits loud enough to wake the dead on Martinique, and I learned to water ski. I've always been a sports nut, just not very good at playing them. So when I realized that I was not only somehow built for this invigorating aquatic pastime but also really good at it, it became my obsession. Before I knew it, I'd graduated from two skis to a single ski, and slaloming like a pro. Eventually, I could dock start and beach land, both pure show-off tactics guaranteed to impress the equally impressive sand candy.

My instructor, and the man who got me up out of the water and into the big leagues, was Jiggs, a fearsome-looking local with a physique like Sonny Liston and a technique so adept that he skied on the balls of his feet. If Jiggs was gruff and reserved, then Ronald, his boatman, was the polar opposite. A live wire of wicked charm with personality to burn, he was gregarious, devastatingly handsome, and the possessor of the whitest set of teeth I'd ever seen.

In the interim between water sports and decibel-defining disco, Elton and I allotted ourselves the task of making the acquaintance of two of Barbados's most notable residents. The tropics have always had a calling for the patently British, the lure of its temperate climates agreeing with and inspiring all manner of artistic and literary greats. The coast of Jamaica notably drew Ian Fleming, the creator of James Bond, to his estate, known as Goldeneye; while Noël Coward, that quintessential of all Englishmen, languished in the midday sun of Firefly, his own Caribbean refuge. Respectively, these residences drew legendary houseguests, whose memoirs and diaries record the cornucopia of pleasures afforded by these celebrated homes.

In Barbados, we had Verna Hull, a fantastic old lesbian who lived next door to her ex-lover (rumored but never proved), the acclaimed actress Claudette Colbert. A falling out between the two best of friends had driven Colbert to build a Berlin Wall of sorts between the two homes, further sealing the legendary Hollywood icon away from her former companion. Hull, on the other hand, aside from being a talented artist, photographer, and Sears Roebuck heiress, was a constant and indomitable presence. Hefty and vivacious, she was a fireball of goodwill. Kaftan-attired, rum in hand, she entertained and was in turn an essential fixture at all manner of dinner parties and festivities the island over. Some of this may have had to do with her royal connections—Princess Margaret and Antony Armstrong-Jones being her token ticket "in" via convivial nepotism. Be that as it may, she turned up at the drop of a hat, twirling around our living rooms as music played and her whoops of joy ricocheted off the walls.

The other was Oliver Messel, an expat who as a young man went from being a celebrated portrait painter to acclaimed recognition as one of the finest set and stage designers of all time. The complete Renaissance man, he did it all. His costuming talents are ubiquitous in countless classic films from the 1930s and '40s, while in the most off-the-wall of all wartime gigs he became a camouflage officer in charge of disguising gun fortifications along the south coast of Britain. With true theatrical flair he dressed them in all manner of quirky Englishness, including haystacks, cafés, and castle ruins.

By the time we caught up with Oliver, he was in his early seventies and recently retired from designing what seemed like half of the homes in the northern and western hemisphere. He was, although frail and small, the possessor of a sparkling personality and was genuinely appreciative of the goodwill afforded him by those he might imagine to be totally unaware of his extraordinary artistic achievements. Motley group that we were, we had had the luxury of being raised in an era where, although we may have been on the cusp of cultural change, we still basked in the glow of an era that gave rise to such unparalleled talent and cultivated thinking. This is to say, we knew who they were and were duly impressed.

So it was that we celebrated Oliver's seventy-fourth birthday in the rotunda of Elton's rental. A cobbled affair thrown together in haste, the fete was hamstrung by the island's lack of what we imagined a man of his standing would be accustomed to in the way of gifts. It was decided that in the absence of a Van Cleef & Arpels, the local drug store and tourist emporium would be our best bet. Figuring if we couldn't go grand we'd go kitsch, our plan was a decision that he fortunately found righteously amusing. With great vigor and accompanied by our egging him on, he tore into a colorful mountain of tissue-wrapped junk. Pez dispensers, snow globes, paper parasols, and refrigerator magnets piled up before him, each offering being thoroughly scrutinized by his bright and childlike eyes. It was a win-win for us due to the pure delight on his face and his profuse enthusiasm providing a benediction by way of our humble altruism. This tiny man who had brought joy and exquisite taste to the world through the sheer alchemy of his visionary innovation was momentarily a child again. Oliver passed away four years later, while Verna Hull continued to twirl and whoop until dying in California in 2002 at the grand old age of eighty-six.

FOR THE REMAINDER of the '70s, when gray days descended on LA, I would hop aboard that silver tube, returning again and again to this tropical Oz, always renting homes in the Saint James area, always with some accomplice or on occasion amorous companion in tow. My mornings would be spent skiing and writing, if a project were in the works, whereas the rest of the day and late into the night my propensity for the local rum shacks and establishments of entertainment meshed immaculately with my current hedonistic temperament. Freedom was of great value to me at the time, and while on paper this attitude had earned the right to exist, it also came with a price. I wouldn't call it selfish necessarily, but there was definitely a gremlin strapping blinders on and fogging my sensory perception. Poor judgment might be the simplest way of putting it, but any way you looked at it, it could only end badly.

You would think that the tropics with its balmy winds, warm nights, and leisurely pace would be the perfect blend of intoxicants to make romance a natural accoutrement to everything else the island had to offer. The twinkling stars and the unbridled perfume of a wellspring of multicolored foliage and flowers could only be correlated with l'amour of the most passionate kind.

Not really. I lived and lusted on the island and loved absolutely no one. It was all tropical hypnotism in a limited expanse of geography that threw up the beautiful and the damned simultaneously.

When I said earlier that I wouldn't call it selfish, I believe I was referring to my occasionally unhinged nocturnal escapades rather than any coupling that transpired over the years, because in this area I was indeed unequivocally selfish. It certainly wasn't confusing romance with convenience because, believe me, love was nowhere in the equation. On the island it was always on my terms.

Linda Field was the first white Miss Barbados in 1974. White Bajans were rare on the island in those days, and in my opinion the possessors of an interesting accent, not dissimilar to that of white South Africans today. Linda, as you might imagine, was a looker, curvy and built in a way similar to many beauty contestants of that era. She was, however, relatively volatile and certainly made no effort to appear to be a convincing competitor in the "question and answer" portion of the pageant game, if you get my drift.

Our meeting was inconsequential, but in the aftermath of it, I was not convinced it was the best decision on my part. While there were obvious benefits, her habit of running up and down the shoreline screaming "Skiiiiii Meeeeee!!!!" while I was out on the water should have tipped me off. Sounding like Joss Ackland's smarmy South African envoy braying "Diplomatic immunity," in *Lethal Weapon 2*, she cut a bizarre and unsettling presence on the beach. In the boat, Jiggs would roll his eyes, Ronald would smile that smile, and we would simply ski beyond the sound of her voice.

If you're wondering, it didn't last long. I had borrowed her rather splendid jeep and failed to turn up for a date. I imagine the afternoon's intake of rum, pool, and chicken wings had wiped my memory slate clean, leaving me unaware of my negligence and up to my ears in too much fun. That feeling came to an abrupt end the moment I returned home and heard my phone ringing off the hook. Needless to say at the other end of the line was an inconsolable berserker, hellhound nuts and not someone you'd want to be within a mile of at that moment. Bawling for the return of her jeep along with a series of not-to-be-divulged consequences for yours truly, I, erring on the side of caution, thought it best to let her stew for a couple of hours before returning her vehicle.

The next morning as the sun broke the horizon, I threw back a few morning vodkas, and clambered into her jeep. Smarting from the tongue lashing of the previous night, my confrontational armor began to fall into place and Mr. Hyde returned to the wheel. With a head full of steam and a serious buzz going, I tore through the dawn, my petulance accelerating along with Linda's misappropriated automobile.

I arrived in her driveway to find her large front doors wide open and her expansive entryway beckoning. Without thinking twice, I gunned it and with great dexterity drove up the front steps and into the house, parking the jeep conveniently in her front room. And that, as you can imagine, was that.

I FIRST MET Oliver Reed at The Bagatelle, a former sugar plantation house reformed into the island's most glamorous restaurant. Unlike Oliver Messel, this other Oliver was cut from a distinctly different cloth than that of his gentle namesake. A renowned hellion and first rate actor, he roared into the 1960s as part of the unholy quartet of Richard Harris, Peter O'Toole, and Richard Burton. After cutting a swathe through swinging London and expunging all rules of civilized etiquette, they picked up and blew like the four winds to spread havoc worldwide.

The Bagatelle was owned and operated by a splendid Englishman called Nick Hudson. Nick, also a product of London's golden era, was the complete bon viveur. An accomplished sailor and pilot with a background in entrepreneurial expertise, he excelled as a restaurateur, having laid his Midas touch on Nick's Diner, the legendary London eatery. With a passion for fine wine, polo, and beautiful women, he was for me (minus the polo) the perfect man to know in Barbados.

This turned out to be a wise choice as Nick was a certified conduit into the regulatory balance of what made the island tick. From the far-flung fringe eateries and inland bars where flying fish and chicken were the staple dishes, to the hip hangouts and nighteries that drew those hesitant to frequent the latter, Nick knew them all. He was also a magnet for celebrity and that is how Oliver Reed ended up plonking himself down at my table one night early on in one of my initial visits to The Bagatelle.

Seating himself without invitation and only going by Nick's whispered aside as to who I was, Oliver took me for a likely chap and fair game for a good time. As with all things involving him, alcohol was of primary importance and the common language with which business was conducted. "What are we drinking?" he roared good-naturedly, and with that my entire fate with this incorrigible rouge was sealed. Bear in mind, Mr. Reed was an imposing fellow, lacking in forbearance and built like a brick wall. Succinctly, he was not one to be trifled with. Steering the choices as far as I possibly could away from gin (a drink I've had an absolute loathing for since the age of fourteen, when I drank so much of it that I woke up in a friend's house wearing a polo neck dickey and nothing else), it was decided that the island's fine white rum seemed appropriate.

For half an hour or so, we imbibed while our interloper in a voice dialed to "pay attention to what I'm saying" regaled us with anecdotes, opinions, and lurid tales of debauchery. I'll admit he was seriously good value for money, although I'm unsure as to how our fellow diners took to this entertaining foghorn monopolizing the evening air.

Suddenly, his narrative trailed off, his attention span seemingly excommunicated. Draining his glass he took stock of us, smiled devilishly, and said, "Well, I'll be off then," and promptly leaped over the wall to the left of the table, which to the best of my knowledge was about twenty feet from the ground. Obviously, this couldn't have been possible, but there was serious height involved that would lead one to believe that he was either totally deranged or uncharacteristically agile.

The next morning I was out on the water, skiing, when I spotted a lone Oliver walking slowly along the beach. Docking myself in the vicinity of his promenade, I hailed him with a wave and approached to find him in a seemingly meditative trance. As cheerily as possible I floated another greeting, which this time elicited a sloth-like turn of his head. Seemingly awakening from a deep slumber, he caught me in his periphery and in a voice no more than a whisper bid me, "Good day." This was an altogether alternate Oliver, quite far removed from the bacchanalian fireball of the previous evening, so much so that he was almost genteel and monastic in his countenance. He was so soft-spoken and mannerly in his demeanor that one couldn't help but wonder if, as it is in the case of so many, alcohol was the fuel that fended off his insecurities and bolstered Dutch courage. There was no doubt in my mind that he was 100 percent aware of this self-inflicted transformation and totally committed to it taking place. What was a mystery to me was if he also enjoyed the tranquility of this flip side, the real Oliver as it were, or if it was just simply downtime to regroup. That morning he reminded me of the wild beast who having a thorn drawn from his paw lapses into a benign and ingenious disposition. A little unsettling, but good to know. I'm just sorry that more people didn't get to experience, or weren't familiar with, the other Oliver.

IN ORDER TO remain on the island in chronological fashion, we'll reconvene with Oliver a little later. For now my relationship with Nick blossomed as did my friendship with Jiggs and Ronald through whom I gained access to areas of Barbados where tourists were not in danger, but not necessarily welcome. With Nick, I flew above and sailed around the island, becoming increasingly familiar not just with avenues of pleasure but also with the pacing of everyday life and how Barbadians balanced joyous recreation with a commendable work ethic and immense pride in this harmonious slice of the Caribbean. This cultural assimilation may have suffered at times from serious contradiction where I was concerned, but even if it sounds ambiguous, I truly loved this place unconditionally. Though I behaved on occasion with juvenile irrationality and in a manner where my actions were seriously questionable, at no time did I disrespect anyone but myself. Ultimately, my delinquency left me the recipient of my own bad behavior.

In an earlier adventure, Nick had suggested flying to Martinique for lunch at the island's splendid Grand'Voile restaurant. With me and a couple of Elton's houseguests in tow, we took off for what was to be a long and languid afternoon. At its conclusion, satiated and in possession of fine vibes, we dutifully returned to the airport and took off back to home base. Once airborne, however, there was some consternation with the tower regarding flight formalities and the approaching evening's rulings on Nick's instrument panel. Whatever the reasons, we had to turn back and spend the night on Martinique. Unfortunately, this information was not relayed to Elton correctly and it was presumed our plane could not be located. Back on Barbados, a panicked household, thinking we'd gone the way of Amelia Earhart, spent a fitful night pacing and imagining the worst until we nonchalantly sauntered in early the following morning.

Somewhere around this point, I had been in London to promote a book and taken up with the diminutive English pop singer Lynsey de Paul. Vivacious and with a knack for potent melodic compositions, she was at the forefront of music's female liberation and making headway in a male-dominated music scene. One had to respect her for these achievements, and while her accomplishments included a myriad of collective creative irons in the industry fire, I was poorly versed in her history, being blithely uneducated and not terribly interested in British Top 40 pop. She was a headstrong woman, talented and smart and used to getting her own way. What she wasn't was an equal opportunity partner in certain areas and prone to a dictatorial tendency when it came to decision-making. Of course from the get-go this wasn't going to make for plain sailing and probably accounted for the number of celebrity boyfriends she had left in her wake, both before and after me. The thing was she was a looker, and I'm sure this had been the key ingredient that had caused my predecessors and me to be reeled in.

Needless to say we eventually ended up vacationing in Barbados, and while I wouldn't call our relationship one of harmonious compatibility, it wasn't initially without moments of mild reciprocity and a truce-like sharing of entertainment options. I'm not sure when things started to go pear-shaped, but it may have had something to do with my inordinate time on the water and lack of time indulging her increasing demands to be catered to. This escalating fractious atmosphere came to a head when I forgot her birthday, a slight that incited an award-winning meltdown. I might add here that she had made no mention of this impending event, and I can only imagine she had expected me to be aware of it by way of mental telepathy.

Inconsolable, her lower lip protruding in a sulky pout, she proposed that if I cared at all and wished to rectify my oversight, I might hop a flight to New York and purchase something shiny to place around her tiny alabaster neck. What I'd like to have put around her neck at that particular moment wasn't jewelry, but before I could contradict her demands a thought occurred to me: Escape!

"Absolutely, of course, my darling, happy to oblige, anything to make you happy." Well, perhaps not quite as sugarcoated as that, but solicitous enough to sound sincere. Dang, twenty-four hours in the Big Apple, no bickering, no constant wet hornet in my ear badgering me to bend to her will and pave her way with rose petals.

In need of an accomplice, I enlisted a rakish island charmer by the name of John. A good-looking blond and buoyant Brit, John was always good value for money and able to defuse any ruction by way of his beguiling personality.

We landed in New York midafternoon and wasted no time checking into our hotel and tarting ourselves up for a night on the town. After buffing up the edges of my tarnished fidelity we hit the hotel bar for a couple of belts before heading down to Little Italy. Little Italy in lower Manhattan simply oozed Old World charm. From the get-go in 1970, I'd been drawn to this Neapolitan wonderland. Its atmosphere was completely magical: the sights, the sounds, the glorious smells, its colorful complexity intermingling into a scintillating concoction of celebratory tradition.

Over the years I'd been drawn to the Feast of San Gennaro, an eleven-day blowout of street vendors, games, and cultural attractions all culminating in the Grand Procession where the statue of Saint Gennaro, bristling with dollar bills, is transported through the streets of Little Italy to its home in the Most Precious Blood Church. When I was younger I would get lost in the crowd, gorging myself silly on sausage and Chianti followed by fresh *zeppole*, and if luck would have it, a slice of the world's largest cannoli.

For now I was merely initiating John into a slice of my New York passion while rekindling my affection for this unique neighborhood where committed Catholicism and religious fervor coexisted implicitly with organized crime. Tacit approval made this alliance curious bed-fellows, and out in the streets a code of honor ensured that the patron-age of one turned a blind eye to the other.

Umbertos Clam House at Mulberry and Hester was our destina-tion. It was here only several years prior that the infamous mobster Joey Gallo was gunned down while eating dinner with his family. This glamorous bit of bloody folklore aside, not to mention its effect on my impressionable friend, was a moot point given the good eats I was familiar with at this simple but palatable family-style joint. Barbados was in my blood, and a haven of alternate cuisine, but when it came to *linguine vongole* and *pasta marechiaro*, no place delivered like New York City.

From here on, the rest of the evening went according to plan, which meant cramming in as much crazy-assed night crawling as possible in the limited time allotted. An introduction for John to the whacky weirdness of the Gilded Grape was essential, while a strategically sit-uated table in the musty splendor of Max's Kansas City could always be counted on for excellent people watching and liberal amounts of cheap booze.

Max's had recently undergone a transition, morphing from a social club and magnet for the New York School, a collective term for radi-cal artistic scions like Warhol, Rauschenberg, and John Chamberlain, into a home base for the emerging new wave movement. Where Allen Ginsberg and Philip Glass once rubbed shoulders, it was the grand racket of the New York Dolls, Blondie, Television, and the Talking Heads that now took center stage. It was also at this very table several years earlier that I had spent the evening with Loudon Wainwright III and a pregnant Kate McGarrigle sifting through names for their soon-to-be-born son. We all agreed that Rufus was a fine choice!

By the time we hit the Village, we had a serious buzz on with no inten-tion of surrender. Putting the pedal to the metal, we caroused up Bleecker and down Mercer checking in at The Bitter End, The Bottom Line, and every hole-in-the-wall bar that beckoned with trashy complicity.

At some point we connected with a group of fellow revelers, several of whom I was vaguely aquatinted with. Of course vaguely acquainted is not always necessarily a good thing, however in keeping with our propulsion into alcoholic anarchy, it seemed fitting at the time.

Back at the hotel, mayhem ensued, minibars were consumed, and many pizzas were ordered. The group appeared to grow larger, although that might have been because by that time I was seeing double. It was only when I found myself alone in the bedroom with one of the female partygoers, a willowy brunette resembling a sexed-up librarian, that things took on a distinctly debauched turn. A willing participant was one thing, but the modus operandi of this cracker in a cardigan and horn-rimmed specs was beyond the range of my personal proclivities. "I like to be whipped" are words that thankfully have not entered my personal space other than this one time, and with them came a swift expulsion and an end to the night. My scruples may have at times been questionable but physical violence against women, invited or other-wise, is the loathsome proclivity of cowards and bullies.

Next thing I knew, an alarm was ringing in and outside my head. John was banging on the door, sirens were screaming in the streets, and seemingly above and below construction drills were roaring with pneumatic convulsion. In a somnambulistic state, we staggered out of the hotel into the blazing day and poured ourselves like liquid gelatin into the back of our waiting limo.

I was nodding off in the back seat, cruising down Fifth Avenue on the way to the airport when it hit me. Sitting bolt upright it occurred to me that I'd absolutely forgotten the one thing I'd come here for in the first place.

Frantically looking up and down the street it was as if by a sheer miracle that Tiffany & Co. appeared, a life preserver tossed into the midday traffic, a means with which to salvage my ass and not go down with the *Titanic*. With little time to browse I grabbed the first thing I saw, a moderately priced small gold box housing a petite diamond and anchored by a thin chain. *Unique*, I thought, but then again jewelry not being my thing it was always going to be a crapshoot.

Luckily, we made our flight with seconds to spare and headaches like Hell's bells. Fortuitously, with a sympathetic stewardess admin-istering Bloody Marys at a rate that could have only been matched intravenously, we soon overrode the hair of the dog and got back in the saddle. Bolstered by this aerial imbibing and with my secured trinket tucked away, I felt little regret for our mild turpitude in the Big Apple and became fully resigned to reconnecting with my tiny blond fireball.

While not terribly impressed with my purchase, Lynsey seemed appeased by the gesture and like a magpie toying with something shiny turned it over in her hands as if quizzing its value and sentimental worth. Almost expecting her to bite down on it like some backstreet Fagin, I made nice and promised myself that I'd endeavor to improve the status quo.

Of course this promise lasted about as long as the sun took to rise and set, and a lull in my cease-fire was staved off only by the arrival of a golf ball. This rolled through my living room the subsequent evening followed by the unexpected appearance of my dear old friends, Sheryl and Alice Cooper. This beautiful diversion thus saved my vacation and defused an increasingly hostile environment, putting a buffer between our dwindling romantic tryst.

For the next ten days, harmony was temporarily restored as Alice golfed, I skied, and we all lounged poolside reading Anne Rice's *Interview with the Vampire*. In the evening, we would decamp to Alexandra's, the island's premier nightspot, where we would while away the time eating, drinking, and watching white couples dance atrociously. Alexandra's was owned and operated by a smooth as silk Trinidadian called Noel Charles. Noel dressed immaculately, purred like a kitten, and moved like a cat. Never solicitous, always charm personified, he'd opened this extension to his collective club consortium only recently, and it had been a hit from the get-go.

Noel had a way that charmed women and had the social damsels flocking to his club falling over backward to get his attention. I was never really convinced that Noel cared for me too much, although I'm not sure as to why being that on a scale of cool to humid I was a tarnished and incorrigible contender by comparison. Perhaps I'm overthinking this because he was always happy to have me in his club and was nothing but accommodating to those I brought in as guests. The only time in fact that a modicum of friction materialized was when we both were vying for the attention of a certain Wendy, the daughter of harmonica virtuoso Larry Adler. In this instance I bested his efforts, which I have no doubt only momentarily ruffled his very expensive loafers.

So it was that we idled away the nights here, and while the clientele were enchanted by Alice's presence, it was obvious that Lynsey was more than a little miffed by the lack of attention offered her given that her celebratory status was not international and her star shone only for those who might be visiting from the UK. I can't say that I was terribly sympathetic to this issue being that I was the recipient of fame in name only and quite satisfied to remain generally anonymous although, aside from the fleeting tourist quota, everyone on the island knew who I was . . . which didn't sit well with my petite songstress.

In the heat of our revelry one night, Lynsey challenged Sheryl to a bout of arm wrestling, a not particularly good idea I thought, given that Mrs. Cooper was a professional dancer, toned, and muscular.

I wasn't wrong, and within seconds Lyndsey was flipped across the table like a dime unceremoniously deposited onto the banquet in a crumpled and indignant heap. It was the beginning of the end.

Eventually, she followed me to LA and briefly hung in until finding comfort in the arms of actor James Coburn, a wise choice and one that proved to be successful for quite some time.

The last great hurrah came later in the following year when the celebrated illustrator Alan Aldridge and I were dispatched to Barbados by Universal Pictures to write a script for a proposed animated movie of *Captain Fantastic and the Brown Dirt Cowboy*.

Alan, who had created all the original artwork for our conceptual record, a worldwide bestseller that had the distinction of being the first album ever to enter the Billboard charts at number one, was not only an impressive conspirator but a collaborative architect of great mischief.

On the rear jacket of Alan's delightfully illustrated autobiography *The Man with Kaleidoscope Eyes*, I described our relationship as this: "In the mid-seventies Alan and I were inseparable friends. It was a curious collaboration of eccentricity and dangerous curves taken at ever increasing speed and joyous abandon."

The word *genius* is bandied about far too liberally these days and attached more times than not to individuals unworthy of that label. Mark my words, Alan Aldridge was a genius. He was also a little bit nuts in the most delightfully irresponsible way imaginable. So, to be brutally frank, the idea of dispatching Alan and myself to Barbados to create anything was about as sensible as sending the Marquis de Sade to Victoria's Secret to buy stationary.

Alan's resume was impeccable. Coming to prominence in the '60s, he was responsible for *The Beatles Illustrated Lyrics*, album covers for The Who and Cream, along with the notorious poster he created for Andy Warhol's *Chelsea Girls*. He'd also designed the Hard Rock Cafe logo and had been at the pinnacle of the animation and illustration game for over a decade.

Our rental in Barbados was in familiar territory. A splendid villa in walking distance of the Sandy Lane Hotel, it came fully staffed and appointed with a grand selection of bedrooms and a perfect view of the ocean. I reconnected with Jiggs and Ronald, Alan took in the sun, and we both proceeded to get no work done at all. We just couldn't focus. In fact in the entire time, the only profitable moment came when Elton called me from Toronto one evening to play me a backing track he'd just cut with the band. Half cut myself by this point in the day, the afternoon's poolside cocktails having muddied my brain waves, I listened and took note. Elton was in need of a lyric that could be done as a duet, something along the lines of each of the old Marvin Gaye recordings with either Kim Weston or Tammi Terrell. I listened, told him I'd give it a shot, hung up, and stuck my head in the ice bucket. In ten minutes I'd thrown something together that was simplistic without being overly trite, and that is how "Don't Go Breaking My Heart" came about. Not exactly "Sad Eyed Lady of the Lowlands," but the second biggest selling single of 1976 and our first UK number one. Believe it or not, it also scored an Ivor Novello for best song musically and lyrically. Not bad for ten minutes of drunken scribbling. Elton would go on to rerecord it years later with RuPaul and have a number one in Iceland, a fact that I didn't fail to see the irony in.

You'd have thought our failure to deliver anything resembling even a script synopsis would have weighed heavy and resulted in embarrassment on our part for taking advantage of Universal's generosity. Hell no! It never even crossed our minds as we accelerated into inertia with surprising ease. It's not that we didn't discuss it, it's just that the grown-up part of sitting inside hammering out cohesive storylines and sizzling dialogue when so many congenial distractions spoke to us outweighed any work ethic. It was easy to conjure up colorful vignettes and think you were terribly clever for it, but when you're wading about in a concoction of self-appropriated shenanigans, self-medicated ideas aren't always the best in the clear light of day.

About a week into our aborted creative clinic, Oliver Reed returned, and havoc with him. Not unlike myself, Ollie had a penchant for the mountain rum shacks and life in the edgier interior. So it was that the three of us found ourselves one afternoon cracking jokes and gabbing over fried chicken in one of the most remote shanties on the island. At a certain point we were approached by a sullen group of locals whose obvious intent was to intimidate. This, as you might imagine, meant about as much to Oliver Reed as a feather on a bull's ass, and in no certain terms he took them at face value and challenged them to a drinking contest. Naturally, this was done with no confirmation that either Alan or I was agreeable. Oliver, being obviously drawn to people who weren't intimidated, took us for a couple of nervy Jack the Lads who weren't about to let a bunch of wannabe Rastas get the upper hand.

The game, as Sherlock Holmes famously said, was afoot. Steeling myself like Karen Allen in *Raiders of the Lost Ark* and with a tentative Alan alongside preparing to "take one for the crown," we proceeded to do battle. Drink of choice? What else but white rum, of course, a clear, lethal concoction brewed locally.

In a matter of minutes the shot glasses were piling up and the wicked spirit was already taking effect. The locals, though mouthy and animated, were lacking in livity (a Rasta term for a life force that is not forthcoming) and looked as if they might be regretting their provocation. One caved in almost immediately with Alan following close behind, having already topped up on Banks beer and Bloody Marys for the last couple of hours. The second opponent was the next to go with yours truly, hallucinating heavily, tagging on behind him, all surrendering gestures and gills of green. This left only a barely stewed Ollie and a rapidly faltering final adversary who raising his glass slowly to his lips followed through by falling backward on his stool and crashing unceremoniously to the ground. The crowd that had gathered to witness this feat of absolute stupidity burst into applause. In the spirit of all chugalug champions, Oliver roared out as one does: "Drinks all round!!!!"

It was relayed to us later that Oliver slept for the next three days, which was understandable given that his drinking didn't end with his victory, and while we were carted off to repair, he barreled on through the night draining the island dry till the morning light.

From here on, things really started to get out of hand and were only temporarily restrained by the arrival of a calming presence in the form of one David Nutter. David was the younger brother of the iconic London couturier Tommy Nutter. Tommy's designs reinvented Savile Row and he was famous for dressing three out of four Beatles on the cover of *Abbey Road*. David was a talent in his own right, a wonderfully candid photographer who'd been the exclusive lensman at John and Yoko's wedding along with chronicling numerous Elton performances and personal informalities.

I adored David. His humor was as dry as a bone and his temperament gentle and positive. He was an elfin presence whose conviviality endeared him to everyone he came in contact with. Even the unconditionally hetero Ronald, for whom David harbored a major crush, played along, laughing uproariously at every camp come-on and thinly veiled innuendo. When David was present, any romantic pairing I may have had at the time inevitably wound up wrapped around his little finger, an agony aunt to whom they poured out their frustrations and girly machinations.

With his mellow presence installed, my disorderly antics were curbed slightly, although Alan continued to cavort as if his life depended on it. By now, the project that we had been dispatched to create had dissipated from even the vaguest attempts to completely neglected. Where Alan went I wasn't quite sure, but there were times he'd take off into the night like some clandestine Nosferatu not to return for a couple of days. Funny thing is I never really inquired as to where he was going, simply presuming it was some feminine nest or Barbadian opium den.

This short reprieve saw me commence to ski like the dickens and deepen my impressive tan. While I took to the water, David would recline in his deck chair on the beach knitting and taking in the scenery, which for the most part meant Ronald in a speedo.

With David's departure, the mellow embrace that had found me temporarily tamed simply melted away, and I'm at pains to admit left me beating a drum for which I had no control over tempo. I believe some of us have times in our lives that we feel we are losing control and that stupidity might somehow be a temporary substitute for rational behavior, but if intelligence is judged by deeds committed, then my last island infraction left me a bulb of flickering wattage.

In the waning days of our botched assignment, I simmered under a dark cloud of overindulgence. Alan was gone, David was gone, and any true hard-earned relationships I'd developed locally had been neutered or teetered on the edge of extinction. Feeling sorry for myself and in a maudlin state of mind, I reflected on the path I'd chosen years earlier. Embarrassed and resentful that barely out of my teens I had made choices so completely asinine at a time when I was still developing socially left me contemplative in the most unhealthy way.

Attempting to shake myself free of the funk I was in, I spent a long evening propping up the bar at Alexandra's before meandering morosely into the parking lot to find my vehicle locked, and me minus the keys. Yes, I went back into the club to look for them; no, I didn't find them; no, I didn't ask anyone for a ride home; and no, I didn't call a cab. These options aside, I made the extremely wise decision of stealing a bus. Opposite the club was a line of them, orange school district ones that just seemed to scream availability. As was the way on this trusting island, the keys swung conveniently in the ignition, an inviting solution to my stranded predicament. So off I went, traversing the late night highway all the way home, where I left my ride in the driveway and went to bed.

I awoke late the next morning to a pounding on the door. As expected, I was confronted by a collection of individuals of no good intent and whose collective objective was to chastise, arrest, and harangue me in no particular order. The only smart thing that I did in the ensuing twenty-four hours was to fall on the sword and call in a few favors. Luckily, several friends in high places lent their assistance, and I was able to weasel out of incarceration and promise in no uncertain terms that I would vacate from my vacation by the next day. Feeling as if I'd run my course and that it was in my best interest to reconvene with the mainland, I packed my bags and didn't look back. However, I took my ski just in case.

Showdown at the Gilded Grape

I like boring things.

—ANDY WARHOL

It was cold; I mean really cold, New York City cold circa 1974. I loved it; it was brutal and malevolent then, a time of dystopian landscapes and raw interludes of shock and awe.

The winter chill was fully in character with the Babylonian years long before Giuliani's whitewashing of the city. The cold embraced that fabled Mecca in a way that humidity and summer sunshine could never hope to achieve. It swept along the avenues, scything through the bundled masses and driving a diverse quantum of the populace into queer and odd places free of labels and organized structure. Here they shed their protective outer skins and became denizens of the night, owners of their own obsessions, plumed and sequined, leather bound and bad to the bone, which of course they weren't, just wishful thinking for the most part, a posture of attitude as amour, a self-inflicted coterie inhabiting a debauched pantomime.

An enema was immanent and altogether necessary. Things got out of hand, caution was thrown way beyond the wind, and the in-house nature of what I perceived as a much smaller circus exploded into a mammoth bacchanalia of sex and violence that sowed the seeds of calamitous and darker times to come.

Back then, at twenty-four, I was fearlessly quizzical, the settings on my moral barometer hovering somewhere in the vicinity of nonjudgmental. I was a fly on the wall rather than a voyeur. I had no desire to either view or include myself in any nocturnal shenanigans that might transpire in the back rooms of the torrid but highly entertaining hole-in-the-walls that throbbed away, oblivious to the external Nordic chill. I was a straight man-child immune to danger, looking for love in all the wrong places yet learning life lessons from an alternate nether world of the baroque and the bizarre, and for that there was no better place than 719 Eighth Avenue.

It was easy to see why this place in particular fascinated me. Felliniesque to the core, the Gilded Grape claimed to be a drag bar, but on closer inspection was a magnet of solace and strange comfort to a myriad of both colorful and buttoned-up characters. Looking like an English transport café designed by Disneyland, it adopted a distinctly laissez-faire attitude in regard to its clientele. I can't say that I have ever frequented a place then or to this day where no one cared a tinker's toss who they were sitting next to. On one hand you'd have a mascara'd bald queen in a pink tutu passing ketchup to a wise guy from Jersey while a Wall Street warrior and his bejeweled hottie swapped war stories with an oiled up muscle stud in a rhinestone codpiece and leather chaps. I once went there with Little Tony, a Hells Angels friend of mine from Brooklyn, and he didn't bat an eyelid.

This same come one, come all attitude permeated the staff, who if memory serves me correctly, had the habit of inhabiting the personas (in drag of course) of dead movie queens and obscure theatrical divas. On one occasion, I turned up with my amusing expat friend from Barbados who with no sense of irony whatsoever inquired of the stately trans bartender.

"Hello mate, d'yer sell fags?"

"Not personally dear, but I'd entertain an offer" came the swift reply.

One regular was Andy Warhol. I was a tremendous admirer of Warhol's work and to see him in person was initially thrilling. The revolutionary New York movement of Abstract Expressionism and Pop Art had had a profound effect on me, and along with Warhol, the likes of Robert Rauschenberg and Jasper Johns were akin to rock stars.

Warhol was so enamored with the Gilded Grape that he was persuaded by Italian art dealer Luciano Anselmino to create over two hundred paintings and prints of the club's transvestite staff. Ultimately, this spilled into the streets to include a phalanx of similar drag queens and transwomen. Predominately Latin and African American, the collection titled *Ladies and Gentlemen* was exhibited for the first time in Ferrara, Italy, in 1975.

Unfortunately, while Warhol's work was groundbreaking and captivating, his personality, most certainly, was not. Talking to Andy was like conversing with an eight-year-old girl. I was going to say thirteen-year-old girl, but reflecting on my daughters at that age they were George Plimpton by comparison. He would whimper things like "The color of your shirt is really great," or "I like your hair." Much has been made of this, and indeed, it might have been his shtick, but if it was I'm not sure why. If dull is how he wanted to be perceived, he came through with flying colors.

His accompanying acolytes and Factory posse weren't much of an improvement. Painfully at odds with convention, their sole concern seemed to be acting as aloof as possible while projecting a huddled and slouching agglomerate of stereotypical pretentiousness. I can't be certain, but depending on any given night the group might include the likes of Paul Morrissey, Joe Dallesandro, Jackie Curtis, and, on one occasion, fashion designer Halston. Not one emitted any shard of personality, they simply hunkered like crows around the cadaverous pancake-white carriage of their mentor.

My most memorable evening at the Grape, however, consisted of what I look back on in retrospect as a simply excellent mélange.

I'd met Billie Jean King through Elton, who had befriended her through his passion for tennis and his ability via his significant and emerging fame to make the right connections. Billie Jean was a force of nature, a former world number one and the winner of thirty-nine Grand Slams. She was tough, passionate, and a genuine maverick not to mention lots of fun. I'd first encountered her at John Gardiner's Tennis Ranch in Phoenix where she had attempted to turn me from a scrawny rock 'n' roll miscreant into an agile and bronzed athlete. Undoubtedly this is the only time Billie Jean King has ever failed at anything.

Rounding out our intrepid trio was Queen's magisterial front man, the irrepressible Freddie Mercury. Freddie was what they refer to in the UK as a diamond geezer. He was absolutely infectious, a one-off, irreverent but in a way that was too endearing to be offensive. Freddie on occasion had dragged me to similar dens of iniquity that had seriously tested the mettle of my broad mind, so to my way of thinking the Grape was middle ground, and to my relief Freddie loved it.

I'm sure the evening for us had begun elsewhere, and as was the way things transpired back then, various factions of a larger group would splinter off into smaller ones with plans to hook up at another location later in the night. So it was that the three of us found ourselves sequestered around a rickety table, drinking champagne and conversing in the tangerine glow of the Gilded Grape, a triangle of social and sexual variation basking in idiosyncratic safety until the unheard of happened, a fight. This you must understand was anathema to the usual benign bedlam in an environment that fully embraced eccentric creativity but drew the line at physical violence.

In all honesty it was a pretty girly affair, the two drag queens involved flailing their arms wildly, squealing like drunken mice scratching and pummeling as they groped at each other unconvincingly. Sequins scattered, wigs went flying, and mascara and tears ran in rivulets.

While I was mildly amused, Freddie was positively ecstatic, getting into the spirit of things by egging them on with a gleeful commentary of camp encouragement—that is until the floundering lady-boys wrestled each other squarely onto the center of our already impaired table, which under the weight of their intertwined aggression collapsed into a twisted heap of crinoline, metal, and Formica.

Call it speculation, call it poetic license, but I imagine it as one of those moments when the world stops and everyone freezes in place, a momentary deathly silence as all eyes focus on one calamitous spot. Maybe not, but one thing I can tell you is suddenly it was as if it never happened: within a flash the tattered pugilists bounced to their feet, embraced, and vanished while the debris was removed and our table was replaced with a sturdier substitute. All this was done without any fuss or word of apology. To their way of thinking, it really *had* never happened. It was matter of fact, purgatorial in nature, a series of sideways smiles as complimentary champagne was offered and genteel mayhem resumed.

John Lennon's Not So Lost Weekend

What you leave behind is not what is engraved on monuments,
but what is woven into the lives of others.

—PERICLES

"I don't know if you've ever heard it, but I wrote this song called 'Across the Universe.'"

OK freeze, stop right there, hold that thought and picture this. I'm aboard the *Starship*, Elton's private touring plane, flying out of New York to play Boston Garden on November 20, 1974. Cozied up alongside me on the padded couch that runs horizontally along the central wall of the plane is John Lennon, whose utterance of the aforementioned information has me wondering if he's (A) pulling my leg, (B) placatingly humble, or could it really be (C) honest?

The cause for this conversation and the reason that John is on this flight are altogether unconnected. The latter is that John, having lost a bet to Elton regarding the unqualified success of "Whatever Gets You Thru the Night," John's latest single, has found the former Beatle in the unavoidable position of having to join Mr. Big Glasses onstage eight days hence at Madison Square Garden. The Boston gig is to be an EJ primer, a close look at the Elton spectacle (no pun intended), and, in a nutshell, what Mr. Lennon is more than likely getting himself into.

OK...back to John's offhand, but ineffaceable reference to a Beatle classic that unless you were born in a crater on the planet Pluto or cryogenically frozen for the duration of the '60s, you'd have to know.

"Er, yeah, of course," I laconically respond, fidgeting with my eye and attempting to maintain some sense of body language that doesn't involve sliding off the silky suede like a slice of hot buttered toast.

Sorry, I haven't the foggiest idea as to what was the kernel of our discussion. Why? Because it was frigging *JOHN LENNON* that's why. John Lennon, one of the architects of the greatest musical force in the history of pop music, a breath of fresh air that energized a nation in the wake of a political assassination and blew out the last vestiges of what was the flickering flame of Elvis Presley.

I'd like to believe we were kindred spirits grappling with the fundamentals of lyrical anarchy, delving deep into the literal value of shopping for inspiration in the everyday world. Perhaps it was a discussion fueled by mutual appreciation of current philosophy driven by society's hamster wheel of ever-changing points of view, and then again, perhaps it was just "Yeah, thanks, love your songs too, man."

With the Boston gig in the books, it's back to New York and time to pay the piper. Which is why John Lennon can be found sequestered in a bathroom stall backstage at Madison Square Garden. It's Thanksgiving night, November 28, and the reality of performing live after such a lengthy absence from the stage has our hero purging his nerves into the porcelain throne.

Nerves aside, John looks every inch the quintessential rock god. Tip to toe in black, including smoked glasses, he sports a gardenia in his buttonhole and a circular medallion around his neck, emblazoned with studded diamonds and spelling out Dr. Winston O'Boogie, his nom de plume du jour!

As countdown becomes inevitable, his insecurities resurface and he relapses into a state of faltering paranoia, his black Telecaster shaking in his hands. I know this because I'm standing next to him in the wings, ready to propel him physically onto the stage should he book out and attempt a runner. As Elton begins his introduction, John begins to plead. "You have to come out with me." And it's here that I will defer to my partner's description of this moment in his excellent autobiography *Me*. "Bernie always hated the limelight, and not even a desperate Beatle could convince him to change his mind." Indeed, plus as I venture to steer my anxious charge toward his date with destiny, I offer little in the way of comfort other than "And do what?"

I refuse to dwell on the ultimate significance of this event and its placement in John's legacy. Yes, it was the last time he would ever appear onstage before his untimely assassination in 1980, but I prefer to recall the decibel-defying hurricane of adulation that night and the pure volcanic eruption of applause that saw the floor of the Garden do more than its usual reverberating seismic roll. The building seemed to briefly levitate off its foundations, and in all my years of concert going I have never heard or witnessed anything like it.

Triumph is an understatement. Elton was at the top of his game and the sheer electrical force of his personality and the propulsion of his crackerjack band energized John's confidence, spotlighting what always made him great: the stance, the voice, the undeniable charisma.

What I wasn't ready for was the encore situation that had me transported by one ecstatic ex-Beatle whose previous snubbing of aid in regard to his entrance wasn't going to wash in the euphoria of his return to center stage. How could I refuse? He was engulfed in glory and undeniably so. Adrenaline pumping and with his arm wrapped around my submissive shoulders, I was extracted from the wings and dragged before the massed and mesmerized crowd. Let's face it: no one cared. I may as well not have existed as all eyes were rightly fixed on his presence and not on some uncomfortable totem moronically flailing away on a perfunctory tambourine.

After that euphoric evening, I didn't see John again until July of the following year when we reconnected in LA to see Bob Marley at the Roxy Theatre on Sunset. Much has been written about John's LA exploits, but bear in mind that the most unpleasant and notorious of these incidents happened earlier, in 1973, in the company of Harry Nilsson, when the two of them carved a not-too-memorable path through Tinseltown's night life.

Harry wasn't a bad guy. In fact he was fiercely intelligent, just not terribly entertaining when under the influence of his many addictions, which apparently included the acquisition of Beatles for buddies. He could be imposing, intimidating, and loud. Sweating beneath his old cloth cap and herringbone overcoat, his confrontational nature drove a wedge between good, clean fun and dark, destructive nihilism. I, for one, wondered if the man ever slept. He just wasn't one of those people you could imagine tucked beneath the sheets in his jammies enjoying nocturnal rest no matter how brief. He always seemed to be roaring, wide-awake in a sort of gestating bestial netherworld. I'm not sure I'd call it pandering, but then again for a man who in his best moments could create such beautiful music and sing with a God-given voice, his obsession with John seemed humiliating to me.

It's not that I didn't have any entertaining moments with him, in fact I once spent a robust and riotous evening in his company at Johnny Gold's legendary London nightclub, Tramp. Things were trotting along in an intellectually stimulating way up until the point that it became blindingly clear he couldn't differentiate between Mozart and Mantovani. It was obvious that his alcoholic and pharmaceutical intake had surpassed his ability to function capably, and in a matter of ten minutes turned him from a knowledgeable debater into a lowland gorilla.

And so it was that in the early hours, I suggested (delicately) that he take his blitzed and pickled self to the exit and ask my driver to give him a ride home. Heeding my advice he stumbled up the stairs and jumped into the closest available vehicle. Unfortunately, it wasn't mine, but a seventy-two-foot Mercedes limousine belonging to the Sultan of Brunei.

The terrified chauffeur acquiesced rather than engage the monstrous and fatigued songwriter, feeling it in his best interest not to question why and just do. Which is exactly what he did, because that's how I found out when I ran into a bleary-eyed Harry at lunch the next day. "Fuck man, you've got a nice car," he said.

Bob Marley and the Wailers did a blinding set, and afterward John and I repaired to On The Rox. On The Rox was actually more like a large living room for owner Lou Alder's friends and those he perceived as quirky or interesting. This included, of course, a wide cross section of movie stars, character actors, and rock artists, some currently hip, many legendary, and some of a distinctly vintage nature.

Top-shelf classics like Nicholson and Beatty propped up the bar alongside neophyte Eagles, and on occasion when not hunkered down in the swamps of Jersey, a fledgling and wiry Bruce Springsteen. Old guard Whisky a Go Go stalwart Johnny Rivers was a regular, as were James Taylor (trying to retrieve his coke spoon from the men's toilet) and legendary scene stealers like Seymour Cassel and Harry Dean Stanton.

I loved Harry Dean, and on many occasions he would return with me to my house not five minutes away, where we would stay up until dawn sipping tequila and singing old cowboy songs. Years later I would pay homage to him by writing a song called "The Ballad of Dennis Hopper & Harry Dean," which I performed in the early '90s with my sidebar roots band, Farm Dogs.

The mix at On The Rox created a continually compelling atmosphere. There was a certain sense of security, the diversity of the members working as a sort of aphrodisiac to settle everyone into unity. No pressure, no competitiveness, just a level playing field devoid of any rubberneckers and voyeuristic interlopers who might tarnish the vibe. That is, of course, as long as the vibe wasn't tarnished by inappropriate behavior or the occasional loudmouth. I once punched John Belushi out cold for insulting my girlfriend, an act that impressed him so much that he called me the next day to apologize.

So Messrs. Lennon and Taupin are settling into a nice cozy corner when up the stairs and through the velvet curtains saunters Bob Marley, trailing in his wake the Wailers and what appears to be half the population of Kingston. Immediately they engulf us, two white minnows sucked whole into the belly of Rastafari. Their presence is mesmerizing, a small army of seemingly willowy and towering regality, all billowing shawls, turbans, and knitted berets of red, green, black, and yellow. They drape themselves and lounge around us, occupying the space with a combination of confidence and gregarious camaraderie, seemingly thrilled (in the coolest way possible) to be languishing next to the legend that is Lennon. It appears that even Jah this evening bows out as his apostles succumb to Fab Four fever.

Marley is diminutive by comparison to his compatriots, but by no means a lesser individual. It's obvious he's the engine, the focal point, the very eye of this mystical hurricane. He is nonchalant and ethereal, distant and sanguine in equal measures, the movement of his eyes and the contours of his features giving away nothing that would allow you to put a finger on what flips the switch electrifying his mesmerizing and shamanistic performances.

It's a surreal scene kicked up a notch when Marley reaches into his shoulder bag and produces a spliff the size of a baby's arm. Apparently that's all it takes, as if on cue his Jamaican brethren follow suit producing their own large and lethal looking joints. *Aptly named*, I think to myself as they strike up and light up.

And this is when things get fuzzy. Up to that point hanging out around weed was as common an occurrence as coffee at breakfast. My immunity to secondhand pot smoke had never been a problem, and aside from its rank odor that I didn't care for then (and care even less for now) my tolerance for it was rock steady.

This was, however, an altogether different animal. Although "monster" might be more descriptive, for John and I soon found ourselves encircled by a fierce tsunami of wicked-ass ganja. Voices became incoherent and visibility shrank as Marley and company seemed to shape-shift in a somnambulistic state beyond a veil of sweet blue smoke. Slowly, I began to feel totally immobile as if I were epoxied to the couch by some Rastafarian superglue. John looked at me, and I looked at John, but no words were forthcoming, our vocal cords on pause, our tongues in limbo.

I've been pretty stoned at several points in my life. In fact I once ingested half a block of opium on a night flight from New York to Barbados and spent two days in the airport because I had no idea where I was. This wasn't like that. This was like when you hear about those people who are pronounced dead but they're really still alive and inside they're screaming and praying for a tear to appear in order to save them from a premature burial.

Unable to move my head, the best I could manage was a sideways glance. At this point the smoke cleared slightly and in my narcotized state, I saw the citizens of Trenchtown on fire. Or so it seemed. For as they toked in tandem and exhaled, the smoke crawled in serpentine swirls up across their chests and into the density of their heavily coiled braids. Here it lingered momentarily before exiting their dreadlocks, billowing forth like some simmering Rastaman Vesuvius.

Frankly, in my state it was alarming, and quite honestly if Haile Selassie had floated into the room riding a lion it wouldn't have been any less disturbing. In a matter of moments, they had transformed from picturesque performers into smoldering gorgons laughing maniacally at the traumatized and paralyzingly stoned duo in their midst.

The rest of the night is unrecountable for obvious reasons, and only the good Lord knows how we managed to wake up in our own beds. I can only imagine Good Samaritans had a hand in it, and except for the occasional flashback we both emerged from it none the worse for wear.

Sadly, my last encounter with John was several days later when we reconvened to attend a party at the home of Jeanne Martin, the recently divorced wife of the incomparable Dean. In retrospect, knowing that the two were still on good terms, I imagine that for many of the attendees it was the chance of a possible encounter with the King of Cool that made the invite more potent. I say this because for me it most certainly was, Dino being the quintessential symbol of grooviness, the Rat Packer with the most, the living embodiment of the bachelor pad pulse. In fact the serial stalker (fanboy?) in me had on several occasions made a point of dining at Carmine's, an Italian eatery on Santa Monica Boulevard—a known Dean hang. It was here that the effortlessly charismatic crooner could be found most nights propping up the bar, cigarette and drink in hand.

Still recovering from our encounter with Bob Marley and the deadly spliffs, a relatively sane afternoon soiree seemed a genteel alternative to as John put it, "Seeing Bunny Wailer in a steaming tea cozy."

It was all terribly Hollywood with an array of current celebs and beautiful people relaxing, and as is always the norm at such events, the air of "I belong" and "I don't wish to seem impressed that John Lennon and David Bowie are mingling in my branded space" was evident.

In all honesty it wasn't at all bad, and cynicism aside, I'll admit it was an airy to-do that was quite jolly and easygoing with little to do but wallow in the carefree and Dean-less conviviality. That is, however, until the somewhat hefty presence of Brian Wilson plopped down beside me and whispered breathlessly into my ear, "Bernie, Bernie, will you introduce me to John Lennon."

OK. I'd met Brian on several occasions, and though we couldn't in any way be regarded as close friends, we were acquainted to the point of nodding acknowledgment and casual conversation. I was also convinced in this instant that there must most certainly have been some time in the not-distant-past that the Beatle and Beach Boy had crossed paths. But then this was Brian Wilson circa 1975: the acid aftermath, the paranoia, the sandbox years. Still a lovely man, and in spite of being toasted by demons and lost in a fog of fragility, he was still someone to respect deeply and treat with TLC.

So naturally, I acquiesced and turned to John relaying that Brian would like to say hello, and of course, he did gently and pleasantly with no hint of surprise at the request. They conversed briefly and very soon John and I found ourselves in some other corner of the room where Brian found me and whispered once again into my ear that he'd like to meet John Lennon.

Surprised but not terribly unprepared given the individual at hand, I remained unfazed and once more turned to my party date inquiring with a raised eyebrow if he would once more like to meet Brian Wilson? Similarly unruffled but obviously amused, introductions were made and small talk was made.

Groundhog Day resumed and not more than ten minutes later Brian, wide-eyed and insistent, waylaid me pleading in no uncertain terms that he must be introduced to John Lennon. By this time the hunter seemed transfixed on the game. It was as if they had never crossed paths and that Brian needed the introduction like a junkie needs a fix. It was somewhat unnerving, but still harboring the belief that the genius that was Brian Wilson was temporarily on vacation, what could I do?

Thirty years later from the date in question I sat alone in a studio with an engineer and watched as Brian Wilson stacked a twenty-part harmony on our 2010 song "When Love Is Dying" with as little effort as it takes to blow smoke. What did he ask for in return? "A really big hamburger." Yes, genius unquestionably.

Slightly exhausted but prepared to remain sympathetic, I approached John and ventured somewhat uncomfortably to once more relay Brian's request. Straight-faced and unwavering, John once more turned to engage the clearly overheated Beach Boy.

Before long he was back and we made a beeline for the door rather than fall into the same trap a fourth time.

"What did he want to talk about?" I had to ask.

John shook his head. "'Across the Universe.'"

"Sorry about that," I said

John looked at me, smiled, and in that unmistakable Liverpudlian drawl just said, "Bless him, he's not well, you know."

Weird Scenes from the Old World

A crown is merely a hat that lets the rain in.
—FREDERICK THE GREAT

Truth be told, I've never been terribly enamored with royalty. Even in my rural childhood, the several dozen cherry trees planted in our village to celebrate the coronation were just that, trees, charming enough in their pale pink uniformity, but registering little relevance to the pageantry they represented.

From an early age, the reverence and fascination afforded the British royal family completely eluded me. It wasn't any sort of juvenile anarchy on my part, just a total mystification as to why we clung so dearly to this cobwebby institution. In the parlors of our neighbors, embroidered pillows, chipped enamel tea sets, and faded portraits of miscellaneous monarchs established an allegiance as if by proxy. In hindsight, that distinctly black-and-white world that was Britain before the 1960s had elements of Pythonesque forelock-tugging subservience, a cloth cap in hand subjugation to colonial rule and an antiquated world of tiaras and toffs.

It was reported that twenty-seven million people in the UK alone watched the coronation of Elizabeth II in 1952. OK, that's fantastic. Impressive numbers indeed, given that in the boonies back where we were, crawling out from under ration books and powdered orange juice, the idea that twenty-seven million people owned or had access to a TV before I even knew what one was is astounding.

While I had no doubt that Queen Liz was a wise and benevolent matriarch, it just didn't translate that way in the turgid newsreels of the day. Her gloved hand slightly tilted and proffered unenthusiastically, as if limply bestowing acknowledgment, could easily be misread as an appendage in fear of fire. Then there were the lusterless inquiries, routinely asked questions that were easily dispensed and in no danger of confusing the beneficiary. "And what do you do?" "Do you enjoy your work?" and "That must be terribly interesting," all doled out while the ever-present handbag swung silently on her wrist, an accessory one imagined only an operation could remove.

As I write this I think to myself, *Am I being unreasonably negative?* But given that this is all from the perspective of a curious child weighing the components of his rural simplicity against something almost fictitious in its grandeur is hardly surprising. My father had come home from the war and was struggling to establish a foothold in the challenging terrain of a bleak and isolated Northern England. So any news from Buckingham Palace filtering down to us plebs behind the plough in the hinterland was met, as you might imagine, with a certain degree of shoulder shrugging indifference. On the other hand, albeit less rustically, they had their own rows to hoe and I imagined it was hard work having to muster enthusiasm to clamber onto the hamster wheel of social obligation with harrowing regularity—exhausting but necessary for those for whom tradition was indeed cathartic. We were out there on our own, but for an enormous slice of the populace, royalty was both a distraction and security blanket for a nation recuperating from such universal upheaval.

The history was fascinating of course, a lineage stretching back centuries, a family tree littered with an assortment of thick branches and brittle twigs. Murderers, madmen, sadists, rapists, pedophiles, alcoholics, bigamists, and buggerers, batshit crazy were a great proportion of them. It's no wonder an aura of nuttiness enveloped them, a peculiarity inhabiting their bloodline, and a testament indeed to he who said, "The poor are insane but the rich are eccentric."

So it was that destiny did indeed have the last laugh, for in the years following my earliest successes, I was to have several interesting encounters with the House of Windsor. This was obviously due to my close proximity to a certain rock star and our friendship with an influential neighbor and royal conduit.

Bryan Forbes was a highly esteemed postwar inhabitant of the British film industry. Coming up through the ranks he ran the roughshod route of dogsbody acting, all the way up to directing influential English classics, finally becoming chief of production and managing director of EMI Films before retiring into an enviable life of doing what he damn well pleased. He penned two autobiographies, multiple novels, and dabbled once more in direction while simultaneously hobnobbing with screen legends and royalty. He was witty and charming with an encyclopedic knowledge of both literature and film, constantly crackling with joie de vivre. He along with his elegant other half, the actress Nanette Newman, and their delightful daughters, Sarah and Emma, became a fixture in both my and Elton's lives for a number of years.

Although he came from humble beginnings and grew up in what then was the low-income area of West Ham, Bryan, most likely through theatrical ties and his obvious desire to adopt a more upper-class persona, became quite grand in his diction and delivery. An animated conversationalist, he would wield his ever-present cigarette like a baton as he held forth on all manner of anecdotal vignettes and trivia. Everything from the last deathbed words of George V, "Bugger Bognor," apparently, to stories of the Queen Mother shopping unrecognized at Fortnum & Mason. The upshot of this one being that when a hapless sales representative did finally pay attention to her and condescendingly inquired as to how her husband was, she airily replied, "Oh, he's still the King."

Our collective company also afforded us many memorable moments. There was a highly entertaining dinner where I watched incredulously as an immaculate Peter O'Toole ate and drank with one hand while simultaneously chain-smoking and ingesting alpine lines of cocaine with the other.

And it's hard to forget Yul Brynner educating me in the alarming origin of earrings. In gruesome detail he informed me that Tartar warriors, in a gesture of seemingly antagonistically driven respect for their enemy, wore large hoops in their ears so that in the event of their decapitation their adversaries had something with which to hang their heads on their saddles. True or false wasn't important; what was, was that when the "King of Siam" extols on the virtues of extreme courtesy, young men with pierced ears pay attention.

Bryan—bless his heart—did on occasion have a habit of lapsing into overarticulated pretension. One only has to tune in to the flowery narrative he provided for *Elton John and Bernie Taupin Say Goodbye Norma Jean and Other Things*, the documentary he directed in 1973. While very much a product of its time, it's Bryan's commentary that gets most of the laughs today: *There is a scent of fresh mown grass outside but not a suspicion of it inside, He writes self-isolated in a nostalgic ivory tower*, and the eternally classic reference to me as *the Cartier-Bresson of rock and roll*. This is at a time when the compliment compared with my not-altogether-eloquent presence in this feature made for an absurd comparison, not to mention my then-complete ignorance as to who the legendary master of 35 mm candid photography was.

Through Bryan's involvement with the National Youth Theatre and its patronage by members of the royal family, Elton soon fell into favor as a charitable source of revenue for this worthy cause. However, after a couple of benefit concerts, his generosity was hijacked by the crown and channeled into securing his services as an in-house jukebox. On the cusp of global superstardom, Elton John became the musical brandy and cigars for a motley group of blue bloods and upper-crust insiders.

In effect, this was entertainment provided gratis simply by token of "Think yourself lucky." In the minds of royal procurers, it mattered not a wit, the privilege of royal request outweighing all else. While this is a bit like "Mr. Sinatra, would you mind singing while we take tea, but keep it down a little," it's not totally unrealistic, and was quite honestly in my mind a little presumptuous in its assumed antiquated obligation.

I've never been a pitchfork and torch revolutionary, but I couldn't help but equate the underappreciated indulgence of satiated nobility reclining free of charge inches away from a pop megastar with the working stiff who had to fork out a fiver for a nosebleed seat. "Let them eat cake," indeed I thought.

Inseparable as we were in those early days, suffice to say I duly accompanied my obliging buddy, quizzical and happy to be a fly on the wall for this initial foray into the surrealism of an intimate royal gig! Apart from the possible suggestion that Elton refrain from playing "The King Must Die" or standing on the piano to proclaim "Are you ready to rock, you royal motherfuckers!" I remained on the sidelines a mere tag-along and inconsequential shadow masquerading as a genial factotum.

The gig in question took place in what seemed like the bowels of Windsor Castle, the Queen's country residence in Berkshire, twenty-five miles from central London. Like everything associated with the monarchy, the room in which Elton was to perform was musty and drab as if hanging in a capsulated time warp waiting for some new age prince to come and kiss it into the twentieth century. The audience was slim but packed with enough overdressed patricians and eccentricity to warrant weirdness of the first order. The only recognizable presence and actual product of modernity was Patrick Anson, Fifth Earl of Lichfield who, while well respected as a celebrity photographer, was equally renowned as a notorious libertine. This fact was soon established when during a particularly genteel rendition of "Your Song," said earl keeled over and crashed to the ground in an intoxicated stupor. Not a head turned and no attention was payed to this unfortunate interruption. It was as if it was a standard procedure, something expected and simply a repetitive occurrence. In its immediate aftermath, the Queen simply turned her head slightly, said, "Lichfield's gorn again," and in came the cleanup crew. Four footmen, powdered wigs and all, trundled down the aisle, picked up the unconscious earl, and whisked him out as if under a cloak of invisibility.

Then there was Princess Margaret. Princess Margaret was supposed to be the freewheeling loose cannon of the Windsor household, the token dolly bird counteracting the stiffer upper lip of her anointed big sister. She floated out of the '60s bitter and burnt, albeit not surprising I suppose given the prices paid and the ultimatums forced upon her by a primitive set of values both archaic and cruel. Society enjoyed her as much as she enjoyed it, but there always appeared to be the notion on display that somewhere on her person nestled an icy dagger, a cruel streak that seemed impossible to hide.

It was after another charity concert at the Festival Hall that I found myself along with Elton and the band at a reception and dinner hosted by the princess at Kensington Palace. Kensington Palace isn't one of Christopher Wren's finest moments, a Jacobean-styled pile of bricks that stretches to an excessive length with no interesting angles to make it seem comfortably habitable. Situated directly off Kensington High Street down the road apiece from Harrods luxury superstore, it was back then fronted by an unimaginative set of wrought-iron gates and guarded by a lone bobby, unarmed and seemingly uninterested in anything including security.

The reception was in a large sitting room where waitstaff passed hors d'oeuvres, and the prerequisite liveried footman lined the walls and flanked Her Highness. Princess Margaret was positioned at the far end of the room, regally situated at the head of the receiving line. OK! Here we go again! No problem lining up and saying thanks for having me, common courtesy as you would at a wedding reception or the like, but no, not here. Royal protocol insists on subjugation, in the presence of royalty you must bow from the waist, or if female, curtsy with flair. Believe me, I have no problem with bowing if it's a custom created on equal terms. Take the Japanese who are adept at making this formality a greeting that is altogether charming, but when it's one-sided with no reciprocation from the opposite party, and when the blood that runs through your veins is exactly the same, it just seems simply elitist.

All that aside, and not wishing to ruffle feathers, I duly got in line and waited my turn to genuflect accordingly. In my estimation, I was sartorially presentable in a well-tailored but snug white velvet suit that screamed pop star chic. Fully on course to do the right thing, circumstances as they were, and within feet of feigning allegiance, you can imagine my surprise to witness the nicotine-addicted princess, Countess of Snowdon and second in line to the throne, turn to the nearest footman available and proclaim in a voice loud enough to cut glass, "Where are my fucking Winstons?"

This unrefined demand happened to coordinate itself to the exact moment of my introduction, which, as fate would have it, included me bowing low and splitting my pants from crotch to shirttail.

I'm not sure whether it was my look of extreme consternation or my unfortunate body language, but I must have given the game away for while I attempted to nimbly back out of my predicament and into the ether, Fagash Maggie homed in on my fashion malfunction like a buzzard on a gut wagon.

"Did we have an accident?" she inquired dryly.

Unable to retreat into my vortex of humiliation, all I could do was confirm her assumption, a response that elicited a sly smile and two sharply snapped fingers. Out of nowhere a smart young woman appeared, curtsying profusely and paying heed. After a few whispered words from the princess she turned and with charming authority said, "Follow me, please."

Trailing in her wake, I learned that this personage was Margaret's lady-in-waiting, a sort of upmarket PA, but with better manners and none of the attitude. She informed me that Her Highness had allotted her the task of "sewing your trousers back together," a daunting enough proposition given the inevitable questions of how and where.

Was she going to sequester me away into a vacant loo and have me pass her the offending article through a crack in the door? Was I to sit naked from the waist down in some chilly vestibule for Lord knows how long, ruminating on my righteous humiliation?

Not on your life. I was handed a nice fluffy robe and ushered into Princess Margaret's private study where I duly disrobed and dropped my ripped britches into the outstretched arms of my very own personal royal tailor.

To be left unattended in this intimate space initially left me not so much agitated as perplexed. There was some concern on my part that a total stranger left unattended, not to mention in a state of undress in such privileged quarters, might be discovered by parties unaware that I was there by invitation. Invitation, I might add, that could be miscon-strued as something other than what it was. Don't think it didn't cross my mind that a certain Antony Armstrong-Jones, aka the First Earl of

Snowdon, might barge in at any second to find yours truly comfortably situated sans pants in his wife's inner sanctum.

With this unsettling thought in my mind, I attempted to offset it by focusing on the memorabilia and personal effects littering her desk and strewn around the room. With an absent conscience and my scruples unchecked for any hint of tarnished values, I did a Loony Tunes eye scroll up, down, and all around in search of any hidden cameras. In those halcyon days prior to cell phones only my tainted memory was to be the archivist of this surreal interlude. I just recall a lot of framed photographs of family members and general hobnobbing, none of which gave any great insight into her proclivities other than a fondness for alcohol, cigarettes, and celebrities, and these in no particular order. What I do recall was coming to my senses and succumbing to my better judgment. Best not to push it and be caught red-handed rifling through her drawers or caught with my feet up on her desk thumbing through her diary. A wise choice, indeed, for as this sense of contrition washed over me the door opened and in came my pants.

I returned to the gathering as dinner was being served, at which point Lord Snowdon did turn up channeling Joe Pesci and demanding to know where his fucking dinner was. Apparently, this adjective and the demand to be fed straddled a shared line between monarchy and the working class. With this volatile invasion, the princess fled in tears and that was pretty much it.

Surprisingly, and to her credit, I was amazed when many years later at a party held in her honor in Beverly Hills she recalled the incident with the same clandestine good humor as she had on the evening it happened. For all the talk of her using the world as her ashtray, some small fragment of my cynical arsenal crumbled away that day, and I was left with a momentary sense of sympathy for this careworn scion of British nobility.

My last dalliance with the House of Windsor took place ironically at Elton's house in Windsor. It was a delightful summer day and the Queen Mother was coming for tea. Of course this sort of thing happens when you're best friends with Elton John, a proverbial magnet for an oasis of cultural and exalted personages. The Queen Mum, as she was referred to in the old country, was perfectly delightful and, in a generous but experimental gesture on our host's part, was seated directly opposite yours truly. This turned out to be no cause for alarm as I and the old girl hit it off, breaking bread over summer pudding and baseball, a game that I was fanatical about and of which she seemed unnervingly knowledgeable. I think it was because she didn't look down on the boys of summer that warmed me to her and put me completely at ease. As we conversed, I had time to observe her at close quarters and couldn't help but find it charming that if you imagined this wasn't the matriarch of the British Empire, she could easily be your quirky old granny, a fact made more so by her lipstick-smudged teeth and chipped nail polish.

With lunch at an end, I presumed she'd be hopping in the Daimler and be whisked away to wherever she was residing these days. Not so! With a breezy après-tea glow in her cheeks, she expressed a desire to stroll the grounds. What was even more surprising was that she chose me to be her guide, and with that, rather than choosing the front door, she stepped through the picture window and into the garden. Following behind and aware of protocol, I kept my distance until she motioned me over and took my arm, further breaking down my apathy for royalty and only endearing me to her further. Sallying forth we meandered along the side of the house until we reached a spot where upon Windsor Castle could be seen clearly in the distance, its flag unfurled and flying all the way up indicating the Queen was in residence.

"Oh look, Mr. Taupin, my daughter's home," remarked the Queen Mother nonchalantly.

Indeed!

Tumultuous as they were, the war years, due to friendships my father made, were some of the happiest times of his life. My father (*center*) remained a soldier long after his military service ended.

Bernie Taupin Archives

Without my mother and grandfather J. L. P. Cort (aka Poppy), my education in the arts would have been nonexistent. School taught me nothing I cared about; they taught me all I wanted to know.

Bernie Taupin Archives

The Fauntleroy years. Posing for the camera around the age of three.

Bernie Taupin Archives

Back to square one. With my father's desire to become self-employed, we returned to spartan conditions. Situated in the quaintly named village of Owmby-by-Spital, this crumbling relic's lack of utilities tested our resolve.

Bernie Taupin Archives

Making our preferences clear. I load up as my brother Tony (*right*) dreams of soccer stardom.

Bernie Taupin Archives

More elaborate than a tennis racket in front of the mirror. I get up on a chicken crate and channel Eddie Cochran playing a guitar with no strings!

Bernie Taupin Archives

The original manuscript for "Scarecrow," the very first song Elton and I ever wrote. Even though I had no idea of lyrical composition, Elton managed to make something of my free-form take on what I felt was currently in vogue. Note Elton's chord chart scribbled in the margins.

The ad that started it all. *The New Musical Express*, June 17, 1967. My submission was far more bizarre than most people have been led to believe.

Bernie Taupin Archives

The Kaftan Kids. Starting out in '68, this was one of the first shots of Elton and me taken together.

David Larkham © 1969 HST Global Limited, Rocket Entertainment

He told us to quit writing for others and write for ourselves. Elton and I with our mentor and friend Steve Brown (*center*) and our pal and cover designer David Larkham, April 1969.

Photo by Gill Brown; Courtesy of David Larkham

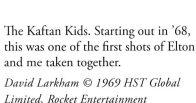

Elton and I take on Hugh Hefner and Barbi Benton at foosball at the Chicago Playboy Mansion, 1975. We won!

Image courtesy of David Nutter

They say you shouldn't meet your heroes. Wrong. Frank Sinatra was charming, hospitable, and made me feel like a million bucks. Backstage with the Chairman at the Universal Amphitheatre, 1978.

Alice Cooper Archives

John Lennon was at his most disarming and delightful during the short time we spent together. Aboard the Starship on route to Boston (*above*), November 20, 1974. I'm obviously amused by his self-deprecating inquiry as to whether I'd ever heard his song, "Across the Universe." *Sam Emerson*

Eight days later, performing with Elton at Madison Square Garden (*right*). He refused to return for the encore unless I came with him. A year later, we would have a reunion in LA, during which fortuitous encounters with Bob Marley and Brian Wilson were had.

Sam Emerson

For a decade, I competed on the circuit as a nonpro cutter.

Midge Ames Photo

The cowboy ethic holds no room for playacting. Saddled up and ready to go, I was one hundred percent serious in my goals.

Christine Lester-Deats

With my mother on a trip to New York in 1999, two years before the Twin Towers fell.

Bernie Taupin Archives

Arguably one of the greatest and most prolific songwriters of all time. Willie Dixon was a generous friend who welcomed me into his family and remains one of a few individuals whose charisma, wisdom, and knowledge have had a profound effect on my life.

Bernie Taupin Archives

What benefits a legend most? Our song, "The Ballad of Dennis Hopper and Harry Dean," performed in the company of the man himself during our Farm Dogs residency at the Mint in 1998.

Katrina Plummer

Live in the canyon. Fronting Farm Dogs at an outdoor festival in Topanga Canyon, 1998.

Katrina Plummer

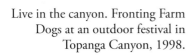

Fate lent a hand at a time I thought I'd never get it right. Meeting Heather in 1998 restructured my entire life and ultimately led me to realize what love really means. Taken at the ranch two years after we met. We were married in 2004. *Bernie Taupin Archives*

The King. Found in a hole in the ground in the ass end of California. Bunker was my canine soulmate. Like a cranky old man in a dog suit, he was as devoted to me as I was to him. I still miss him.

Bernie Taupin Archives

Visiting backstage at Staples Center, Los Angeles, 2014, (*clockwise*): Elton, the author, Heather, Charley, and Georgey.

James Marcus Haney

With paint a thing of the past, I gravitated toward more eclectic work modeled around found objects like "American Burka," a 1995 mummified mannequin; 68 X 17 X 12, fabric, stain, cord, wire, barbed wire and metal.

Photo by Michael DiDonna

Playing with fire. At work in my studio sometime in the early 2000s.

Bernie Taupin Archives

Elton and Whoopi Goldberg look on as I attempt to keep up with Robin Williams's tsunami of ad libs. I was saddened immensely by Robin's death. He was a thing of beauty in a cantankerous world. *Jeff Christensen*

The Taupin family, Christmas 2021: the author, Charley, Heather, and Georgey.

Lauren Mauve Photography

Still connected after all these years. If a picture paints a thousand words, this is it. One of my favorite photos of us and one that says it all.

Lester Cohen

Rocky Mountain High for Real

I ain't stayin' at no ranch.

—AL GREEN

S tanding next to a white stretch limo the length of a city block, Al
Green issued the above statement with succinct aplomb. Immaculately
attired in a suit matching his ride, the Memphis hit machine was making
his preferences abundantly clear.

He'd been offered accommodations after performing with the soft
jazz-rock combo Chicago, and he was not impressed. While his sights
might squarely have been on a five-star Denver hotel, his assessment
of Caribou Ranch was unsubstantiated. He may have equated such a
place with hillbillies and horseshit, but I'm only too sure that was the
stereotypical observation of a flashy Memphis urbanite.

Caribou Ranch Recording Studio saw all nature of famous visitors
during its years of operation. In January 1974, we arrived for the first
time just as Mr. Green was making his dramatic departure. So while
the "Last of the Great Soul Singers" drove off for an appointment with
a pot of boiling grits and his spiritual reawakening, Elton and myself
along with the boys in the band checked in and checked it out.

Named after a local ghost town, Caribou Ranch sat on four thousand acres in the Rocky Mountains near Nederland, Colorado. Two
years previously, producer James William Guercio bought the property
and spent mucho dinero building a state-of-the-art recording facility.
With the same foresight and a dream of attracting an international
clientele, he had surrounded it with an agglomeration of comfortable

cabins. This was a far cry from the Château d'Hérouville where we had recorded our previous three albums. While the accommodations at the château had been functional at best, everything at Caribou Ranch was tweaked to massage its guests into feeling spoiled. Every cabin came with roaring fireplaces, Chesterfield sofas, and comfortable beds, including Grover Cleveland's in the master suite. Ornamental rugs covered antiqued hardwood floors and an array of exotic taxidermy covered the walls, guaranteed to keep Paul McCartney recording elsewhere. There were TVs, stereos, and a fine mess hall where decent food was prepared and amazing ice-cold fresh milk was available 24/7. Foreshadowing my future in ranching and embracement of the Western lifestyle, Caribou also boasted some decent trail horses, which I would take out regularly into the mountains to an abandoned silver mine standing on the edge of a small creek. The tranquility was sublime, the only sound being the wind sighing in the depleted timbers and the rippling water gently flowing past thickets of huckleberry and wild rose. A far cry from rock and roll, it was an embraceable equanimity in the eye of a hurricane.

In keeping with Château d'Hérouville, it even boasted a haunted cabin named Running Bear. It was supposedly built over an Indian burial ground and tales were rife of wailing and weirdness year-round. The Rockies were indeed home to a handful of Native American tribes including Arapaho, Ute, Cheyenne, and Comanche, so it's entirely possible that some traversed this area and elevated their dead. Personally, I think a little snake oil was being peddled here, especially given the abundance of hallucinogenics on hand. But never having stayed in that cabin, I'll refrain from a conclusive opinion.

I did have one startling encounter that, while not qualifying as spooky, was temporarily unsettling. It was always pitch-black at night in the mountains and what little light there was came from the moon, and the brightness varied depending on whatever phase it was in. I was taking out the trash and the alleyway next to the cabin was lit up by a waxing crescent that shone a clear path to the receptacles. As I was approaching the cans, one of them tipped forward with a loud crash depositing not only the contents but a rotund black bear. The bear did a perfect circus roll and stood up. I backed up and froze, and the bear did the same thing. As if on cue I yelled, he growled, and simultaneously we both turned tail and fled.

After France, being back in the States had its perks. The luxury once again of TV allowed me to indulge in my passion for football. In my cabin on my couch, a couple of cold ones close at hand, I got to watch Super Bowl VIII. It was January 1974 when the Miami Dolphins took down the Minnesota Vikings, 24–7. Fullback Larry Csonka dominated the field, the Dolphins all-time leading rusher with 6,737 yards and 53 touchdowns over his career. Csonka was the game's MVP.

Writing songs and making music is always either partly cloudy or completely unrecollectable. Why this is I'm not completely sure, but I imagine it has something to do with the concentration involved and the mental fatigue that follows. I love what I do—I always have— and the satisfaction I receive from it is immeasurable. But at times, it wears me out and the inspirations and specific locales where they were created occasionally take flight once the work is done. What's important is what's on the page. As long as it moves me, that it's equipped with something unique, then I've done my job. Once Elton guides it through the next phase and ultimately commits it to tape, *voilà!* written in stone. What I'm simply saying is that as long as it's preserved indefinitely, it's not terribly important how or where it was conceived. The meaning of it, if not obvious, should be open to interpretation without any explanation from me. It's like abstract art: you stand in front of it and use your imagination. Thousands of words have been written about Jackson Pollock's drip paintings, but in all honesty he probably just woke up one morning and said, "Ooo, I've got a good idea."

We were recording the *Captain Fantastic* album and John Lennon turned up to help cut our version of "Lucy in the Sky with Diamonds." Now, I stand to be corrected, but I really believe this was my idea. I'd been in the UK the previous Christmas and was watching *Yellow Submarine* on TV. Under the influence of an excellent bottle of Château Margaux and a nascent sense of mellow yuletide ingenuity, I'd heard the Beatle classic with appropriating ears. Wouldn't it be the absolute apex of presumptuous cheek to hijack this psychedelic anthem, steal the definitive article, and appropriate it for our canon? Elton was the biggest star in the world at this point and I felt he could get away with it. He'd done it magnificently and with great success a year earlier with "Pinball Wizard," so why not let lightning strike twice. I called him and he probably paid no heed, rationalizing that I was drunk and nuts, and forgot about it until its author showed up at Caribou, at which point he suggested it, and *ta-da!* No pushback for me, just the simple pleasure of keeping our name in lights.

After we'd completed the *Captain Fantastic* album, Elton decided to change the band. We returned to Caribou to make the next record with only Davey Johnstone and Ray Cooper retained from the old lineup. The rest were a completely different crew and with it came a distinctly different sound. Nigel Olsson and Dee Murray had been with Elton in the original trio from day one, so their departure was radical, and I'm sure traumatic not to mention disappointing for them. As a rhythm section they were unsurpassable. One has only to listen to *17-11-70*, the live album we recorded in a New York studio, to know what I mean. It has remained a travesty that they along with Davey have never truly earned the recognition they so richly deserve.

Nigel and Dee returned to the band in 1980 and would continue recording and performing live sporadically throughout the following decade. Sadly, Dee developed skin cancer and battled it for several years before suffering a stroke and passing away in 1992. His singular style and the percussive complexity of sound he rang from his instrument define him as one of the best there ever was.

Dee was a good guy, his only flaw being his inability to handle liquor. He wasn't a mean drunk, just an annoying one. It didn't appear to take too much to tip him over the edge, and when it did he'd revert to boorish behavior. Once, at Canadian customs in an exaggerated stage whisper he suggested we all hide our drugs. The Great White North harbors some of the world's most ornery immigration officials, and they tore us to bits. Then there was the time on a private flight that after one too many he began jabbing everyone on the plane with a fork. This incident got him rechristened the Stabber by the band and reprimanded heavily by all parties assaulted. My last recollection of his overdoing it was one morning on the island of Montserrat. We were recording there and I was driving to the studio in my rented jeep. Nonchalantly looking around and admiring the scenery, I saw Dee fast asleep in a cow pasture, curled up in the fetal position, an egret perched on his head.

It was a scrappier band that congregated to record *Rock of the Westies* in the summer of 1975. The raw edginess of that album is not to everyone's taste, but it is totally indicative of the exposed wires that propelled it. Drugs had been slowly creeping into the equation, addiction by increments if you will. Elton readily admits that his first brush with cocaine came during our first trip to the ranch and the recording of the *Caribou* album in early 1974. It didn't infuse the time period nor did it overwhelm the *Captain Fantastic* sessions later in 1974. However, by the time *Rock of the Westies* arrived along with the new band a blizzard was brewing and it wasn't coming out of the mountains.

If you compare the modish-looking bunch in the gatefold sleeve of the *Captain Fantastic* cover with the band that graces the rear of *Rock of the Westies,* you'll witness a sort of tribal transformation. The motley crew you see is every inch the motley crew you got: individuals who look more likely to be clearing a log jam on the Columbia River than creating mayhem in the mountains of Colorado.

I'm sure each member of the new band bought with them their individual vices. Alcohol and drugs were the prime suspects, but along with that were botched romances, failing marriages, and hallucinatory depression, the latter I'm sure instigated by overindulgence in all the former. In a bizarre *Valley of the Dolls* scenario, our new bass player, Kenny Passarelli, had entered into an affair with my estranged first wife, taking her and setting her up in his Boulder home while simultaneously working on our record. Salacious and grubby maybe, but in this case redemptive, for by doing so he did me the tremendous service in alleviating me of what had been for a brief spell a monstrously depressing marriage.

In other incidents, we had several band members in various snowmobile accidents. In a potentially deadly one, percussionist Ray Cooper left the designated path along a mountain ledge to be saved only by the outstretched limbs of a strategically placed lodgepole pine. Instead of plunging to his demise, he was cradled like a baby, in turn living to bang his gong again and again.

It was like hitting a piñata every day and waiting to see what would come out. One of the more unsettling incidents didn't have to do with a member of the band but with our engineer, Jeff Guercio, and brother of the owner of Caribou Ranch, James. Sadly, after ingesting a little too much doobie magic he decided to make the ill-advised choice of going hang gliding. His faculties impaired, he managed to kill himself by flying into the side of a mountain.

There seemed to be mini dramas and soap operas unfolding all the time. It was like a chess game played by individuals who should have chosen checkers. The elaborate intrigues combined with an unhealthy dose of self-pity made for moves overamplified and more complicated than they needed to be. Obviously, cocaine played an enormous hand in this, and when combined with lethal weed and bourbon, not to mention the altitude, the outcome isn't pretty. When not defended, king takes pawn every time.

We were all playing with fire, but some were getting burned more than others. Whether it was Davey Johnstone on acid sitting in a wheel-chair watching Indian war parties burn down our cabins, Elton OD'ing on valium, or random members of the band staggering around like Jack Nicholson at the conclusion of *The Shining*, the emulsification of vari-ables proved the inmates were running the asylum. I'm not sure how, but with all this insanity we still managed to make a record.

Luckily, there were moments of levity to offset the constant drama and soap opera nature attached to *Rock of the Westies*. One day, Stevie Wonder turned up and in the process played a couple of tricks on me. Far more amiable than Al Green, Stevie seemed to enjoy his surround-ings and got into the spirit of things by convincing everyone that he could see perfectly well. Emerging from my cabin one morning, I was surprised to see Stevie out front sitting at the wheel of a jeep. Bidding me a good morning he asked me if I wanted a ride to the studio. Now the studio was only about five hundred yards away, but it was still a daunting prospect. How could I refuse? What was I going to do? Insult him and say, "No, thanks, I'll walk." Of course he drove there perfectly, and looking back it's obvious that this was his party piece. He'd had someone coach him several times, and being highly intuitive, his sensory perception honed to perfection, it was a trick quickly mastered. He did the same thing with a twenty dollar bill. He'd stand next to you and say, "I think you dropped a Jackson" and, of course, one would be there right between your feet.

In the wake of Dee and Nigel's departure and before decamping to Colorado for *Rock of the Westies*, Elton had hauled the new band to Amsterdam. The reasons were twofold: rehearse for a major show at Wembley Stadium and see how everyone gelled musically. Depending on how you looked at it, Amsterdam might not have been the wisest choice given the nature of this band and the reputation of the Netherlands capitol. Legal weed, copious amounts of drugs, a thriving red light district, and a roaring club scene so morally unrestricted that they should have renamed it Sodom on the Grachtengordel. It might have been home to the Van Gogh Museum and the Anne Frank House, but this lot turned it into the *Village of the Damned*. My liquor bill at the hotel alone came to more than my room, and the lobby at times was invaded by roadies in nothing but their underpants hiding in the potted plants and biting the ankles of guests.

Unfortunately, during this trip Elton had sequestered himself in his suite at the Hilton, and with the exception of rehearsals, he pretty much stayed there. Nursing a bad case of the blues caused by unrequited love, he placated his pain by playing "I'm Not in Love" by 10cc repeatedly. Luckily, I didn't mind the song, and while sustained listening sorely tested one's mettle, I felt it important to lend my support. On hand to assist in this job were Elton's longtime confidant and friend Tony King and Connie Pappas, part of our US management team. Elton loved and respected Tony ever since we crossed paths with him in our nascent days at Dick James's offices. He was flamboyant, smart, and witty, and he was a conduit to all manner of musical connections. Originally, he'd worked in A&R and promotion, but conventional business had restraints that couldn't corral his panoptic vision. He would go on to work for George Martin's AIR Studios, individual Beatles, and for a time was personal assistant to Mick Jagger, but I truly believe it was

Elton he had the most empathy for. He genuinely cared and could make him laugh and maneuver him out of a funk. These are things that I could not always do, and for this Tony commanded my respect. I was highly suspicious of people who gravitated into Elton's personal space. I consider myself an excellent judge of character and can sniff out a phony like a polar bear smelling a seal through three feet of ice. I know if I like someone within minutes of meeting them, so I could get pretty mama bear when it came to my best friend. If someone was good to my buddy and had his best interests at heart without looking for a handout, they had my trust. There were many who didn't make the grade and thankfully fell by the wayside, and there are those who were and remain the genuine article.

Connie Pappas was another gem. An efficient and hardworking staple of our organization, she got things done with zero fuss and charming expertise. I admired her and we had a congenial relationship from day one, but in Amsterdam her stock rose in my estimation. We bonded over our concern for Elton, and in doing so initiated a repartee that was akin to that of sibling fusion. She had a positive outlook, and simply put, she was just plain sensible, her matter-of-fact rationale eschewing general histrionics with unadorned practicality. In this she was unique in our world, and in that short time it helped massage a little sanity into the circus that was our perpetual pinwheel. Connie has remained my friend. She is a woman of deep faith and is married to the remarkable, multitalented musician and songwriter Chris Hillman. They have been together for over forty years now, have a beautiful family, and are both an inspiration.

In writing this and thinking back on that lengthy era of Elton's ever-changing mood swings, I've had time to consider the consequences of it on my own psyche. His reputation for erratic behavior manifested itself in many different forms. I'm not a psychologist, but I know he was angry and unhappy inside. His success and the pressure of enormous fame coupled with the ever-increasing amount of drugs and alcohol he was consuming so that he could decompress was having an adverse effect. Sometimes it was just moodiness, sometimes it was raging irrationality, but what was hardest on me was that he was uncommunicative. In our younger struggling days, it was simple disappointment that hampered us. We felt we were never going to get a break, and it played havoc with our dreams. However, we had each other, and each other only, to lean on. We were an army of two against a phalanx of nos and maybes. Still we soldiered on because of one simple thing: we talked it out. We regrouped, we immersed ourselves in the inspirational music of the times and were rejuvenated by it. We went home, metaphorically slapped each other in the face, and wrote another song. We believed in tomorrow because we believed in each other.

Now, an instant wall appeared whenever displeasure or an arbitrary tantrum ensued. If it was disruptive and unsubstantiated, he'd avoid addressing my body language that spoke volumes about my displeasure. In truth, I would feel physically sick. And I know internally he was embarrassed. It was an uncomfortable standoff, but his rage always won the battle. He would just ramp it up in order to stifle the negotiators until the tempest subsided on his terms. I wasn't always there, but when I was it was a masochistic force that compelled me to stay the course even when there was nothing I could do about it. Ultimately, I'd wind up exhausted somewhere, angry at my inability to solve the problem, and performing my own exorcism by any means necessary.

Meanwhile, with rehearsals in full swing, it became apparent a fly was swimming in the ointment. One member recruited for the new outfit who seemed excessive was guitarist Jeff "Skunk" Baxter. Since we already had two incredibly versatile players filling this spot, the addition of one more was in my view and others as over the top. Baxter was a proficient axe slinger who'd played with The Doobie Brothers, Steely Dan, and Spirit, dressed like Che Guevara, and was obsessed with military defense. It was apparent from the get-go that he was the odd man out, and while he was a genial enough guy, it was obvious that he just didn't gel. I think this is proved correct by the rumor that when we played the following gig at Wembley Stadium his guitar was turned off at the soundboard. Either way, it proved to be Jeff's one and only show with the fledgling Elton John Band.

Amsterdam was diabolically unfettered, but the rehearsals that took place in a giant warehouse were dynamic and successful, and often went ten hours a day. It was the downtime that was a liquid river of insanity and marching powder.

Our most hedonistic achievement was renting a luxury barge stockpiled to the gills with alcohol and drugs. With the band and road crew aboard, and joined by a visiting Ringo Starr, we took off down the Herengracht for a day that will live in infamy. By the time we'd got back that evening we had acquired, along with our complete intoxication, an undetermined number of female pedestrians; we had also lost several roadies in the canal and had an ex-Beatle ask if he could join the band.

It was insane, and for the ten days or so we were there it remained the pinnacle of our excess. It was also the one time (outside of rehearsals) I imagine we were all together at the same time. As is the way, factions form and individuals peel off into cliques, couples, and loners. While I have always fallen into the latter, I wasn't averse to joining in. I'd drift in, I'd drift out, but arrangements weren't key. I didn't make plans. I'm not sure anyone did as we were all a little too toasted for regimentation, but there were those who had aligned themselves over the years and felt the necessity for the camaraderie they had forged. I never had that. I never felt obliged to and never felt comfortable with being joined at the hip. My soul brother was Elton, but even then, we swam in completely different currents, both socially and sexually.

I did spend some time in the company of Ringo, his girlfriend photographer, Nancy Andrews, and Ringo's genial financial advisor, Hilary Gerrard. It was in this coterie of friends that I found myself slipping into a clandestine relationship that might not have been wholly honorable. No question about it, with the exception of Nancy, we were all alcoholics in the textbook sense. However, I believe I was what is termed as a functioning one, and this is what had Nancy gravitating to me over their week in the city. Ringo was a jovial drunk, loved to sing, loved to stay up late, and loved his brandy Alexanders. Hilary was more level in his imbibing. The straight man in the comedic duo, he was quirky and bright in a sort of artsy Gandalf way. Sensibly, *he* drank his brandy with milk because he had an ulcer!

It may have been a wishful mea culpa in order to ease my guilt, but I believe things were winding down with Ringo and Nancy. I got the impression she was tiring of playing second fiddle to a bottle of Courvoisier and a group of boisterous friends. When you had to compete with the likes of Harry Nilsson and Keith Moon on a daily basis, it'll wear you down eventually. I don't know, I could be wrong. I know she loved him and she adored his friends. Hell, she took enough pictures of them, but in our late-night calls I sensed her frustration. Intricate details crumble to dust over the years, but the ultimate upshot was that soon after this, they split and we took up with each other for a short time back in LA. I adored Ringo, as I still do, and justify this as a simple respectful romantic transition much in the same way that Pattie Harrison segued from George to Eric Clapton. Nancy was as smart as she was beautiful, and it was an emancipation of sorts, given my recent track record at the time, to be involved with someone with sophistication and class.

The plan for now was to fly to the UK and headline the show at Wembley Stadium. It would be the first for this current band and was, unfortunately, not a success. Elton chose to perform the *Captain Fantastic* album in its entirety. Not a good idea, since the record had only just been released and hardly anyone in the crowd was familiar with it. To add insult to injury, it was a glorious summer day and the Beach Boys had just vacated the stage after wowing the crowd with a solid set of back-to-back hits. The audience was ecstatic and spent and in no mood to listen to an unfamiliar set of autobiographical tunes. They left in droves, administering a sting to our egos and a dark cloud to a clear day. With our tails between our legs, we flew back to Caribou and commenced recording *Rock of the Westies*.

In a telling finale, and as history informs us when plague and pestilence ravage society, nothing heals like tongues of fire. Caribou Studio burned down in 1985, never to officially reopen.

The Days of Wine and Noses

Vices are sometimes only virtues carried to excess!

—CHARLES DICKENS

Perched on a sloped embankment of emerald green grass, it sat on the corner of Cordell Drive and North Doheny Drive, no more than a minute from Sunset Boulevard. Ensconced in the wishbone of the two streets, it was both exposed and secluded, its facade naked to the eye of traffic, yet its internal demographics wrapped within walls of white stucco and twisted foliage. Its secrecy assured, as it would be for years, it was my first and most quintessential of LA homes, its inner design ever changing over several decades, from stark rock star oblique to art nouveau pretension to a cornucopia of acceptable taste. Like most things at the time, it was afforded by success. I saw such a kaleidoscopic turnover in both relationships and personal development that it almost feels like I lived several different lives there. If the road of excess does indeed lead to the Palace of Wisdom, the ensuing years did, in reality, become a path littered with constantly evolving fads, pastimes, and recreational diversions either interesting, educational, or narcissistically irrelevant. Although I wrote a great deal of my work in the vicinity of recording studios and rented homes around the world, the lion's share of everything from 1974 to 1989 was executed in the office of that house at 1320 North Doheny Drive.

The revolving door was already operating, and as I moved in, my first wife was preparing to leave after barely breathing enough air into the place to register her presence at all. I was soon solo with little company in the way of furniture. Outside of a wicker kitchen table and chairs, a sofa and barstools in the den, a desk and chair in my office, and a bed, its interior was design-free. I doubt whether it was out of lack of interest, because I liked *stuff*. Most likely, the cost of a complete decorative do-over was not in my budget at the time, so it was necessary to just make do with what I could afford. It wasn't a bad deal. The house was airy and cool with plenty of sunlight shooting in to make it feel habitable without clutter. It had a mixture of Mexican tile and hardwood floors, an attractive winding stone staircase with a woven wrought-iron baluster leading to the second level, several bedrooms, a kitchen with character, and an elegant dining room. I wasn't complaining; it was mine, I was perfectly located, I was in LA, and most important, I was where I felt I belonged.

It also had a splendid backyard, completely cordoned off from any outside observation. It was all laid out in red brick, the encircling adobe walls dotted with stained glass portholes, a sizable pool, built-in barbecue, and avocado trees surrounding a firepit on the upper level. Along with all this, I also had a diverse and interesting collection of neighbors.

Directly across from my carport on the Cordell side of the house was the home of the legendary director George Cukor. Cukor was an enigma. A leading light in Hollywood's gay subculture, he had managed to survive in an era where his outing would surely have cost him his career. During his tenure in the director's chair, he had made fifty-odd movies. Many of them are certified classics, including *The Philadelphia Story*, *Gaslight*, *Adam's Rib*, *Dinner at Eight*, *Born Yesterday*, and *My Fair Lady*. A dapper man of impeccable taste, he was notorious for his Sunday afternoon parties attended by closeted celebrities and the attractive young men they'd hooked up with in gyms and bars around town. Like myself, his compound was enclosed to any snooping, so whatever funny business that was going on behind his fence, I was never going to get a look-see. Our only interaction was a friendly wave back and forth when he'd venture out to be chauffeured to and fro by the gentleman I assumed was his caretaker. I imagined he might see me washing my car, find me interesting, and invite me over. It never happened.

Outside of his clandestine festivities, he would also host soirees for his more aboveboard Hollywood chums, who on occasion I'd see either exiting or entering. One day, I saw an elegant middle-aged woman in an ugly old clunker stalled in the street not fifty feet from Cukor's front gate. The car was belching huge plumes of blue smoke that for some reason didn't seem to have the occupant of the vehicle unduly concerned. Coming to her assistance, I realized why. The driver was the no-nonsense and unflappable Katharine Hepburn. As valiantly as possible, and with the help of a couple of gardeners, we got her car to the curb. Inquiring if she would like me to call AAA, she delivered a line as classic as the woman herself, "Good Lord, no!" she said. "Just leave it there, I'll buy another one."

The other notable visitor worth mentioning was the great Anglo American novelist Christopher Isherwood, whose 1939 book *Goodbye to Berlin,* about the dying days of the Weimar Republic, was one of my very favorites. In 1951, it had been adapted into a Broadway play, *I Am a Camera,* and later into the 1966 film *Cabaret* starring Liza Minnelli, Joel Grey, and Michael York. York, as it happens, was another neighbor who lived just around the corner.

The buzzer on my side door rang one day, and when I opened it there was Isherwood. Because I was so familiar with his work, as well as a collector of it, I recognized him immediately. I think from the get-go he realized he'd made a mistake, got turned around, and hit the bell on the wrong side of the street. I'm not sure if he'd imbibed in a couple of pre-excursion cocktails or was merely momentarily distracted, but he was positively profuse in his apology and was absolutely delighted when I told him that Christopher Isherwood could ring my doorbell any day. He didn't invite me over either. I was beginning to get a complex.

On the opposite side of the house, directly to the right of me on Doheny, was an individual who was the absolute antithesis of George Cukor. Art Metrano was a big, loud, mega-macho, Brooklyn-born character actor best known for his role as Lieutenant Mauser in the lowbrow comedy series *Police Academy.* Every Saturday morning, he would play basketball with his cronies on his home court; it was so raucous and profane that at times it felt like they were located in my living room. On Saturday nights, he'd play another game with his wife that was so raucous and profane that at times it also sounded like it was in my living room. The thing is I rather enjoyed him. Like a big cartoon character espousing all the traits stereotypical in a prodigious good-natured palooka, he was like Peter Griffin, Bugs Bunny, and Bluto all rolled into one.

In the '80s, ambulances, sirens blaring and lights flashing, turned up on either side of my house. The first was in 1983 when George Cukor suffered a heart attack and died. The next was in 1989 after Art Metrano fell off a ladder, breaking his neck and seriously injuring his spinal cord. Their presence when I was in residence there, however, remains memorable. Sandwiched between refined culture and unfettered mayhem was a unique experience not easily forgotten.

Overlooking me at the very top of Cordell was the home of the mega-successful record producer Richard Perry. His home's most interesting feature was an outdoor glass shower located front and center and fully exposed to anyone driving or walking up the street. I couldn't tell you what soap he was using, but nothing else was left to the imagination.

My favorite neighbor without a doubt was the brilliant jazz pianist and composer Herbie Hancock. Me being a self-confessed jazz nut, Herbie's presence in the 'hood was thrilling. He lived several doors down to the left of me on Doheny, and he is one of the most charming and distinguished musicians I've ever met. A complete class act, his pedigree is impeccable from his rise to prominence taking over Red Garland's keyboard duties in Miles Davis's second great quintet to his classic recording *Maiden Voyage*, and on into the '70s with his jazz-fusion ensemble The Headhunters. Just being around Herbie made you stand up straighter, feel smarter, and invest your time wisely in becoming more aware of the intricate nuances of modern jazz. While not exactly bosom buddies, we did become friends. I didn't see as much of him when I left the area, but when I did run into him on occasion he was always a magical presence to me. I'm sorry to say I haven't seen him since he turned up at my sixtieth birthday party with Wayne Shorter! Who needs presents when you bring a gift like that?

I never lacked for company, and the considerate space of time between my first wife's departure and my second coming into the picture years later was an interesting mix of varying longevity and radically different personalities. I'm not going to rattle off a list of girlfriends here, that's not the point. What is, is the way that I interacted with them and how each one was appreciated. I never felt I was ever just using someone for a select purpose, and in the case of several of them they were good friends as much as bedfellows. From Day One I'd written lyrics that depicted the seedier side of life, many of them featuring unsavory characters, both male and female, although invariably with a sympathetic slant. An astute journalist once asked me if I was aware of how filthy an album *Goodbye Yellow Brick Road* was. Well, no, actually I hadn't until it was pointed out. I just thought it was poetic license. There was more meat on the bone in songs that depicted hardscrabble opportunists and questionable professions. Sure, there was an element of naivety to some of them, and, yes, a couple may have been inappropriate (the less said about "Island Girl" the better), but compared with what gets said in hard-core rap today, they're Hallmark friendly.

The point is, I was making this stuff up, not living it for real. It was my job to conjure up an illusion of something without people imagining I moonlighted as a dockland pimp or lived in a trailer park. So the women who came into my orbit for real did so for different reasons, but for the most part because they didn't feel threatened or put upon. One of the first girls to hang out at my house was an insanely cute Texan who was one of the original hostesses at Lou Adler's recently opened On The Rox. Linda was petite, completely adorable, and sweeter than homemade molasses. Looking like a sexed-up Betty Boop but unaware of it, she was a little shy, softly spoken, and didn't have a mean bone in her body. She had a roommate who, oddly enough, considered himself her boyfriend. They lived in a small apartment at the bottom of the hill behind the landmark West Hollywood liquor store, Gil Turner's. She hung out and stayed with me intermittently because she felt safe and was intrigued by the things that I liked. She'd never known anyone who read, listened to the kind of music I did, or watched movies that weren't box office hits. In turn, I gave her a copy of Dee Brown's *Bury My Heart at Wounded Knee*, took her to see Willie, Waylon, and The Outlaws at the Hollywood Bowl and to the Cinerama Dome to see Richard Harris in *The Return of a Man Called Horse*. Don't think this makes me look gallant or smart. When we went to catch The Outlaws I'd forgotten that I'd originally invited someone else and ended with two dates turning up at the house at the same time. Linda being Linda, she couldn't have cared less. Not so much for the third party, who turned a hose on me before peeling rubber out of my driveway.

If Linda was sweet natured, earthbound, and reserved, Cynthia was from another planet. Cynthia was never a girlfriend. Cynthia did what she wanted, with whom she wanted, whenever she wanted. Completely uninhibited, she was the dictionary definition of free spirit. In fact, I swear I don't recall knowing anyone who tore through life with such gusto. Cynthia was a law unto herself, immune to rules and social mores, and she lived life completely on the edge. She also had a heart as big as a house and would have taken a bullet for you if she thought you were worth it.

I first encountered her at Rodney Bingenheimer's English Disco where the nymphet groupies and Sunset Lolitas were so dangerously young that it would make you uncomfortable just to look. Bingenheimer, a sort of groupie himself, was an odd character. With his thatched mullet and whiny way of enunciating, he worshipped at the altar of glam rock and pandered to the fad with breathless adoration. The music was loud and predominately English-pop, leaning distinctly in the direction of the mother church of David Bowie, for whom the club seemed to be designated as a shrine. It really was an unhealthy mix of children and men that over the years has cast a dark shadow over the advantages taken by some of the top tier rock gods of the era. When you're twenty-eight and dating a fourteen-year-old, don't try to blame it on the way it was back then. In any era it would be a fractured judgment call, tantamount to cradle robbing; it's indecent and degenerate, a salacious proclivity for which there is no excuse.

Leaving on the first and last night I was ever there, I noticed a young girl shivering on the sidewalk. Instinctively, I asked her if she was OK, only to find out that she'd just arrived in town and had nowhere to stay.

She was a little more heavyset than Rodney's normal crew of skinny nubile groupies, and she'd been given the cold shoulder by the brat pack. Afraid of what would undoubtedly happen to her out on the streets, I made a dangerous decision. With explicit instructions off the bat that this was by no means what she might think, I offered her the couch back at my hotel. I'm not sure she believed me, but I imagine she was fine with it either way. It happens I was staying at the Beverly Hills Hotel, so with this added bonus she was saucer-eyed and mightily impressed. She was a good kid with a budding personality and the capacity for serious street smarts while at the same time unable to conceal the sub-urban naivete filtering through. I think she was surprised that I didn't demand anything of her, which allowed her to dispense with the feigned maturity and let her inner child embrace the luxury she was obviously unfamiliar with. I gave her a robe and some blankets and left her in the living room. In the morning, I fed her breakfast and took her to the bus station. She left, but not for long.

I didn't know this until several years later when I was at On The Rox and met a full-figured and striking young woman with an effervescent personality. There was no pretense about her and it was obvious from the get-go she had one thing in mind. Up to that point I'd seldom encountered anyone with such a sexual potency and succumbed easily to her advances.

As she made her way to leave the next day, she looked down at me, laughed, and said, "You don't remember me, do you?" Cynthia had changed only in age and physicality. She had achieved her goals and was the queen of all she surveyed, party animal number one. She knew everyone and moved in their circles like a whirlwind, captivating social movers and shakers along with movie stars and fringe elements like me.

Now with the legality of things in proportion, our friendship became a crazed collision of circumstances. Arrangements were never made, ours were chance encounters that happened when they hap-pened, spontaneous and in the moment. We once spent a weekend dazed and overstimulated at a languorous house party held at the home of one of Elizabeth Taylor's sons somewhere off Laurel Canyon. In the days at the dawn of true excess, she was a captivating guide and made such events seem like summer camp. She was a mustang never to be broken, like roping the wind she was impossible to restrain, her loyalty to me harkening back to the night when I was Androcles.

I don't think she was ever designed to live long, and when she OD'd she was abandoned by her friends, left blue, cold, and alone. It broke my heart. Not one of the celebrities who benefited from her tangible virility attended her funeral. In 2006, from the song "Blues Never Fade Away," I remembered her this way.

> *She was twenty-one with her life ahead*
> *You don't need to know her name*
> *She breathed her last on the cold stone floor*
> > *of a Hollywood arcade*
> *But fate's right hand isn't always just*
> *Puts a lot of pressure on your faith and trust*
> *She was just a little girl; ain't that enough*
> *To rage against the day*

It was around this time that I began my first long-term relationship after the collapse of my first marriage. It was also the time that I got a housemate in the form of my old friend, the album designer David Larkham. David, whose marriage was on the rocks, needed some refuge, and as he was an easygoing guy with a mellow disposition, he was most welcome. I wouldn't call it a frat house, but it did have a pretty loose open-door policy. Whereas my status of availability had been curtailed by monogamy, David's freedom at certain points afforded him company that I wasn't always a party to. Sometimes I'd return to the house and wonder if it was mine. There were often strange bodies in the pool, and on one occasion in the middle of the night an attractive blonde in a full-on French maid outfit wandered into my bedroom and asked if she could grab a beer from my bedside fridge.

Then there was Loree. Loree had caught my eye a few years earlier at one of producer and manager Allan Carr's festive wingdings in Benedict Canyon. Due to Allan's hospitality, I'd made the acquaintance of some interesting people. Allan was totally over the top, flamboyant, and unnecessarily closeted. Eventually, he would go on to work on *Saturday Night Fever*, coproduce the movie *Grease*, and later mastermind the Broadway version of *La Cage aux Folles*. Later, when Loree and I were a couple, along with the restaurateur Patrick Terrail, the owner of Ma Maison on Melrose Avenue, Allan had put together an eclectic group of individuals that flew to Moorea in Tahiti for the opening of a new primitive-style oceanfront hotel. On this trip I met a young chef named Wolfgang Puck who was on the verge of making something of himself. Also through Allan, I'd been befriended by the actress, singer, and dancer Ann-Margret and her husband, Roger Smith. I've never been one to hang my tongue out to dry, but from the time I had a pulse Ann-Margret could get it racing, so to call her a friend after the likes of *Bye Bye Birdie* to *Carnal Knowledge* was an unexpected source of pleasure. Let me tell you, there is only one reason to watch the otherwise awful Elvis movie *Viva Las Vegas*. Come on, who wants to look at Elvis when Ann-Margret is dancing next to him in tights and an angora sweater?!

The night I met Loree was a mere introduction, and it would be over a year and a half later that a sly orchestration by Betsy Asher, the former wife of record producer and recording artist Peter Asher, got the ball rolling. On the night of Allan's bash (a party in honor of the Rolling Stones), I'd managed to charm my way into giving Loree a ride home. She was renting the home of former evangelist preacher and actor Marjoe Gortner on Lookout Mountain off Laurel Canyon. Things didn't go well, and I think I jumped the gun because I was unceremoniously sent packing due to my heavy-handed approach. Thank you very much, Stoli and tonic.

It's QUESTIONABLE WHERE I was when I wrote the lyrics to "Candle in the Wind." It could have been anywhere as I was continually on the move. What is the case is that Marilyn Monroe wasn't my first choice. It all started with a play and a movie. The play was Aleksandr Solzhenitsyn's *Candle in the Wind*, his 1960 mash-up of repression, survival, and the gulag-style world of Stalin's oppressive totalitarian regime. Not unlike Ray Bradbury's sci-fi classic *The Illustrated Man*, a book of short stories that had spawned the song "Rocket Man," a rubric it shared with one of Bradbury's far-out tales, "Candle in the Wind" was an impossible to resist title for a song.

It wasn't until I was watching John Huston's 1961 American western drama *The Misfits*, featuring a last-gasp starring role for the great Clark Gable and costarring Marilyn Monroe and Montgomery Clift, that the inkling of an idea began to form. Arthur Miller's low-key script was powerful and understated, which may account for it not being duly recognized as classic cinema on its release. Both Monroe and Clift shone, although the latter had a deeper effect on me, possibly due to his rodeo chops and the fact that he cowboy'd up while Monroe's character stereotypically whined about animal cruelty.

Inevitably, it's a dark salute to the end of an era, not only in its plot line, but in terms of the actors entrenched in its muted and collective aftermath. Gable may have seemed old when he passed away back in 1960, but in today's terms he was impossibly young at only fifty-nine years old. It could be said that in comparison to his costars, he did OK. Monroe exited at thirty-six in 1962 either, depending on your beliefs, dying by her own fragile hand or by the shady fedora'd forces of Joseph Kennedy. Clift stayed the course, hanging in until 1966 when he died of a heart attack at forty-five. Drugs played a hand in both deaths, thus committing each one to live on eternally, frozen in time, charismatic and beautiful creatures impervious to the ravages of age.

Clift was my first choice for "Candle in the Wind" simply because he was more appealing to me. As personified by James Dean, the ethos of live fast, die young, and leave a beautiful corpse had a lyrical ring that wasn't lost on me. After some consideration, though, I switched gears. It wasn't a difficult decision. I just decided that Marilyn was more iconically recognizable. More sympathetic in the minds of the masses, she was inconsolably vulnerable, the perfect metaphor for the song's title, a fragile flame flickering away into immortality.

An early death, especially when attached to a hedonistic musician or actor, whether warranted or not can elevate their talent level by leaps and bounds. Then again, by the same token it can in some circumstances, like for instance Robert Johnson, solidify their credentials. Had Johnson not died so violently and young with such a tremendous backstory, his blueprint for the blues might not have emerged to become legendary classics of the genre.

So many have attained death's seal of approval by drowning in the fountain of youth. We've all played games with the 27 Club and ruminated on an idealized concept of worthiness and "where would they be now?"—a macabre scrutiny overkill and a thirst for glamorous tragedy that sets us pondering. In all honesty, any one of many could have wound up as the protagonist of "Candle in the Wind." To be honest, I'd have preferred to eulogize someone I had more empathy for, but then that would no doubt have diminished the commerciality of the song, and ultimately the lyrical agenda. This, in turn, could have hijacked the melody, which is in my mind one of Elton's finest, and ultimately I might not even be discussing it here. Am I searching for shock value by overemphasizing my indifference to Marilyn Monroe? Could be, but the celluloid nirvana she inhabits was never my thing. I'm glad, though, that I rethought my game plan, as the overall universality of the end product has been overwhelmingly generous.

Purse strings aside, this has a comical conclusion. With the song's grand success, I became the beneficiary of more memorabilia than I could handle. Understandably, it was presumed that because I'd composed such a moving tribute to the golden goddess that I was conceived to be a huge Monroe fan. Before I could say *Seven Year Itch*, my house became a shrine to Norma Jean. I was so inundated with vintage movie posters, lobby cards, calendars, and multiple ephemera that my home looked like Joe DiMaggio's basement. I guess I'd never completely emphasized my lack of interest in the subject matter, because Elton himself presented me with the coup de grâce: a Marilyn Monroe mannequin dress form in a five-foot Lucite case adorned with flashing bulbs and a plaque of authenticity. Apparently, all her most famous movie outfits, plus her JFK birthday spangle fest, had been molded on this bit of busty hard foam. In tandem with this, Sharon Arden (later Osborne) bought me another museum-like presentation featuring Monroe's silver satin wrapped slippers. Overload indeed. If memory serves me well, all this may have invaded my easily manipulated propinquity. Without really thinking about it, I just added fuel to the fire of fandom by beginning to contribute myself. Imagining I'd been ordained a gatekeeper, I bought books (all unread) and rummaged through memorabilia stores for further collectables. Of course, it didn't last long and, like Kenneth Grahame's fabulous faddist, the eminent Mr. Toad, it all ran out of steam and I moved on.

At one point I even threw my hat into the acting ring. I'm not sure why. It wasn't something that rang my bell, but with certain parties massaging my ego, I was willing to give it a go, succumbing to it and engaging a topflight Hollywood agent. There were glossy full page portraits in the trades announcing my signing that were so highly stylized and obviously touched up that I looked like the pinstripe-suited and embalmed corpse of Bugsy Siegel. My overamped appearance on the scene was most certainly snorted at by casting agents and derided by skeptical parties in the movie community. These expensive photographic propaganda were most likely interpreted as "bored celebrity lyricist looking for something else to do!" They were completely correct in this assessment, but interestingly enough, I eventually got calls. Not that I ever got the parts, but I did have some interesting interactions that gave me some insight into how things got done.

I couldn't act my way out of a paper bag, and even though I'm certain that I'd have gained traction over time and developed some thespian props, I'm just not sure if I was ever that committed. Certainly not then, which is one more example of the floating inconsistency I was currently adopting. Immediate gratification not forthcoming, all bets were off for serious commitment. If I couldn't see the light at the end of the tunnel, I would hang limply onto the tail of an idea and fly it intentionally into a brick wall.

I read for the movie *In Country* with the actress Emily Lloyd, and likewise for a project with *Sid and Nancy* costar Chloe Webb. At the behest of my friend, Harry Dean Stanton, I was asked to play a club owner in the neo-noir thriller *Slam Dance*, but due to a lax attitude on my part I lost out to the British pop star Adam Ant. Funnily enough, the only role I'd pursued in earnest had been years before my official leap into the game when I was somehow contacted about perhaps trying out for my neighbor George Cukor's remake of *The Corn Is Green* with Katherine Hepburn. It had appealed to me, and I'd reread the book, studied my lines, and saw myself as an emerging Daniel Day Lewis. Fate was not kind, and it never happened. I believe given the chance this might have changed the course and integrated a foothold on some kind of serious acting trajectory.

In all honesty, in regard to my present acting status the only thing I had fun doing was an episode of the popular TV series *The Hardy Boys/ Nancy Drew Mysteries* with my good friend Shaun Cassidy. I'd known Shaun since Elton and I had first arrived in LA, and my partner was, as you might imagine, drawn to Shaun's elder brother, the hugely popular global heartthrob David. Shaun was about eleven at the time, ready for bed, and trying to figure out why his classic showbiz parents, Broadway legend Shirley Jones and her husband, the debonair singer and director Jack Cassidy, had Elton John and Bernie Taupin over for dinner. Not exactly a household name at the time and a million miles from their showbiz chops, it was impressive that our hosts were hip enough to recognize something fresh infiltrating the staid vortex between the Great White Way and the Great American Songbook. Shaun, not exactly young enough to be crawling under the table and biting our ankles, viewed our presence in his parents' house as a coup. Not old enough to join the grown-ups, he sat at the bar in his pajamas playing "Your Song" on his tabletop jukebox, a distraction no doubt in order to alert his parents' guests to his burgeoning hipness.

Shaun would go on to follow in his brother's footsteps and in some ways eclipse his sibling by not only stretching his musical chops, but by gravitating with ease into a successful acting career in TV and theater, both on Broadway and in the West End.

Shaun was selling boatloads of albums and was a huge star by the time I found myself on the Universal lot playing a vagabond gypsy musician oddly called Tim Carstairs, a name that brought to mind a character from *The Four Feathers* rather than a transient guitar picker. It was a two-parter entitled "The Hardy Boys and Nancy Drew Meet Dracula" costarring the diminutive songwriter Paul Williams and the Ponderosa patriarch Lorne Greene portraying the legendary lord of the undead.

The whole thing was typical '70s TV, mirroring the times with a perfect blend of attempted social simulation and a plotline drenched in hokey stabs at imitating what I imagine the writers thought the young'uns would "dig." Part Inspector Clouseau, part *Beyond the Valley of the Dolls*, it was a blizzard of wide-collared shirts, crocheted vests, and gyrating extras. Heavy on mullets, teased hair, and the odd rubber horror mask, it was, in a word, glorious. Like *American Bandstand* in a cardboard Transylvanian castle, what was not to like?

Shaun, as it happens, went on to forge an extremely successful career in TV, writing and producing many successful shows. He remains at the top of his game, lives around the corner, remains a close friend, and on occasion, still calls me Tim.

My agent, Keith Addis, was a sharp guy and socially entertaining. Aside from hosting parties in his characteristic corner apartment on Fountain and Sweetzer, he had on one occasion asked me out to join him for dinner at the currently uber-popular Moroccan restaurant Dar Maghreb. At the last minute, he'd called to ask if I wouldn't mind if we were joined by one of his other clients, the semi-androgynous elfin actress, Mia Farrow. *Not at all*, I thought. With a backstory like hers, it might prove to be an interesting encounter. *Rosemary's Baby*, Roman Polanski, and Frank Sinatra alone had to be fuel for some interesting dinner conversation.

Dar Maghreb was one of those hip, go-to places that was all about the atmosphere and infusion of celebrity rather than the food. With its muted lighting, Spanish tile, and cozy design of catacomb-like nooks and private rooms, it invited a laissez-faire postwar North African pretense.

Things went easily enough, for a while. I wouldn't say she was shy, but she was certainly somewhat reserved. It wasn't until the subject of music came up, however, that she became markedly more vocal and things got distinctly uncomfortable. She was at that time married to André Previn, the highly respected German American classical pianist, composer, and conductor, which apparently had had a marked impression on her way of thinking. In no uncertain terms, she made it abundantly clear that she and André never, never, ever let their three children listen to any sort of music other than classical. She did this with such relish and complete disregard to the fact that a pretty successful practitioner of rock and pop was sitting directly across from her that it resonated like a slap in the face. Although I bit my tongue, it wasn't lost on me that this pompous and pretentious school of thought was being delivered by a former hippy wannabe who, a little over ten years prior, was shimmying to Sly Stone and Johnnie Taylor at The Daisy, a discotheque on Rodeo Drive. Soured by this turn of events, I chose to tune Ms. Mozart out and leave her to her admonishment of my bread and butter while I decided to have some fun with Donovan.

But first, I need to introduce Tommy Cooper. During the golden age of British comedy there was a marvelous prop comedian and magician named Tommy Cooper. Cooper was an ungainly, lumbering man of six foot three inches who in reality was magically proficient, but he invented an act where all his tricks failed. Like so many English presenters and comics, he had several catch phrases, most notably, "Jus' like that!" which he gruffly delivered in a drunken growl while performing his shtick. Whether or not it's true, he was known to be the tightest man in showbiz. One of his stunts was to pay the exact taxi fare, and when exiting a cab slip something in the driver's pocket saying, "Have a drink on me." That something would be a tea bag. Genius. However, his most distinguishable accessory was that he always wore a red fez exactly like the waiters at Dar Maghreb.

Donovan, the popular Scottish folk rock singer of "Sunshine Superman" fame, was dining with friends in one of the restaurant's private rooms. Picking out a likely candidate among the waiters, I offered the most sizable one a hundred dollars to follow my instructions and take a crash course in a passable Tommy Cooper impression. Cooper had a gruff and very identifiable way of speaking, which I did my best to pass on to my puzzled, but eager, impersonator. I instructed him to present Donovan with his lamb tagine by adopting his best Tommy Cooper voice, using some exaggerated hand movements and saying, "Would you like your lamb jus' like this, or jus' like that?"

It worked, as after a lull in the interior conversation, laughter ensued and the proud waiter walked out triumphant.

It sure made up for the stagnant performance that dinner had become. It's interesting to note that some years earlier I had through my friend, actress Brenda Vaccaro, made the very pleasant acquaintance of André Previn's former wife, Dory. At that point Dory had her ground-breaking *Mythical Kings and Iguanas* album in her back pocket and was just releasing her follow-up, *Mary C. Brown and the Hollywood Sign*. Dory was a delicate flower. Beaten by betrayals and a tumultuous past, she had suffered a psychiatric breakdown but emerged from it a startling and provocative songwriter. Tragically underappreciated today, she has for me always been the missing link between other undervalued artists like David Ackles, Judee Sill, and Steve Goodman. She was a remarkable lyricist and totally unafraid of wearing her heart on her sleeve. Ironically, her bitter lament "Beware of Young Girls" leaves little to the imagination and makes "You're So Vain" look like a slap on the wrist. It is, in fact, a flaming red flag warning André Previn of Mia Farrow's machinations to usurp her marriage and court Dory's friendship to her own ends.

I got a call one day from publicist Gary Stromberg asking me if I wanted to have lunch with Cher. Whether this was intended as introductory in terms of a musical collaboration or a "date-date" I don't know. Cher had recently separated from husband Sonny, so either one was possible. I certainly don't want to presume that she had expressed any interest on her part, but being that Gary represented both Cher and Elton, and that both Cher and I were currently single, he may just have been playing matchmaker.

We met at The Daisy in Beverly Hills and sat at a table on the patio in plain sight. I can only imagine the jungle telegraph that this elicited among the contingent of movie agents and ladies who lunch. Cher was a big deal. Fresh off a hit TV variety show, her every move and what she wore was of major interest to people who obsessed over that sort of thing. There was none of the preamble that comes with these orchestrated dates as I believe we had enough in common to dismiss any trivial banter. She was unquestionably a striking woman, but it was her personality that was the most engaging thing about her. She had a dry wit that paired with her distinctively husky voice, making her an entertaining, not to mention self-deprecating, charmer. It was an easy and casual lunch that included her partaking in a glass of wine, something she claimed she'd never ever done at this time of the day. I refrained, of course, from telling her that I didn't recall ever not having a drink at this time of day, but rather concentrated on being as winsome as possible.

At the conclusion of our lunch, she invited me back to her house on Carolwood, not more than ten minutes west on Sunset. The purpose for this alludes me, but what doesn't was the unexpected presence of Sonny Bono in the kitchen. Obviously, he and she were still on speaking terms and had an understanding. Hell, for all I know he might have still been living there. Plainly, he was not happy to see me and elicited a curt grunt in response to my introduction. Thinking it best to avoid any domestic spat, I wandered out of the kitchen and wound up in a large, relatively sparse living area where a small girl with curly blonde hair sat looking distraught in front of a large box.

Not wishing to alarm her, I approached her tentatively and asked if there was something I could help her with. Apparently, inside the box was a large inflatable trampoline that was beyond her capabilities in assembling. Offering to help and imagining there was a pump somewhere in the packaging, I rolled up my sleeves and got down to it. Problem? Yup, no pump. Was I going to let her down? Nope. It might have been gallant, but not only was it a daunting prospect, it was sheer madness. It took me over an hour, and by the end of it my cheeks were cramped, my head ached, and my entire body was on the verge of asphyxiation. I felt the effects of this good deed for days. It hurt when I ate, my equilibrium was off, and my ribs were tender to the touch. Still, I got Chastity's trampoline up and running.

My relationship with Cher never amounted to anything romantic, even though we ran into each other continually over the next couple years. She was always one of the guys, one of those women who simply liked the company of men outside of the obvious ways. We may have flirted, and if I did harbor a crush there is evidence that I didn't handle it well. I don't recall us ever falling out or there being any animosity between the two of us, but the proof of some imagined slight still lives on in a disparaging lyric.

"Snow Queen," the flip side of "Don't Go Breaking My Heart," wasn't a very good song, and it wasn't a very good idea. There was no real purpose for it, the lyric portraying a version of Cher that didn't exist. I'm still embarrassed by it now, "Arms are spread like icicles." It wasn't warranted, and even though both Elton and I apologized for it long ago, it was still dumb, dumb, dumb.

Early on, I took a sabbatical from Doheny and rented an oceanfront home in Decker Canyon, fifteen miles north of the Malibu Colony. I'd never spent any extended time living close to the water, and with the exception of a couple of weeks at Elton's Malibu rental some years previous, this was to be a completely unfamiliar exercise. Why I did it can only be explained through a retrospective microscope, gathering the components of what my life consisted of during those heady days and examining the overall collective. It was prior to drugs and during the death throes of my failed and ruinous first marriage. Elton's fame was unequaled, and the magnitude of his success was unprecedented. Over the years, his history in certain circles has been rewritten to downplay the phenomenon he was. I can only imagine that this has been reinterpreted and underplayed by captious parties who deemed certain elements of his persona facetious. His taste in costuming at times may have been questionable, but believe me, underneath the triviality of them lay the bloodred heart of someone marinated in primal boogie and more rock and roll than any of his current contemporaries, a fact confirmed in recent years by Jerry Lee Lewis who said, "You're the only one around that plays like us old guys." Allow me to defer to the words of a rational online pundit.

Unless you were there, it's hard to appreciate just how big a star Elton John was in the 1970s. Perhaps you imagine him as being on a par with other stars of the era, such as Billy Joel or David Bowie or Bruce Springsteen. He was bigger than all of them. In an era in which rock stars were larger than movie stars, Elton John was the biggest star in the world.

Temporarily extraditing myself from the eye of the storm might have been a good idea, in theory. However, putting it into practice was another thing. I was still a restless individual seduced by my newfound fame and happily reveling in its rewards. Cutting myself off wasn't going to be easy, so inflicting myself to a self-imposed exile no matter how temporary was a challenge. It's no secret that I set myself an onerous obstacle course that even my impulsive nature wasn't stupid enough to attempt. Deterring me from pursuing any escape back to whatever mischief might be lurking in wait for me back in town was forty-five miles of arduous driving. A traffic-clogged Pacific Coast Highway was one thing, but the winding cop-plagued stretch from the Sunset entrance to the heart of the Strip was not something even I would attempt given my drinking habits at the time.

There was no doubt I got what I paid for. It was by no means remote, but it was secluded enough to imagine I was in some isolated jungle compound. My closest neighbor, not more than a stroll away, turned out to be the Chicano actor and comedian Cheech Marin (as in Cheech & Chong). Cheech, who was far less irreverent than his public image would suppose, had recently married his first wife, Rikki, and was currently enjoying some laid-back downtime. Blindingly intelligent with a fierce passion for the arts, he was loose and lovable with a devilish smile and a congenial warmth. For the short time I was there, he was a good friend and together we'd shoot the breeze and visit with each other on a regular basis.

My favorite feature of the house was the deck, and it was here that life's conundrums were contemplated and mulled over. I loved the warm balmy evenings when the breeze would lift the smell of the sea into the air, blowing it through the Jeffrey pines and primrose to blend into an intoxicating mix of vanilla and salt. I had a wooden rocker, two oil lamps, and a cassette deck. It was bliss, and for a brief moment in time, as the sun fell into the ocean, I'd drink Mickey's Big Mouths and unwind to the sound of Mississippi John Hurt and John Coltrane.

What was foremost on my mind was where I was heading with my work. It had been a number of years since Elton's auspicious debut at the Troubadour, and in that time we had moved like a proverbial freight train tearing along nonstop without giving a thought to where the journey might end. The pinnacles our output had reached were record-breaking. Our last two albums *Captain Fantastic and the Brown Dirt Cowboy* and *Rock of the Westies* hit Billboard's number one spot on the day of their release, the first two to do so in the magazine's history. Basically, there were no records left to break, and the best we could hope for was to maintain an acceptable level of popularity that kept us in the public eye rather than having that train drop us off in a town called Obscurity. I documented this dilemma in the song "The Bridge" on the *Captain Fantastic* sequel *The Captain and the Kid*, in 2006. *And every one of us has to face that day / Do you cross the bridge or do you fade away? / And every one of us that ever came to play / Has to cross the bridge or fade away.*

Was this the time to change the game plan and rethink the blueprint? I'd always been a storyteller, scripting mini movies, creating characters both real and imagined. My lyrics were invested with vignettes of life, cinematic parables, cryptic mythology, and science fantasy, and romance hardly came into the equation. If you think about it, "Harmony" is the only track on *Goodbye Yellow Brick Road* that could even be considered a love song. Collectively, there is only a handful of songs from *Empty Sky* all the way through ten studio albums to *Rock of the Westies* that could be deemed love songs in the traditional sense. "Pinky," "Don't Let the Sun Go Down on Me," "Blues for Baby and Me," and of course, "Your Song." That's pretty much it. "Tiny Dancer" I think of as a collective salute, and even a song like "We All Fall in Love Sometimes" is more of a metaphor for solidarity and camaraderie than romantic intent.

The shift I made wasn't subtle, and for the first time my instincts were self-centered and conciliatory. If I hadn't penned much relationship-themed material up to this point, I made up for it on our next album, the aptly named *Blue Moves*. After several years of wasted time, bitter disappointment, and betrayals I unloaded in the only way I knew how, which was by interspersing the more diverse tracks with a scattering of morbid and mawkish humdingers. I regretted it immediately. It would take some time, and a trial separation from my soul brother, before I reconvened with romantic balladry and up-tempo love anthems. By then, for the most part, I got it right.

The track on *Blue Moves* that saved my bacon and proved to be a classic, "Sorry Seems to Be the Hardest Word," worked because it had absolutely nothing to do with my personal life. It was the odd man out and unrelated to the other wrist slitters. In fact, it was one of the few songs that Elton and I ever wrote that emerged from an original melodic idea he had. In his rented home on Tower Grove Drive off Coldwater Canyon, Elton sat down at the piano, something he never usually did in his own homes by that time, and surprised me by playing the fragment of a tune. Not being the way we normally operated I was thrown until, out of nowhere, the muse was forthcoming. *What have I got to do to make you love me*, I kept repeating to myself, *What have I got to do to make you care*, I continued. By the time he quit playing I had those two lines and the title, and a day later we had the song wrapped up.

I'm sure the time spent away from town was beneficial, but in reality it was just a temporary bandage. I was simply going back and picking up where I left off. Fundamentally speaking, I was still adrift in a world that I had no control over. I was a mass of contradictions with habits that were irresponsible and would eventually get much worse.

LE DOME ON Sunset was our de facto hub. It wasn't just a popular restaurant frequented by multitier Hollywood players and rock nobility, it was vibrant mutuality, an interactive playground, and safe haven in which to indulge and unwind. The comfort of familiarity made it a magnet, its close-knit clientele assured of affirmed amity and consistency. During its tenure, its clubby atmosphere created an industry of table hopping that promoted new friendships, renewed old acquaintances, and frequently evoked eye contact that orchestrated couples to harmoniously collide. While I'll admit to having been the benefactor of all three of the previous incidences, that isn't to say that there weren't also some introductions that panned out a little differently than expected. Let's just say, like a book of short stories, some were better than others.

First impressions can be deceiving, which in my case can be annoying. As someone who considers himself a good judge of character, and who as I once wrote "can sniff out a weasel in a three-piece suit," I'm rattled when I'm wrong.

I met, well . . . let's just call him "Leo," through the usual channels of networking at Le Dome. Leo was successful in the entertainment business, trim, personable, and good-looking. He was also disarmingly funny and very soon we found ourselves connecting and enjoying long casual lunches lubricated by abnormal amounts of Beaujolais nouveau. Leo was a great conversationalist, and interacting with him was never dull. Eventually, we would gravitate to each other when attending the same parties, something that is normally only done when you are completely at ease with the individual in question.

One day, lunching as usual, the topic of conversation turned from rational to certifiable. Unbeknownst to me, Leo was a complete conspiracy theorist. I'm not talking gunmen on the grassy knoll, or even cryogenically preserved aliens. No, those topics made perfect sense compared to what Leo believed. What he espoused was such a tidal wave of complete insanity that it was all I could do to maintain my composure. Besides the fact that we're all microchipped at birth and that a group of international elites controls governments, industry, and the media with the goal of establishing global hegemony, he also claimed that 297 years of our history didn't exist. I'm not sure how I wound up reacting to his philosophies on New World Order and Phantom Time Hypothesis, but I knew in all good consciousness that I couldn't maintain these rendezvous. If he were to inadvertently advocate these theories in front of some of my less than tolerant friends, I surely couldn't vouch for their tact and ridicule. It wasn't exactly like discovering that the clown at your party is John Wayne Gacy, but it was a definite aspersion on my better judgment. It's a shame because the side of him that wasn't down in the balmy basement was quite delightful. If only he'd kept that part of himself tucked away, we might still be friends.

Leo might have had some seriously malfunctioning ideas, but he was an absolute angel compared to Don Simpson. I'd been courted at lunch by an executive from Paramount about possibly penning some lyrics for the title song of a new movie produced by the burgeoning team of Don

Simpson and Jerry Bruckheimer. Rather than read the script, I agreed to a screening of a rough cut minus the music. I'd been given a rundown of the story in as much as it had one and was left less than enthusiastic. The movie was called *Flashdance* and the plot involved an eighteen-year-old welder played by Jennifer Beals (already it was far-fetched) who aspires to be a professional dancer. She lives in a warehouse with her dog (you heard me right) and moonlights at night in a sort of titillating combination of burlesque and cabaret that in the real world didn't exist anywhere that I'd ever heard of. The whole thing was clumsy and manipulative, soft-core porn masquerading as a fairy tale while pandering to a demographic of horny teens and lecherous middle-aged men. Enter Don Simpson.

Simpson was the only other person in the screening room when I arrived to check out the movie. From the get-go, he creeped me out. It was as obvious as the nose on your face that he was vain, egotistical, and brash. He also had a very silly haircut and was extremely high. Skittish and fidgety, he insisted on giving me a running commentary of everything that was unfolding on screen as if I were watching it with a blindfold on. I'm no shrinking violet, but he may just have been the crudest man I've ever met. Everything that came out of his mouth was either sexual innuendo or just blatant filth. It was unsettling enough to see him so aroused by the female actors, but this doubled with his observations as to their anatomy and sexual capabilities was nauseating. What was most upsetting was the fact that he assumed I had no problem with this sort of behavior and was equally complicit in his misogynistic degradation. By the time the final spool ran out, I was ready to hurl and left with little said.

Don Simpson, along with Jerry Bruckheimer, went on to become enormously successful. Don also became notorious throughout Hollywood for his unquenchable thirst for cocaine, prostitutes, sadomasochistic sex, and prescription drugs. In 1996, he was found dead on his bathroom floor with twenty-one different drugs in his system. A lineup of 2,200 prescription drugs were found in alphabetical order in his bedroom closet. It was also reported that his drug tab amounted to $60,000 a month.

Not much happened after that. I gave the song a shot but it was half-hearted. Giorgio Moroder had created a track that really wasn't in my wheelhouse, but I'd thrown something together and submitted it. They didn't use it and went with a lyric written by Keith Forsey and the singer of the song, Irene Cara. There were suspiciously some elements of my original in the final track but hardly enough to complain about. The song "Flashdance . . . What a Feeling" won a Golden Globe, a Grammy, and an Academy Award, but I'm not sure even that would have been worth running into Don Simpson again.

I didn't know what Marilyn Grabowski did for a living. She was just another Le Dome regular who I got to know. I figured she held a position of some importance as she was chic, smart, and obviously the possessor of high intelligence. The only noticeable flaw in her trim and tidy presentability was a slight deformity. I learned that she'd had a facial injury that had been botched up by a careless plastic surgeon, almost resulting in her losing her nose. After countless skin grafts and surgeries it had been saved, but had left her slightly disfigured in that area. She carried herself remarkably well with this minor impediment, and in many ways she resembled a slightly contoured Joni Mitchell.

At a collective dinner one night, she asked me what I was doing the following weekend and, if I was free, did I want to go to a party at the Playboy Mansion. Let me tell you, "Playboy Mansion" are the last two words I would have ever expected out of her mouth. She just didn't fit the composite of anyone who would have the slightest interest in that whole stridently fabricated concept. If that was a shock, the follow-up was a doozy. Ascertaining my perplexity, she realized immediately that I was unaware of her occupation and laughed. For the last twenty years she had been the photo editor for *Playboy* and was responsible for over-seeing every aspect of the layouts with complete ascendancy, answering only to the alpha bunny.

Before you jump to conclusions and think I might have been excited by this prospect, think again. Even in my younger years, the whole *Playboy* thing really didn't do it for me. I'd certainly seen plenty of the magazines, but the only time I've ever bought one was, yes, for an article, the much-publicized Marlon Brando interview in the January 1979 issue. Even at its height, *Playboy* seemed to have a smug self-importance that gave the finger to the common man. There was nothing natural in the fantasy, just an airbrushed world of make-believe that demeaned femininity and created an unobtainable illusion. The fact that it was all the erotic visualization of a self-ordained libertine who smoked a pipe and lived in his pajamas only added to its camouflaged vulgarity.

Sometime during the Louder Than Concorde Tour in 1976, Elton and I had been invited to the Playboy Mansion in Chicago. Why did we go? If it wasn't my scene, it certainly couldn't have been Elton's. I can only imagine there was some promotional connection somewhere and we'd simply gone along to honor a commitment. I brought along a six-foot-tall model named Cynthia Russell who was built like an Olympic athlete and rode a 500cc Harley. Cynthia wasn't part of the Playboy stable, although she had done a layout, which featured her depicting strictly masculine, blue-collar roles: coal miner, oil rigger, construction worker, that sort of thing. Again, it reeked of male fantasy, but in contrast to the usual formulaic subservience and boudoir props, at least it had some edge to it.

Hefner, who was partnered up with the aptly named Barbi Benton at the time, was cordial and perfunctory if not a little bland and stiff. The thing I noticed most distinctly then and in any repeated encounters with him years later was that he was the possessor of a perpetual, passive smirk that I found unsettling. There was a degree of condescension in it that made any conversation with him seem like an exercise in futility; if he was listening at all, it was most likely falling on deaf ears.

Back in real time, I was loath to refuse Marilyn's offer. I didn't want to be rude and, besides, the ever-present sense of curiosity in me was adamant I attend. I've experienced many things in my life that have proved to be a letdown, including Graceland, the Orient Express, and blowfish, so believe me my hopes weren't high for the Playboy Mansion. I wasn't wrong. What a dump. Popular folklore might have built it up to be a louche Mecca preeminent in sensual sophistication, but I can assure you it was none of that and a lot less. Like a miniature House of Usher, it was a gray collision of Tudor and Gothic, all faux turrets, battlements, and way too busy in its attempt to be anything more than a kitsch architectural mess. Arguably, this could be a matter of taste, and if indeed the exterior might have thrilled a certain sector of impressionable fanboys, nobody could argue that the interior was anything but a huge disappointment.

Even glitzed up and lit like Knott's Berry Farm at night, it wasn't hard to tell that maintenance was not a priority and that the efficiency of cleaning crews was lacking. The place was like a courtier in the Palace of Versailles, constantly powdered and perfumed to mask the unpleasant odor beneath. The place simply had no style or character, the furniture looked old and ugly, the alcoves were murky, and the carpets were balding and frayed. The upper levels were cordoned off, and whatever went on up there most likely was also conducted in the infamous grotto. Imagining what went on in those furtive waters wasn't something I wanted to dwell on while eating at the same time. Needless to say, all the chlorine in the world wouldn't have got me to go commando in there.

I seemed to be surprisingly young in comparison to the majority of male attendees there, who varied from old Borscht Belt comedians in polyester suits to second-tier TV personalities and tough guy actors like James Caan and Hugh O'Brian. I'll admit that everyone there looked like they belonged, a demographic certainly sculpted to be attracted to this form of thinly veiled debauchery. Lascivious older men in abundance looking to hook up, codes of honor be damned. In this garish cyclone of tertiary color, I imagined demand took precedence over anything consensual, a fact that proved to be correct in the ensuing years.

In fact, speaking of the House of Usher, the character of Roderick in Edgar Allan Poe's novel suspects the house controls its inhabitants. Not a bad analogy for the Playboy Mansion. It wasn't a prison, but it certainly held sway, mesmerizing generations of young women and marginalizing them into an army of fembots devout in their allegiance to one man.

As much as Hefner thought of himself as an avatar of the sexual revolution, I don't believe he knew how to engage the emerging personalities of the counterculture. He certainly didn't understand rock or its purveyors even while pandering to them. He may have made overtures, but in reality he never really emerged from the penthouse mentality of his syndicated TV shows such as *Playboy After Dark*. He was simply treading water, an anachronism forever inhabiting a sky-high man cave of chrome and Formica. Manhattans, old-fashioneds, shag carpeting, and Buddy Greco on the hi-fi . . . every day was Groundhog Day for Hugh Hefner.

ONE OF MY favorite clubs of the era was The Palomino Club. "Club" actually might be misleading as it was more like a roadhouse, something that wasn't necessarily indicative of LA. Located in North Hollywood over the hill in the Valley on Lankershim Boulevard, it was LA's premier country music venue. Less precious than many of the city's rock joints, it was more blue-collar, and in the early days was open all day to patrons and regulars who would wander in and hang at the bar while top-line acts set up and rehearsed for the evening's show. It could get a little rowdy at times and that wasn't just the clientele. I once witnessed the rebel country singer Johnny Paycheck, incredibly coked up and standing on a table waving a gun and screaming, "This motherfucker's my wife, anyone wanna meet her?" Then there was a cow punk band that got into a fistfight with each other in the middle of their set, demolishing their equipment in the process, and a member of Billy Joe Shaver's band who coldcocked a heckler with his bass. Of course, all this sounds a bit hairy, but I never once felt threatened there. In fact, if you just settled into the rhythm of the place, it was a dynamite space to watch live music. George Thorogood duckwalked across the tables, George Harrison, John Fogerty, and Bob Dylan sat in with Taj Mahal, and Jerry Lee Lewis played there once a year.

When I needed my jazz fix there was no better place than Catalina Bar and Grill, a small venue on a shabby stretch of Cahuenga just off Sunset in Hollywood. For the most part, the performers here were a little less unruly, although Nina Simone could be a bit prickly if the mood suited her. This I was willing to put up with as the High Priestess of Soul was beyond transcendent and always mesmerizing in her performance. In the first batch of albums I ever owned, her *Broadway-Blues-Ballads* was one of my most treasured. At this point in time and in years to come before it closed its doors and moved to a less intimate location, I saw many classic performances there: a late-night set by Dizzy Gillespie with no more than a dozen people in the room, and such a laid-back set by Mose Allison I thought the walls would melt. No matter what rough seas my life might be sailing at any given time, I could always count on these kind of musical moments to rehabilitate my soul.

At one point Elton was playing the Forum in Inglewood and asked me to pick up Dusty Springfield en route. Dusty had been one of Elton's idols when he was a boy, and with his escalation up the pop-rock ladder, Dusty had cemented this adoration by befriending him and singing backup vocals on our 1970 album *Tumbleweed Connection*. I only knew her fleetingly but was aware that at times she could be highly strung and a little difficult. Of course, I was also a fan, her *Dusty in Memphis* being an all-time classic. I was a little apprehensive but was immediately put at ease by her amiability, even though she did seem a trifle fussy. Although tiny, she was a larger-than-life character, a little overdressed, over made-up, and most definitely over-coiffed. Even with these personal exaggerations, she was a handsome woman who, no matter how much I tried to refute my perception, reminded me of a really fabulous barmaid. From the get-go, she immediately began patting her hair and checking her makeup in her compact mirror. Because of this, our conversation was limited and constantly hampered by her obvious dissatisfaction with some area of her preparations. Finally, she let out a deep sigh and inquired if we could perhaps stop at a drug store. This not being a problem and without inquiring what it was she needed, we pulled into the closest one at hand. Dipping into her bag, she pulled out a can of hair spray and handed it to the driver requesting, "Please buy me the largest can of this you can find." In minutes, he returned with a can of hair spray the size of a howitzer shell, and off we went. Curious as to why she felt a can of this size was necessary when I imagined a little misting here and there would do the trick, I made some amusing remark in regard to this. She looked at me like I was mad, and as if to show me, she lifted the can to her head like a loaded gun and started spraying. Stopping only intermittently to shake her head and look in her mirror, she continued in this fashion for the duration of the journey. Even a slightly cracked window was no means of escape, and by the time we rolled into the backstage area she'd emptied the entire contents of the can not only onto her rock solid hair but also into my lungs, the driver's eyes, and every stitch of clothing we all wore. For the rest of the evening, I walked around like a human fly strip smelling like I'd spent the last twenty-four hours in a Tijuana whorehouse.

I don't know how it happened, but for a short period of time in the dying embers of the '70s my house became the Doheny Social Club. Late at night it was the place to be, an after-hours establishment for a ragtag clique of like-minded partygoers whose nocturnal interests and aversion to pjs and a nice glass of milk found them swarming my living room and knee-deep at the bar.

There was most decidedly at that time a cross-continental gravitational pull among Britain's rock exiles and LA's close-knit American counterparts. All bonding in a protective circle secured by an epoxy of drugs, liquor, and inertia, it was codependency on a hedonistic level.

For such a sprawling metropolis, our world was incredibly confined. It was like a small village where all the inhabitants knew each and everybody's business. For anyone familiar with that time period in LA's incestuous and some might say vacuous history, a lot of us were coasting on the fumes of our earlier success and languishing in various addictions before getting serious about a second act. Though I'm loath to admit it, those in attendance could most definitely be described as the "usual suspects."

You never knew who was going to turn up at the house on any given night, and that wasn't necessarily a good thing. Quite honestly anybody could have walked in, and did! After all, since Charles Manson, extending a little caution might have been the sensible thing to do. On one occasion, a stoned interloper crawled in through a bathroom window at the back of the house and was immediately collared by one of the more sturdy of my guests. When the police arrived to haul him off, they quickly eyeballed the rock star quota in the room, and after handcuffing their charge in the back of their cruiser joined the festivities. No one had security or bodyguards back then, so on one hand it was nice to feel protected while at the same time it was incongruous to have law enforcement interacting with teeth-grinding celebs fresh from ploughing through several lines of coke in the bathroom. If they sussed it out they couldn't have cared less, which I think was the case, and if my memory serves me correctly they were a couple of the last to leave. Along with collecting autographs and allowing attractive female guests to take Polaroids wearing their hats and brandishing their guns, nothing about it seemed out of step with the times.

Speaking of intruders, I did have a disturbing home invasion that caused me to get distinctly badass. Hearing someone break into your home in the middle of the night is unsettling and scary, and when this happened to me, I figured the best thing to do was to make a lot of noise. Throwing open my bedroom door, I hurled a volcanic barrage of violent threats by way of screeching profanity that achieved the desired effect. It's obvious they were amateurs, as my verbal assault caused them to scramble out the rear entrance and into a waiting car. With adrenaline pumping and still unsettled by this transgression, I scrambled out onto the balcony of my bedroom and unloaded the entire cylinder of my .35 caliber revolver into the trunk of their fleeing vehicle.

Not unlike our Troubadour opening, I have met innumerable individuals who have claimed to have passed through the Doheny Social Club in the time it was open for business. The truth is, mostly it was the double trouble drummers Messrs. Ringo Starr and Keith Moon, my best pal Alice Cooper, and an assortment of folks like Harry Dean Stanton, various Monty Python alumni, and, on one occasion or another to the best of my recollection, folks like Stephen Stills, Susan Sarandon, Ryan O'Neal, Marty Feldman, Ronnie Wood, and Rod Stewart.

My friendship with Rod went back to the days in the early '70s when I still maintained a residence in the UK. He'd first recorded our song "Country Comfort" on his second solo album *Gasoline Alley*, but it wasn't until we'd given him an original number "Let Me Be Your Car" for his *Smiler* album that we met when Elton played on the track at Morgan Studios in London in 1973.

Rod was immensely likable. He was easy company and had a particularly distinct sense of humor. He was still dating his first major girlfriend, Dee Harrington, at this time but was at a point where they were squabbling intermittently. I liked Dee; she was cute and funny, modish, and completely in vogue with the era. She probably had her hands full with Rod, who, by that time, was most definitely affected with a wandering eye. I recall him on one occasion coming over to Bourne Lodge, my home on the Wentworth Estate in Virginia Water, to retreat from confrontation when things with Dee got overly heated.

On the weekends, we'd roust about with a group of friends and associates, including Rod's PR rep and general factotum, an extraordinary human specimen called Tony Tune. Tony looked like a turtle stripped of his shell. Gangly and painfully thin with wispy shreds of hair and bulging eyes, he was a character who'd be completely obsolete in today's delicate culture. Solicitous, gossipy, and dangerously attracted to very young men, he did copious amounts of cocaine, was irresistibly camp, and in turn uproariously funny.

Rod liked to go to cheesy places like The Penthouse Club near Piccadilly Circus, and if someone struck his fancy, he would send Tony to reconnoiter and attempt to score for him. I never thought this was a particularly good idea given that a pretty girl being descended upon by an obviously gay man with the charm of a debauched locust was certain to send her screaming into the night like a barmaid in a Hammer horror movie.

Not to be self-righteous, I wasn't complaining; wherever we ended up was usually fun. Because of Rod, I developed a proclivity for frilly shirts and loud jackets, which made me end up looking like I was auditioning for a Faces cover band. We'd glide through the evening in a large Mercedes limo driven by Rod's genial driver, Cyril, and were at one time or another glommed on to by the hugely popular glam rocker Gary Glitter. Wherever we went he seemed to turn up wearing a ridiculous full-length fur coat and his preposterous mile-high hairpiece. One night after dining at the Hungry Horse, a favorite restaurant of ours in Fulham, and a little tired of Gary's hulking presence and incessant prattle, some member of our party tore his wig off and threw it out the car window into the oncoming traffic on Fulham High Road. Had I known what I know now about Gary Glitter's future exploits in child pornography and attempted rape of minors, I'm only sorry we didn't toss him out along with it.

With all this in mind, I always wondered why Rod moved to LA in the first place, his fervor for Scottish Nationalism being what it was. Obviously, he was wrestling with his dueling images of Jack the Lad Brit and his desire to play the part of well-heeled Hollywood playboy.

Indeed, Rod was part of that quirky breed of Englishmen who emigrate to the US then proceed to fervently cling to every bit of Britishness they can. It never made much sense to me. It might have when C. Aubrey Smith came to Hollywood in 1932 and founded the Hollywood Cricket Club, bringing a distinct whiff of tea and crumpets with him, but then again, back then actors couldn't move around with the ease that entertainers can today.

Don't get me wrong. I don't care if you want to come here and play soccer seven days a week. You can eat roast beef and Yorkshire pudding till it's coming out your ears and sing "Maybe It's Because I'm a Londoner" while playing darts in a faux pub in Santa Monica. It's just that you can do all this with more authenticity back in Blighty. So why come here? The weather? Best of both worlds? Perhaps!

I'm certainly in the minority. I left because I wanted an alternate lifestyle and was driven by an Americanism that was always in my soul. I excommunicated myself from a culture that I didn't feel I belonged to or was terribly interested in and embraced one that had inhabited my imagination since I straddled a broom and galloped across my old front lawn.

I guess the thing that I found odd, more than anything else about the ex-pat mentality, is that it has at times brought with it a form of new colonialism. Cliquishness is one thing, but I've witnessed self-importance manifest itself in condescending ways. It's an unattractive elitism that professes to assume our stuff is better than yours. This has never been more prevalent than in terms of professional sports.

On several occasions, I've heard Rod belittling American football. It just seems petty coming from a man who, as a sports enthusiast, I'd imagined would respect professional competition on all levels even if his interest in it was a big fat zero. To live here in this country and be derisive of anything that isn't soccer is patently incongruous. His wisecracks about NFL team names was bewildering. Soccer teams have names like Hotspur, Hornets, Wanderers, and Rovers. How is that different from Raiders, Titans, Cowboys, and Broncos? Don't pillory the fabric of a nation that has invited you with open arms and piss on its pastimes. This all may sound petty and inconsequential in the big picture, but I happen to be as rabid in my love of football and baseball as Rod and his buddies are about soccer. I don't watch soccer, but I certainly respect it as a highly athletic and skillful game.

It's like the ridiculous notion that's floated around that rugby is American football without the padding, thus intimating that it's a rougher sport played by tougher men. Obviously those who subscribe to this theory have absolutely no concept of either game. Aside from the fact that the rules are completely different, the contact involved is of an entirely different nature, the average height and weight of an NFL defensive tackle being six feet three inches and 310 pounds. If rugby players were this size and played their game by NFL rules with no protective padding they'd be crippled, paralyzed, and dying like flies. I've spent a good amount of time on the sidelines of pro football games and it's like wandering around in Brobdingnag. The players are humongous. You have no concept of the size of these guys when you're watching on TV. The balance between the proportions of rugby players versus football players is completely erroneous. The physicality and speed isn't remotely comparable. Rugby is a tremendous game played by committed, tough competitors but it's in slow motion when compared to the speed of NFL running backs and wide receivers. Rugby players tussle and wrestle, football players are gladiatorial freight trains who interconnect with massive impact.

At one time or another I'd sat up until dawn watching old movies with Boz Scaggs, thrown out Chevy Chase for playing my piano and being a total dick, and watched Timothy Leary spend the best part of the evening talking to my jukebox. On one occasion, the wonderful English actor John Hurt stood on my coffee table reciting the "gravedigger scene" from *Hamlet* using a snow globe as Yorick's skull. Christopher Reeve, fresh off his first blockbuster, crashed in my guest bedroom one night, compelling me to have a plaque made for the headboard that read "Superman Slept Here." Through Christopher, I met Robin Williams who was just starting out in the TV comedy *Mork & Mindy*. I adored Robin, and, outside of being an absolute delight, he was the funniest human being I've ever encountered. He was constantly on. I truly believe he was not of this world. He was wired differently than the rest of us. His mind worked at such a frantic pace, it was as if he had to continually release stream of consciousness lest his brain get overloaded and his head explode. Whether or not his exhaustive verbal deluge was a shield, a smokescreen to cover some deeper frailty, I'm not qualified to ascertain. I just know that on any occasion that I got to interact with him, he always brought his wonderful smile and tremendous joy. The last time was no exception. It was at Elton's sixtieth birthday party in March 2007, and my wife Heather and I were seated next to him at a table that also included my friends Whoopi Goldberg and Kiefer Sutherland. Robin was in fine form, greeting Kiefer with feigned surprise and theatrically shouting, "Jack Bauer, you're alive!" He was so funny that I couldn't catch my breath for laughing and literally had to beg Whoopi to get him to stop before I choked. Everything on the table was fair game, from the cutlery to the items on the menu. Blue-footed chicken, imagine what he did with that! I was literally sore the next day. He was unique, brilliant, and disarmingly lovable. His death was a tragedy, and I felt enormous sadness in his passing. He was completely without equal, the like of which we'll never see again.

Some years ago I ran into Ringo at a friend's party where he reminded me of an amusing anecdote from the Doheny days. I apparently was fond of tequila at the time, especially Jose Cuervo, and was despondent by a rumor that they were going to discontinue making it. Ringo claims he turned up at my house a few days later to find my hallway stacked from floor to ceiling with several dozen cases of the stuff. In a panic, I'd called every local liquor store and purchased all the surplus stock I could find. The rumor proved to be false and I was ultimately stuck with a lot of tequila. As previously noted, Ringo and The Who's atomic drummer Keith Moon were conjoined at this point and would turn up at any given time of the day or night. Sometimes, if I was feeling fragile, I would assume the fetal position behind the front door and pray they would resume their plundering and pillaging elsewhere. If not, I'd throw caution to the wind and unleash the dogs of war. Keith, for all his notoriety, was awfully sweet. Far brighter than he would have you believe, he could charm the pants off Mary Whitehouse and talk turkey on any kind of highfalutin topic. The fact that he was an unconscionable rogue, mad as a sack of hammers, and lit with a short fuse occasionally slipped my mind. Everything was "Dear boy" this, and "Dear boy" that, and hypnotically like Kaa in *The Jungle Book,* he'd have you transfixed with beguilement while simultaneously slipping a jar of nitroglycerin into your microwave.

When the house was eventually sold to the actress Winona Ryder in the '90s, I heard that it wasn't purchased so much for its architectural allure but for its history of celebrated attendees and haunted rock and roll residue.

In a multitude of musical memoirs, the elephant in the room is inevitably the drug thing. Life gets darker and more unpleasant with these reminiscences. You might hear it from some that I did a lot of drugs, then again if you listen to others I didn't do nearly enough to be considered a heavyweight. Well, yeah right, I was never going to be Keith Richards but then again in my own small world I wound up teetering on the lip of the volcano quite prepared to free fall into the magma.

It's a weakness we sink into due to casual circumstance. Wanting to belong socially, the romantic allure of imitating musical icons, or just blind stupidity. Pick a card, any card. Regardless, that dangerous road traveled is always going to turn out badly. Any way you look at it we choose our poison and suffer the consequences.

I'm shrinking time periods here. From day one at Doheny, the distribution of furnishing was bare bones. The alcohol content of the house was of far greater importance. I had a small refrigerator by my bed filled with Stolichnaya, orange juice, and beer. My dog was called Vodka. What does that tell you? Reaching over for a morning buzz was my way to start the day, and a plastic jug containing a combined cocktail accompanied me everywhere.

Alcohol was always my friend. Certainly before any narcotic got involved, it was the most important accompaniment to anything that came after. Ultimately, they became entwined with each other, the instructions reading snort, drink, cigarette, repeat ad infinitum.

I never enjoyed smoking weed, and when I did I simply became immobile. I had no tolerance for it and was always impressed by associates who doobied the day away while efficiently conducting business and making career-defining decisions. I once smoked a Thai stick with an impossibly gorgeous young woman and imagined I'd had the best sex ever when in actuality I'd rolled over and gone to sleep before the first kiss.

Hallucinogenics weren't a big thing either, although my only experience of them was relatively traditional and not "the bum trip" one reads about. On my first tab of acid, I spent an enlightened afternoon watching Stanley Kubrick's *2001: A Space Odyssey* on a colossal screen that, if memory serves me well, was only colossal in my altered state and was, in reality, my own small bedroom TV. You'd think Kubrick would be the way to go on a maiden voyage, and, yes, it was everything you might imagine in terms of visual distortion and mind-expanding psychotropics. Monkeys bounced around the room, alien voices beckoned from the bathroom, and inevitably the ceiling blew away. This was only eclipsed by my second stab at the tab when my sensory perception went on overload watching Walt Disney's animated *Alice in Wonderland*. Hard to imagine the visionary auteur of revolutionary cinema being out-stoned by old Uncle Walt. Let me tell you, if you are ever inclined to test the waters of LSD and want a suggestion, strap yourself in and watch this insane take on Lewis Carroll's drugged-out odyssey. It's batshit bonkers, and if the animators weren't tripping when they made it, they were certainly anticipating those who would.

Magic mushrooms were my last flirtation with organic drugs, and again it wasn't altogether unpleasant. I was on the island of Maui staying at a friend's house when after a days' gentle rain, the hills were alive with an abundance of the potent fungi. Duly collected, I proceeded to clean them, chop them, and make a delicious omelet. Post breakfast, all I remember was wandering down to the beach where I lay down on the sand and slept for two days dreaming about Eleanor Roosevelt and cheese.

I don't remember when I first encountered the powder, but I do know that it accumulated gradually until it was an omnipresent part of my life. It started when I began to toy with it in the mid to late '70s, only to escalate into what might be termed "a problem" by the '80s. It would be easy to enter into my own take on cocaine, but no dissertation from me is going to cover ground that hasn't already been done to death. Let me just say that it is indeed the big lie, a horrible drug that makes you feel witty and wonderful and far smarter than you really are. What it does in reality is not that; in reality it causes you to launch into verbal diarrhea, increases your paranoia, and keeps you coming back for more. It is a highly addictive and brutal narcotic that has for decades turned well-educated men and women into saucer-eyed, motormouthed buffoons.

In 1978, Alice Cooper and I had written and recorded an album together chronicling Alice's experiences drying out from alcoholism in a New York state asylum. Both the album *From the Inside* and Alice's treatment proved to be a success, but unfortunately, as is often the case, he swapped one addiction for another. For this, I take full responsibility, for which I am not proud. Alice and I were joined at the hip, spending most days together in the recreational den, a converted pool house at the rear of his property in Benedict Canyon. Before his drying out stint, we would while away the day playing pool, watching TV, and yes drinking, and drinking some more! When he returned from rehab clean and sober, I inadvertently introduced him to the white lady. The addictive personality in Alice took to it like a duck to water, and although it was in minor quantities at first, the damage was done.

We got a lesson in how things could get worse when we traveled to the UK to do some press for the *Inside* album and were interviewed in our hotel suite by the highly regarded *NME* journalist Nick Kent. Aside from the fact that he didn't seem terribly interested in being there, it was painfully obvious he was currently in the complete embrace of heroin addiction. Maintaining some sort of strung-out equilibrium until his next fix, he stayed the course by draining our minibars of tomato juice. A well-known junkie antioxidant, he fortified himself with it while feigning interest and vaporizing the room with a jonesing nihilistic presence. It was just another quintessential example of heroin's allure and perplexing drudgery, an undeniably talented writer seduced by the desperate machinations coursing through his veins. Outside, it was a sunny London day, but in our hotel room his opiate eyes, dead and dark like a shark's, was a depressing continence compared to our formative baby steps into what was to be and not to be.

Back home, the warning signs, if they'd had any momentary effect at all, were fleeting. We were soon back in the bag, hoovering up lines with frightening regularity, when one night out of the blue Alice suggested we try freebasing. Freebasing involves boiling and melting cocaine over a flame until it vaporizes. This increases the potency of the substance, which is inhaled using a small glass pipe. The effect is an intense euphoric rush, like an internal orgasm swimming through your body leaving you swaddled in a rapturous embrace. Of course this is temporary, half an hour tops, and very soon you crash with all the side effects of coming down. Anxiety, irritability, paranoia, and depression overwhelm in the aftermath. Yeah, all that good stuff that makes you wanna reconnect with the pipe as soon as possible. Get back on the train and drop me off at Ecstasy and Serenity. Not me. I'm not sure where I procured the momentary sound judgment, but I was overwhelmed with a sense of foreboding that if I didn't get away from this concoction ASAP, I could die on its high. There was just this little voice cutting through the fog in the back of my addled head that said, "This is a rabbit hole you do not want to go down." I'm glad I didn't, but it had its consequences.

I regret that this is where Alice and I parted ways for a while. The times were torpid enough without allowing this seductive siren to lay waste to me by drawing me into complete narcotic destruction.

Alice had his own battle to fight along with his own choices to make, and for a while it was touch and go whether he'd pull through. Luckily, he had an extraordinary woman in his corner who had so much faith and love in her heart that the pure strength of her belief helped him rise from ashes and regain his theatrical crown. Sheryl and Alice have been married over forty-five years, and he still looks at her like they met yesterday.

Was I abandoning my friend to save my own soul? It's a question I've wrestled with, and in all honesty the answer is probably yes. I didn't have the stability or the moral perception to engage in arbitrating or assembling friends for an intervention, something I might add that was not common back then, not to mention hypocritical. We were all in the same boat, some in deeper waters than others, but collectively in a canoe paddling against the current. None of us wanted to float off the edge of the world, so selfishly we battled our personal demons on our own ground. Invariably, many lost the fight.

Eventually, even the help inadvertently got both dosed and tainted. I had in my employ a low-key and sweet young housekeeper who'd run my home efficiently for several years before she accidentally fell foul of some spiked baked goods. A friend of mine had whipped up a batch of marijuana brownies and left them in a bowl on the kitchen counter. Unaware of their ingredients, my housekeeper consumed two or three and went berserk. Screaming that she was dying she ran around the house hysterically until the true reason for her malady was explained to her and she calmed down. Whether or not this was a tipping point, I'm not sure. After her episode with the brownies, she was certainly on high alert to what was transpiring around the house drug-wise. So much so, in fact, that she morphed from a demure and efficient domestic to a covert mule running bags of blow for one of my dealer friends. This transformation took me completely by surprise as I'd never in a million years imagined her succumbing to work as a *narcotraficante*. She was eventually busted and did time in the Sybil Brand Institute, an unfortunate end for such a delightful lady. I was completely shocked by this fall from grace; after all, good help is hard to find.

The pointlessness of it all was only emphasized by its drudgery. The need to become excommunicated from it came somewhere in the late '80s. It ended in a whimper with no dramatics. Giving up was easy. I was lucky in that respect; I just woke up one day and said I was done. No rehab, no cold turkey, no nothing. I just set all the worst aspects of it front and center, and for a couple of years referred to them if ever the inkling to do it again crossed my mind. If I felt the urge, all I had do was close my eyes and refresh my memory.

Staying up for two days straight, confined to one room, rooted in the same spot for fear your disorientation would get you lost in your own home. Immobility punctuated by grinding teeth, your nerve ends like exposed wires crackling with jittery fatigue. The sensation of sandpaper behind your eyes, your mouth dry and racked with stale wine and nicotine, your churning guts needing food but unable to stomach the sight of it. Overflowing ashtrays, the paranoia of sirens, wastebaskets full of empty bottles and bloody tissues, your hands shaking as you picked through the carpet for the last remnants of the final gram. After playing Trivial Pursuit for hours on end, so long in fact that the same questions occurred again and again, and with no drugs left, we would surrender numb and neutered into a brume of finality. In bed, I would stare wide-eyed at the ceiling, a balled-up Kleenex gripped in my fist, the bright sunshine outside, mockingly cruel. With tongues of fire, it pierced the cracks in the drapes seeking entry, tormenting my charred mind as a barrage of leaf blowers roared across the neighborhood and the voices in my head screamed for them to stop.

I'm uncomfortable with the term "survivor." It has a heroic ring about it that does disservice to those who credibly warrant that distinction. Disappearing into the black hole of addiction and emerging free and clean at the other end is hardly something that warrants a medal. It might be commendable, but it's hardly courageous and, at best, is simply brow-sweeping relief that you weren't quite the idiot you were when going into it in the first place.

Rehabilitation works better for some than others. I've seen people completely change from short-tempered, irrational, and unpleasant brutes into completely levelheaded and thoroughly charming individuals. On the other hand, don't mistake sobriety for responsibility. I've known several who fit the bill for what a wise man once said, "You can cure a drunk, drugged-out asshole by eliminating the liquor and drugs, but you're still left with the asshole."

Did I write under the influence of drugs? Unquestionably, no. I can't recall one instance. But then if I did, how would I remember? With an alcohol buzz on? Absolutely. Late at night, hotel room, post-concert, a little Mingus on the Walkman, Ronald Colman muted and flickering on the box, sure as hell I'd be jotting down ideas on the hotel stationery. On planes comfortably ensconced, several Bloody Marys under my belt, you bet. In fact, planes were a favorite. Back when flying was fun and I loved nothing more than being on the move, it was a comforting and perfect environment to compose. I read a *TIME* magazine article on the Tet Offensive traveling on a 747 from the UK to the West Coast that got me thinking and sketching ideas in the margins of the mag.

I had tremendous empathy for the veterans returning from Vietnam who faced a barrage of verbal abuse from those who opposed the war and saw the US troops as government-programmed baby killers. The war was wrong and our reasons for being there were questionable, but for the honest grunt in the field it was an unfair assessment. There might have been some rotten apples, but there were multitudes who had little choice but to go when the call came. No loophole escapes, no blind allegiance, just dutifully caught up in the web of the times. The emotional scars they brought back were varied and this was the seed that eventually sowed my story line. While some were derided on their return, there were by the same token those who came home to farming communities and small Midwestern towns who were feted as heroes, not pariahs. They were paraded on floats along Main Street, flags flying, brass bands playing. Like Ira Hayes in Peter LaFarge's classic ballad, the veterans were "wined and speeched and honored." Their dress uniforms and medals were impressive, the cheering crowds delivered a vocal four-gun salute, and kisses were bestowed by corn-fed beauties and older veterans sang their praises. For some vets, the backslapping became overbearing. Rounds in the tavern were never on them, well-wishers and grateful citizens were a constant, their patriotic fervor impervious to the fragility of their experiences. Some cried out for a return to normality; some, I imagined, might find solace far away.

Written through the eyes of a younger brother, that was "Daniel" in a nutshell. It's simplistic and straightforward, and, on reflection, a little confusing lyrically. If his eyes have died does that mean he's blind? If he is, how does he know Spain is the best place he's ever seen? Let's see. Perhaps he is blind, blinded in action, and is returning to somewhere he's been before, somewhere familiar, a comfort zone for the future.

He also may not be blind; his eyes having died simply meaning that he's refocusing away from a past he'd rather forget and preferring to only look forward. Creating these kind of conundrums is sometimes unintentional but ultimately proves to be a completely alternate entertainment. Some people won't give it a second thought while others might agonize over the true meaning. That's the beauty of songwriting. Having those listening use their own imagination and draw their own conclusions is half the fun. It's like abstract art. What do those configurations of color mean to you, what's it saying? Quite often people's interpretations of my work have been far more entertaining and ingenious than the original concept.

It was floated around that "Madman Across the Water" was about Richard Nixon. A novel idea given his prominence at the time and affiliation with paranoia, but not what I had in mind when creating the song. I'd never thought that the content was vague or in any way hard to understand. It's obviously about institutionalization and isolation, about someone whose mental instability is driving them slowly deeper into insanity: *Is the nightmare black / or are the windows painted?* Then again, on second thought, maybe it is about Richard Nixon!

In the same way, I didn't have British glam rock star Marc Bolan in mind when I wrote "I'm Going to Be a Teenage Idol." It should have been though, because after reassessing the lyrics, it fits the elfin electric warrior to a tee. Likewise, "Idol" on the *Blue Moves* album wasn't about Elvis. I don't think either one was modeled on anyone in particular, but I do know in all certainty who they weren't about. They're lyrically hazy, and indeed they contain enough fragments to warrant speculation that I had both of them in mind. What I can assure you is that I never sat down with the preconceived notion that I was going to specifically write about either one. In these instances, I think what happens is you fly with a loose idea, a phrase, a title, a few random spot points, which eventually gives way to a sense of direction. When you're done and look it over there's a good chance you might say, "Hey, you know what, this could be about Little Richard." Yet again, that doesn't constitute saying that you consciously set out to write about Little Richard. If you're going to run with the fact that you did, you're simply fabricating a lie to gain a little ink and give it more weight. Believe me, I've penned plenty of lyrics outside of "Candle in the Wind" where I sat down knowing full well who I wanted to write about. They're diverse and plentiful from "Empty Garden" (John Lennon), "Roy Rogers," "American Triangle" (Matthew Shepard), and "Oscar Wilde Gets Out." Then there are the slightly more obscure "Jimmie Rodgers' Dream," "Whitewash County" (white supremacist David Duke), "The Ballad of Blind Tom" (house slave turned musical prodigy Blind Tom Wiggins), and "I've Got Two Wings" (guitar evangelist Elder Utah Smith). The same can be said about dedications. Just because you dedicate a song or an album to someone doesn't mean that either one is about that person.

Of course, the story exists that there was a final verse to "Daniel" that made the meaning of the song much clearer. In all honesty, at this point in my life I'd be lying if I said I remember. However, there is the sharper recall of others and enough evidence out there to suggest there was. The problem lies with who you believe. Guitarist Davey Johnstone's take on it is that the verse was so completely out of character with the rest of the song that Elton tore it off the bottom of the page and threw it in the trash. According to our erstwhile axman, it had something to do with a ship's captain and a one-legged dog named Paul! Being that I didn't start taking drugs until a couple of years later, this is pretty funny but highly unlikely. I'm sure the truth is far less colorful and that in fact the final verse was simply a continuation on the same thread where nothing was made any clearer than what had come prior to it. It's become a moot point, and unless someone comes up with the original manuscript, it will remain a half-truth at best.

The house on Doheny served me well. It represented such an important chapter of my life right up to the point when that life was once more changing gears. I guess when I left it was done with me, it needed a new perspective. I'd worn it out, and it was most likely happy to see me go. I not only left disruption and confusion behind, but a chunk of my history that I couldn't take with me and a part of my soul the house couldn't exorcise. I must have been torn to pieces by mixed emotions to leave that place, the brutal honesty of my departure being the truth after the lies I'd recently lived with. Beyond the ever-churning change that threw up dramatically different sets of circumstance over the years—amid the frivolity, philandering, and procrastination—in the final analysis creativity rose above it all.

My office was Doheny's constant and a big mahogany desk was my anchor, an inanimate bastion of reason, a concentric mainstay where I escaped. In this cocoon surrounded by some of my most reliable friends, thousands of records, and literally hundreds of books, I would sequester away and summon the muse. After John Lennon's assassination in 1980, I was so upset I confined myself to this room for two days and wrote "Empty Garden." Temporary anger saw me pen "I'm Still Standing" there, and in the ebb and flow of conciliatory gestures made in Elton's and my reuniting after our temporary split, I wrote the olive branch that is "Two Rooms at the End of the World." Most notably perhaps is "Sacrifice," in my estimation one of the very best songs we have ever written, and one that foreshadowed my departure. It was my subconscious on a metaphorical soapbox screaming in silence that I could no longer live here honestly. *Some things look better, baby, just passing through.*

The Little White Wonder

It was but a small affair.

—GENERAL ANTONIO LÓPEZ DE SANTA ANNA,
on the Alamo

I t wasn't a particularly good idea, but if it was mine then it was hardly
surprising. It might have made a little more sense if I'd put some
thought into it, but rational thinking not necessarily being my forte at
the time, I decided to declare my independence and make a solo album.

But first things first. With our burgeoning success, we'd decided to
get all entrepreneurial and form a record company. Why not? If the
Beatles could cock it up, who's to say we shouldn't have had the opportunity to do the same thing? The principals along with Elton and myself
were producer Gus Dudgeon, current manager John Reid, and in-house
coordinator and guru Steve Brown. Rocket Records was launched in
1973 with a label that depicted a . . . well, not a rocket, but a cartoon
Thomas the Tank Engine kind of train! I'm still wondering why.

In its infancy, it was definitely more idealistic than successful with
the first batch of releases winding up in the bargain bin pretty much
out of the gate. Our offices, deep in the heart of Soho on Wardour
Street, were a perfect reflection of both the idealism and the guileless-
ness that the label copy depicted. Topsy-turvy and cramped, they were
located up a rickety flight of wooden stairs in a narrow old building
surrounded by porn merchants and strip clubs. In other words, it was
quite fabulous, Soho at that time being a slightly more concentrated

and less treacherous version of New York's Times Square of the same time period.

It was a clubby little place with three or four offices and a makeshift reception area. Elton's manager, John Reid, had an office in the back and Gus had one to the left of it. Steve's, however, was where we'd hang since Steve was more apt to compose a more laid-back environment. Embracing the hippie manifesto, he'd painted the walls to mirror Rocket's motifs. Sky blue with puffy white clouds and tranquil pastoral scenes, it was like spending time in a peacenik nursery. Steve burned incense, drank a lot of coffee, and smoked a great deal. It was here, though, that a lot of plans were made and ideas, both good and bad, were discussed, many regarding album design and titles. Although Elton was not an artist on Rocket Records at this point, everything pertaining to his career was in-house at Rocket. I remember one afternoon, Monty Python alumnus Eric Idle came in to help us with the ad campaign and titling of what would become the *Caribou* album. As you can imagine, his ideas were both ingenious and absurd. Best of all was his suggestion that the commercial voice-over should have the announcer continually get the name of the album wrong, "Get the new Elton John album *Elk*, no, sorry, sorry, *Moose*, no *Yak*, *Aardvark*," while a frustrated voice off-screen shrieks, "It's *CARIBOU!*"

By the mid-'70s, Rocket had established offices in LA and were flush with the success of several career comeback albums by the hit-making '60s pop star Neil Sedaka. It was around this time that I had the idea that if everyone else (band members Davey Johnstone and Nigel Olsson) was making solo records, it might possibly be time for me to get my oar in the water. With Sedaka's albums making waves, it was suggested that his producer, Robert Appere, might be a good fit for me. I wasn't so sure, for while Neil's records were impeccably produced, I had in mind something a little rougher round the edges. My tastes were not really leaning to glossy power pop, so I imagined someone perhaps with a foot in both minimalistic rock and raw country. What in fact was really needed was someone who could control and work around my increasingly unpredictable behavior. Robert Appere actually turned out to be that guy.

The whole affair was slapdash from the start, beginning with my decision that it would be all cover songs with the exception of one self-penned number. The reasons for this were twofold: One I was too lazy to round up any potential cowriters, and two, there were some songs around currently that I loved and wanted to record, things like Tom Waits's "San Diego Serenade" and Mickey Newbury's "Mobile Blue." The problem was dissenting voices, while placating me with much of what I was desirous of, wanted their two cents worth. So while I was allowed Buck Owens's "Crying Time" and Curtis and Delanoe's Everly Brothers classic "Let It Be Me," I was press-ganged into making a stab at things like the Atlanta Rhythm Section's "Cuban Crisis" and for some odd reason two songs by the rudimentary pop duo the Sanford-Townsend Band, a macabre story song entitled "Squire James" and a forgettable feel-good number called "Mississippi Sunshine." They did come up with one interesting gem, a sort of meandering Dylanesque parable by Tonio K called "Ain't You the One" that eventually turned out to be one of the album's best. The only track I really put up any resistance to was Eddie Cochran's "Twenty Flight Rock." Not because I didn't like it; I loved it. It's just that I found it difficult to sing and knew it. They got their way, but I was right, and it sucked.

The players we assembled were a crack team. Ace session drummer Jim Keltner, guitarist Ben Benay, Elton band member bassist Kenny Passarelli, and keyboard wizard and future nine-time Academy Award nominated film composer James Newton Howard. Passarelli was my cowriting partner on the album's only original, a slow laconic cowboy song called "Blood in the Dust."

Because Elton had completed much of the tracking for the *Blue Moves* album at Eastern Sound in Toronto, it was decided that we fly over the forty-ninth parallel to do the same thing. A bonus to this strategy may have been to extract me from LA, relocating me somewhere I'd be less likely to be distracted by familiarity. How wrong can you be? I laid waste to Toronto like the Visigoths sacked Rome.

To ensure I complete the task at hand, I was put in the care of a very large ex-football player named Bill Hodge. Bodyguard is a term usually used to describe someone whose job it is to protect their client from others. In Bill's case, I imagine he was assigned to protect me from myself. The head of his own private security company, Bill was a good guy: easy going, levelheaded, and not easily ruffled. This was a good thing because I tested his patience like no man deserved.

I liked Toronto and still do. Through my friend Alice Cooper, I made the acquaintance of a very handsome and stylish Indian bass player called Prakash John. He'd made a name for himself after being recruited by George Clinton to share bass duties with Bootsy Collins in Funkadelic and had gone on to play with Lou Reed as well as Alice. Prakash had excellent taste. Not only did he have a very beautiful girlfriend, he also had an amazing car and knew the city inside out. Being tapped into what's what, they immediately made the mistake of introducing me to the city's best bars and restaurants. It was a hip town, and I took to it immediately, filling in the hours between recording by staying lubricated and well-fed.

The one major mistake made in the scheduling was that we usually tracked in the daylight hours and left the evenings free for vocals. As you might imagine, by this time seeing the microphone was hard enough, never mind singing into it. Propped up on a stool with a diligent Bill Hodge hovering close by lest I topple sideways, we laid down some surprisingly effective weather-beaten vocals. Not everything worked, but the songs that benefited best from this kind of treatment had an eerie quality to them that was most effective.

After the studio, at night I'd hit any spots still open for an abundance of nightcaps before retiring to my hotel where I'd keep Bill up to all hours manning a movie projector at the end of my bed. Since I was clueless as to how the thing worked (VCRs being a thing of the future), I required Bill's assistance in changing the reels. At times he'd nod off on the couch, so I tied a string around his wrist and yanked it when the spools ran out.

One night in a desperate attempt to reach a particular watering hole that was near closing time, I persuaded Bill to make a detour that required some off-road driving. Jumping off the curb we cut a path across a national city park and shaved off several miles to our destination. The incredulous looks we received from late-night joggers and dog walkers was one of open-mouthed astonishment as our fire-red jeep tore an uncompromising path, uprooting restrictive signs and floral borders. Luckily, we weren't spotted by the cops and apprehended. Knowing the rigidity of Canadian law, I'd most likely still be languishing in Kingston Penitentiary, "He should have kept off the grass" forever stamped on my criminal record.

At some juncture in the proceedings, we got a flying visit from Elton, who, newly indulging in white line fever, fit right into the unfolding madness. The most notable act of foolishness that took place while he was with us was an impromptu game of cornhole conducted from my hotel bedroom window. Collecting all the glass ashtrays we could find, we took turns in attempting to sail the circular missiles into a large metal dumpster seventeen floors below. I've been informed since then that Elton promised the winner a lifetime supply of cocaine, a thoughtful offer that, happily, he welched on.

With our work in Toronto completed, the flight home proved to be an entertaining highlight that surprisingly didn't involve bad behavior on my part. Bill Hodge, frazzled and sleep-deprived, but no doubt delighted to be unshackled from his exasperating charge, celebrated by doing serious damage to the cocktail cart. Delighted at this Declaration of Independence, I egged him on while making sure not to let myself fall behind. There was nothing surreptitious in Bill's quest to drain the plane, and being a big guy, with his normally calm voice dialed up to a gridiron bellow, he began to illicit uncomfortable squirming in our fellow passengers. In due course, a call of nature uprooted Bill, sending him on a heavy-hoofed stumble beyond the purple curtain. Five minutes later, after a lull in the disruption, a familiar voice roared out over the plane's PA system singing an off-key "California Girls." With this, the curtain flew back exposing Bill surrounded by several crew members hovering like angry birds pecking at an oak tree. As the outstretched arms of pleading stewardesses did their best to reclaim their property, Bill directed his attention toward the rear of the plane. "Hey, fat lady in the back, sit down!" was just one of several directives he managed to impart before the mic was wrestled out his hand and order restored.

With beverage service to Bill discontinued, he immediately sat back down and fell asleep. Good thing, too, as it probably saved his ass from being greeted at the gate by the LAPD. With rules and regulations not being quite so stringent in the days long before 9/11 and COVID-19, Bill got a pass. Me, too. I got to get another drink.

Back in LA, we booked ourselves into Sunset Sound for overdubs and guest vocalists. The latter consisting of a couple of friends and an equal number of folks we reached out to in hopes they'd say yes. These included Phil Everly, who graciously agreed to sing with me on "Let It Be Me," and country singer Jessi Colter, wife of Waylon Jennings. The fact that I had the audacity to presume I could go toe-to-toe with an Everly Brother was beyond ballsy. Phil, though, proved to be a delight and was, as expected, harmoniously sublime. Jessi sang on "Crying Time" along with Ringo, who in the same straights as me at the time, added a vocal full of well-lubricated pathos.

While these additions were most appreciated, there was the participation of a newer friend that I got an extra special kick out of. As a founding member of The Band, Rick Danko was not only the bass player in a group that changed my life like no other, but he also sang like a tarnished angel and pretty much could play any instrument you threw at him. We clicked immediately, and to call him my friend was an honor, The Band's music having been so instrumental in getting me to the point I was at.

Rick was one of the most kinetic human beings I'd ever befriend and, in turn, one of the most soulful. Admittedly, he did vast amounts of blow that might have contributed to his restless energy, but in all honesty, it didn't seem to invest him with the vexatious characteristics it manifested in others. On "Blood in the Dust," my sole contribution to the album as a writer, he vocalized with such aching intensity I was moved to tears.

To promote his own eponymous debut album, Rick played a show at the Roxy, parking his tour bus directly in front of the club. Holed up inside, he spent the hour before showtime bouncing around, knocking back shots of tequila, and plowing through an abundance of marching powder. Admittedly, I wondered how someone with this amount of debilitating toxins in their body could possibly perform a comprehensible show. I was proved wrong; he was simply great. Entering through the back to the dressing room located directly above the stage, Rick and his band began singing an a cappella version of the Four Tops's "Loving You Is Sweeter Than Ever." The club fell silent as the boys trooped out of the dressing room and down the stairs to the stage while singing together in perfect harmony. Still singing, they picked up their instruments and on cue fell into the song with razor sharp precision. It was dramatic and impressive and set a tone for the whole show.

Post-gig, we wound up back at my house on Doheny where the concert continued with assorted pickers and grinners dropping by to join the fun. Rick never lagged, and while continuing to partake of his preshow diet, played mandolin to Harry Dean Stanton's strummed guitar. The night however belonged to Paul Butterfield, the legendary virtuoso blowing some of the wickedest harp I've ever heard. It was otherworldly, filling the house with a combination of spine-tingling magic and ethereal chromatics. Butterfield was an interesting cat, not unfriendly, but reserved and intense, obviously high, and possessing what I imagined might be a darker and potentially dangerous character simmering somewhere below the surface. I don't remember who else was there, but I do know that a lot of music was played, including spirited versions of "I'll Fly Away," "Down to the River to Pray," and "I Like the Christian Life," songs that seemed at odds with the harmless, yet vice-ridden revelers. Still, 50 percent of the Lord was better than 100 percent of the Devil.

The last time I saw Rick was in New York in May 1985. After The Band's farewell concert, The Last Waltz, in 1976, the group had splintered but reconvened in time without Robbie Robertson, their guitarist, main songwriter, and de facto leader. Augmented by several other players, they were playing the Lone Star Cafe on the corner of Fifth Avenue and Thirteenth Street. Rick, learning I was in town, got in touch and insisted I come down and get reacquainted.

I didn't have to be asked twice and was there as requested, still drawn by their spiritual earthiness, a devoted disciple still worshiping at the altar of their incomparable convergence. What I wasn't expecting was a glowing introduction and an invitation to come up and sing one. Trapped and terrified, I had little choice. Singing in front of that rhythm section, one of the best on the planet, was hardly comprehensible. I managed, and singing two on mic with Rick and Levon Helm's backbeat driving an impossibly savage shuffle, completed a passable take on Johnny Otis's "Willie and the Hand Jive." I went to bed that night euphoric and warm with tequila, my heart racing in the realization I'd fronted The Band!

As of this writing, with the exception of Robbie Robertson and Garth Hudson, they're all gone now, the victims of suicide (Richard Manuel), cancer (Levon), and in 1999, after succumbing to heroin addiction, Rick passed away in his sleep at the age of fifty-five.

Rick was a gentle soul who chased the tail of the dragon just a little too recklessly. He put on weight, and, ultimately, his heart couldn't withstand the years of abuse. Some years after Rick's death *Rolling Stone* published an article recollecting The Last Waltz concert. In it, the writer described both Rick and Richard Manuel as "looking worn down by the effects of drug addiction." I was incensed, especially in Rick's case. Rick may have been indulging, but he was far from looking worn-out. On the contrary, if you watch the movie, Rick is clear-eyed, focused, and singing and playing beautifully. He also is immaculately turned out and looks like a handsome twenty-two-year-old. How the writer of the piece ever got that perception was beyond me, and I fired off a letter expressing my feelings stating my displeasure at his assessment. They printed my letter, and I felt a sense of satisfaction that I had in some way vindicated my friend from what I perceived to be an inaccurate form of character assassination. Reacquaint yourself with the movie and watch him singing "It Makes No Difference." You'll have to agree. It's Rick at the height of his powers, the quintessential golden god.

Oh, right, what happened to my solo album? It never saw the light of day. Slipping between the cracks of distribution changes at Rocket Records, it simply evaporated in the corporate crossover. There wasn't a tremendous amount of enthusiasm for it anyway, the consensus being that it was a hodgepodge of confusing styles not likely to excite radio listeners and enthrall consumers.

I WENT ON to make two legit solo albums before my tenure with my roots band, Farm Dogs, in the mid-'90s. *He Who Rides the Tiger* for Elektra Records in 1980 was a lyrically satisfying but melodically wanting dark noir storytelling outing that got decently reviewed in regard to . . . drum roll please, the lyrics. *Tribe* for RCA in 1987 was a more mainstream rock/pop album. Produced and cowritten by the very talented British bassist and songwriter Martin Page, it was high energy and technically polished with, for the most part, excellent songs and an overall look of sophistication and well-thought-out design. It also spawned two singles, "Friend of the Flag" and "Citizen Jane," which were accompanied by highly stylized videos, a fad I loathed but went along with in order to adhere to the times.

Concurrently with this, Martin and I wrote a couple of songs that unintentionally overshadowed my own erstwhile effort. Anathema to critics and sophisticates alike, the anthemic "We Built This City" became a colossal worldwide hit spawning a publishing bonanza that still ricochets through commercials, TV, and movies to this day. Derided by *Blender* magazine as "the most awesomely bad song of all time" (a compliment I wear as a badge of honor), it has refused to die, steamrolling on long after *Blender* magazine bit the dust. Even Grace Slick, the lead vocalist who sang it with Jefferson Starship, chose to trash-talk it once she was sure the success it afforded her group had dissipated. In later years she even took time to step up the heat by trashing the absurdity of the lyrics, which coming from someone whose earlier career included its own quota of songs riddled with unfathomable mumbo jumbo should get her equal billing in cheesy detritus. When you spend the best part of your adult life painting pictures of white rabbits because it references the only song of yours that anyone remembers, I wouldn't go knocking one that people are going to remember long after the rabbit's dead.

Do I like the song? It's a moot point. If I hadn't written it, no, but I did, so I stand by it. It's been good to me and my family, and for that

I thank the more commercial minds that took it from a dark brooding demo about the eradication of LA nightclub life and turned it into what, at one time or another, has become a giant sing-along, jerry-rigged for every city in the nation. On my desk I have a framed cartoon of *The Argyle Sweater,* drawn by Scott Hilburn. It is entitled "Torture Methods Listed by Pain Levels." The first four are thumb screws, the rack, the pillory, and the iron maiden, and the fifth, you guessed it—"We Built This City" on replay. Me, I'm always happy if I can rub the wrong people up the right way.

Along with "We Built This City," Martin and I also wrote a song called "These Dreams," another huge hit for Heart. Both songs reached number one on the Billboard charts six months apart making our collaboration a resounding, but short-lived, success. I've always been proud of the fact that I can navigate my way through different styles, even if some of them are not to my own personal taste. It makes for interesting challenges, and besides my day job with Elton, my music making both back then and now was built on an ever-evolving appreciation of multiple genres that we have continually incorporated, which is why our catalog is so diverse.

Sometime in the 2000s, the tapes of the Toronto sessions came into my possession after turning up during a spring clean at Rocket. They were in poor shape and possibly unsalvageable, but after turning them over to my old friend and studio owner Mark Paladino, through the process of baking them he was able to bring them back to life. Baking tape is a process that temporarily removes the moisture that has accumulated in the binder. This restores the tapes and enables them to function like new for a limited time, thus allowing you to transfer them to another format. Mark saved the bulk of the tracks and cut a CD for me. Listening to them after all those years didn't alter my outlook. The tracks I liked back then were the tracks I liked again when reacquainting myself with them. The rest were not good, so much so that the discomfort in my delivery is clearly apparent.

After listening to them once, I grabbed a sharpie to title the jewel case. Pausing, it occurred to me that in my hand I had the only surviving copy. Reminded of Bob Dylan's legendary late '60s bootleg the *Great White Wonder*, I tipped my hat and titled my own pirated memory *The Little White Wonder*. After this, I threw it in a drawer where it remained until it went missing in a move many years later. It was always a project sabotaged by my own inconsistency, a deformed vanity never meant to survive.

The Ragtop Leaves on Friday

Now is no time to think of what you do not have.
Think of what you can do with what there is.

—ERNEST HEMINGWAY
The Old Man and the Sea

Mexico before the cartels governed was a magical land. Assuredly the country and the people remain unique, but where once its borders invited unfettered adventure on the open road, they now only promise instability and tremendous danger. Mexico is rugged and primal, so steeped in tempestuous history that it unfortunately harbors the perfect stage for violence, an outlaw terrain channeling itself all the way back to the spirit of Pancho Villa and Joaquín Murrieta. It's no wonder then that this rustic template for the songs and movies that instilled my childhood and ignited my writing should one day envelop me in its embrace.

It all started with a fishing trip. I'd always liked throwing a line in the water, but I'd never taken my limited skills to the open sea. Up to a certain point, my angling endeavors had been of a freshwater nature. Lolling around in a bass boat with little expertise and more interest in the tranquility of it all, I felt it was time to kick it up a notch and get serious.

Through a mutual friend who was more adept in this kind of thing, I was directed to Cabo San Lucas on the southern tip of Mexico's Baja California peninsula. Back then, Cabo was still under development and had not even come close to the exclusive enclave of ritzy hotels and luxurious vacation homes it eventually morphed into. The likes of the Palmilla, Bajo Colorado, and Finisterra were adequate, but it was the characteristically unadorned Hotel Cabo San Lucas that exacted the most old-world charm. It was perched on a rocky bluff with magnificent views and had a plugged-in connection to the vibrant fishing scene. Here, where the Pacific Ocean meets the Sea of Cortez, was where I proposed to live the Hemingway dream.

October and November were the prime months. It was at this time of the year that the coveted black marlins ran and sportfishermen worldwide would flock to these fertile seas. Unlike in years to come, the primary reason for heading here was to fish, and no shortage of vessels were at hand for hire. Hooked up with a couple of likely locals and a no-frills thirty-four-foot boat, I set out to be tutored in the art of big game fishing.

Little did I know how fertile these waters were. No doubt my two experienced and supportive crew knew every square inch of this ocean, and as we made our way past the iconic El Arco de Cabo San Lucas with the sun leisurely ascending above the horizon, the water seemed to come alive. Someone once dubbed the Sea of Cortez the "World's Aquarium," and it was easy to see why. Almost immediately, bottlenose dolphins were flanking our boat and flying fish were zipping in and out of the water beyond our bow. Not to be confused with dolphin fish (also known as dorado), these charitable mammals converged as if possessed of a protective quality that my shipmates, through hand gestures and broken English, assured me was a sign of good luck. In those moments, it wasn't hard to feel fantastically free and very much alive. These guardians of the ocean had a calming effect, an almost transmorphic ability to assure us safe passage and good hunting.

The next thing I knew, the captain was cranking the engine and pointing port side. About half a mile off, the sky was full of birds and not just any birds. These were *tijereta* (frigate birds) and a sure sign of fish . . . big fish! Snapped out of my idealistic reverie, my heart started pounding and I began pacing the deck like an expectant father. Damn it all, I hadn't even had a starter kit lesson on something manageable, and now, here we're steering into the motherlode.

The guys were already in the process of baiting and trailing the lines of all four rods into the wake of the boat while I swiveled and undulated in an effort to look confident. Too fast, too fast, I wasn't ready! My idealized aspirations of emulating the literary aquatic battle was possibly imminent and I was unprepared.

A reel screamed and for the next minute my world became a blur, impossible to recount. The next thing I knew I was strapped in the fighting chair, feet planted in the footrests, the rod in my hands, the base set firmly in the gimbal mount. The captain hovered, gesticulating wildly, and I pulled back hard at his command thus setting the hook and baptizing myself in a rite of passage.

It was a sailfish and a beauty. As the line went taut it reared from the ocean and arched above the water, the turquoise blue of its writhing form catching the sun in a shimmering rainbow of spray and sunlight. Diving back down and deep, it ran taking incalculable feet of line with it. Shocked by its speed and strength, I set my torso down hard in the chair and prepared to do battle. Aided and abetted by the steady direction of my instructors, I was able to find my rhythm and come to grips figuratively with the technique. Reeling in the slack line and allowing some give in return to the fish, I slowly but surely maneuvered it closer to the boat. In a little over forty-five minutes, sweating like a docker, my entire body torqued like a pretzel. I had it on the gunnel.

Back then, the catch and release laws were lax, but in all good consciousness there was no way I could take its life. To watch the color drain from its body, its ebony eyes, marble-sized and bright, abate and die, its magnificence extinguished, was not an option.

Believe me, apart from the fact that I'd hit the big time in no time, it wasn't lost on me that this accomplishment and my refusal to retain a trophy would most likely place me in the pantheon of great angling liars. As prepared as I was to face the skeptic who may deduct pounds and feet from my claim under the assumption "he's exaggerating," any eye-rolling could be rendered null and void by simply keeping it to myself and be satisfied with that.

The rest of the day was a blinder as we hit more bountiful schools of fish and I managed to bring in a couple of healthy-sized dorado and a nice yellowtail. It was a pretty exhausted, but hubristic, angler that disembarked later that afternoon with heady expectations for the following day. My cockiness, however, came to a crashing halt when I awoke the next morning and couldn't move my arms. I felt like I'd bench-pressed two hundred pounds for an hour, which in theory, I had. Embarrassed, I had to cancel my trip while compensating the crew for their inconvenience.

I got over it soon enough though, but I'd been bitten by the bug and I vowed to return, which I did. Fishing, whether fresh water or salt, is philosophic meditation. As someone once said, "It transports us to a special world, and a state of mind, where we are free." Whoever coined the phrase "carpe diem" was undoubtedly a fisherman.

Over a decade later, I would go sharking on the Great Barrier Reef in Australia and experience my *Jaws* moment when an eighteen-foot great white shark strafed our boat in an attempt to overturn us. When you've got about two thousand pounds of frenzied fish determined to dislodge you for a snack, it's cause for both alarm and "a bigger boat." Luckily, there was a sister hunter close at hand, and between the two vessels, we managed to not only get the predator to cease and desist but gaffed it and hauled it in. A set of jaws three feet wide hung in my garage for years!

I would on occasion bring a friend, but in all honesty my solo excursions were both the most liberating and beneficial. Paradoxically, the less of me I had to spread around the more time I was afforded with my ruminations. In Mexico, inspiration was in the air and in particular on the water. With no one to placate, I'd simply drift into thought and the muse would be generous. I've no doubt much of my early works, whether it be titles, character, or conceptualization, were formed on the deck of a fishing boat.

Likewise, the evenings were equally inspirational. Back before Cabo's transformation into the Riviera of the Baja, there was no nightlife to speak of and what there was were simple cantinas designed for locals with tourists as an afterthought. My go-to hole-in-the-wall was just down the hill from the hotel. I really don't think it even had a name. To the best of my recollection the only text on the crumbling white stucco was *cerveza*! It was open fronted, no doors just three walls, a bar, and a small kitchen in the back. It looked like a set piece from a Sam Peckinpah movie and exuded a vibe of timelessness, a south of the border Brigadoon that existed as if only to stubbornly resist change. Laid-back is an understatement. The food came out when whoever decided to cook felt like sending it. The staff seemed to consist of everyone in the place, and slow motion was apparently the primary choice of inclination. The only thing that appeared as if by telepathy were the drinks. They were always there, no request necessary. A shell game in which bottles and glasses moved from table to table, an unwritten rule governing distribution by sleight of hand. It was fantastic, and only got better when the musicians arrived.

They ambled in individually, no formulaic set pattern to their regime, just a bunch of working stiffs congregating to unwind, shoot the breeze, and swap songs. It was all guitars, no trumpets, violins, or *guitarróns*, the bulky acoustic bass so identifiable with Mexican ensembles. This wasn't a performance group, it was simply local players who came together to eat, drink, and sing on their own dime. It was unvarnished and raw, not your sequin and gold braided mariachis playing "La Negra" and "La Cucaracha" over family fajitas at El Coyote on Melrose. These guys had a vibrant camaraderie. Playfully competitive, they harangued each other in a guttural singsong cadence that filled the night with laughter and stars. Hunched over their instruments, they sang of love, oppression, and revolutionary heroes, *corridos* and *rancheras* invested with the melodious history of generations. It was magical and romantic, once again investing my imagination with cinematic vistas. Transfixed by this acoustical mesmerism, the sultry arid evening air fanned my propensity to fictionalize. Written in my mind and recorded there, *vaqueros* and *banditos* thundered across the Sonoran Desert past pueblos, saguaros, and towering mesas. Purloining from the very best, I stocked my mental arsenal by invoking the ghosts of the nefarious and noble, the hoofs of their horses setting rhythmic patterns to my already formulating ideas.

Acapulco in 1976 was the polar opposite of Cabo's early hardscrabble years. A reverse situation that would see what was then a thriving vacation hub bristling with countless entertainment amenities vaporize over the decades into what it has become today. Acapulco is no longer safe to visit. It is gang ruled, racked with political assassinations, and in 2016, rechristened with the unwanted accolade of Mexico's Most Violent City.

This would have been inconceivable and impossible to predict when I had my "get the hell outta Dodge" epiphany in the fall of '76. Worn out from all manner of excess and in desperate need of a cerebral recharge, I chose to seek sanctuary in Acapulco. LA had suddenly felt claustrophobic, and in the aftermath of such a tumultuous year, detoxification could only be achieved by relocating to fresher air.

Through Alice Cooper's multifaceted manager, the eternally laid-back Shep Gordon, I was directed to the services of one Jaqueline Petite. In the business of real estate and securing rentals for a select few, she was an extroverted Tilt-A-Whirl in perpetual motion, irrepressible, spinning from A to B like the Road Runner in Gucci.

I've encountered many eccentric women in my life, but Jaqueline was a different animal. A socialite with character to burn, her backstory was murky. Never one to give up any information, she lived in the moment, orchestrating every introduction and event as if it were of monumental importance. Detective work has turned up nothing, but you didn't have to be Kreskin to imagine her history was checkered and littered with romance, opulence, and intrigue.

Alice and his fiancé, Sheryl, had engaged her earlier in the year to assist with their wedding. What they got was pure Jaqueline. Turning up an hour late with a bemused minister in tow, she arrived soaked to the skin, her dress clinging to her body, saturated and completely see-through, a bathroom towel still wrapped around her head.

The location I got was a gorgeous rental. Jaqueline showed it to me while dressed in a gold lamé bikini and heels. It was owned by Marie Fisher, the widow of legendary New York mayor Fiorello La Guardia. Just what the doctor ordered, it was spacious, airy, and open fronted, boasting a substantial patio, generous pool, and a phenomenal view of the Zona Dorada, Acapulco's premier bay. It was a far cry from my humble digs in Cabo, and a total 360 in regard to environment. Acapulco's golden era began in the 1950s and escalated with the construction of the iconic hotel Las Brisas, the pink and white palace that became synonymous with the rich and famous. On into the '60s, it remained a magnet for international celebrity, its colorful cityscape encompassing world-class beaches and an abundantly upmarket nightlife. By the time I blew into town, there was a little more modernity thrown in the mix, but just enough of the old glitz to keep it unique.

My initial mantra was to go it alone, be my own Zen master and recharge my depleted batteries. Once again, alone was never my problem, and, elevated in my Olympian retreat, it was easy to segue into a behavioral pattern of semi-abstinence. As long as Zeus stayed put and didn't descend into the 24/7 Hades at the bottom of the hill, this might actually be achievable. Catered to by a terrific housekeeper, I hiked, swam, read voraciously, and lived on ceviche and white wine spritzers.

It's the hiking part and Jaqueline's involvement in it that fractured my monastic stability and kicked the ass of my inner yogi. She arrived early one morning requesting I join her for an exciting and vigorous ramble. Dressed like Coco Chanel about to traverse the Amazon, she hustled me into her car and tore off down the road as if she were piloting the *Millennium Falcon*. In no time, we were screeching to a halt in some scrubby shrubland close to the ocean. Up front and setting the pace, she looked every inch the determined explorer, her course charted, her bemused batman picking up the slack. We marched on, and for a while the going was easy enough. The sea breeze was invigorating, keeping the humidity at bay, the thermals bouncing the birds around as they dove and rose beyond our sightline. Rabbits skittered around in the bushes and lizards sunned on the rocks, and for the moment all was pleasant enough.

Before long, however, foliage seemed to become scarcer and rocks more prevalent. Also, what was initially a relatively even surface was becoming increasingly craggy. I'll be honest, I wasn't paying a whole lot of attention, and in my attempts to keep up I failed to truly access our current status. The gradual curve upward was deceiving but it was soon apparent that not only was the hike intensifying but our trajectory was becoming steeper and steeper until we were almost vertical and literally climbing. Within minutes I was grappling with jutting rocks and digging my feet in for support. In a disorientated state of momentary perplexity, I rationalized that this was no longer rigorous exercise and that looking back might not be the best idea. Like the button that says DO NOT PRESS, I did exactly that; I looked back, or should I say down, and my blood froze. We were quite literally on a rock face and a good forty feet up. I can't begin to truly explain how I felt in that moment, my memory withers at the thought of it. The absolute fear that racked by body completely immobilized me. With grim thoughts of imminent demise racing through my mind, I was slowly aroused from my bleak assessment by a voice from above. Without leaning my head back, lest the weight of it dislodge me, I tilted it sideways and rolled my eyes upward. There she was, the cause of my predicament, a good twenty feet above, all smiles and beckoning brightly, sitting on the cliff's edge swinging her legs like some overstimulated teenager. In a fog of fear, I calculated that this was a fight for survival. Driven by a desire to strangle this mad bitch with my bare hands, I exorcised my negative demons and began my ascent. Embracing the precipice, I embarked on a slow diligent crawl targeting any indentation that might offer the best support. It was during this final leg of my ordeal that I began to hallucinate, or that was what I imagined. In my periphery to the left I saw arched bodies falling through the air, gracefully down and out of sight. Was I mentally predicting my imminent fate; were these bronze angels here to bear me aloft into the arms of my maker? These thoughts rushed through my confused and tortured brain as I finally clambered out of that hell at odds with my equilibrium and too fatigued to commit bodily harm.

The angels? Well, they weren't angels, but they were real. This crazy cow had had me climbing up the cliffs of La Quebrada where, for a paltry fee, local lunatics risk life and limb by diving from over a hundred feet up into a narrow strip of water below. Acapulco's number one tourist attraction could have been embellished by a sidebar snuff movie free of charge had I not made it out alive.

From then on, avoiding any further contact with Jaqueline was of primary concern. With complete exhaustion having stifled any retribution on my part, I set to reestablish the status quo. After my ordeal, along with its life-threatening overtones, it was time to sever my ties, not just with Jaqueline, but with my hermetic alter ego. It was time to summon the troops. I was desperate to take the edge off, my nerves having been exposed, the raw fragility of aftershock leaving me in need of detonation.

Back at Casa Taupin, reinforcements duly arrived nullifying the contemplative nature of the previous weeks. Rooms got occupied and provisions became more substantial. The spacious open floor plan echoed with multiple footfall as friends and lovers repopulated my transitory ashram with liquor, laughter, and the respiratory hum of conversation.

First up was Loree, my current flame. Raised in Chicago, Loree Rodkin was a raven-haired beauty who'd headed west to LA in 1969. With a natural affinity for interior design, she was the possessor of immaculate taste and a dry sense of humor. After spending time in New York, she had returned to California in the early '70s, entering into a relationship with Don Henley of the Eagles. It had come to an end, and Don, stung by its disintegration, had aimed his exceptional songwriting skills by skewering Loree in a verse from the title song of his band's current album *Hotel California*. You know, the bit about antique lamps, expensive cars, and attractive young men. Ouch! As if in an act of contrition, Don had had second thoughts and softened the blow in "Wasted Time," another song from the same album. The last verse is a lamentation of sorts, a more reflective and poignant adieu.

Loree's search had wound up discovering yours truly, and whether or not that was a step in the right direction is not for me to judge. As always, Loree brought with her a sense of style that smoothed out my rougher edges but could never quite extinguish my singular addiction. That is to say, I liked to drink, she didn't. But to her credit, I'm imagining she saw it as a romantic consumptive poet sort of thing and navigated it accordingly. It helped that I was a contemplative and creative drunk, never ever mean or violent. I wasn't Dylan Thomas and she wasn't Caitlin MacNamara dolling out cynicism to her man's suicidal decline. This balance of an alcoholic and a teetotaler cohabitating wasn't unusual for the time, and with Alice Cooper, my congenial best bud due in anytime soon, I'd have the quintessential drinking partner to quantify the guilt I never really had in the first place.

I'd been in Acapulco since early November, so there were two major holidays on the agenda. In due course, the ragged influx of revelers consisted of a serious grab bag of conviviality. Before and during Thanksgiving and into the buildup to Christmas and after, we were joined at one point or another by not just Alice and Sheryl, but my dear friend and Elton's management wrangler, Connie Pappas. Also along for the ride, but holed up elsewhere, was another longtime buddy from my UK days, the consistently creative screenwriter, Ian La Frenais. Along with his delightfully bohemian future wife, Doris Vartan, Ian was the very personification of meticulous observation. I guess that's what made him so good at what he did. Ian was figuratively like a ribald old pirate scouting out prospects for plunder. With his fruity laugh and direct assessment of what makes human nature consistently humorous in its perplexity, he had always commanded my deep admiration. His longtime partnership with coconspirator Dick Clement had birthed the finest British TV comedies of the '60s and '70s.

The camaraderie was infectious, and it was magical in all manner of combinations. We lounged, we took the sun, we read, we fed, and we took in the town. Snapshots show bronzed vacationers cozied up together in all manner of booths from Boccaccio to Carlos and Charlie's. In loud shirts and linen pants, kaftans, and sundresses, we align along the balcony of my rented home, an embracing body of twilight smiles. Big drinks, long straws, shot glasses, and water backs all incorporated into a colorful hue of carefree intimateness. It's incongruous how the camera freezes you in time. How it solidifies you momentarily and never lets go. It doesn't lie, it just browns and dissipates with age, chronicling an instant but refusing to follow its subjects into the future. It's a license to reflect but holds no notion of what's to come. What once was a constant becomes slowly pulled apart until we grow into a set pattern where old friends remain under an umbrella of reflective familiarity, yet seldom return in the same orchestrated formations. Partners change, friends shuffle like a deck of cards, dealt out into geographical settings that make reuniting infrequent. I regret this; these people are still my friends. There is no encumbrance that prevents me from making an effort other than my own reclusive nature. I hope to do better as I age.

Another of the incoming was my old friend from England, photographer and creative designer David Larkham. David had been in the mix from mine and Elton's earliest days working on all our album sleeves from *Empty Sky* to *Rock of the Westies*. He'd taken candid shots of us in our formative years when we were fledgling songwriters still knocking on doors and honing our craft. Very much a part of that simple time when innocence outweighed the consequences of the future, he'd arrived in California with us on our first visit, one of the select few to accompany us on that history-making journey. Like myself, he had embraced LA and returned to live and make a qualified success of himself, owning his own independent company and designing album covers for many classic rock albums of the '70s.

David, who had recently separated from his wife, Janice, had been living in my house as a caretaker during my extended absence. Five years previously, Janice had embroidered the album cover of *Madman Across the Water* and was the main inspiration for *the seamstress for the band* in "Tiny Dancer," a song inhabited by fragments of a handful of LA females: a Whisky a Go Go waitress, a girl who worked in a Beverly Hills shoe store, and a hitchhiker in cutoffs on Pacific Coast Highway.

It was close to Christmas, and David, in an inadvertent pretravel questionnaire, had thoughtfully asked me if I needed anything exported from the home turf. Well, of course, big mistake. Dumb stuff naturally: decorations, tinsel, and copious amounts of aerosol snow. Most important, though, was a fresh twenty-pound turkey that accompanied David on the flight, occupying its own first-class seat.

It was a mellow enough threesome who dined on the terrace that Christmas, presided over by our first-class turkey. At that time there was much on my mind. After two months escaping into an alternate world, I was creatively estranged from my oldest friend and about to run slipshod into a purgatorial hiatus.

We all flew back in the New Year, our futures in question. Loree and I made it on into the following year, but ultimately she couldn't handle my excesses and her requests for me to desist fell on deaf ears. Much as I thought I might be, I wasn't in the "true love" business, and she was far too smart and driven to deal with my escalating dependencies. It was a relationship destined to falter, which it did eventually in a fog of acrimonious recrimination somewhere between LA and New York. Did

I write a song about it? Yes, in something I'm ashamed to say is fired up with more venom than "Hotel California." I'll fess up that "I'm Still Standing," a song that has become synonymous as an anthem for Elton's steely quest for survival (and quite rightfully so), was originally written in response to Loree's and my failed love in a time of impossibilities. My exercise in bittersweet black humor was certainly something she didn't deserve given my previous disasters. What she did get out of both mine and Don's relationships were three good songs. As they say, all's well that ends well, and Loree and I are now the very best of friends, as are Don and I. Both are unique and tremendously successful people.

After a couple of years of interchanging collaborations, solo ventures, and a multitude of personal misadventures, the dynamic duo ultimately returned, two rooms at the end of the world reconnected without ever falling out in the first place. Reconciliation be damned, it's a moot point because it never happened in terms to define that characterization. We simply made up for our *Lack of communication on the telephone line* and *Got that aching feeling / to look up one another one more time.* Yup, we simply hooked back up easy as Sunday morning. Pulled the waterlogged wagon of overkill out of the corporate ditch and hooked it back up to pen, paper, and piano.

It was a 1964 fire-engine red Plymouth Signet, and starting sometime in the early '90s it transported Mark and I on any given weekend into the Mexican heartland. The ragtop did indeed leave on Friday, and with it a categorical sayonara to whatever was impeding our daily lives.

Mark Paladino was a wiry, good-looking Italian kid from Jersey. The possessor of serious street smarts, he was bright, adroit, and completely incorrigible. A composite that made him the perfect partner in crime. I was at that time by no means done with the specter of mischief while at the same time retaining an ever-present need for discovery, inspiration, and intelligent interaction. Mark was able to achieve this status by bookending my much-needed renaissance, and in the process accompanied me on some of the most dubious and entertaining exploits of my post '80s years. I have never in my life laughed with any other individual as much as I laughed with Mark.

He'd come to LA in 1967, bummed around, and inhabited a series of bands before forming his own at the onset of the new wave movement. Playing the Sunset Strip's usual suspects, he'd entered into a romantic relationship with the model Rene Russo. Rene, a world-class beauty and later a first-class actress, had ultimately forsaken him for some other rock stud, leaving Mark adrift and working for Modern Records. Through Rene's sister and my younger brother, both of whom were familiar with him on one level or another, Mark slowly drifted into my orbit. Soon we became inseparable.

Our collective passions collided, annoying all those who chose to believe themselves the logistical and assumed purveyors of stability. A tier above this domestic tyranny we were full-on bro harmony, personifying a diverse entanglement of unashamedly macho camaraderie. Boxing, football, sex, and booze were a shared cache unavailable to outsiders. Mick and Keith were the Glimmer Twins, Steven Tyler and Joe Perry the Toxic Twins, Mark and Bernie euphemistically and with tongues planted firmly in cheek became the Scum Brothers!

We did so much together. We invaded the UK several times, and on one trip set about sampling every craft beer in every county we visited. Bear in mind, English ale is not the overcarbonated kitty piss that constitutes domestic US beer. We are talking hardcore locally brewed stuff where only a couple of pints can transform you from a country bumpkin into a Hopi shaman. Some of it was like liquid peyote and, much to the infuriation of our female companions, kept us on a permanent high. We were, of course, insufferable to anyone but ourselves, rewriting the rules of both tourism, etiquette, and the English stiff upper lip. On a one-note assessment, we just found everything funny.

On another excursion, I took him on a crash course of my past— careening along country backroads deep into the heart of darkest Lincolnshire. With a definite *Reader's Digest* approach to my fractured history, I attempted to recall any points of interest. A mile from my childhood stomping grounds a sharp S-bend jogged my memory.

"Hey, I came up with the first verse of 'Rocket Man' right here."

Before he'd had time to ingest that tidbit of trivia we were roaring through the village of my youth and on into the barroom of what had supposedly been the inspiration for my most famous brawl. Seven miles farther on up the road was Market Rasen and the Aston Arms. Apparently, there's a plaque there now indicating that this is where I did indeed conjure up the kernel of a seed that grew into our rowdy classic. I'm not sure that's altogether true, but I imagine if "Saturday Night's Alright for Fighting" was birthed anywhere, I think many of its references are indebted to this drinking establishment.

Three miles northeast of the bruising déjà vu of Market Rasen's hoary past we took in Tealby, a delightful confection of sleepy tranquility. Winning an unparalleled number of awards as one of England's most beautiful villages, it was traditional overload of the first order—a predominant collection of thatched cottages and impeccably orchestrated floral imagery. I briefly owned my own dwelling in this idyllic setting in the belief that I was somehow married to the traditionalism of a UK utopia. Celtic and gnomic traditionalism aside, I'd left my A. A. Milne and Kenneth Grahame version of pastoral Edwardian England lying dormant long ago.

Hainton was yet another tiny village in the spider web of civil parishes and communities that dotted the landscape. Many of them date back to the eleventh century, and most of them grew out of medieval settlements. In time, a village was deemed a village if it had a house of worship and a gathering place. No doubt this is why every village in England has a church and a pub, a sort of unwritten British law that binds you to faith and fermentation.

It was Hainton that I switched to Hienton, and thus wrote my first lyrical reflection on young love. Not to confuse matters, but the subject of the song actually lived two miles up the road in a hamlet called Six Hills. Being that neither Hainton nor Six Hills sang that well melodically, I took poetic license by gussying it up with a bit of elevated Lorna Dooneism. The song, "First Episode at Hienton," might have been composed around the same time as "Your Song," but whereas "Your Song" may be more familiar, its protagonist was most definitely a figment of my imagination.

The Valerie in "First Episode at Hienton" was very real and was my secondary school girlfriend. I suppose, my first real girlfriend. I perceived it as a romance, when you're fifteen or sixteen, love in such a relationship is totally inapplicable. You loved your parents and your pets, but the utterance of such an unfathomable realization was never going to materialize. Crushes back then were the exclusive domain of sexual stirring. Postpuberty, the discovery of an erection in a warm bathtub wasn't going to give insight into something it takes decades to truly understand.

The song is a fanciful reflection, a tribute I suppose to someone who left an impression. By the time I came to write the song several years later, it was embellished with an almost Harlequinesque nature that took immeasurable liberties with the truth. But then again, unbuttoning a blouse in a youth club closet, inept fumbling on her parents' couch, and questionable kissing techniques do not present an aura of mystique. The song as recorded was a theme that boded well for the era in which it was written. Valerie was well worth the time I invested in the relationship nearly sixty years ago, and if I wrote it again, I believe I'd write the truth.

At some point in our journey, Mark and I stopped off for Sunday lunch at my elder brother's home. The one member of our family who had remained in Lincolnshire, Tony had separated from his first wife, Belinda, and was recently married to a boisterous and somewhat overbearing woman called Jenny. When they had traveled to the US and visited my parents in North Hollywood, my father, never one to let affection get the better of honesty, decided he couldn't stand her and proceeded to completely ignore her. I'm not sure she deserved such a caustic freeze-out, but he did have a point: she could overwhelm with mind-mincing exuberance.

We duly congregated at a nearby pub for several jars before repairing for lunch. Apparently, according to Tony, Jenny had been busy in the kitchen all morning preparing the classic Sunday roast with all the trimmings. It did seem to be taking an inordinate amount of time, which meant more drinking. By the time we got the word, Mark and I were three sheets to the wind and famished. Fussing like a mother hen, Jenny ushered us to the table and assured us that this would be a meal we would never forget. Well, she was right about that. It was completely inedible. Everything was either burnt to a crisp, completely overcooked, or tough as mother's old boots. Nodding appreciatively in answer to her consistent requests for culinary validation, we attempted to consume what was indigestible. What did we do? We filled our pockets with gristle, seared flesh, and incinerated potatoes while slugging back copious amounts of wine to neutralize the nestling taste of acrylamide. The problem was she read our empty plates as plauditory kudos, a license to refill them one more time. Eventually, Tony divorced her and remarried his beloved Belinda, who, as luck would have it, is one of the most inventive and fantastic cooks imaginable.

In our trio of UK jaunts, with or without accompaniment, Mark and I seemed to have the most fun on any highway moving between A and Z. At one point we stopped at a Dartmoor pub straight out of *An American Werewolf in London*. Two freakishly large Irish wolfhounds lay like snoozing props before a fireplace big enough to park a bus in. At the bar, a couple of surly locals, like character actors from a vintage Hammer horror flick, huddled over pints complaining about "queer things happenin' about." You couldn't make stuff like this up, and as if in juxtaposition to this craggy antiquated watering hole, a mile up the road you had Gidleigh Park. Here, for a hefty price, you could take a time machine ride back to Downton Abbey. In a word, it was Westworld for the lace and hanky set.

Learning to wear different hats is par for the course in rock and roll, and over the years I've learned to switch character to accommodate all manner of the world's social inhabitants. Bikers and cowboys, divas, gangsters, eccentrics, and the most pretentious and affected personages imaginable. I've met and dealt with 'em all. Never once have I felt like I was patronizing, just always imbibing of the moment, loving and learning, enchanted and intrigued by life on both sides of the tracks. You never can presume what you're going to encounter and learn from any given collision of cultures. I once spent the evening in a Glasgow hotel bar deep in conversation with Jimmy Boyle, Scotland's most notorious gangster and hard man. This is a guy who had been sentenced to life in prison and preserved himself in solitary confinement by covering himself in his own excrement in order to parry the guards who clambered to administer daily beatings. He was erudite, charming, and completely engaging. Jimmy Boyle went on to write the most electrifying memoir, *A Sense of Freedom*, and after his parole in 1982 became one of Scotland's most acclaimed sculptors and novelists.

On our home turf back in the US, we had continually done much more of the same thing. We took frequent trips to Vegas for championship fights, on one occasion encountering a fellow ragtop enthusiast. Retrieving his fight tickets in the VIP offices of the MGM Grand was a completely windblown and dazed looking Nicolas Cage. Gingerly inquiring how his drive in was, he turned to us and with shell-shocked fragility assured us that "It was not without its ramifications." Seeing that his companion and shotgun rider was Charlie Sheen, we totally understood.

Our eventual decision to make the liberating pilgrimages into Mexico was the last hurrah in an escalating, inadvertent attempt to change my life. While it was still infused with all manner of freedom's follies, it also purged me of roadblocks that might be hindering my quest to reconnect with the honest realizations of growing older.

The emancipation of the wind, the warm night air, and the mingled fragrance of jasmine and gasoline made for a heady concoction. Something about leaving for Mexico was always invigorating. My desire to recharge made those Friday evenings an incomparable safety net. After a week of work interspersed with the stifling interrogation of inconclusive romantic relationships, I was ready to go.

We blew straight down Highway 5 through San Diego and across the San Ysidro border entry into Tijuana and on down State Route 1 all the way to La Fonda, a beachfront hotel. Thirty minutes south of Rosarito Beach, La Fonda had been a destination for wayfaring strangers, all manner of celebrities, surfers, and ne'er do wells for longer than I'd care to take a stab at. That ageless frat boy, Ted Kennedy, was said to have used it as his own personal knocking shop, hence La Fonda being nicknamed The No-Tell Hotel. It was a rambling potpourri of hacienda-style guesthouses, a restaurant, bar, and terraces that could only have been constructed by a team of blind designers lost in a fog of absinthe. That, of course, was its charm, the unparalleled clash of color, the construction of everything seemingly built from found objects, and a floorplan that after a pitcher of margaritas had you so confused you'd need a compass to find your room.

After the night ride in, it was unparalleled in its hospitality. Exuding an illicit air tailor-made for conspiratorial dalliances, its cozy dark corners and taffeta-hued terrace were intoxicating medicine. With two fingers of tequila and the warm Baja breeze at my back, the tensions I'd ridden out of town with fell away like the sun into the ocean.

Nothing was relative to time. We owned it and acted on a whim without a watch. We played Tecate-fueled touch football on the beach and built huge driftwood fires. We wrapped ourselves in ponchos, cranked up the boom box, and tried to make sense of life. Nights on the beach turned into bull sessions where everything was up for discussion. Soul brother bonding over politics, history, and the magnetic power of our sexual counterparts. The euphemisms might have been more direct back then, but my recollections have undoubtedly softened with age.

We fed ourselves from roving taco trucks and roadside produce stands, practically all of which were run by entire families. From the matriarchal *abuela* down to the youngest child, all served a purpose. It was a hierarchy of understood camaraderie carried out with efficiency, the long arduous days seeming to do little to dampen their good spirits. They were upbeat to a fault, never did we ever encounter anyone along the road who wouldn't have given you the shirt off their back. From dawn to dusk and into the night for surely what could have only been enough to keep them solvent, they were one more reason why that stretch of blacktop to Ensenada was more than just a road trip. They were a lesson learned, feeding not just the hungry, but serving up serious food for thought.

Ensenada was always a destination point. It's good to have something in life to aim for, and back then it was Hussong's Cantina. The oldest bar in town, it never failed to make you feel it was worth the trip. One of the world's greatest gifts is a good bar, and Hussong's was a doozy. We'd perch ourselves on a couple of stools there and not leave until we practically fell off them. We loved it there, and like in all good drinking establishments fell into the philosophical.

Vacationing with a group of friends is easy: conversation is shared and separate entities can break away for a breather. Burning up the road one-on-one over forty-eight hours sharing every moment together is a whole different ball of wax. It ain't easy to do, and you've got to have some kind of chemistry to make it work. I'm a solitary soul at heart, and admittedly, my attention span is limited when not stimulated. I have many friends whose company I cherish, but each one constitutes a different social interaction, a different way of playing against each other that makes every one of them interesting and entertaining in their own way. Back then, it took a certain availability to be as free as Mark and I were. In the allotted amount of time, we shared the spirit of individuality collided in a perfect blend of like-minded emancipation. What am I getting at? Only we could have done the things we did.

The last time we took the ragtop south was April 1993. The Branch Davidian compound in Waco was burning, and Elton's stage in Melbourne, Australia, had just been invaded by grasshoppers.

As always, we ended up in Ensenada but then decided to head on down the road apiece, winding up in La Bufadora. Not sure how it's fairing now, but back then it was infested with tourists and populated by an inordinate amount of tacky gift shops offering kitsch souvenirs. It was totally at odds with my rustic and timeless vision of this unbridled territory. This was not my Mexico.

The draw at La Bufadora is "The Snorter," a blowhole above a series of underwater caves that suck in the sea. The pressure of the intake, the result of air trapped in the caves, explodes upward, shooting the water a hundred feet in the air. It's an impressive sight that's cheapened by its overcommercialized surroundings.

Not to deny the public's opportunity to witness such a wonder or the local merchants' chances to extract the gringo dollar, but selfishly in my own mind I craved a purer finale. I later learned the legend behind "The Snorter." Supposedly, a whale became trapped in the rocky point and blew water to attract its pod's attention. Eventually, the whale turned to stone, staying there forever. In some way, I found this pro-phetic. Mexico was an exorcism. So many of my experiences there had a purity that shone a light into my restless heart, propelling me across one more hurdle on the road to redemption. Like the whale, my time south of the border is frozen in time. It will always be what it was back then and not what it has become.

Bad Day in Montserrat

I have no house only a shadow. But whenever you
are in need of a shadow, my shadow is yours.

—MALCOLM LOWRY
Under the Volcano

AIR Studios on the Caribbean island of Montserrat is decaying. Unlike most traditional ruins, it's disintegrating more rapidly by way of modernity. It was, after all, a recording facility, not Stonehenge; it was never rock solid, probably never built to last. Perhaps it was always meant to simply be a testament to a short-lived period of artistry. Sooner or later, due to its affiliation with collective bouts of hedonism and creativity attached to the obscene recording budgets of the time, it would ultimately be swallowed back into the earth by the competitive forces of nature.

We, as in Elton John and different musical formations, recorded three albums there before Hurricane Hugo hit in 1989, leaving over one-quarter of the population homeless. That was just the beginning. Not more than a couple of years later, the Soufrière Volcano (dormant for centuries) erupted and eviscerated the remaining landscape in a cascading lava flow of apocalyptic proportions. That was pretty much it. Sadly, the island was done and its moment in the sun, if you will, has become a footnote in the annals of "getting away from it all."

There's a 2021 documentary entitled *Under the Volcano* (not to be confused with the booze-soaked 1947 novel) that shows many of rock's premier performers utilizing this high-tech compound. Simultaneously, we see them basking by the pool, goofing off, and generally behaving like rock stars are supposed to. Dire Straits recorded their classic 1985 *Brothers in Arms* album here, while The Police knocked out two platinum-plus biggies, and Paul McCartney brought in Stevie Wonder to help him cut "Ebony and Ivory." Likewise Duran Duran, the Rolling Stones, and multiple others dug in and got stuff done while enjoying everything else this hospitable island had to offer.

That being said, I didn't really like it that much. Odd, given my inclination toward tropical retreats. The people were delightful, the staff at the studio couldn't have been more accommodating, and the island in general was composed of some truly stunning topography. Selfishly perhaps and due to my loner nature, the "communal thing" didn't always play into my over-romanticized ideology. I shouldn't have complained; it's not like we were living on top of each other. Unlike the Château d'Hérouville in France and Caribou Ranch in Colorado, where we'd all bunk up collectively, here we were living in a series of rented villas. Still, there was on my part a pervading sense of melancholy that I, for some unbeknownst reason, was feeling at the time. Perhaps the continual shamming and malcontent back home was messing with me more than usual. Still at odds with traditional domesticity, escape was supposed to be beneficial. This time, though, it didn't seem to be working. I'm not sure why; I didn't feel stifled here, there was plenty of breathing room, and I wasn't chained to the studio couch.

From the get-go, I've never been overly fond of studios. Back in the day, my work was usually completed up front, and outside of genuinely enjoying a great take, my contribution was usually nothing more than an enthusiastic nod or some simple lyrical jerry-rigging. I've always believed that a fraction of my phobia for studios stems back to my earliest inhabitation of them. They were always intimidating, not my terrain, and occupied by individuals better equipped to dwell in them than myself. There was an almost feminist inequality involved back then, a boy's club where I was playing the dumb blonde. "You sit and look pretty, let the boys do the heavy lifting." If you substitute "write the words" with "look pretty" you'll get an inkling as to what I'm talking about.

I had and still have the highest regard and greatest admiration for our earliest studio commandants. Guys like Caleb Quaye and, in particular, the outstanding and innovative Gus Dudgeon were exceptional in the control room. Gus's production on the bulk of our '70s output has never, I feel, been recognized with the reverence and respect it duly deserves. Those records are sonic masterpieces. Whether you care for the song content or not, any audiophile worth his salt still refers to the sound on them as one of the templates by which all others are judged.

That being said, this is the main reason we were never particularly close. I think I was ultimately invisible to Gus, his priority being completely aligned with those who powered the engine, not those who provided the coal. In my youth, this alienated me and made me feel somewhat insignificant. Of course this wasn't intentional, but it did disable me for some time, neutering my learning process. Back then, in terms of studio dynamics, I was without a doubt a second-class citizen.

In retrospect, had I been of a different temperament things might have gotten ugly. However, not being prone to amateur dramatics, the whole situation probably played to my advantage. My personality wasn't combative and my ruminative camouflage helped me develop an outsider identity. Always at arm's length from overt familiarity, things developed in a way that validated my characteristics. In hindsight I guess I didn't have to fight to belong, when, perhaps, in reality I didn't really care.

In terms of the core musicians, Gus was joined at the hip with the boys in the band. They developed a singular camaraderie, and it was impressive. It's not hard to understand why their friendship was so intertwined whereas mine was nonexistent. It was a unity I had no understanding of. I was a fly on the wall, they were the web weavers, tirelessly and effortlessly stitching together the necessary alchemy. As a combined force they would spend days getting drum, bass, and piano sounds before we even started recording. I might add that Elton didn't have the patience for this strategy but at the same time was as committed in his own way to the science of sonic perfection. As usual and as always, Elton was my anchor. From day one, without his constant presence in the studio, I'm not sure I wouldn't have preferred to just come in at closure and listen to the final results. The subduing nature of the environment was at times equal parts mind-numbingly dull, slightly claustrophobic, or satisfyingly euphoric. Being that Elton and I did absolutely everything together there was no question of me not being present. "Wherefore he goes, there go I" was my mantra. It all boiled down to the fact that it began with us and that everything after was icing on the cake. It was expected that I be present as the recipe was prepared, even after I'd helped supply one of the two main ingredients.

The earliest recollection I have of studio phobia dates back to around 1968 when we were cutting tracks in Dick James's studio under the auspices of Caleb Quaye. Caleb was an immensely talented guitar player and a proficient engineer who ran the DJM studio operation and would go on to be the guitarist on so much of our early work prior to Davey Johnstone joining the band. He was also the possessor of a raucous laugh, and to the uninitiated a somewhat intimidating and slightly sarcastic sense of humor. He was a great guy, just a tad too happy to find the chinks in my parochial armor. Caleb had been the finger pointer when I'd arrived at DJM to meet Elton for the first time. It was he who had turned on me from the control desk and demanded to know what I was doing there. This was strike one and had left me shaken. Sometime later when we were cutting demos, someone stuck a tambourine in my hand and suggested I play along with whatever we were working on at the time. Naturally, as a newbie I was clueless as to tempo and made a total cock-up of the whole thing. Rather than let it slide and cut me some slack, Caleb found it hilarious and made much of my rhythmic ignorance. It was hugely embarrassing, a minor incident that left a temporary scar. Proficiency comes with time, and five years later I was playing tambourine along with John Lennon at Madison Square Garden while extending a middle finger to the past.

I should add that later producers were more accommodating. As time marched on, so did my knowledge of studios. It didn't mean that I warmed to them particularly, but at least my presence in them wasn't ignored. My knowledge all around had experienced serious schooling, and on every level I was better educated. I earned my wings by paying attention and simply maturing in musicality and auditory awareness.

In this way I gained a respect that I hadn't enjoyed in the past. In time, everything changed, including how I wrote. Initially, my ideas were presented in unformed and meandering phrases, sometimes hammered out on a typewriter, sometimes simply handwritten in my spidery naked scrawl. As structure became apparent and rhythmic meter began to make sense, so did my cognizance of verses and bridges. In time, I couldn't write without a guitar in my lap and a legal pad at my fingertips. Like Linus with his blanket, it became a necessary psychological support. Simple chording aided me in making things flow more evenly, the natural singability of things being way more palatable. It's still how I write today, my '92 Ovation being my singular weapon of choice, and a word processor conveying the completed article once it has been transcribed from reams of yellow legal pad pages.

All this being said, I've certainly enjoyed intermittent in-house experiences in regard to making records. Usually, they're sessions that have an organic base to them. Projects that are recorded live with revelatory instrumentalists and set down on analog rather than digital technology. Tape, like vinyl, just resonates with more depth. I love that kids now can cut tracks in their bedrooms and formulate careers on social media. The opportunities for them are in their own hands and that is empowerment of a righteous kind. However, I'm a little long in the tooth for that. I still love that meat on the bone kind of music making that emanates from the core instruments of rock and roll. There's more pleasure in it now that my voice is louder. Explanations are given, ideas ruminated on, and direction of personal opinion is not trashed.

I've been more comfortable in diversified settings. A couple of examples: the 2001 Pat Leonard–produced *Songs from the West Coast* was an irresistible breath of fresh air, while due to Leon Russell's charismatic presence, 2010's *The Union* was a similar pleasure. In 2013, *The Diving Board*, like *The Union*, both produced by T Bone Burnett, was a healthy return to a piano, bass, and drums lineup, making it a cathartic experience all around.

Without a doubt the polar opposite, with no disparagement of the participants involved, would be 1997's *The Big Picture*. This release, while harboring some decent songs, has to be the singular most boring control room containment of my entire musical career. If a real instrument ever came into play, I've no recollection of it. The whole thing seemed like a series of programming and triggering devices that were all computer generated. Whether this was a decision made to give us progressive credibility I've never ascertained. Aside from the fact that I had to travel over five thousand miles to the UK to sit in a boxy control room and watch indiscriminate individuals press buttons all day, every day was enough to cross my eyes and drive me to the edge of insanity.

By the way, when I said "villas" earlier, I was being a bit charitable. Some might have been better than others in Montserrat, but none were what I would term luxurious. I'm not fussy, and after reading this book you'll be aware that I've crashed in enough places that could be termed either sketchy or spartan. However, in most cases, they came with conditions that stipulated a drawing of the line. I'll get to that later.

My digs were nothing to thumb your nose at: one level, simple, and elevated on a rocky plateau directly adjacent to a convenient backroad. All bleached stucco and tourist approved, it also had a nice-sized pool and a roommate in the form of band guitarist Davey Johnstone. If you're going to be saddled with a roommate, Davey was back then the best sort to have. Easygoing, far from needy, and totally independent, he was the band's go-to guy when I was feeling sociable. I wasn't uncomfortable with him as we'd shared some memorably bonkers excursions together around the world. From Amsterdam to foggy locations where stimulants can erase recollection, let's just say there were a couple of times we'd burned it down in complicity.

All this being said, what amplified my negative attitude to this particular patch of the Caribbean outside of human nature was a collective series of misadventures. On top of my complacency in regard to whatever might be happening elsewhere, I attempted to settle in in the best way possible. It barely lasted. Within the first few days, I was both burglarized and paralyzed.

Two nights in I returned to find my bedroom ransacked. What few valuables I had were gone and any initial complaint I made was countered with the fact that this was not unusual, pretty much "Oh yeah, it happens all the time!" In context to my earlier assessment as to the populace, allow me to make an amendment.

The next day while ruminating by the pool on the island's leniency toward thievery, I was zeroed in on by a hellacious local insect called a Jack Spania. These beyond badass Caribbean wasps seem to circle like mini-Chinook helicopters, zero in, and attack for no other reason than pissy aggression. The sting was like Max Muncy hitting you with a baseball bat. This fluorescent orange drone left my right arm paralyzed, painful, and inflexible. Embarrassingly, my infected arm was so catatonic in its rigidity that its undeniable upward slant gave anyone approaching me the impression I was proffering a Nazi salute.

With my writing arm incapable of function and my wallet empty, I attempted to make the best of my recovery. Of course, I made good on hanging out with the gang and especially spending time with Elton. I'm not really sure what my friend was imbibing at the time, but it was most assuredly something that had him amped up to the max. One night after work in the studio was completed, or at least Elton's input was, we retired to the pool for a little extracurricular aquatic recreation. Elton being Elton (intoxicated and possibly as high as Saturn), he tried to drown me. These sort of jousting tournaments between the two of us went all the way back to the days when he took great pleasure in placing a hot teaspoon on the back of my hand at any given opportunity. This along with farting silently in the back seat of a car and awaiting my reaction with a silly grin on his face were early juvenile but harmless party tricks. They, however, tended to get a little more aggressive as we aged, and when alcohol and drugs came into play. Point in fact was an evening at LA's Le Dome restaurant when after a bucketful of martinis he slapped me so hard across the face that I almost fell over. I might add that Elton was Herculeanly strong and built like a proverbial brick shithouse. So, liberally soused and not knowing his own strength, what was meant as a loving tap felt like a sucker punch. When he called me the next day, he had no recollection whatsoever of the incident and was sincere in his apology. The fact that he'd done it while conversing with the venerated song stylist Anthony

Newley cemented forgiveness and, in turn, gave good humor to these kinds of recollections.

Meanwhile back in the pool, the two of us were thrashing away like a pair of combative porpoises. His strength being far superior to mine and my arm only now recovering from rigor mortis, I attempted to scramble out of the water. It was at this point that the studio dog, a very large, yet normally complacent German shepherd, decided to join in the fun. Imagining me to be some discarded pool toy, he locked his ample jaws around my flailing leg, clamping down on my thigh with precise intent. It didn't really hurt, but then again, like my friend, I was seriously blitzed and numb by way of intoxication. The puncture was deep and obviously in need of medical assistance, a fact impeded by the island's lack of anything resembling *Emergency Ward 10*. What I got instead was *The Island of Doctor Moreau*!

Aware of my predicament, the altogether sober staff at the studio were on it in a jiffy. I wasn't even dry before they'd tossed me in the back of a jeep, wearing little more than a pair of shorts and nursing a bottle of Wild Turkey. With the latter in hand, I alternated by taking slugs from the bottle while simultaneously dousing my wound with generous splashes of the rapidly dwindling bourbon. Whether or not this dramatic form of vintage sterilization was something I'd picked up from too many westerns or in reality it really worked was inconsequential since the wound was starting to sting considerably and I was freezing my ass off.

The wind whipped around us as we tore an unsteady path into town. Unbeknownst to me, a call had been made ahead alerting the local sawbone as to my condition. Rousted from his slumber, he met us at the door. His office, it turned out, was located in the cellar beneath his house. I have to say, he was pretty damn jolly for a man recently turfed out of his bed to treat a half-naked drunken lyricist. If he looked like a caricature of Boris Karloff, his consulting room looked like it had been designed by Josef Mengele.

In a word it was a mess. It wasn't that it was dirty, although the dispersion of tongue depressors, thermometers, and other sundry medical items in random jam jars and old San Marzano cans gave off the distinct impression that a sanitized medical facility might be a little late in catching on in this corner of the tropics.

Teetering piles of journals and files were everywhere, drawers were half open and filled with what looked like hundreds of pens and discarded syringes. The furniture was threadbare, either patched up with gaffer tape or sprouting little clouds of synthetic fiber. Along the wall, to my relief, were a series of framed certificates reassuring anyone being administered to on these premises that they might indeed be in the hands of someone who knew what he was doing.

If you've ever had a rabies shot, you'll be aware that the needle looks like it's three feet long and hurts like a son of a bitch. The implementation of it into your leg, especially administered by someone you're not completely sure is actually in the medical profession, is frightening at best. So much fluid was injected into the locality of the wound that it caused my quadriceps to spasm and my leg to kick uncontrollably. It was not, I can assure you, a pleasant experience, but in all fairness this funny little man was the model of efficiency and more than competent. In fact, because it was so completely surreal, a margin of my fear was alleviated, not only by the booze but by his boisterous bedside manner. I've no doubt he, like the old island, is long gone.

Burglarized, paralyzed, and now punctured, I wondered how things could get worse. What happened next didn't harm my physical being but it certainly contained a biblical element that continued to hamper with my quest for peace of mind. When it rained on Montserrat, it rained, and when you have to maneuver home in an open jeep along roads so potholed they could swallow a dog, it's an exercise in absolute concentration.

It was already dusk, the skies were teeming, and I, soaked and hunkered down over the wheel, was cursing the elements and squinting into the distance, trying to navigate this forbidding thoroughfare. Not under the influence of anything debilitating, I was taken by surprise when the road ahead seemed to undulate. I slowed to a crawl, shook my head, and blinked profusely. No, it was still moving, but now it was no longer a singular hallucination but a sea of shadowy silhouettes accompanied by a low monotone of guttural croaking.

Oh, great. Mountain chickens. These creatures are not chickens at all. They're frogs. Really, really big frogs. In fact, the largest frogs in the world. Up to eight inches long and weighing around two pounds, "chicken" refers to their large hind legs. A local delicacy and a traditional Caribbean dish.

What happens is that when it's wet, they for some un-frog-like reason gravitate toward the highways in order to secure solid ground. I won't go into detail, but let me just say that forward movement along a road overrun with quaggy amphibians is completely unpleasant. If you're lucky and if the rain's heavy and your engine's loud enough and you're singing maniacally at the top of your voice, it's possible to render inaudible the sound of exploding frogs. This is how I made it home, leaving under my wheels and in my wake a trail of pancaked croakers. I've since learned that they are now on the critically endangered list, a fact that I can't help but feel I've somehow contributed to.

Soaked in tropical rain and remorse while averting my eyes from the slick coating of death on my tires, I abandoned my vehicle and headed for dry land. My reception committee was obstacle number two. Tarantulas also hate the wet ground, and a dozen or more had decided to seek shelter on my front door screen. I might add that I'm extremely fond of these arachnids, having had many interactions with them in my life, and as a rancher I've become appreciative of their individualistic and dignified presence. However, when you return to your rental late at night after some major frog genocide and find scores of tarantulas eclipsing your entrance, it's a different matter. Tired and a little freaked out from my drive, I simply retrieved a branch from the side of the house and with as much delicacy as possible bumped them off the screen and shooed them into the foliage.

Phase three was the worst. On a par with rats and maggots, there is one other species that I detest. Sliding open the door and flipping on the lights, literally dozens of cockroaches fled for parts unknown. This was way worse than all other things combined. It hadn't crossed my mind that these fast-moving, armor-plated, heebie-jeebie-inducing nightmares were under my roof. Lord love a duck, it was like having Freddy Krueger living in your house. The simple fact that you had no idea where they were, that they were most active at night, and supposedly could survive a nuclear attack left me riddled with a combination of paranoia and insomnia. I didn't sleep much after this, not in this house at least, but the lingering recollection of *The Swarm* stayed with me for the remainder of this trip. I stripped my bed, I vacuumed underneath it, I circled it with prayer. Did I mention I didn't particularly like it here?

THE ALBUM WE were currently making turned out to be the best we made on the island. A consolation of sorts for my bouts of indecision and concurrent bad luck. From day one and down through the decades, it seems like we've intermittently made an album that has reestablished our credibility and kicked our careers back up a notch. *Too Low for Zero* was undoubtedly that album for the '80s. It was a huge worldwide success and spawned several hits including "I'm Still Standing" and "I Guess That's Why They Call It the Blues."

All three albums recorded on the island were produced by Chris Thomas. The first album, *Jump Up!*, which I hadn't been a party to, was an unremarkable record featuring a mash-up of songs written by Elton with various collaborators including myself, having recently reconnected with Elton after our temporary separation. "Empty Garden" was the diamond in the rough, and to this day still one of our best and most poignant songs. The remainder of my contributions on this album were, for the most part, tragic. They included a couple of things I'd attempted to go against the grain with. I don't enjoy writing lyrics to existing melodies, but I attempted to do so when Elton, lost in a fog of drugs and holed up in Paris, was staying up late into the night hammering out an endless stream of compositional ideas. I tried to oblige but couldn't keep up with him. I simply did what I could, which, in essence, was nothing but blundering unimpressive schlock. "I Am Your Robot" anyone?

After *Too Low for Zero*, in 1984 I returned to Montserrat for the last time. The results were rewarding and the trip far less stressful. The album we made, *Breaking Hearts*, while by no means a classic, contained enough strong material to deem it noteworthy. That album produced four Top 40 singles, including "Sad Songs (Say So Much)" and "Who Wears These Shoes?" It was strong driving pop that, in retrospect, deserves some reevaluation. Deeper cuts like "Did He Shoot Her?" and "Slow Down Georgie (She's Poison)" are by no means filler, having strong melodic drive and smart effective lyrics.

With my allotted time for *Breaking Hearts* at an end, I prepared to erase the unpleasant tribulations of my stay by leaving. Happy to see the back of Jack Spanias, cockroaches, and giant frogs, but with a modicum of clemency for the studio dog, I flew to Antigua but had forgotten to pack my passport.

Unable to go any farther and stranded between my island nemesis and home, I managed to get through to the studio and beg for help. Davey, luckily, retrieved my passport, but it wouldn't be able to be delivered to me until the next day. Thankfully, someone in the know directed me to lodgings where I could spend the night.

Once again in keeping with the oddities that continually seemed to confront me, my hotel (and I use the word loosely) seemed at odds with the nature of accommodation. By the time I arrived, it was late in the day, the sun was setting, and I discovered a meandering property that sprouted from the vegetation like some stumpy collection of bleached topiary. Oddly enough, they were expecting me and were most generous in their welcome, excitedly fussing over me as if I were the first guest they'd had in years.

Outside of the staff, I don't recall seeing anyone else. The lobby, dimly lit but not without charm, smelled of wet earth and cleaning products. It was impossible to get a sense of the general structure as at intervals around the reception area, hallways like mysterious portals gave no indication as to what lay beyond. From the outside, it looked like there were multiple buildings, so I could only imagine that these darkened passageways led to accommodations elsewhere on the property. I proved to be correct in this assumption, but first I had dinner.

This was surprisingly excellent; in fact, the best food I'd had in a couple of weeks. Not that the studio kitchen didn't provide decent fare, but there was something about the nature of a candlelit dinner in a surreptitious setting that appealed to me and relaxed me after an altogether taxing day. Even the curious absence of fellow diners didn't really cross my mind. The waitstaff were so friendly and attentive that from my table, sequestered in a cozy nook, the place might as well have been alive with action. With the help of an excellent claret and some über-fresh fish, even my healthy imagination couldn't get the better of me. If I'd been lured here by white slavers to be drugged and shanghaied, waking up in two days on a Malaysian steamship bound for Mombasa, well, OK then.

Relaxed from the wine and engulfed by a sense of well-being, I reported to the front desk in order to locate my room. All I wanted now was a decent bed and a good night's sleep; as long as it didn't involve cockroaches, it could be as basic as a stable for all I cared. Careful what you wish for!

With a smile and a hearty good night, I was assigned an ancient bellman and no key. The old boy seemed hardly capable of standing, never mind handling a suitcase, and when I offered to carry it, he seemed offended. Shuffling across the lobby, we did indeed enter one of the black holes, a long nebulously lit black tube; it was humid and eerily silent. Like an escape route on the Underground Railroad or a drug lord's getaway, it seemed to stretch indefinitely. Perhaps because we were progressing at a snail's pace . . . that's an exaggeration because within minutes we'd turned a corner and we were out in the open. I didn't see anything resembling bungalows, only the thick vegetation at our back and before us an open field, complete with several mangy-looking cows. The old man started out into the field, and I, by now a combination of intrigued and slightly leery, followed dutifully. Within fifty yards of our trudge across the meadow, a slog that I might add involved sidestepping innumerable cow patties, the silhouette of a structure loomed before us. It was circular and tall, probably no more than four meters in diameter with a shale roof and, as I remember, no windows. This was my room, and whether it was the only one on the property, I never found out. It seemed a waste of time to either question my guide or drag my ass all the way back to request an upgrade.

It was lit by a single naked bulb and had an exposed toilet against the wall. There was also no furniture, no closets, and the shower was a hose hanging through the roof in the center of the room. The most bizarre twist was that the bed looked comfortable and clean. It didn't have a mint on the pillow, but there was a bottle of Evian on the nightstand. Yeah, it ranks up there in the annals of the idiosyncratic and wasn't going to be featured on *Lifestyles of the Rich and Famous*, but after everything else that had proceeded it of late, I found it strangely pacifying.

I slept surprisingly well, rose the next day, and without much effort located the entrance. Waiting on my passport, I did inquire as to the locations of the hotel's alternative rooms. Apparently, they existed. Exactly where remained a mystery, but I was assured that mine was the finest accommodation on the property.

Overdone Down Under

Such is life.

—NED KELLY's last words

I t's estimated that almost 20 percent of modern-day Australians are descended from transported convicts. It's also said that a convict in one's lineage is a cause for celebration. I can see why. Since the ships of the First Fleet deposited prisoners at Botany Bay in 1787, shackles and chains can be credited as much for their liberation as to their initially intended purpose. I mean the way I see it, the British government thinned out their putrid prisons by sending men and women of dubious character from a dank and fog-bound England to a sun-drenched land in the Indian Ocean. Alright! It wasn't all surfboards and shrimp on the barbie initially, but ultimately after brick making and timber cutting under sweltering conditions and brutal overseeing, their ever-evolving genealogy and fortitude paid off in spades. Probably not what His Majesty George IV had intended, but a good poke in the eye for those who imagined that these colonial castoffs would remain just that. The founding of Sydney and its evolution into the Emerald City is a perfect metaphor for the tortoise and the hare. Decades later, young men and women also of dubious character came in droves. From all across the globe, they came to serve time, not in chains, but in electric boots, mohair suits, and with really loud guitars.

There is a heightened light about Australia, and Sydney in particular. It shines with a crystalline radiance that bounces off the harbor and engulfs this architecturally magnificent city with a cone of complete clarity. I'll draw the line at utopian comparisons, but making my first trip there in early 1984 was like diving off the deck of the *Flying Dutchman*. I needed some breathing room, and the coasting nature of things back home wasn't providing me with lucidity in my work or an honest equilibrium in my personal life.

Arriving in this city built on the crack of the whip and the muscle of sweating human chattel was both refreshing and stimulating in equal measures. The country itself and its distribution of cultural diversity was enlightening. Like a colossal cake of unequally proportioned slices, it's a big-ass island harboring a divergent collision of all things UK and USA.

The cosmopolitan elements of its cities are built around hip universal themes while its boomer populace retains a proclivity for British humor hinged on a very tea and crumpets familiarity. Recording artists, comedians, and television personalities purely connected to the United Kingdom and nowhere else have found continued popularity and healthy shots of career stability in Oz.

On the other hand, the immeasurable acreage of its interior mirrors the American West. The outback is unforgiving with one of the most inhospitable terrains imaginable. This is where you'll find characters comparable to their distant forefathers, what I imagine to be the closest in temperament and durability to those who cast off the yoke of their oppressors almost two hundred years earlier. Hardened is an understatement. There is a faction of individuals inhabiting Australia's remotest outposts, places like the Kiwirrkurra Community in the Gibson Desert west of Alice Springs, that make the redneck element in *Deliverance* look like Amish doily embroiders.

Of course much of this was unfamiliar to me when we checked into The Sebel Townhouse, Sydney's very own rock and roll mecca. The Sebel was a boutique operation with a mere 160 rooms, 40 of which we initially occupied. It was modern, comfortable, and had a surreptitious vibe, sort of like a hip Chelsea Hotel without the bacteria and weird smell. It was located in the Kings Cross area of the city, none too savory, but edgy enough to heighten its desirability. Being that it catered to the idiosyncrasies of its guests, offered the ability to turn a blind eye to indiscretion, and had a tiny world-class bar, it was irresistible.

One of its greatest attributes was the night manager, Steve Rowland. Steve became like an extra wheel in our touring party due not only to his sublime affability, but his prowess in making over-padded bills go away and seeing that anyone in our tribe knew how to find anyone else at any given time. This latter quality got him christened "Reuters" by Elton, a man who felt everyone needed a sobriquet. Rod Stewart was Phyllis, Freddie Mercury was Melin as in Mercouri, and I for unknown reasons was briefly christened Mavis!

Things got interesting the minute we arrived. During the recording of the *Too Low for Zero* album on the Caribbean island of Montserrat, Elton had struck up a close friendship with a German sound engineer called Renate Blauel. It was an odd set of circumstances, and while everyone found Elton's fixation with this perfectly delightful young lady curious, the mere fact that he was spending so much of his free time with her made for circulated speculation. During that period, Elton had been more in the habit of flying his infatuations in and out of whatever location we found ourselves in. He seemed to be in love with someone different every week. Usually young men who were either smitten with his attention or the occasional hustler on the make. Either way, they would come and go in a revolving door–like manner: here today, gone tomorrow, and on occasion back again the day after they'd gone the first time.

So it was a shock, nonetheless, when Elton returned to The Sebel one night after an Indian meal with Renate and announced that he was getting married. Whether the strength of the curry was to blame for playing havoc with his mental state rather than his digestive system could not be determined, although the collective reaction of the band and crew was certainly one of emotional indigestion. "Oh good grief, here we go again." Memories of Furlong Road came flooding back along with those of Elton's first sabotaged stab at wedlock. In actuality it made even less sense now than it had in 1968. Back then at least he was still in a quandary over his sexual orientation, an excuse that can't be discounted. Now, however, he had fourteen years of nothing but gay relationships, both committed and recreational.

The absurdist nature of it was solidified by the two individuals he chose as his best men. One, his manager and first live-in lover, John

Reid, the other, his spiritual boyfriend, yours truly. Impulsive and dead set against anyone getting the last laugh, my friend was not joking. His irascible nature currently was not something anyone wanted to argue with or question. It just wasn't worth it, and while most of us doubted this was a union that would be any more successful than attempting to raise the *Titanic* with tweezers, we just shrugged our shoulders and took advantage of the festivities.

As you might imagine, everything was done to excess, especially in regard to alcohol and marching powder. The Sebel bar was practically drained dry as we smashed all previous records for the amount of money taken at the bar in one night. The reception also held at the hotel was stuffed to the gills with all manner of exotic food stuffs and ridiculously high-end wine. I mean, we're talking bottles of Margaux and Montrachet of collectable vintage that I imagine went unnoticed by many of the revelers whose main objective appeared to be waste not, want not and damn the torpedoes.

During the evening, I entertained an obviously booze-motivated proposal. Russell Mulcahy, the flashy and inventive director of MTV's most groundbreaking videos including Elton's iconic *I'm Still Standing* among others, was moving into motion pictures and currently planning a time-traveling fantasy/action-adventure called *Highlander*. It should be noted that grand plans made under the influence of weighty drinking and drug-fueled nights lose gravitas in the morning light. That being said, he actually sent me the script and even indicated a part I might be interested in. The role in question was that of Kirk Matunas, a crazed ex-Marine gun nut who attempts to exercise (by way of immense firepower) a citizen's conclusion to a back-alley sword fight between two immortals. For his interference he receives a large sword in his belly and is lifted off his feet by the Kurgan, ultimately played by the always-affective and imposing Clancy Brown. Who wouldn't want a shot at that? Queen doing the soundtrack and a Sean Connery cameo. Although Christopher Lambert in the lead role was adequate but not terribly strong, I took the offer seriously for five minutes. When I couldn't secure an AFTRA card in time, I let it go.

It was a completely bonkers time and just one more episode in a decade when things were careening all over the place, illogical and out of control. The '80s were the apex of our drug intake and alcoholism, yet it saw some good work, the *Too Low for Zero* album (which we were promoting in Australia) in particular being an admirable return to form. Yet in terms of low points, things like *Leather Jackets* (made in a complete blizzard of nihilism) and the abysmal *Jump Up!*, which had it not been for the exceptional Lennon tribute "Empty Garden," are among our most erroneous. The problem with the rest of our output is that while it was interspersed with some very good songs, they got lost in our catalog due to a couple of things. In the wake of punk and new wave, we were not terribly hip, and with our addictions marring our sense of purpose I imagine we believed ourselves better than we really were. We had our moments in the sun, but since being reunited at the offset of the decade, we were still not connected the way I would have preferred, our inner demons and dependencies taking pride of place, our social interaction restricted to not much else but the studio.

That being said should I, still his devoted friend, stick my oar in once the nuptials had been announced? Maybe, but what would have been the point? It would have just fallen on deaf ears and caused a rift that I wasn't about to induce due to my own personal life. I'd recently remarried, pondering, "How could it be any worse than the first time around?" It wasn't, not even close. But eventually it was still a mistake. Initially, it was a pursuit that in its subsequent achievement should have remained a temporary relationship rather than a fully announced, "I do." By the time she arrived in Australia to perform bridesmaid duty, I was seriously doubting my commitment.

Not that we had a lot of time to ingest the absurdity of our first few days here. Following Elton's wedding and its complete bacchanalia, we were winging our way to New Zealand. Not sure how we made it, but the following night I was standing backstage in Christchurch, New Zealand, gazing at the aurora australis. I might not have been terribly educated in celestial science at the time, but boy in the aftermath of the last few days this heavenly theater left me completely lost for words. It was so magnificent and compliant of God's hands that I only wish it had had as much of an effect on my morality back then as it did my vacuous ability to stare skyward and simply say, "Whoa, cool!"

After more dates in New Zealand, a beautifully anachronistic country that was at the time belittled by the Aussie elite as tragically outdated, we returned to the hatchling incubation of The Sebel bar and the company of John, its smooth and gossipy barman.

In The Sebel bar we would encounter all manner of diversity. While it attracted emerging Australian movie heroes like Mel Gibson, it was the British oddities that made it unique. They were more than likely to be familiar only to we children of the English '50s who had grown up on radio and the offerings of TV's black-and-white era, but still there was a well-worn familiarity to them that made us chuckle with realization and nostalgia.

One of the more impressive regulars at the bar while we were there was England's original guitar god, Hank Marvin. Marvin was legendary in the UK as the former lead guitarist for the Shadows, Britain's premier instrumental combo of the pre-Beatles '50s and '60s. They had risen to fame as the backing band for Cliff Richard, England's Elvis and a British institution from the dawn of rock to the modern day. Marvin would later relocate to Perth, Australia, in 1986, but due to whatever performing duties he had currently agreed to wound up on a stool at The Sebel bar. Odd considering that Marvin was a confirmed Jehovah's Witness, which meant abstaining from alcohol, serving in the armed forces, voting, singing the national anthem, and pretty much anything else of a celebratory nature you can think of.

The oddest of all bar sightings on this trip, and one who fit into the criteria I outlined previously, emerged from the density of the crowd one night when the band and myself were taking in a preshow cocktail. Not sure who it was among us who spotted him first, but due to his boisterous outcry I'm imagining it was guitarist Davey Johnstone. "Fuck me, it's Jimmy Edwards!"

Well, yes, it was and who is Jimmy Edwards you may well ask?

In postwar England, on both radio and TV, we'd grown up with Jimmy Edwards. He was a man of ample girth, booming voice, and a splendid handlebar mustache, a trademark that flared out from beneath his nostrils like a hairy pair of angel's wings. He'd become enormously popular in the '50s as a radio performer in Frank Muir and Denis Norden's *Take It From Here*, a show that achieved even more success for him when it introduced *The Glums*, a deadpan spin-off. His career was varied and high profile, especially his early TV sitcom *Whack-O!*, a sort of *Sergeant Bilko*–styled comedy with Edwards playing the scurrilous drunken headmaster of an elite public school whose cane-wielding character, a tyrannical schemer, was continually attempting to fleece his pupils out of their pocket money in order to finance his get-rich-quick schemes. It was a huge favorite of mine and one of the first things I recall watching on our black-and-white box when the world was younger and I was still preadolescent.

I'm not altogether sure where Jimmy's recognizability stood at this particular point in time. He'd remained visible in the UK and Australia throughout the '60s and '70s working in residencies at the Shaftesbury Theatre in London's West End and closing Melbourne's Tivoli Theatre in 1966, but by then I imagine he was becoming a bit of nostalgic trivia.

Faking heterosexuality, he'd been married for years before being outed as homosexual in 1979. Whether or not this played any part in his fading to black, I'm not sure. What was a bit "six degrees of separation" was that in the late '70s, my former PA, Pete, was dating Jo Turner, the daughter of celebrated British comedian and singer Joan Turner. Joan Turner (a genuinely acerbic wit) had at one point been the highest paid female vocalist in Britain, however her proclivity for drunkenness and volatile behavior (fired from the musical *Oliver!* for throwing empty wine bottles out of the window of her dressing room) banished her to seclusion and eventual destitution. At the point Pete was seeing her offspring, she was holed up in a small mews cottage somewhere in London's interior drinking herself to death and acting as Jimmy Edward's beard. Weird it was, and Pete would return from dropping her off with sad tales of fading vaudevillians hunkered down on a threadbare couch sucking up the booze and slurring out tales of a bygone era.

Meanwhile back in The Sebel bar, the old geezer seemed amiable enough and was up for anything if a free drink was involved. Did I mention he played the trombone? Well, he did and this is how Jimmy Edwards wound up walking onstage at the Sydney Entertainment Centre playing "I'm Forever Blowing Bubbles" on the trombone during an instrumental lull in "Rocket Man."

Elton later admitted that he thought he was hallucinating, and I've never actually ascertained as to whether he recognized his interloper. One's things for sure, I can absolutely, categorically attest to the fact that 99.9 percent of the audience didn't have a clue as to who he was and were as perplexed by his invasion of Elton's space as the star himself. It wouldn't be the last time that "Rocket Man" drew a bizarre comedic accompanist to the stage. Several decades after William Shatner's inexplicably surreal reading of the song, Jim Carrey walked on, sat himself down next to Elton, and attempted to play a piano solo with his head!

Nowhere near as outlandish, but still odd, was a phone call I received in my room early one morning. At the other end of the line in a weary but not unfriendly Texan drawl, the caller introduced himself to me as Mickey Newbury. I was immediately skeptical. It wasn't unusual for fans to purloin the personas of notable people in order to make contact, but Mickey Newbury?! If this indeed was an imposter, they'd certainly chosen the identity of someone I was certainly aware of but not a name familiar to the average man in the street. Mickey Newbury was the original country outlaw, bucking the Nashville system and forging his own path as a songwriter of tremendous diversity. His songs had been a great success since the early '60s when he'd penned the iconic "Just Dropped In (To See What Condition My Condition Was In)" among others. Perhaps his most significant cover had been Elvis's version of "An American Trilogy," his stirring medley of Civil War standards that became the grandiose highlight of Presley's live shows. I'd been a fan of Newbury ever since hearing "San Francisco Mabel Joy," which was, and remains, one of my favorite songs. Funnily enough, I'd also recorded a version of "Mobile Blue," another of his songs that I loved, although it was on the album I made that was never released.

I'd never met or ever had any interaction with him, so it was anyone's guess if it was indeed him or not. What made things stranger was his reason for calling. Did I know anywhere he could get some guitar strings? Well, let's bypass any small talk and get straight to the reason you're calling me, Bernie Taupin, a man not particularly known for his guitar playing skills, at 7 a.m. in the morning in Sydney, Australia, to see if I know where you can pick up a packet of 12-gauge strings. Sorry, but that's a little strange and warrants serious scrutiny, least of all: Why me, and how the hell did you know I was here and where? I could have assumed, logically, that he'd been up a little longer than was good for him and had stuck a pin in a who's who map of musicians currently in Oz, but still I think you can sympathize with my skepticism. While too polite to recommend certain options, like maybe the yellow pages or corralling his own booking agent, I simply pleaded a lack of geographical information and suggested he call an actual guitarist. I was never completely sure that it was him, but in doing research for this book I found out that Newbury toured Australia in 1984.

By the time we got back to Australia in 1986, things had gotten progressively more stagnant on the home front, and I was desperate to find a more liberating release anywhere other than where I lived. Even at my worst, and during times of extreme bad behavior, I can honestly say I remained on an even keel in regard to my morality. However, there are times that try a man's soul. And in order to assess my state of mind at this particular time, I'm reminded of the lyric of Tommy Collins's confessional ode to infidelity. "Carolyn" delivered so impressively by Merle Haggard says it all. *Yes, Carolyn, a man will do that sometime on his own / And sometimes when he's lonely / And I believe a man might do that out of spite / but Carolyn a man will do that always / When he's treated bad at home.*

I'm not proud of the fact, yet in retrospect I feel no guilt or remorse that I found favor in the arms of others. A marriage without passion is a marriage of convenience. Without a fire in your heart you're just coasting and running out of time. I was still young, and while I like to think that had the circumstances been different I would have remained true blue, it just wasn't in the cards. Terms like "codependency" fit the bill to a certain extent. And while not technically agoraphobic, due to various forms of low self-esteem she wanted to leave the house less and less, which yet again was ultimately fine with me. How do you go from writing declarations of love like "I Guess That's Why They Call it the Blues" to aching admissions of adultery like "Sacrifice"? Live life like I was living it, desperately unhappy, and without even realizing it looking for ways to screw it up.

One beacon of joy in the year prior to my return down under was Carlene Carter. I had rented an old farmhouse in the UK and was recording an album with Elton at a studio in Cookham, a historic old village in Berkshire. While there I was invited by the singer Kiki Dee, Elton's duet partner on the wildly popular "Don't Go Breaking My Heart," to see her act and sing in the West End production of the American musical *Pump Boys and Dinettes*. Along with Kiki, in the cast was Carlene. Carlene, who had recently separated from the exceptionally talented recording artist and producer Nick Lowe, was a singer-songwriter in her own right and the offspring of country music royalty. Her father being Carl "Mister Country" Smith, her mother being a former Carter Family member, June, who later married Johnny Cash and became June Carter Cash. I believe it's safe to say we were attracted to each other immediately. Carlene was a complete spark plug, lighting up the dressing room where we met with a hundred watt smile and a twang in her voice to die for. She was witty, warm, and sassy, not to mention remarkably pretty and petite.

Within days we were seeing each other every night. I'd be at the studio during the day, then I'd head into London hopping off the M4 at Hammersmith, and picking her up in the parking lot of the Hammersmith Odeon theater. These, being the '80s, were drug days, and after scoring a couple of grams of what she comically referred to as bat food we'd drive back to my rental, the colloquially named Swilly Farm. While I was not homesick for home per se, I was missing the US and all its levels of tradition and Americana, hence our tendency to spend the night listening to Emmylou Harris CDs and watching repeated viewings of *The Long Riders*, Walter Hill's saga of the James-Younger gang. Interestingly enough, the Emmylou album I'd play constantly was her

1978 gem *Quarter Moon in a Ten Cent Town*. The lead-off track, "Easy from Now On," contained the album's title and had been written by Carlene along with Susanna Clark, wife of Texan legend Guy Clark. Surprisingly, I wasn't turned off by the accusatory key line, *Harder to kill the ghost of a no good man*!

Of course it couldn't last, and it pains me to say I wasn't aware at the time how ultimately hurt Carlene was that it didn't work out. She retreated to her stepfather's home in Jamaica to lick her wounds and nestle under the wing of her sympathetic mother. I found out years later that Johnny and June would counsel her by recalling their own perils in matrimonial deceit. June would tell her: "If it was meant to be it would be," but sadly it wasn't. Carlene has remained my dear friend ever since, and I'm indebted to her for lighting up a very dark corner of my life.

Back in Australia, Elton was about to embark on a hugely ambitious tour incorporating the eighty-eight piece Melbourne Symphony Orchestra and a stage costume that I imagine was supposed to be a cross between Mozart and eighteenth-century formal wear. Either way, it was over the top and totally in character with my friend's determination to always set the bar a little higher than what anyone was expecting. Bear in mind, this is the same tour that in the band portion of the set he sported a two-foot-high turquoise mohawk and dragged it up in a full impersonation of Tina Turner. There was an awful lot of people about, and quite honestly I felt a little lost. Not in a bad way just *in the way*, which I didn't mind. It wasn't my wheelhouse, so in lieu of having anything to do, I stayed under the radar and rolled solo. For a while.

Nights would find me occupying a table at La Strada, my favorite restaurant in Sydney's Potts Point. Owned and operated by a former Italian immigrant called Giovanna Toppi, it was a magnet for visiting musicians and celebs who flocked in droves to her establishment. More important than merely having a "cool hang vibe," it was the food that kept me coming back. Giovanna had arrived in Australia penniless and had started her escalation to fame as a dishwasher in all manner of establishments before rising through the ranks to become the queen of

Sydney eateries. She cooked, bussed tables, berated the inefficient, and was perfectly charming to those of us paying homage. I loved both her and her stylish room. Decorated with movie stills from the 1954 Federico Fellini movie that lent the restaurant its name, it was like my nighttime office. It was here I'd round up a few waifs and strays not directly needed during showtime and carouse for an evening before heading back to The Sebel bar.

I'd like to make a point here. For those who might assume that I was simply coasting on a wave of Elton's tour dollars and flaunting around as if I was owed this luxury by way of my lyrical contributions, take note. I was continually observing, always in the minute, drawing my blueprints from every single thing that steered into my path throughout the day and into the night. My penchant for observation was a constant. I loved writing, I loved chronicling life, and every moment whether I was cogent, sober, or blitzed, I was forever feeding off my surroundings, making copious notes for future compositions. I was deadly serious about my work and even in the times when I may have turned out material that was subpar, I'm not altogether sure it was due to excessive intakes of alcohol and narcotics. As I recalled previously, I believe there were times we were coasting and not as committed as we should have been, but as is the way of things we ultimately took our trip off cruise control and got back to laying down some serious rubber. The thing is, good, bad or indifferent, I never stopped writing. It was as addictive as any drug. I was forever traveling the track and transporting the information back to the terminus. It might not always have been first rate, but the masses of what I accumulated, once sifted through, offered glimpses of things worthwhile and worth pursuing.

Elton was appearing at the Sydney Entertainment Centre for eight nights with his orchestral show, and I was continuing my marital indiscretions. I'd embarked on a very freewheeling and secretive fling with Elton's lone female backing singer, Shirley Lewis. It was dumb fun and, once again, an excuse to feel wanted rather than endure sterile cohabitation. Our friend, Steve Rowland, was no longer working at The Sebel, so with the regime change it was a slightly different environment, no less fun, but without his presence questionably less personal than it was when he was running the night show. It was perhaps for the better: the less anyone knew about what I was up to, the less anyone got hurt, which in itself is an anachronism in retrospect. I was simply floating free and easy, always waiting to see what tomorrow had to offer.

THE MATCH IN the powder barrel at home came when I made a conscious decision to go back on the road with Elton to promote our *Sleeping with the Past* album in 1989. Once again, it was an excuse to leave my domestic woes, but this time it was fatal. The clairvoyance of the album title notwithstanding, I was dead set on delivering the final nail to a coffin filled with too much remorse and one hell of an arsenal full of confessional material. That album for the most part is a veritable cypher of cryptic confessions of what was happening in and away from the home front. "Blue Avenue," "Whispers," "Stones Throw from Hurtin'," and, of course most tellingly, "Sacrifice," spelled out how rapidly the ship had been sinking. By the end of the year, we'd pitched our tent at the Turnberry Resort & Spa in Miami, using it as a staging ground to fly in and out for shows in the South.

It was here I met the PR director for the facility, and everything at home went south very fast. There were obvious elements to the rapidly escalating relationship that factored into the demise of the dying embers at home. I don't wish to sound superficial here because I've spent a lifetime paying for the stupid mistakes I've made, but in the moment as a red-blooded male, any man worth his salt would in all honesty agree that you may try, but sometimes you just can't win.

Fun might sound like a shallow moniker in the big picture, but without surfing on a broken record, I needed these experiences to keep me alive and functioning in dalliances that I would pay for (literally) for the rest of my life. Certain parties have and remain living high on the hog from my poorly executed moves. Do I regret it? Not for a moment, with the exception of my first marriage. That was a litany of stupidity on my part: too young, too naive, and unaware of the machinations of deceit that allowed it to happen.

Denise, the young lady in question, was exceptionally attractive. An ash-blonde dynamo who carried herself straight as an arrow and parlayed her obvious efficiency with a personable dynamic that was both conservatively sexy and exuberantly captivating. Needless to say, we tore it up. Reckless, dangerous, call it what you will, it was completed by the fast-paced and celestially lit dynamic that inhabits Miami. A sort of cross between a bloodless *Scarface* and the Buena Vista Social Club, we shared a passion for great restaurants, Miami Heat basketball games, beach bars, and ultimately each other.

Obviously, as things got progressively more serious she questioned my marital status. Was this a fling, was this serious, was I planning on divorcing? Ultimately, as I dug myself in deeper and deeper, and while I had no intention of getting out of one stranglehold into another, it did force me into making the ultimate decision to lower the boom on my marriage. This took place in a phone call from a hotel room in Boston and, as you might expect, did not go well.

My eventual return home was an ugly affair, and while I went along with the charade of trying to patch things up and make a go of it, in all honesty, I had no skin in the game. It was messy, at times hysterical, and for all the fake commiseration I made available it just wasn't possible to fake my determination to move on. It dragged out, there were lulls in the storm, but it was just a matter of time. It was hard to live with and would suddenly manifest itself in accusatory outbursts that didn't seem to really matter at that point. Funnily enough, the one affair she accused me of was one that didn't actually happen! She was convinced I was engaging in a nocturnal tryst with the lovely Nancy Wilson of the band Heart. It was a ridiculous accusation of course; however, it wasn't for a lack of trying.

It wasn't helped by a package that arrived one day containing a skimpy bikini that only a body of extremely nubile proportions could inhabit. Denise had left it in our room during a weekend at Little Palm Island Resort, a romantic getaway in the Florida Keys, and the hotel, determined to be efficient, had mailed it back to the residence of the dumbass who'd filled in the registration card.

Well, that was about it really. One morning it all came to a head and I simply said, "I'm done," and left taking literally nothing and leaving her everything. Oh, I grabbed enough for a couple of nights and had a close friend retrieve some other items at a later date, but quite honestly, I had no qualms about leaving everything and starting anew.

Gladiators in ancient Rome wore thirty-pound helmets with meshed eye slits that impaired their vision. Armed with heavy weapons they were expected to kill an opponent they could barely see. Leaving my home on Doheny Drive was like leaving the arena. I threw down my sword, pulled off my helmet, and never have I felt so free.

In-Between

Change is inevitable. Growth is optional.
—JOHN C. MAXWELL

1990 was undoubtedly a liberating new chapter. At the same time, that liberation was etched with a degree of self-absorbed mechanics that drove me to ignore some primary concerns. After my arbitrary retreat from Doheny, and with the towel thrown in on my second marriage, I simply went off the grid. The only place that this erratic action caused any real grief was for my parents. For while I don't believe anyone else was put out by my vanishing act, the singular fact that I couldn't find the time to keep my parents abreast of my whereabouts goes to prove how adrift I really was.

Out of my temporary digs at the Sunset Marquis and settled into my new apartment on Robertson, I was commuting regularly to Miami to visit my girlfriend, Denise. Most days there were spent hanging out at the pool bar of the Turnberry Resort where Denise worked in public relations. As hard as I tried to convince myself that I was investing my time discovering the meaning of life, in my heart of hearts I knew that while this might indeed be *The Razor's Edge*, I was no Larry Darrell. No matter how many transcendentally styled books I thumbed through, all the Carl Jung in the world wasn't going to help when a more pragmatic solution was easily obtainable. I just wasn't ready to simplify things and preferred to wallow in a self-designed torn and frayed persona.

I knew perfectly well that this current relationship was temporary. While it was casual and fun, there was no getting away from the fact that Denise wanted more out of it, a dream I couldn't fulfill. I was beginning to feel a certain amount of pressure that was only adding to my emotional upheaval. As things were coming to a head, all this changed with a phone message and some distressing news.

Stephanie Haymes was the very popular maître d' at Le Dome, the legendary industry restaurant on Sunset. I'd known Steff since she'd started working there, which was several years after Le Dome opened in 1977. The only daughter of world-class crooner Dick Haymes and singer and actress Fran Jeffries, Stephanie was a familiar presence and friend. Back when Steff was married to her then-husband, Bill Oakes, an executive in the Robert Stigwood Organization, my second wife and I double-dated with them occasionally, an irony that would play its hand in years to come. Like everything that transpired at Le Dome, familiarity drew everyone into social groups, and in my case it was one that included Steff. A lot of this centered on co-owner and French expatriate Michel Yhuelo, a magnet to whom it was impossible not to be attached. Stephanie's disturbing message pertained to him.

Michel Yhuelo was my earliest real friend in LA. I first met him when he was running Le Restaurant, his elegant French establishment on Melrose Place. Handsome, gregarious, and gay, he immediately made an impression and endeared himself to the close-knit group that constituted the Elton John inner circle. Le Restaurant was our original dining hangout in LA, well before Michel partnered with Eddie Kerkhofs (the manager of Le St. Germain) to eventually open Le Dome.

From the get-go, we became a sort of de facto odd couple embarking on everything from professional sports events to chaotic European vacations and spontaneous local outings. It wasn't in Michel's nature to consider the finer details of anything, and flying by the seat of his pants was very much his preferred method of traveling. Any bee in his bonnet was completely embraced and entered into with unbridled enthusiasm, even if his comprehension of the fine print was limited.

He had a delightful patriotic flair and loved his adopted country, putting as much fervor into celebrating American national holidays as he did French ones like Bastille Day. He also loved professional football, and when the Oakland Raiders relocated to LA in 1982, I'd occasionally drag him along where he'd exuberantly revel in the ardor of the crowd while at the same time having absolutely no idea what was going on down on the field. He just adored the vitality of it all: instigating stadium crowd waves, high-fiving anyone for no reason, and showing a remarkable interest in the tightness of the players' pants.

We'd go sailing with his great friend, actor, comedian, and director Charles Nelson Reilly, an unlikely nautical aficionado who, in actual fact, was a competent, if not facetious, sailor. Charles was like a gentler version of Paul Lynde, less abrasive and terribly sweet. He possessed a wonderfully dry wit, his humor edgy and off-the-cuff, which he imparted while standing erect behind the wheel, like some incredibly camp commander of the high seas.

Michel also loved to host dinner parties at his home, usually on a Sunday night when the restaurant was closed. Unfortunately, Michel's organizational skills being what they were, dinner would invariably be an hour or two later than everyone had presupposed. With copious amounts of wine on hand and hunger pangs gnawing at the bellies of his guests, people got drunker faster, thus helping to erase the fact that when the food did arrive, it was always the same old thing. Why this was, I have no idea since Michel on his home turf of Le Dome was positively Mr. Efficiency and uncompromising in his expectations of the food. At home it was chicken pot-au-feu. Pot-au-feu every weekend, or as it became known among the attendees, bones-and-gruel.

Our trips to Europe were never normal, normal meaning they were never simple tourist episodes that went according to plan and were completed without incident. Of course, that's what made them so memorable and made Michel's company so infectious. We'd wind up in the wrong places, lose track of each other, but still always have fun. In France, a country that he concluded would be far better off if there were no French people in it, he had enough contacts to steer us right when the going got erratic. We were certainly creatures of habit returning to familiar haunts where our most memorable experiences occurred.

In Paris an absolute must was Chez Michou, the celebrated drag cabaret in Montmartre. Like the Birdcage in *La Cage aux Folles,* it was colorful, wild, and uncompromising fun. The Michou in question was

Michel Catty, a bona fide Parisian legend. The two Michel's were old friends and air kisses abounded on any occasion we happened to drop by. A front-row seat was always guaranteed and Michou is a memory not easily forgotten. It was a warm and welcoming place filled with so much joy and fun, the personnel and performers irreverent and kitschy in the most pleasurable way.

We traveled to the wine country and Champagne, veering into the Loire Valley and making our way to Reims. It was in the Loire Valley that the hotel and restaurant Le Coq Hardi was situated, and no trip we made was complete without a pit stop at what Michel gleefully referred to as Le Hard Coq. In Reims, we went to the movies to see the erotic drama *The Story of O,* an adaptation of Pauline Réage's 1954 novel about sexual subservience. Of course, Michel loved it and insisted on sitting through it a second time, fascinated by what twisted fantasies took place in the minds of straight men. In the same way, he adored the Crazy Horse Saloon in Paris where naked symmetrically matched bombshells danced like a chorus line of R-rated Rockettes. He was just a big curious kid, the mystery of things exciting him, and he indiscriminately took interest in anything classified verboten by the morality police.

My parents adored him, and we visited them in England prior to their move from rural Lincolnshire to a new home in California. It so happened that this coincided with a dinner and dance benefiting the local cricket team with which my elder brother, Tony, was involved. I'd helped him out in the entertainment department by securing the services of my old friend, the hugely popular Scottish comedian, Billy Connolly. A tad radical perhaps since Billy's style was improvised obser-vation bordering on the seriously profane.

As expected, the dinner was pretty much the usual for these sorts of functions in the provinces at the time. Something resembling chicken surrounded by a sad assortment of frozen vegetables, followed by a sorry-looking confection of some sort. Michel, soaking in every bit of village life on a grand night out, lorded it up while seemingly undeterred by Lincolnshire's very own pot-au-feu. As the food was set before him, he politely inquired of the crinolined old serving crone if he might see the wine list, a request that prompted a bony finger to stab at the flimsy menu sheet beside his plate. Under the heading "Drinks" was the answer: "Wine, Red or White." I believe he kept that menu till the day he died. As expected, Billy managed to offend pretty much everyone in the room outside the hardier youth element, and of course Michel, who, due to Billy's thick Scottish accent, couldn't understand a word he was saying, yet laughed uproariously in all the wrong places. This wasn't to be the last time Billy's accent proved unintelligible. Out of sheer love for the man, Elton made the mistake of taking Billy as his opening act on his 1976 American tour. Not a good idea since the crowd hated him and made him, to paraphrase Billy, "As welcome as a fart in a suit of armor."

In time, things started to go wrong. Complications arose in Michel's health, odd maladies that went undiagnosed, all of which he shrugged off with his usual bonhomie. At first I took him at his word, but during our last vacation I became concerned. I'd rented a luxury yacht to sail us through the British Virgin Islands from a starting point at the old pirate stronghold of St. Thomas in the USVI. We stayed the night before our departure at a waterfront colonial-styled hotel that reminded me of the sort of place where W. Somerset Maugham may have written the short story "Rain." It had an architectural atmosphere that made you want to dress in white linen suits and panama hats and drink Negronis. I loved it. I felt like I was in another time, and it was the perfect spot to embark on a little decadence.

Lasting about a week, the voyage was uneventful except that Michel would tire easily, complained about swelling in his legs and groin, and, at times, became uncharacteristically cranky. His normally healthy appetite was noticeably suppressed, unusual food being one of the great bonding requirements of our collective trips. His weight loss was certainly becoming apparent, and the fact that he seemed unexcited by the abundance of fresh seafood being scooped out of the water by our accommodating crew was alarming

Admittedly, he would bounce back and regain flashes of his old self but no sooner than this happened, he would fall back, felled by some new complaint. It wasn't long after our island voyage that everything went pear-shaped in my life and my own troubles washed me away into what William Butler Yeats called "the abyss of himself." After I'd hung up my "Gone fishing" sign and unplugged from the mains, it would be weeks of commuting back and forth from Miami, running away from goodness knows what, when I got the call.

The voice mail I received from Stephanie was conclusive and emphatic. Michel's health was declining, and as one of his closest friends I needed to get my butt back and lend a hand while preparing for the worst. During the early stages of his erratic health issues, the common name for the plague that was preparing to sweep the country and decimate the gay community was not completely entrenched in the public mindset. There was so much misinformation and misunderstanding floating around that AIDS, in Michel's case, was not considered the culprit. By this time he was properly diagnosed and, with the advancement of ways to combat it still in the exploratory stages, his outlook was critical.

From the time I returned and got involved, there was a small group that congregated at his house holding a sort of constant vigil while aiding and assisting wherever possible. Aside from Stephanie and myself, there was Michel's Le Dome partner, Eddie Kerkhofs; their business manager, Connie; Maggie Wilde, a producer for Richard Gere's company; and Virginie Ferry, who was partnered with her husband, Gerard, in the elegant restaurant L'Orangerie.

For the most part, Michel was in and out of a sort of hazy delirium that didn't make much sense, but I saw him questioning the air with odd snippets of familiarity and the occasional brickbat aimed at his surroundings. I don't recall, but I'm sure as a collective, we swapped stories and regaled each other with the humorous exploits of "Zeee best in the west" as Michel would repeatedly refer to himself. It was during one of these bull sessions that an extraordinary thing happened. He got out of bed and wandered into the living room where he became remarkably lucid, which, in all honesty, was slightly unnerving. He even attempted to drink a glass of red wine, which I thought was absolutely the perfect last declaration for an epicurean like Michel. Wandering around the room, he took us all in with a stoned irreverent gaze, commenting here and there, and digging deep to find an appropriate insult for each of us.

It was both magical and surreal, the final rallying of a man determined to make exiting this mortal coil hard to forget. In due course, he wandered back into the bedroom, lay down on his bed, and four hours later he was dead.

A year later, in a poem from my self-published book *The Devil at High Noon*, I wrote the following in a piece called " . . . But the View Outside My Window Never Changes." It was dedicated to Michel.

> *His fragile heel has stumbled*
> *His incomplete encasement*
> *Braves the burning day*
> *What aid in light makes sense*
> *When logic curves and drifts away-*
> *But the view outside my window*
> *Never changes*

After Michel's passing, the close proximity in which Stephanie and I had found ourselves during our stakeout at his house somehow wove a connecting thread that drew us closer together. Soon this evolved into a relationship that we kept completely to ourselves and a secret from our closest friends. In retrospect, I'm not entirely sure why, but for whatever reasons there may have been, it just made the intimacy surreptitiously more alluring.

Held at the popular night spot the Roxbury on Sunset, my fortieth birthday party, while successful on many levels, was most memorable for one thing: it was in many ways a coming out party for the freshly minted new me. Returning to active interaction and embracing a heady sort of acclimatization, I'd arrived solo but with a romantic secret circulating among the revelers.

Before I'd even made it into the main room, I was waylaid by an associate who informed me that my presence was requested on the second floor. Curious, and in no hurry to join the party, I dutifully did as I was requested. Heading upstairs I walked into one of the balcony rooms and there he was, a large glorious, glowing hunk of blues history. Resplendent in a white safari suit, panama hat, and leaning on an ivory-handled cane was Willie Dixon. In the pantheon of musical greats, Willie Dixon was a titan. The greatest blues songwriter of the postwar era, he was pretty much the heart and soul of Chess Records, producing and writing songs that defined an era.

How Willie Dixon wound up at my birthday party needs no detailed explanation. It was simply a question of "be careful what you wish for." Someone in my management office had casually asked if there was anyone they'd forgotten to invite, and being in a flippant mood I chided, "Yeah, Willie Dixon."

Ta-da! There he was, and what a wonderment he was. Genial and imbued with charisma to burn, he was a man in touch with his history. Sharp and incisive, it wasn't hard to deduce that there was a lot going on behind the beatific smile.

I first became aware of Willie through his work with Howlin' Wolf, the six-foot-three-inch, three-hundred-pound gravel-voiced blues howler from White Station, Mississippi. Wolf had been the first real blues artist I had ever heard. Back in my hoboing teens, my friends and I had stumbled upon a college keg party in a windswept barn in the Lincolnshire backcountry. The music they were playing was eerie and primal and like nothing I'd ever heard before. It was unsettling, and initially I dismissed it and pretended I didn't care for it, only I couldn't get it out of my head. Imbedded in my brain were songs like "Back Door Man" and "I Ain't Superstitious." Prowling hypnotic riffs crackling with raw intensity, their irresistibility sent me in search of my own black magic.

Eventually, the name Willie Dixon became synonymous with every Chess Record I picked up. His writing credits were all over everything, not only the songs, but production and arrangements also. These included Muddy Waters, Little Walter, Buddy Guy, Koko Taylor, Elmore James, Lowell Fulson, and Bo Diddley to name just a handful. And the songs, Oh my!

"Hoochie Coochie Man," "I Just Want to Make Love to You," "Wang Dang Doodle," "Little Red Rooster," "The Seventh Son," "Dead Presidents," "My Babe," "You Can't Judge a Book by Its Cover," the list just goes on and on.

It was obvious that I'd made a friend, and rather than hang around and distract me from the festivities, Willie took his leave and snuck out the back, promising to be in touch. The rest of the night was celebratory, but nothing was going to top my surprise guest.

Willie, true to his word, proved to be the gift that kept on giving. We had lunch a few days later at what would turn out to be our regular dining spot. Musso & Frank, the Hollywood Boulevard landmark that has been steaming along since 1919, was a perfect location that Willie was unfamiliar with but came to love. Willie was by no means wrapped up in the past or cruising on fumes. He was acutely aware of the current music scene and had a fascination for rap, which in theory wasn't that strange to wrap your head around. In many ways, the cadence of some of his earlier work wasn't a million miles from the grassroots of hip-hop. At this initial lunch I also met his eldest daughter, Shirley, a devoted right hand who would blossom into a reliable friend in the coming months.

During our conversation, I happened to mention that I was planning a trip to Chicago. Elton had recently decided to change his life drastically and had checked into a hospital in the city to undergo rehabilitation from a handful of addictions. Coincidentally, Willie was planning a trip to visit his Blues Heaven Foundation, a Chicago-based organization he founded and developed to encourage a new generation of blues greats and to provide for the ongoing welfare of senior blues musicians. With this we made plans to meet in Chi-town.

For this special trip, I was joined by Elton's and my old friends, Eddi and Johnny Barbis. Johnny had worked in association with us for a long time, mainly in promotion and radio, and he would eventually graduate to a managerial position during the 2000s. It was a trip with two goals: one tentative yet full of hope, the other less strenuous.

Seeing Elton drained of the poisons that were eating him alive was an emotional event that pushed a lot of buttons. During the autumn of 1989, I was privy to the months of physical decline that were hampering his better judgment during the North American leg of his Sleeping with the Past Tour. The fact that it was at this point that I'd entered into the affair that was the catalyst for calling it a day on marriage number two didn't exhibit any general equanimity on my part. Elton's mood swings had become increasingly more erratic and his nocturnal post-show behavior was so desperately out of control that it caused an alarm and anxiety in me that I'd never experienced before. It was a downward spiral that could have only one conclusion. If he didn't get help, he was most assuredly going to die. His inner rage was his worst enemy, and any form of verbal confrontation would only up the ante. I felt completely powerless as if the intimacy of our mutual affection had been boarded up and wrapped in razor wire. Those withering days were an incongruous mix of melancholy that left me torn between a liberating romance and blood on my hands.

After a rocky start, Elton had persevered and overcame the initial horrors of detoxing. Smooth sailing has no place in rehab; it's painful, depressing, humiliating, and above all else, lonely. You're there to make it on your own with only a hefty dose of psychoanalytic tough love to ease you along. Encountering him clear-eyed, lucid, and mastering menial tasks that had become incomprehensible to him since our days at Frome Court was an enlightening amusement tinged with pathos. Making his own bed and learning to operate a washing machine might not seem earth-shattering, but for Elton John they were an emancipating tonic that flushed out another form of equally habitual dependency.

It was the first time that Elton had been allowed visitors, and I think at that point any friendly face would have warranted an appreciative reception. Still, me being there I think meant something, or at least I'd hoped it would. I know for my part it was absolutely necessary on so many different levels. Support might have been the main factor, and while I eschewed any blatantly patronizing overtures, my real purpose was encouragement. He needed to be reassured that his musical genius would not evaporate along with the crutch of drugs, and that a clearer tomorrow spelled a new beginning. It was when he read me his farewell love letter to cocaine that I lost it. It was a simply magnificent piece of writing, a Dear John if you will to the White Lady, and it is printed in its entirety in Elton's autobiography. I was so overcome by this testimonial that my eyes welled and the tears flowed freely. I knew then that my best friend was back.

That night I felt as if a great weight had been lifted, and along with Johnny and Eddi, I reunited with Willie at Buddy Guy's Legends, a blues club on South Wabash. What made the night doubly special was that not only was Buddy playing a set, but that Willie ambled onstage and played his signature stand-up bass on a couple of numbers. It was a fleeting trip but had proved to be both cathartic and pleasurable in equal doses.

Through all this, I developed a relationship with Willie's family members, and in particular, his wife, Marie. Marie was a handsome woman. Effusive and sharp, she managed to juggle the domesticity of the household while sharing Willie's passion for his foundation. After his passing, she took the reins of his legacy and became a force to be reckoned with, moving Blues Heaven into the historic Chess Records building on South Michigan Avenue. Letting nothing slip through the cracks, she was a tough businesswoman and continued to secure the rights and royalties to Willie's music for his family up until her death in 2016 at age seventy-nine.

In January 1991, I attended Willie's seventy-fifth birthday party at the Dixon home in Glendale, California. As you might imagine, it was a boisterous gathering of colorful characters, many of them surviving contemporaries of Willie's golden era. One of the standout guests I got to meet was the great jazz and blues shouter Jimmy Witherspoon, whose early albums like *Evenin' Blues* were personal favorites of mine. Jimmy and the rest of the crowd, musicians, singers, and family friends, interacted with each other with a jousting one-upmanship and colloquial street jive that turned the gathering into a veritable Louis Jordon's "Saturday Night Fish Fry." The good humor abounding was infectious, but it was not hard to see that Willie was operating under some physical duress. Willie passed away the following year on January 29, 1992. He was seventy-six years old.

Even though I was aware he was failing, it came as a shock when Willie died. He wasn't so much a mentor as an inspiration, a fountain of knowledge happy to recount his past in detail while turning me onto artists who were unfamiliar to me, like Harmonica Hinds, Buster Benton,

Leonard Caston, and Luther Johnson. His Vicksburg, Mississippi, birthplace was also an odd coincidence since Vicksburg had been the destination of my very first road trip out of LA. Being able to talk knowledgeably about the demographics of the town paved the way for several conversations concerning the fact that the past wasn't that much different from the present, and that along with some decent down-home folk there still existed closeted nests of racist civic peckerwoods.

Two years following his passing, his daughter Shirley and I produced a Willie Dixon Tribute benefiting the Blues Heaven Foundation. Held at B. B. King's Blues Club in Universal City, it featured some top-tier talent including John Lee Hooker, Ry Cooder, Branford Marsalis, Lowell Fulson, Keb' Mo', and George Thorogood, plus a blistering set by the twenty-eight-year-old guitar phenomenon Becky Barksdale. It proved an unqualified success, but still it got me wondering. Would time be considerate to Willie's legacy, or would the passing of time erode his enormous contribution to the blues? There was an upcoming generation emerging that was rapidly hurtling forward without investing much time in exploring the past. I promised myself that I would do whatever I could to always be available to champion Willie while helping to keep the flame of roots-based music alive. It was this promise on my part that caused me to blow a gasket in 2013.

I'm not sure why, but my wife and I attended the Songwriters Hall of Fame induction ceremony that year and wondered (not unlike the Rock and Roll Hall of Fame) why some of their choices had made it in. It wasn't until I'd returned home that I wondered what year Willie had been inducted. You can't even begin to imagine my apoplectic reaction when I couldn't find his name.

The Songwriters Hall of Fame has been operating since 1969, a period in which Willie's songs were an absolute staple of contemporary recordings and set lists. The Rolling Stones, Cream, the Doors, Led Zeppelin, The Who, Van Morrison, Jeff Beck, Grateful Dead, the Animals, the Yardbirds, and dozens more—every rock band worth its salt had covered Willie Dixon. It wasn't like it was localized to one era either. Decade after decade, his songs would continue to be recorded and sung by dozens of emerging acts, like Tom Petty, Stevie Ray Vaughan, Bruce Springsteen, The Jesus and Mary Chain, Meat Puppets, Sting, and Dr. Feelgood. Hell, even Willie Nelson sang Willie Dixon.

I was simply incredulous that a man who had been called "the Shakespeare of the blues" and penned several dozen bona fide standards of the genre had been snubbed while some mediocre mid-'80s pop songwriters with two or three hits under their belts made it in. It was like shutting out Cole Porter; but then again for an institution that doesn't include Pete Townshend but has Lou Gramm and Mick Jones of Foreigner, it's hardly surprising.

Within days I fired off a letter expressing my utter frustration with the nominating committee for failing to recognize Willie's work, calling his exclusion a "travesty" and "embarrassingly overdue."

I conducted several phone calls with executive individuals, getting to the point where I threatened to return my own award and kick up some real dust if they didn't make amends. It became apparent at one point that posthumous awards weren't popular due to the inductee's unavailability to be present or perform. So that was it. Aside from the fact that had they inducted him when they should have, he would have been fit and well enough to assemble a crack band, it appeared that the night's entertainment value was more important than the legitimacy of the nominee.

In due course, they relented. In 2015, in what ranks as one of the proudest moments of my life, I was able to induct my old friend in what would have been his hundredth year. Accepting on behalf of the family was his daughter Jacqueline, a delightful and enterprising young lady who has since become a friend and is the last surviving lifeline I have to the family. Willie once remarked, "The blues are the roots, and the other music are the fruits." There have been three individuals in my life who I believe were instrumental in the further education of my passions. Mentors who took me under their wing, heightened my awareness, and catered to my curiosity. The great jazz photographer William Claxton, the art dealer and historian Michael Schwartz, and Willie Dixon.

DECIDING THAT APARTMENT life was restrictive, not to mention a waste of money, I bought a delightful house sitting on a hill of bedrock on Devlin Drive half a mile up from the Whisky on Sunset. The house, completely fronted by French doors and horseshoed around a sizable pool, had a panoramic view of LA and an infusion of sunlight that kept it bright and airy all through the day. The view at night was spectacular; the entire city lit up and seemingly stretched into infinity. Sadly, not long after I'd moved in, this view was marred by the grim specter of the Rodney King riots of 1992, which turned the normally breathtaking cityscape into something resembling a war zone. Like having a grandstand seat overlooking Hell, buildings burned and the skies turned a tainted orange. Thick black smoke and the smell of burning rubber filled the air while a cacophony of sirens screamed endlessly through the night. If one disaster wasn't enough, almost two years later in January 1994, we endured the Northridge Earthquake, a twenty-second trembler that registered a magnitude of 6.7 and ultimately caused $50 billion in damages, one of the costliest natural disasters in US history. There's something to be said for a home built on bedrock. In my house, not even a picture frame fell over.

It was uncharacteristically quiet on Devlin. Hard to imagine that one of the city's most infamous rock clubs was so close at hand and that on weekends a minute away was a seething mass of rowdy revelers, choked traffic, and a cacophony of noise coupled with the amplified roar of guitars and drums. Perhaps because the road ended in a cul-de-sac not two hundred yards from my front door, the chance of much traffic was unlikely. I'd see the odd coyote, but outside of that the only interesting oddity was the old lady who'd always be out looking for her cat. The fact that she did this stark naked and weighed about 250 pounds was unremarkable in that it represented a bit of neighborhood eccentricity. I had to notify the cops so often I got to know the desk sergeant on a first name basis: "Hey Frank, she's out again."

A friend of Stephanie's, Nathalie Delon, was the ex-wife of Alain Delon, one of French cinema's most indelible icons. Very much a free spirit, Natalie (herself a veteran of over thirty movies) was at the time in an on/off relationship with record executive and Island Records founder Chris Blackwell. Forthright and fun, Natalie would host us at her LA home and ski lodge in Lake Tahoe.

One night after a dinner party at her LA home, I was challenged to a game of pool by Alexander Godunov, the Russian-born Bolshoi Ballet defector. Very intense and looking like a Soviet version of guitarist Davey Johnstone, Godunov seemed particularly wound up and was pacing around the table while issuing directives, as if he were in the act of conducting war games. Let me tell you, I've never been one to be mistaken for Willie Mosconi, but after several cocktails my game could improve tenfold. To cut a long story short, I beat the pants off him, which sent him ever deeper into a spiral of conniption. For every game he lost he would challenge me again, constantly playing on my machismo in order to induce a rematch. With my energy and interest flagging, he finally won one, which should have brought things to a conclusion. Not so. Claiming I'd let him win in order to bring things to an end, he demanded we continue. My patience at an end, and him buoyed by an ocean of vodka, I threw my stick on the table and suggested he "play with himself." I'm sorry that I never saw a different side of this choleric young man, as a couple of years later he was dead from hepatitis secondary to chronic alcoholism.

Stephanie's and my early courtship was erratic, to say the least. A lot of indecision on her part led to considerable gaps in our ability to truly bond as a couple. Confused at one point with her lack of commitment, I assumed it had run its course and started seeing other people, which led to a couple of casual relationships. Some lasted weeks, some were platonic to a point, and then there was a weekend fling that culminated with the best exit line imaginable.

She was a striking girl who worked for a major record company. I'd partaken of a flirtatious dance with her on occasion. We finally got together and one thing led to another, with us spending a leisurely Saturday of movies, Mexican food, and conversation all of which culminated in what you might imagine. Way too early Sunday morning she rolled over and checked her watch. "Oh crap! I've got to go!" she exclaimed. Drowsy and confused, I inquired as to why the rush.

Grabbing her scattered garments and heading to the bathroom she turned only to say, "Because I'm getting married this afternoon!"

Finally, things got serious on the Stephanie front. She moved in and the two of us further solidified our undertaking by purchasing a couple of birds and opening a restaurant. The birds were a large cockatoo called Hook and a sad little African gray with a perpetual molting problem called Baldy. Baldy, in fact, was quite extraordinary and, interestingly enough, very affectionate. He would clamber down from his perch in the kitchen, make his way through the dining area and into the living room, where he'd scramble up the couch and onto my chest. Here he'd stand, contentedly rubbing his head against my cheek and pecking at my teeth with his beak. He also had an amazing vocabulary and would drive me nuts by imitating the sound of the phone ringing, perfectly. He would then proceed to have a one-sided conversation with the imaginary caller, punctuating his responses to their nonexistent dialogue with responses like "uh-huh," "oh, really?" and "bye."

Hook, on the other hand, was a bit like the avian equivalent of the Disney villain Gaston: vain, handsome, and not terribly bright. Outside of occupying his cage with a sort of regal serenity, he didn't do a hell of a lot other than appeasing you by sitting on your shoulder when scooped up by the beak. Hook's most memorable adventure was when my great friend, David Fryden, one of the world's serious mensches, took him for a ride in his car. Placing him on the center console, he shot off down Devlin, Hook happily bobbing his head to the radio. When David reached Sunset, Hook was gone. Panicked, David looked all around the car to no avail, only to notice the sunroof was open. Hanging a dramatic U-turn, David shot back up the street and came upon one very dazed and confused cockatoo standing in the middle of the road. Lucky for Hook, cats, coyotes, and cars were temporarily absent. Heart attack averted, David breathed a sigh of relief. It was the most distressed I'd seen him since one night in the private bar upstairs at the Troubadour, we'd got plastered on black rum and I'd convinced him he'd propositioned Joni Mitchell.

I suppose it was inevitable that Stephanie and I would open a restaurant. She'd been in that line of work most of her life and I, as a lover of anything gastronomic, made the venture a shared dream that had endless possibilities. While ultimately it proved to be sufficiently successful, I'm sure we'd both agree that it wasn't the slam dunk we'd hoped for. The details of how it all came about are inadmissible. All the fine print, leases, licenses, and hoops you have to jump through to make things like this happen are too tiresome to bother with. Suffice it to say, once it was up and running, we both did our best to make it a warm and welcoming environment. With a mixture of French provincial and Italian-styled food, Cicada (my idea) sat at the intersection of Melrose Avenue and La Cienega Boulevard. Style-wise, it had a Tuscan vibe. A spacious two-tiered dining room, it had stone-tiled floors with the walls and motifs painted in muted colors of terracotta and pale blue. It was light and energized during the day and romantically lit and laid-back at night. Banquettes hugged the room and intimate tables were discreetly positioned around the inner partition walls. There was a small bar in the backroom where we would present live music, a feature that would prove to be our most popular project.

I'll admit it was nice to have a place to go and make like I was Rick in *Casablanca*, but while greeting friends and regulars at their tables was permissible, I loathed the idea of working the door. As a person who could be intensely leery of people, I didn't trust myself to adhere to the "customer is always right" concept. If someone came in with a snotty attitude or appeared condescending, I'd be more than likely to tell them to "buzz off." This was not something I could afford to do, so I just stood back and let calmer heads prevail. My eavesdropping led to hearing a couple of amusing interactions made by Danny, one of our waiters, an effervescent and eager young man we promoted to maître d'. Answering the phone late one evening, he found himself on the line with a grumpy Milton Berle. "You still open? We're coming in for dinner," Uncle Miltie pronounced. Lord knows why, but Danny had to ask. "Do you have a reservation?" You could almost see the phone receiver melting in Danny's hands. "Reservation!" roared the comedic legend. "Reservation, do I sound like a fucking Indian?"

Danny's second bit of blinding brilliance was when an incredibly shabby and poorly dressed individual with a cloth cap pulled over his head came in one night. Attempting to bypass Danny, he was none-theless waylaid by our diligent gatekeeper. Inquiring in no uncertain terms as to where this hobo presence thought he was heading, he sim-ply received a muffled response indicating he was going to the bar in the back. As this was unfolding, one of our sharper waiters appeared behind the raggedy interloper gesticulating wildly to get Danny's atten-tion and mouthing silently, "It's Bobby 'Fucking' De Niro." His blun-der registering, Danny took several steps back, offered a weak smile, and said "Have a nice night then." When Cicada was sold some years later, it went to one Bobby "Fucking" De Niro.

One night I had dinner with the great comedian, actor, and author Steve Martin, who quizzed me intensely on my recipe for the perfect relationship. Why me, of all people? I had no idea. After all, who was I but someone who had gone from twenty to forty making poor deci-sions, entering ruinous marriages, and only getting decent results when I didn't slip a ring on someone's finger. In essence, it made about as much sense as asking Donald Trump his opinion on Kierkegaard. Still, it got me thinking since at that point it looked very much like I might be taking a stab at it again. Stephanie and I may have had our ups and downs and taken a couple of time-outs, but I sincerely thought that this thing might go the distance. Yes, the earliest part of the decade had been a confusing time period, but I'd ridden it out, including making amends to my parents who had never wavered in their support of me even when I went AWOL. Two years earlier, after skating on thin ice, my saving grace had not come in the form of a good woman but some-thing that ran concurrent to my life in LA. I'd looked outside the box and followed the siren call of a voice that had been bouncing around my brain since the day I was born.

At the same time, I was writing again and one song stood out. *And I won't break, and I won't bend / And with the last breath we ever take / We're gonna get back to the simple life again.*

Don't Fence Me In

We can achieve what we can conceive and believe.
—MARK TWAIN

It was inevitable that the time would come. Dreams, whenever possible, should not be waylaid forever. If there is enough tenacity in your makeup to resist the temptations and inconsequential trivialities of hemmed-in social compliance, then it's possible to throw in the towel on one life and lace up your old boots in another.

I was tired of not engaging the Western lifestyle when it was so close at hand, so when a certain business venture afforded me a windfall in 1992, I went shopping. Elvis got Graceland, George Harrison, his beloved Friar Park, and Jimmy Page got the creepy Boleskine House, the former Loch Ness home of occultist Aleister Crowley. Me? I got Roundup Valley Ranch, a thirty-acre horse facility cradled in the hills of the Santa Ynez Valley above Santa Barbara.

Two and a half hours north of LA, I'd happened upon it at the end of a long day looking. I'd never been familiar with the small towns and communities located on the periphery of Highway 101 heading along the Central Coast en route to San Francisco. The Malibu Hills were too close, too socially tempting, and Ventura wasn't far enough away to be credibly authentic. On the northern edge of Santa Barbara, the San Marcos Pass circumvents the 101 and winds up through the Los Padres National Forest past Cachuma Lake for thirty miles, snaking precariously and culminating in the San Ynez Valley where the twin towns of Santa Ynez and Los Olivos are located.

I was tired and a little cranky from traipsing around properties that really hadn't met my requirements, including an avocado plantation belonging to John Travolta and a yoga retreat that may or may not have belonged to Jane Fonda. The latter had been halfway up the San Marcos Pass and my real estate agent suggested we continue into the Santa Ynez area to check out one more listing. I was less than enthusiastic but agreed to take a quick look before heading home.

Paraphrasing, it had me at "hello." I said, "Yes," before our car was halfway in the gate. I knew this was it; this was where I belonged. The property branched off at the entrance into two roads, one leading left up a hill to the main house, the second straight ahead to the right past a man-made lake and into a circular driveway surrounding an impressive equestrian center. This was the real deal, built and designed by someone committed to training and raising horses for the express purpose of serious competition. What that competition was meant to be was initially lost on me and, quite honestly, something I put little or no thought into at the time. What mattered was that the configuration of everything adhered to my momentary desire to acquire something on which to build my American dream.

The main house, in keeping with the area, was Mediterranean in design. Two long, low single levels bookended a two story center point, all of which curved slightly while hugging a generous veranda bordered by rosemary bushes, its beamed supporting columns wrapped in bougainvillea and night blooming jasmine. The garden fronting the house was enclosed and generously appointed with a variety of fruit trees including blood orange, lemons, limes, plums, and figs.

A fountain at the center of the garden babbled reassuringly twenty-four hours a day, and at night in the summer with the bedroom windows wide open, its calming stability would be a pleasant alternative to souped-up sports cars roaring through Beverly Hills. The night skies were staggeringly clear, every star in the firmament pin-spot bright, a billion gleaming testaments to the power of Heaven. I'd walk out into the garden at night and wander up into the pool area located in the far corner to the right of the house. There was a raised observation point directly to the rear of the pool where it was possible to not just marvel at the luminosity of the constellations and asterisms, but it was also the best place to view the Santa Ynez Valley's spectacular sunsets. Giant slashed brush strokes of crimson and orange colliding and churning in a sea of blood red and turquoise, they radiated across the horizon on a pallet of inky black immensity. Along with the proliferation of stars, it was all incredibly moving and shockingly prolific.

In terms of the equestrian facility, the main barn was divided up between luxury accommodation and basic housing. There were stalls of hardwood and wrought iron with sliding doors and solid walled interiors at the enclosed end of the building while a series of simple wire alternatives ran along the exposed center section. Let's just say that including the outlying pastures, there was room for a substantial number of horses. At the far end of the barn was a covered indoor arena of show-sized proportions. There was also a large round pen at the back end of the property that was handy for when we wanted to work outside. This was most of the time and literally where I came into my own as a rider and student of cowboy culture 101. It was ground zero for my education, and at this point in my life I was prepared to go all out and take the reins. Never has a literal saying carried so much weight.

The closest I'd gotten to it in the past was trail riding around the Universal lot in 1971 as well as an unmanageable birthday gift I received in 1977. Outlaw was a testy palomino gelding for which I was unprepared. It was unfair for the horse and unfair for me, a vanity project bestowed on an unwilling participant. Of course, I pretended that it was everything I'd ever wanted, even at a time when it was the very last thing I needed. I imagine the perennial spirit of cowboy culture and the Western history that dwelled within me was not lost on my well-meaning girlfriend, who, thinking she'd fulfilled my heart's desire, inadvertently saddled me (no pun intended) with hell on four legs.

Through an obliging connection, I managed to secure a stable for my horse at Will Rogers State Park between Beverly Hills and the Pacific Palisades on Sunset Boulevard, not more than twenty minutes from my house. Every couple of days, with little enthusiasm and schedule permitting, I headed out there and masqueraded as someone who imagined they were happy in the guise of an urban cowboy.

Everything about this situation was wrong. I was completely ignorant as to how to care for a horse, and with my inexperience dialed into
the red, things did not go well. Horses need to be ridden. They require
commitment and dedication, and if left to idle in their stall will grow
bored and difficult. It's no wonder then that when I did cinch up and
take Outlaw out it was debatable as to who was in charge. If you've
ever ridden a horse that doesn't want to be ridden, and when the horse
you're riding knows you're totally incapable of controlling it, it will certainly forge its own path. This is how things proceeded for the duration
of our time together. It was a miserable culmination of me yanking
helplessly in a vain attempt to reign him in while he plowed forward in
spite of my best efforts.

It came to a head one Saturday afternoon when Outlaw decided to
veer off the designated trail and cut a calamitous path across a pristine
and finely manicured stretch of Will Rogers's celebrated polo field. That
this took place during an active polo match is a memory that is hard to
shake, even at my advanced age. Clinging on for dear life, my runaway
steed, lathered up and snot flying, thundered unchecked across the
playing field while all around me elegantly mounted visions in white
shook their mallets and cursed me in surprisingly obscene vitriol for
country club gents. Like Harold Lloyd in a Mack Sennett comedy, I
barreled on, rolling slack in the saddle as Outlaw's rear hooves carved
great chunky divots out of the immaculate turf.

Roundup Valley Ranch had been built twenty years previously by a
Chicago businessman named George Stout. It had seen a great deal of
action in its formative years, and George was a driving force in popu-
larizing and expanding the highly agile sport of equine choreography
called cutting. It was solely for the purpose of training, breeding, and
working these highly athletic animals that George had created this
compound and had eventually sunk a great deal of money in it in order
to establish it as a one-of-a-kind facility.

From the offset, it would have been way too ambitious on my part
to dive headfirst into the deep end. Cutting was a complex and highly
competitive sport that demanded natural ability and focus. Most of all,
in order to compete you almost had to have been born in the saddle. I

mean you really, really had to be able to ride, because a cutting horse in motion is like sitting on the back of a 1,200 pound Ferrari. Allow me to explain.

Cutting, like most of the events featured in traditional rodeo, has its roots in ranching, especially when it comes to working with cattle. This goes all the way back to the great migratory cattle drives and roundups of the nineteenth and early twentieth century when separating individual cows from the herd was necessary in order to brand or doctor them. This took skill and know-how, and it's how cutting was born.

I'll attempt to explain the rules simply; however, when it comes to competitive horses you learn very quickly that nothing is simple. Your allotted time in the arena is two and a half minutes. This is referred to as a "run." You are assisted by four helpers of your choice. Their job is to keep the cattle bunched together and not allow them to scatter all over the work area when you enter the herd. The two in the front are "turn back riders" the two in the rear are "herd holders." You must make at least two cuts, one being from deep in the herd: this is a "deep cut." Others may be peeled off from the edges. It is advantageous to enter the herd with a prospective cow in mind. A turn back rider will often make a suggestion (if you haven't already decided) as to what cow he or she thinks may work well in front of your horse. A bright-eyed alert cow with its head up is usually a good choice. Once you've made your cut and the cow is driven clear of the herd, you must commit your horse by giving it its head. This is done by placing your rein hand on the horse's neck while gripping the saddle horn with your other hand. At this point, it's all up to the horse, the objective being to prevent the cow from returning to the herd. Outside of using your legs, your hands must remain in place until you decide to "quit" this cow and go back for another. This can only be done when the cow comes to a complete stop or turns away from the rider. Judges score a run on a scale from 60 to 80, with 70 being an average score. If none of this makes any sense, I suggest a YouTube view.

A good cutting horse can anticipate a cow's intended moves. It will stay head-to-head with it, stopping instantaneously, turning on a dime, totally focused, and in sync like any highly conditioned athlete.

Its lateral power dance sweeps across the arena floor, crab crawling at times, its belly low enough to graze the dirt, its legs splayed out, its ears pinned back. This is referred to as "cow smart," and it's a beautiful thing. There's an almost sexual intensity to being on the back of one of these animals, it's extreme yet poetic, a sport condensed into a momentary adrenaline rush that leaves you energized by the horse's power. It's like an electric current surging through your body.

The extent of the ranch's capabilities and what it offered in the way of possibilities wasn't so much overwhelming as it was exhilarating. I just needed a starting point and a baby-steps attitude in regard to moving forward without getting ahead of myself. I had a lot to learn and, as in all things pertaining to learning, mistakes are made. It's important to point out, though, that I was fully committed and serious in my intentions. I learned fast but not without acting the role of dumb beginner. This began with securing my initial equine acquisition.

There was no way I was going to achieve immediate success in terms of Western homesteader and accomplished and all-knowing horseman, and from the get-go I was caught completely in the trap of impressionistic neophyte by falling prey to that most notorious of Western flimflam men: the horse trader.

Buying and selling horses has forever been one of the most dubious and cautionary transactions attached to the Western lifestyle. The dictionary describes horse trading as hard and shrewd bargaining, which to my way of thinking is a description penned by an academic not terribly familiar with some of the people I've met along the way.

I engaged in my first purchase with a slick local who obviously saw me coming. Although it pains me to admit it, it wasn't a good solid horse I was interested in. When I should have been in the market for a seasoned vet to get me out of the gate, the aesthetic idealist in me coveted something cool, temperament be damned. This was clearly stamped on my forehead as I paid through the nose for a coal black stallion called St. Nick. He might have looked like Zorro's horse, but he acted like Holden Caulfield. This I wasn't initially aware of because, naturally, I bought him straightaway, no test ride, no vetting, no nothing. Stupid is as stupid does, as the saying goes.

St. Nick was most certainly not Outlaw, but he did have a decid-edly angst-ridden personality. It was almost as if he knew he was a hot-looking horse and on occasion needed to prove it, the only prob-lem being he didn't know how. This seemed to confuse him and this confusion manifested itself in peculiar ways. At times he preened like a teenage girl while on other occasions he reared and bucked around the arena. Luckily, this was when he was turned out and not when I was on him. Of course, this is not unusual when a horse is freed up and unfettered. It's just that he did it in a perplexing, self-conscious way, throwing his head back to check himself out, unsure if he was doing what he was doing correctly.

Interestingly enough, the only time in my life I've been thrown from a horse was during a video shoot in Fontana in 1986. I was por-traying the Angel of Death in a reimagining of "A Whiter Shade of Pale" along with my old pal, Harry Dean Stanton. My character at one point adopts the guise of a Clint Eastwood–like avenger mounted, yes, on a pale horse. In one tracking shot, I was supposed to gallop across some desolate scrubland to a remote mansion to claim some souls. Dressed accordingly, including a gnarly pair of Mexican spurs, I threw myself up into the saddle and tapped the horse's flank with my heels. The horse reacted as if he'd been shot in the ass with a BB gun. It was totally unexpected, and after bucking uncontrollably a couple of times, he reared up on his hind legs, and off I came. I landed flat on my back, my head inches from a nasty rock, my horse already a cloud of dust in the distance. What the wrangler had failed to tell me was that the horse had never been spur-ridden. It took them two hours to retrieve my terrified steed. They had to shoot around this mishap, and in due time I remounted, minus spurs, and secured the shot. A couple of inches to the left and I might have met the character I was impersonating.

Pretty soon, things started to fall into place. I began some remod-eling, nothing extensive, mostly audio, visual, and minor aesthetic improvements. I was still dividing my time between my apartment in LA and the ranch, but gradually less time in the city and more time in the country. It was a natural transference. I'd always been a country boy, it was where I came from, it was in my blood, only now I had the luxury of making choices as to where I wanted to be at any given time. In my youth I was rooted in one spot, dreaming of getting out and escaping the drudgery and possibility of being trapped on a colloquial hamster wheel. Fresh air and farmland was one thing, but without the freedom—not to mention the finances—to move or have the opportunity of alternatives, the prospects were bleak. I like a good pub, but the thought of spending every night in the same one was not a scenario I wanted to act out. Although it was geographically and socially different, I'd come full circle and returned to ruralism. To paraphrase a popular song, I'd finally decided where my future lay.

I also acquired several more horses. Only this time, I was more apt to listen to reason rather than jump the gun. These were good solid ranch horses, all-rounders not meant for serious competition but capable of handling cattle, trail riding, and team penning. All these activities were soon on the agenda, and as my confidence grew so did my capabilities.

The trails around my property and beyond were extensive. They wound up into the surrounding hills for endless miles through an ever-changing distribution of natural wonders, the terrain changing with the seasons from the lush greenery of spring, through parched summers, into the mellow muted saturation of fall. We would take our horses up into the backcountry through tall grass and brittle bushes of dried blue sage, its pungent fragrance agitated by hoof and flank, its potent aroma rising like shamanistic dust. Leaning down out of the saddle, I'd rip clumps of it off in my hand, rolling it in my palms, infusing my skin, and detonating the twigs into aromatic smudge sticks. It was heady stuff and smelled like freedom.

We rode at a languid pace, no rush, embracing the tranquility, an easy equanimity bestowed upon us by the drone of insects and the dry warm air. There was a time when I'd equated contentment with complacency, but in this setting I may have reevaluated that theory. Contemplation came easy, the installation of change dramatically enhanced in this heady environment. The search for my true identity and sense of purpose was an ongoing quest, but here in closer proximity to the master's hand, it was easier to purify my spirit.

In the high, wild, rolling hills of the Santa Ynez Valley, it was easier to embrace the niche of my lifelong arc and read the fundamental messages ingrained in every little thing. The stateliness of cadaverous trees bowed and twisted into a fossilized form of architecture, the panorama of the mountain ranges, a backdrop slideshow ever constant, colorfully changing with the seasons.

Red-tailed hawks gliding on the thermals, solitarily swooping, their flame-like tail feathers catching the sun, their predatory nature intercepted intermittently by blackbirds and crows that dive-bombed them impressively, bravely strafing their aggressive attempts to pick off their young.

In a melancholy rain, the murmur of the wind sang softly through the live oaks and drummed the leaves above our heads, the rhythmic tattoo of the heavy late summer drops playing into the fantasy of the fine line drawn between who I once was and who I wanted to be. These were the first magic moments of a new beginning, far from complete but heading in the right direction.

During my very first trail ride, I was on a high plateau looking down to the ridge below when a large mountain lion strolled nonchalantly out of the bushes onto the trail. *Not something you see every day*, I thought, but then the things I began to see every day became more frequent and equally as enlightening. Coyotes and deer were plentiful, bobcats and lynx infrequent but visible every once in a while. Then of course there were the porcine rototillers known to us as feral pigs. These guys are the rock stars of rural destruction. They can turn your pristine landscaping into Joe Walsh's hotel room overnight. They'd turn up after dusk, prodigious families of them endemically committed to mayhem, aggressive if confronted but fully aware that shotguns had the upper hand. For hefty hunks of demolition they were stealthy in their activities and well-accomplished in espionage.

Interestingly enough, venomous snakes, rattlers in particular, were rare around the ranch, although at a higher altitude they were occasionally encountered. The only run-in we had with one was a close call. We were on a thin path with a sheer drop to our right when one reared confrontationally out from under an adjacent rock, taking a stab at the lead horse's fetlock. Luckily, the horse's sharp instincts sidestepped it, and a .38 slug took the aggressor's head clean off. Funnily enough, the snakes we had on our home turf were big, harmless, and kind of fun if you like snakes. Gopher snakes, which can average from five to nine feet, are named for their adept ability to slither into the holes of critters whose tendency is to turn pastures and virgin embankments into tenement slums. They take them out like elite Special Forces, and their work is impressive.

TEAM PENNING IS widely regarded as a family sport for obvious reasons. It's also a great deal of fun, a terrific way to unwind, and an excellent opportunity to bring along a case of beer and act silly. In my day, I encountered individuals who took it way too seriously and got uppity when you'd gallop around yahooing and acting like a complete idiot. It's not rocket science, and it certainly wasn't cutting, but it was the first competitive equine sport I indulged in.

Thirty head of cattle are in the arena, each wearing a number from 0 to 9. Each team consists of three riders who start at the center of the arena. A couple of herd holders keep the cattle contained at the far end of the arena, and a small pen is located at the opposite end. A random number is called out and the objective is to separate the three cows with that number and herd them into the pen. You have ninety seconds to do this, the fastest time winning.

It was a great way to spend a Saturday morning and hang out with a diverse group of locals. While everyone had a competitive edge to them, the whole thing was loose, raucous, and completely free of pretension. It was, for the most part, the same competitors week after week riding a mixed bag of horses that ran the gamut of slick and solid to one hoof in the glue factory. Mostly quarter horses, there were exceptions, a mule or two, and one family who turned up week after week on Arabians. This was an odd choice given their high-strung nature and the fact that they're not terribly fond of cattle. When you're participating in a sport where your horse needs to go shoulder to shoulder with the cow, I imagine it must have been frustrating to have your horse running away from them instead of running into them. Undoubtedly, the most entertaining were a group of kids who showed up a couple of times on miniature ponies. When they entered the herd, they were completely lost from sight, their progress monitored only by high-pitched squeals and the occasional glimpse of a small hand fanning the air. Within our ranks they were referred to as the Oompa Loompas.

As much fun as it was, it still required a degree of skill, so it was gratifying that my team, which was made up of myself and two of my ranch hands, often won. This obviously boosted my confidence and improved my seat. In due course, incorporating the ranch's specific amenities and diligently spending every morning practicing, I realized that in order to step up into my big boy pants, I needed to cut.

The first thing I did was to engage a trainer, get some technique under my belt, and hit the road. Based in Ojai an hour and a half south of the ranch, Scott Weiss was one of the winningest pros in the business and a no-nonsense taskmaster. The fact that I schlepped to his facility twice a week every week for a brief lesson, in all humility, proves my commitment to what would be a huge part of my life for the next ten years.

The cutting circuit was a mixed bag of destinations varying in distance from close at hand to the long haul. An hour north, the Paso Robles Event Center was one of the most frequently used arenas of the Pacific Coast Cutting Horse Association. Handy in its proximity, it was state of the art in as much as it was well-appointed and professionally sound in its design. It was also advantageous that Paso Robles itself is a delightful town. Along with the neighboring town of San Luis Obispo, it's a jewel in the crown of the Central Coast, a magnet for tourists traveling on the 101, and is home to good restaurants, great wineries, and comfortable lodging.

Farther afield, but no less appealing, were places like Rancho Murieta in Northern California and Temecula, located about four hours south of Santa Ynez in southwestern Riverside County. They were fun places to show, lush and sunny, with accessibility to excellent amenities. It was easy to spend time in these places without feeling you were cut off from civilization.

I say this because for every Paso Robles, Arroyo Grande, and Temecula there was an El Centro. In equal measures, showing horses will take you to a totally acceptable location for one show, then toss you unceremoniously into the ass end of beyond for the next. I've shown in most of them, and while everything is manageable once you become acclimatized, there are still some that leave a residue of negativity.

El Centro falls squarely into this category. It was, back when I was competing, a tough place to like. By comparison, the desolate and dust-blasted landscapes of places like Tulare, north of Bakersfield in the San Joaquin Valley, and other remote showgrounds where there was literally nothing for miles around, weren't completely without an emblematic sense of Americana. El Centro, however, was precarious, seedy, and smelled bad. Located in Imperial Valley, twelve miles from the US-Mexico border, it had elevated pollution concentrations caused by emissions from Mexico blowing into town. Many of my fellow cutters, when heading for El Centro, would pack heat, be it a handgun in the glove box or a shotgun behind the front seat. It was also sensible to park your truck directly in front of your motel room window in order to assure that it remained unmolested during the night. Sleeping with one eye open was always recommended, which in essence was not hard given the drunken confrontations and spousal altercations that erupted in the parking lot and shook the walls of the adjacent rooms.

El Centro had one restaurant that was marginally above fast food alternatives and a bag of pork rinds. It was Italian and a tough reservation since it was the only game in town. One night, about a dozen of us, fresh from a day of getting down in the dirt, got together for dinner here and, feeling generous, I offered to pick up the tab. On receiving my credit card, the proprietor noticed the name and announced knowledgeably that I had exactly the same name as "the guy who writes songs with Elton John." Hearing this, one chirpy gal in our party couldn't contain herself and assuredly confirmed, "Oh, that's him." The owner, taking in the dusty cowboy before her, smiled benignly and with a sarcastic snort said, "Yeah right, you wish." In a two-bit border town a million miles from rock and roll, who could blame her?

The El Centro showground was on a bleak bit of terrain situated in some blustery scrubland on the edge of an abandoned demolition derby track. There was a wide swathe of dead ground between the trailer parking and the arena, with nothing but abandonment on the periphery. One day in the early afternoon, I was ponying a couple of horses over to the arena when in the distance to my right, I noticed a skinny dog taking frantic laps around the perimeter of the neglected speedway. Intrigued, I handed off my horses and loped over to take a closer look. The agitated dog seemed relieved that her actions had attracted attention and began to tighten her circles closing in on what looked like a collapsed structure at the center of the long-dead venue. What it turned out to be was a massive stone drinking trough purged from the ground and tipped sideways on a pile of regurgitated dry dirt and twisted iron. At the base of this pyramid of junk was a deep round hole the width of a serving platter and coming from within was the sound of scuffling and whimpering.

As I dismounted, the wild-eyed dog stopped dead in its tracks and looked directly at me, its tongue lolling from the side of its mouth with its head cocked to one side. It was obvious this animal had a job to do and was dead set on getting it done. She'd obviously alerted me and led me here for a reason, and now that she'd completed her task, she took off. It didn't take a genius to guess what was in the hole, and after tethering my horse I sat down in the dirt and began to croon some invitational coaxing.

It took some time, but eventually a small pudgy face appeared at the crest of the hole looking out suspiciously. Blinking warily and feigning bravery, this cautious pup inched out into the daylight. This is the exact moment I met my canine soul mate, a sturdy yellow meatball that due to his birthplace came to be christened Bunker.

Within a matter of minutes he deduced I meant him no harm and crawled up into my lap while alerting his siblings all was well. One by one they emerged, all six of them, not one alike. I learned later that a bitch impregnated by multiple partners takes on the genetic components of all her couplings. They were black and brown, big eared, and small. A couple looked like German shepherds, one looked like a

Lab, and at least in an homage to their mother one looked like her, a border collie.

The punk in my lap had one bright blue eye and one green. In time he grew into a giant with paws the size of small fists and the energy and exuberance of an unfettered colt. He lived for fifteen years and in that time I treasured him as much as he was devoted to me. He was the handsomest dog I've ever known and would tear alongside my off-road vehicles, leaping fences, and corralling the rest of our dogs with alpha attitude. He had his own armchair in the living room and in some ways was the embodiment of my dad: cranky, loyal, and lovable. In his declining years as his haunches failed, I would hoist his back end upstairs at night so he could sleep at the end of our bed. When he could no longer stand, I lay on a blanket with him for hours before he was euthanized in my arms. Almost a decade after his passing he still lives indelibly in my memory, and thinking of him still brings a tear to my eye.

While El Centro was not a favored spot to show, there was another that boasted a higher profile and might be imagined as a more desirable destination. Not on your life! If it was comparable at all, Reno, Nevada, was just a different kind of murky disenchantment. If ever there was a town devoid of charm and imbedded with gray desolation, it has to be Reno, a town God must have created as an afterthought at the end of a long working day. It was El Centro on steroids, an amalgamation of tawdry despondency and secondhand glitz, a desperate quagmire of lost souls and seriously acquired taste.

The showground was attached to the town and not outside it, which was unusual. In fact, it was so close that if you took a right-hand turn out the front entrance and drove over the freeway bridge, you were in the thick of it: an abundance of fatigued casinos, greasy spoons, sex shops, and anemic neon. The hotel everyone bunked up at was a Holiday Inn across the highway from the arena. This was another iffy establishment where unsavory characters lurked in the shadows and menacing-looking individuals roamed the halls.

In contrast, Reno made Vegas look like Shangri-la. Speaking of Vegas, showing on the east side of Sin City in Summerlin was what you needed to do if you wanted to up your game and head on out to

Texas. Being Vegas, there was no shortage of hotels, and for myself and others that was the Suncoast. It was slightly odd to be in a casino resort when your sole purpose for staying there was to go to bed early and be up with the chickens. It defeated the very logic of the gambler ethic. Leaving at five in the morning, passing revelers still sipping drinks through foot-long straws, your spurs jingling in time with the jangling of the slot machines was curious, but not without fodder for a mental diarist like myself.

The hotel had one palatable restaurant that was relatively comfortable, exceeded a warm glow, and was inviting after a long dusty day in the dirt. Armed with a good book and a pen to make notes, I'd head there every night for a steak and a bottle of Barolo. Dining solo was my preference and became a revelatory time to ruminate on things outside the arena. As much as I loved the thrill of showing and the good-natured camaraderie of my fellow cutters, the conversations on the whole were decidedly one dimensional. Horse talk was pretty much it. Bloodlines and breeding was fine for a while, but eventually it could become mind-numbingly repetitive. Warmed by the wine and a decent meal, I'd hit the hay early and rise with the sun. Weekends cutting was like being on a movie set, seventeen hours of hanging around for two and a half minutes in the arena. Years later, along with cutting's wear and tear on me physically, it would factor into my retiring from active competition.

It's important to note that cutting in Vegas in 1995 was where I first became acquainted with the PBR (Professional Bull Riders) organization. I had no idea that outside of rodeo, bull riding had become a singular event. There was a reason for this. It was the highlight of traditional rodeo and why it got the prime spot at an event's conclusion. It kept folks in their seats and then kept them coming back for more. It was gladiatorial, brutal, and unforgiving. The maximum in extreme sport, it was eight seconds of treacherous gravitational aerobatics between man and beast.

I'd acquired some nosebleed seats for one of the first events the PBR was staging in Vegas, and I witnessed one of the most notorious and vicious collisions in the sport's history. Bear in mind, riders did not wear helmets back then and had only just started adopting protective vests. During the evening, one of the sport's stars, a roughneck hero called Tuff Hedeman, got paired up with Bodacious, still regarded as the rankest bull in the sport's history. Seconds after leaving the shoot, Bodacious bucked forward throwing his back end high in the air. Doing what riders do when this happens, Hedeman readjusted by arching high over the bull's shoulders. Just as he leaned forward, Bodacious threw his head back full force, smashing Hedeman square in the face. Unbelievably, Hedeman stayed on, his hand twisted in the bull rope, only to get head-butted again, but this time he was catapulted in the air, coming down and bouncing violently off the bull's back like a rag doll. Walking out of the arena, Hedeman recalled, "When I bit down my teeth didn't come together!" At the hospital, doctors diagnosed that every bone in his face was broken. After thirteen hours of surgery and six titanium plates installed, his face was so swollen his son didn't recognize him. Tough sport, tough cowboy.

This one event got me hooked and hooked up. One way or another, it led to introductions being made and some trusted and enduring friendships being forged. One of them was the man that made it all happen.

The PBR was born in 1992 with twenty riders throwing in a thousand bucks apiece. Determined to begin something that gravitated away from traditional rodeo and embraced a more fiery dynamic, they deferred to an entrepreneurial Central Coast–born boy called Randy Bernard. As Randy describes it, it all started behind a desk in a broom closet off a hallway in an office building in Colorado Springs. In 2015, Randy and his cohorts ultimately sold PBR for $100 million. Those twenty cowboys recouped their investment and then some!

Randy's vision was accomplished through a combination of reimagining Western heritage and a complete reconfiguration of rodeo's small-town aesthetic. He took its basic principles and turned the whole thing into a rock concert. He amped it to the max with strobe lights, smoke and fireworks, and a blaring soundtrack of AC/DC and Guns N' Roses. Vigorously promoting the handsome young cowboys, the overtures to the show were a fanfare of explosions and patriotic fervor, the competitors sauntering out along a catwalk to be introduced. Adorned in brightly emblazoned chaps and doffing their hats in acknowledgment to the boisterous crowd, they paraded forth with understated Midwestern swagger. Unlike in showbiz, their names were real, not manufactured, bestowed upon them by their ethnic background and the windswept vistas of Frederic Remington's visuals and Zane Grey's words. Chase Outlaw, Cody Jesus, Ryan Dirteater, and Macaulie Leather were some of the more colorful while the Brazilians brought with them romantic Latin names like Valdiron de Oliveira, Edevaldo da Silva Ferreira, and good friends like Guilherme Marchi and the ultimate powerhouse three-time world champion, Adriano Moraes.

My relationship with Randy and the PBR would endure for years. Up to the point of his departure in 2010, I was a regular at events and became a sort of goodwill ambassador for the sport. It's hard to emphasize how entrenched I was. My friendships were across the board, not just with the riders, but the color commentators, medical staff, point adjudicators, gate men, stock contractors, bullfighters, and of course the inimitable Flint Rasmussen, a guy who took the cheesy, Raggedy Andy cliché of rodeo clowning and turned it into a hyper-adrenalized form of stylized entertainment.

In 2002, North Carolina businessman Tommy Teague, a friend and fellow enthusiast, persuaded Berger Bucking Bulls to sell him a half interest in Little Yellow Jacket, one of the sport's most legendary animals. In turn, Tommy kindly offered me a shared interest, and from the time we gained a piece of him he became PBR World Champion in consecutive years from 2002 to 2004, a feat never achieved by any bull before him. Little Yellow Jacket was an anomaly in the game. He seemed to genuinely enjoy what he did, prancing around the arena shaking his head and acknowledging the crowd once his job was done. He was also docile in his demeanor, only unleashing his athleticism once he was out of the shoot, then with the job done seeming to purposely avoid stepping on a downed rider. A huge fan favorite, he had his own line of merchandise and afforded those who covered him (rode him for the full eight seconds) huge scores.

One of the greatest friends I made along with Randy Bernard in the PBR was World Champion Michael Gaffney. Known to everyone as G Man (as in "defying gravity"), Michael, aside from being one of the most unassuming and soft-spoken gentleman I've ever known, was also one of the most fearless and beautiful riders I've ever witnessed. He also has the distinction of having been one of only two riders to have covered Little Yellow Jacket twice, one of them being in 2004 for a record-setting score of 96.5 out of a possible 100, an achievement not matched until seventeen years later. As for bulls, only Bushwacker in 2014 possibly surpassed Little Yellow Jacket as the best bucking bull of all time.

RODEO, I'M AWARE, isn't to everyone's taste and it has many detractors who see it as inhumane. That's their prerogative of course, but having lived that life and seen this rich American culture up close, I can assure you that where the PBR is concerned, the very last thing involved is cruelty. The bulls are cared for in such a way that it's the cowboys who must travel hundreds of hard miles and sleep rough to make it to their next event. They are the ones you should sympathize with. Listen, there are those who think riding a horse is cruel. So when you have that argument to contend with you're always going to be fighting a losing battle.

While cowboying, I encountered some of the most indelible characters imaginable. If you want to know where some of my song ideas were born, picture Roy Carter, a rawboned hard-ass who traveled with a bobcat riding shotgun in his truck. Or Punk Dexter, a roper who after losing his dallying thumb (the act of securing the rope to the saddle horn) so many times in competition retired it and wore it as a mummified pendent around his neck. I spent a little time with Larry Mahan, arguably one of the most legendary rodeo stars of all time, and along with Ramblin' Jack Elliott the subject matter of a wonderful song by the late great Texas troubadour, Guy Clark.

> *Staying up all night in the Driskill Hotel*
> *Ramblin' Jack and Mahan cowboy'd all to hell*
> *The room smelled like bulls*
> *The words sound like songs*
> *Now there's a pair of drunken boys*
> *I would not steer you wrong*

Mahan was a stoic kinda guy who I hung with a couple of nights on and off in the Worthington Renaissance Hotel in Fort Worth. Taciturn initially, he was obviously in complete sync with his own history and seemingly only somewhat interested in mine. He warmed after a while, and when he realized I wasn't someone glomming on to his notoriety or plumbing the depth of his archives (which I most likely was in a tactful way), he became more open and autobiographical. Jack Daniel's is a subtle lubricant, and pretty soon a spirited one-on-one ensued as the combined forces of our individual backgrounds made for something more than conventional conversation.

Ramblin' Jack, on the other hand, was a completely different interpretation of the cowboy ethic. We met only one time, but that one afternoon and evening was without a doubt a memorable one. First and foremost, Elliott, like myself, was not born a cowboy but was enraptured by the lifestyle after witnessing a rodeo at Madison Square Garden. Brooklyn-born, his father was a prominent Jewish physician who, like so many of his era, expected Jack to follow in his footsteps. Jack, like all good fabricators, embroidered his resume, reinventing himself as an itinerant guitar picker, ultimately melting into this persona with ease. Befriending and becoming a student of dust bowl icon Woody Guthrie helped Jack gain ground and forge serious street credibility, elevating his reputation as a prodigious interpreter of not only Guthrie's music but also with his own take on resurrected obscure traditional American folk music. Later, a nascent Bob Dylan (someone else not unaccustomed to inventing his own personal history) sought out Jack to mentor him in the rudimentary ethics of what it meant to be a soldier in the army of the burgeoning folk militia inhabiting the clubs in New York's Greenwich Village.

Although he got around, traveling to Europe in the late '50s and touring Britain during the height of trad jazz and the emergence of the skiffle craze, it should be noted that Jack's nickname was not bestowed upon him for his traveling habits. Rather, it came from his tendency to expound at length on the most trivial of matters. The moniker is credited to the folk titan Odetta who remarked, "Oh, Jack Elliott. He sure can ramble on."

Jack was a credible legend, and in all humility I saw in my own small way a parallel, no matter how many decades apart I was from the ethos that he had built his image upon. He was, as I always had been, enamored with the world of cowboys, deliberately and actively pursuing his infatuations. Instead of the circus, he ran away to join the rodeo, learning the ropes while mastering his musicality. You have to earn the right to be a cowboy, playacting isn't going to cut it. There are no shortcuts and no pandering to celebrity. Respect comes with pulling your weight, valuing your horse, and tipping your hat to a lady.

Jack and I met in 2000 at the Paso Robles Film Festival where he was attending a showing of his daughter's documentary *The Ballad of Ramblin' Jack*. I was there as a guest of Randy Bernard who was presenting a different documentary on bull riding and the PBR called *This Is Not a Rodeo*. Earlier in the afternoon, all the festival's participants were gathered in the courtyard of one of the host hotels for a tasting of local wines. Not a particularly great idea given that this simply allowed those in attendance a head start on what was to prove to be a long day imbibing.

Imagining that I might be someone who had music in common with Jack, I was hauled away from the bar and into an alcove where he stood cradling a generous pour of Paso Robles's best. Under a very large white cowboy hat with a classic Western scarf tied around his neck, he was not as robust as I'd imagined he might be. In fact he was very small, slight of build, with sparkling eyes that were immediately engaging, canny, and full of history. It's not often that I converse with someone who has to look up when talking to me, but in Jack's case it was a necessity. I'm not convinced he knew who I was since after we were introduced, he remarked dryly, but not without good humor, "You must be a famous guy."

Slightly surprised, given that in my estimation I looked like just another comparatively cleaned up cowboy, I said something like "I may have a degree of fame, but I'm in no way legendary like yourself."

He afforded me a generous smile and a humbling "aww shucks" shrug and immediately proceeded to engage me in an inquisitional line of questioning. Detecting a hint of an accent in my vernacular, he retreated back into the 1950s, peppering me with anecdotes of his time spent in the emerging music scene in England. Our rapport became easier, and after several more complimentary beverages we agreed to meet up after the documentaries were screened. He was due to play a set later in the evening, and since we were both staying at the same hotel we made a date to meet in the lobby. I'm not sure if Ramblin' Jack Elliott ever had a roadie, but if he didn't, he did for that one night in Paso Robles, and that roadie was me.

Right on time, Jack appeared in the lobby with a guitar case almost the size of the troubadour himself. Transportation to the gig had been arranged, and after several more preperformance cocktails, I nipped outside to verify our ride was ready to roll.

At the front entrance as promised was a white van and driver. Taking my cue for the evening, I grabbed Jack's guitar case and ushered him into the back seat while I jumped in the front. Continuing with a nonstop juggernaut of anecdotes and recollections, Jack in every way lived up to his reputation. He was a skillful raconteur, his stories immaculate in detail, always energized by his dry delivery and effervescent wit. If there was one problem, it was that in order to include our driver in his banter he kept saying "sir" and "young man" when it was obvious from my point of view that the driver was neither a sir nor a man. Granted, it was dark in the vehicle and he was buried low in the rear and wrapped up in his own narrative, but even in those slightly less enlightened times it wasn't hard to assess that our chauffeur's gender performance, although certainly masculine in appearance, was in fact female.

Seemingly not offended by this slight on her appearance, she maintained her poise with good grace while I attempted to lighten the old boy's gaffes by indicating my apologies to her by way of some over-effected shoulder shrugging and eye-rolling.

On our arrival, I thanked her for her durability and understanding, and told her we'd be out in a couple of hours. Out of earshot, I set Jack straight on his identity gaffe. If he was embarrassed, he didn't seem so at all. He just looked back over his shoulder, and as if addressing the shadows of night around him, simply said, "Oh."

The event was being held in a large tent in an open field. Minimalistic at best, it was set up with several bars, standing round-top tables, and an abnormally large stage. By this time, most of the festival participants were three sheets to the wind, rowdy, and ready to hear some live music. Feeling an initial wave of trepidation, I wondered if this little old guy with the big guitar could give this crowd what they wanted.

Contrary to my doubts, Jack was completely at ease and after yet another couple of belts made for the stage with me and his guitar in tow. The setup was simple: just a chair and mics and a side stool for his drink. I opened his case and handed him his guitar, which I was charged to see had a bull rider emblazoned on the scratch plate. Nice touch.

I left him to it and shouldn't have worried. He was wonderful. He completely defused the sense of raucousness pervading the tent. His flat pick style and surprisingly strong high lonesome voice, intermingled with his engaging banter, thoroughly disarmed the collective of lubricated cowboys. Caught in a single spot, the beam bounced back from a reflective point at the rear of the stage, shooting through the fine head of white snowy hair beneath his hat and enveloping him in a glowing halo of orange. Tricks of the light can be convincing in their imaginative narrative, and for the short time spent in this translucent light, he weaved a wonderful spell. Like some elfin cowboy angel hovering in the ether above a drunken choir, I witnessed the best of traditional American music salvaged from obscurity by a potent practitioner of authenticity.

He exited the stage to much eeeehawing and yahhoooing and was soon engulfed by a congratulatory pack pressing his palm and slapping him on the back. Concerned for the safety of his instrument, I made sure to sequester it back in its case lest it fell afoul of some overexuberant reveler. A couple more gratis drinks later and we were heading for the door, old fans and new converts trailing us out into the warm night air.

He was quieter on the return trip but obviously satisfied with how the evening had gone. When we reached the hotel, he exited the van a little stiffly, turned to our driver, and, obviously with no recollection of his former faux pas, waved a hand and said, "Thanks again, young man."

Rousting up a lone employee, we managed a couple more glasses and called it a night. In the morning, I found an amazingly spry and refreshed Jack drinking coffee in the lobby. I told him how much I'd enjoyed spending time in his company and we shook hands expressing hope we'd meet again somewhere down the highway. Retrieving my truck, I drove back past the front entrance where he was sitting on a bench outside. I rolled down the window and bid him happy trails, and he tipped his hat in response, the little man with a big guitar and a lot of stories. I never saw him again.

As if I didn't have enough going on, in 1996 I decided to start a band. The reasons for Farm Dogs were numerous, my passion for roots-based music was certainly an underlying factor, but my desire to work with a particular guitarist is undoubtedly what set the whole thing in motion. Robin Le Mesurier was an old friend. He was also an immensely gifted and tasteful guitarist. Very much in the vein of Ronnie Wood, he was the son of beloved British comedic actors John Le Mesurier and Hattie Jacques. Even though he had played a relatively high-profile role in Rod Stewart's mid-'80s lineup, I'd always felt his talent was vastly underappreciated. Over dinner one night at my LA restaurant, Cicada, I proposed we do something about it, describing to him my desire to put together a group that could combine elements of blues, folk, rock, and country. He was in at the get-go, and at his suggestion, because they'd blended so well in Rod's band, we approached fellow UK guitarist Jim Cregan, an alumnus of progressive British ensembles like Family and Cockney Rebel. Jim's other attribute was that he was a smart songwriter, and with his Irish roots had a good ethnic background in the compositional elements I was looking for. He readily agreed, and as an afterthought I suggested my old associate Dennis Tufano to round out the band's first incantation. Dennis had been the lead singer for The Buckinghams, a popular Chicago band from the mid-'60s, and had been my cowriter and associate on my 1980 album *He Who Rides the Tiger*. The idea was to write and record the songs at the ranch, campfire style, in the tradition of bands who'd forsaken hi-tech studios for a more spontaneous, homemade approach. With this decision made, my financial commitment to it ran rampant, starting with the construction of a functional recording facility.

At the rear of my house was an adjacent building that housed a racquetball court and small workout room on the lower level with a guest apartment directly above. This became, then and in years to come, the nerve center of all my creative endeavors. Inside the racquetball court, I installed two isolation booths, one for vocals and the other for overdubs and the eventuality of drums. In the exterior gym, we set up the control room, designed and installed by our engineer and coproducer, David Cole. David had come at the recommendation of A&R man John S. Carter, who had worked with David in connection with Detroit rocker Bob Seger. Carter, as he was known singularly, was our barometer and champion at the record company, although his initial idea of us calling the band Mohammed Chang (the two most popular names in the world) was thankfully outvoted in favor of Farm Dogs. Carter was also a hugely successful producer in his own right who had resurrected Tina Turner's career in the 1980s and guided her 1984 album *Private Dancer* to astronomical sales. He also had the distinction of having written the lyrics to "Incense and Peppermints," the Strawberry Alarm Clock's 1967 psychedelic number-one single, which in my eyes was of equal value.

Facing a large picture window looking out over the valley, we put four chairs in a circle, sat down with guitars, and all wearing A-T headphones, wrote, and recorded the songs that would constitute *Last Stand in Open Country*, the first Farm Dogs album.

The communal spirit was infectious, and we had a lot of fun. Our humor was in sync, and there was enough inside joking to make my recollections of it memorable. There was one in particular that never fails to bring a smile to my face. There would be a market run made every day, and in the evening we would have long elaborate dinners usually prepared by myself with a designated sous chef, usually Robin. Fueled by pitchers of martinis and many bottles of appropriately designated wines, they were bacchanalian evidence of male bonding. How we got back to work after these medieval-styled feasts beats me, yet it's a testimonial to the fact we still had enough giddyup-'n-go in us to go.

Anyway, back on point. I'd usually go to the market, it's always been my thing, plus I was known locally and respected by that time as an entrenched member of the community. During the day, before my grocery run, we would make our own idiosyncratic grocery lists, the more ridiculously eccentric the better. They ended up posted all over the walls of the studio and now probably lie yellowing in some storage file box reading "Farm Dogs stuff."

For example:

> A pound of granulated mouse bait
> Slim Jims
> One packet of interesting peanuts
> Overripe armadillo cheese
> Potatoes
> Edmundo Ross' saddle
> Milk
> Identical kangaroos
> The Piltdown Man
> The Piltdown Man's Wife
> Coal
> Somalian Ice Cream
> Inflatable trousers
> And one large can of invisible peaches

We even gave ourselves rap names. Being that my nickname was Bean, I was Bean Latifah, Robin was Six-Pac-I'm-Sure, Jim was Run-W.C., and Dennis, due to his Italian background, was Snoop Denny Dago. We also planned on making a live album, not because it was feasible, but simply because we liked the title, *Together Again for the First Time*.

To promote our first release, we went out on a radio tour that was primarily focused on making an indentation in local radio around the country. Again, it was fun and on my dime, but not without issues that ultimately reconfigured the ideological gap in the conceptional balance of the group.

At this point, we brought in a serious component to corral our undisciplined childishness. This was totally necessary in order to keep order, maintain stability, and make sense of things. We were overage adolescents inhabiting invented juvenile personas, and Pete Buckland was durable, tough, and possessed of a built-in no bullshit mechanism. He'd been the original road manager for the Faces, and if he could wrangle that rabble, then he'd have little trouble handling us, because we were simply an aged version of the same thing. He immediately gained my respect by watching the bottom line, and although he had no aversion to a breakfast margarita, he got us where we were going and acted like a responsible adult when necessary.

Sympathizing with my monitorial input and realizing the major investment I'd made, he took the reins and monitored the cash flow. Meanwhile my management appeared indifferent to the project. My peripheral desires were of no consequence to the main office, and because there was no percentage in it for them, it was off their books and thus of no interest. Pete, however, stayed true to the band even though he was completely aware that we would never break even. He understood our shelf life was short but genuinely thought we were worth a shot for as long as it lasted. He shepherded the group, engineered our live sound, and simply assisted because he had a heralding desire to be in the swamp with silliness one more time.

Playing live was not something I had envisioned and was yet to come to terms with. Eventually, we tested the waters with some local LA gigs. Nothing overambitious, just some backroom performances at my restaurant and at Luna Park on Robertson. It was breaking ground for me and set up things not only for our future recording but for my confidence as a singer and front man.

In order to amp up the minimalistic arrangements of the first album, we brought in some extra muscle to rearrange the songs into a more powerful live context. We got lucky and got some superior support, not only in Sheryl Crow alumnus bassist Tad Wadhams, but in a coup of genuine kismet snared one of the best time keepers in the business. Tony Brock had been the drummer for the solid pop rock band The Babys and was well respected as an explosive and rhythmic player.

I loved his style and was thrilled to have him aboard. Like Robin, he was a guy who had somehow missed the boat in regard to high-profile recognition. He was so damn good and, if in the right place at the right time, would have been on the raiser keeping time for some stadium filling mega band. For now, though, we were blessed to have him, and he was in my estimation the backbone of the band and the reason for driving forward.

As we prepared to go back in for our sophomore album, it was obvious that things weren't working out with Dennis. Let's just say there were personality traits becoming apparent that didn't altogether gel with the camaraderie of the band. I have to say I felt completely responsible for his removal. I'd brought him in and, with all due respect, had in previous years spent some wonderful times in his company.

The original concept of Farm Dogs had been to form an autonomous collective where I could slip into being just a member of the band. I'd wanted to simply blend in and be part of a democratic ensemble. Good luck with that! It was completely ridiculous. I was paying for everything, housing everyone, feeding them, and lending some of them money while at the same time pretending to be just the singer. It was a pipe dream and totally illogical. The only reason we got ink and were invited to pitch our music on credible FM morning shows and regional TV was because the bus was driven by someone whose recognition value, no matter how unwanted, was the very reason we got to exist.

After Dennis's departure from the band certain members didn't seem to grasp this concept, and ultimately, Jim and I would butt heads. Not in an officious way, just small creative differences that at times seemed designed to assure his ego that this was to continue as a democracy.

It was more prevalent during the recording of the second album and, while Robin in his nonconfrontational English way steered clear from anything quarrelsome, Jim was adamant in pitching in his ten cents. I had no problem sparring with Jim initially, it just seemed part of the process, what group members do. In time, though, whether I saw the writing on the wall or that the financial burden on me was tipping the scales, it started to have a niggling effect that, depending on my mood, would become irksome.

It didn't help either when Jim's wife decided to chime in. It started during rehearsals with her barrage of phone calls intermittently disrupting our run-throughs. We'd be passionately doing our best to improve our game when his cell phone would light up. Instead of ignoring the call and waiting for an opportune time to call her back, he'd quit playing mid-song, wave for us to stop, and take the call. Annoying? Hell yes, but we bit our tongues.

I was sympathetic to a point. For while I was aware he was suffering from marital problems, I was enduring my own. I was in the death throes of my third marriage, but while my wife never called me if she didn't have to, Jim's seemed to have him on speed dial in order to have him twist in the wind and dance to her tune.

The irritation factor was kicked up a notch one night in Vegas. We'd completed our second album, *Immigrant Sons*, a more electric and powerful album than its predecessor, and were at the tail end of a six month tour. Having just played a blistering set opening for Leon Russell at the Hard Rock Casino, we'd all repaired to one of the hotel's better restaurants for a celebratory dinner. We were all feeling the natural high of post-performance bliss when out of the blue a clearly inebriated Mrs. Cregan launched into a Spinal Tap assessment of her proposal for our future. Mouths agog and both horrified yet respectful for Jim's sake, we, like Nigel Tufnel, took it in the shorts. Imparting what I imagine she thought was sage advice, we all smiled benignly as she slowly ran out of words and nodded off, her head genuflecting slowly and hovering precariously until it gently came to rest in her bowl of untouched pasta.

After this, and what seemed like a boisterous packed house swan song at the Roxy in LA, we did a limited residence at The Mint on Pico before fading to black. We were a gang as much as we were a band and of an age when it seemed appropriate to kick up some dust and assume the position that to be entirely politically incorrect was still feasible. The image that we created for ourselves was an important component of the music and was in itself an absolute reality: we complied with our merchandise byline on T-shirts that read "Growing Old Disgracefully" and our logo that was a Milk-Bone in a martini glass. We lived it to the hilt simply for the love of the music we created and the pleasure at (varying interludes) of each other's company.

There are those who might perceive Farm Dogs as one of many things: a midlife crisis vanity project, or a wealthy musician's plaything, his sideshow away from the Big Top. Nothing, however, could be further from the truth. We recorded homestyle, though not exactly in spartan conditions, but on tour we traveled coach, slept cheap, and didn't make a dime. We played street festivals, church basements, in the back room of restaurants, and every kick-start cramped classic rock club imaginable. There were nights when there were more people onstage than there were in the crowd, but I'm thrilled to say that one way or another I got to give forth on the boards of some of America's best. Yeah, we played the Roxy and the Troubadour in LA, but we also covered a wide spectrum of North America's finest: Third and Lindsley in Nashville, the Fenix in Seattle, Denver's Soiled Dove, the fantastic Belly Up tavern in Solana Beach, and the legendary Bottom Line in New York's Greenwich Village.

I'm not by nature a nostalgic person when it comes to my career. I'm always looking ahead, yet the occasional reminiscence of the good old days isn't entirely uncomfortable. For all the daftness and cryptological shenanigans, we actually made some really good music. Not everything worked, but for every couple of things that failed to fly we'd craft something poignant, naturally descriptive, or organically windswept. On the first record, the likes of "Bone of Contention," "Cinderella '67," "The Ballad of Dennis Hopper and Harry Dean," and the title track are really strong songs, lyrically sweeping, and melodically transient. I think "Last Stand in Open Country," in particular, is one of the best songs I've ever written. On our sophomore release *Immigrant Sons*, tracks like "Distance to the Mountain," "Foreign Windows," and "Stars and Seeds" have credible muscle. It's understandable that people are familiar with my more identifiable work, but as someone who has always been driven to create, the motifs and personal observations ingrained in the lyrics of these songs are so closely connected to my ideology that I will be forever indebted for the chance to invest time into my own personal individuality. I'm never happier than when sharing what Elton and I create because it's based on mutual observation, a panorama of varying subject matter, and a completely synchronous union of our combined history. It's my lifeblood. But we, as inquisitive animals, will always seek out alternative productive outlets as a way to stay creatively solvent.

Sometime after the band's demise, "Last Stand in Open Country" and "This Face" from our first album were recorded by Willie Nelson on his 2002 album *The Great Divide*, a testament, I'd like to believe, to their strength and timelessness.

The guys in Farm Dogs were some of the most gifted musicians I have ever worked with. Their contributions cannot be trivialized, and the experience we shared was magic. They encouraged and taught me that I could be a front man, something that in my wildest dreams I never imagined I'd add to my resume. But in the end, economics and reality told me it was time to move on.

My checkbook might have had some regrets, but I don't. Everything has its learning curves. Like I said, we made some splendid music, wrote some excellent songs, and were a pretty competent and entertaining live act, but in the end I'm sure my accountants weren't completely thrilled with the amount of money I ultimately poured into the project. After investing in an LA restaurant and running a high operation ranch, business acumen not being my strong point, I'm sure the suits weren't unhappy to see it go south.

Had satellite radio existed during Farm Dogs tenure, I imagine we would have fared better. There are channels dedicated to the kind of music we were making, whereas on traditional FM at the time there was no niche for us. But as Pete Buckland succinctly put it, ultimately democracy is OK as long as everyone does what you tell them. Pete's influence resonates with me to this day, and he remains one of my most enduring friends, wise and still unafraid of a breakfast margarita.

IN AUGUST 1997, Diana, Princess of Wales, died from injuries sustained in a car crash in the Alma tunnel in Paris. It was a brutal and tragic end to a life turbulently played out in the media spotlight, and while I freely admit I paid little attention to the royal soap opera that seemed to consume so many, there was no doubt in my mind that she was a decent woman with a good heart and enough class to rise above the turgid mire of royal protocol.

I'd never met her but was aware that she and Elton had formed a close personal relationship. That this should happen only a month after a psychopath called Andrew Cunanan gunned down Elton's dear friend, the designer Gianni Versace, outside his home in Florida must have been devastating to Elton. The world mourned for Diana and, like everyone else, I watched as fingers were pointed and theories engulfed the obsessive with a mixture of genuine grief and gratuitous morbid curiosity.

Diana's funeral was planned for the first week of September, and prior to this I received a call from Elton. As is the way with all things that take place when tragic circumstances are involved, recollections can vary.

I don't recall the Richard Branson equation Elton talks about in his book. If he did make the suggestion for a rewrite of "Candle in the Wind," it wasn't discussed in our phone call. As I remember it, we initially mulled over the possibility of a new song, but given the expediency with which something needed to be done, we discarded the idea of an original in favor of reworking the existing lyric. Once we hung up I went straight to work, and within half an hour I'd completed what would become "Candle in the Wind 1997," or as it's more intimately known "England's Rose." If you put a gun to my head right now and threatened to kill me if I didn't recite the lyric, I'd be a dead man. I don't remember a word of it.

Along with 2.5 billion people worldwide, I watched the funeral on TV. I was in a hotel room in New York. The austere solemnity of Westminster Abbey coupled with drifting camera sweeps along the silent thousands lining the surrounding streets invoked a sort of emotional manipulation that made me uncomfortable.

It was hard not to get caught up while at the same time wondering why. Being molded into believing that this was the way you were supposed to feel felt like cheating. It was sad, devastating to so many, yet for me there was a chasm between the reality of it all and the fantasy fairy tale it falsely invoked, like the distance between relatable affection and a faraway star. I shed a tear for the wrong reasons, my focus solely on my friend's burden. I can only imagine how harrowing it must have been to perform at the axis of this sentimental tsunami not only carrying his grief but simply to hold himself together. Ultimately, he was poised, impassioned, and magnificent, and I was immensely proud of him.

From the funeral, he went directly to AIR Studios where, with George Martin in the producers chair, cut the single version of "Candle in the Wind 1997." It would go on to sell thirty-three million copies, raising an unprecedented $38 million for the Diana, Princess of Wales Memorial Fund along with becoming the highest selling single of all time since the charts began in the 1950s.

With all due respect, I did it because Elton asked me to and ultimately that decision was wise because of the immense charitable impact it made. Later, Christie's sold my original manuscript for over $400,000 to benefit Children's Hospital Los Angeles, which was an added bonus.

I was back on a horse loping around a windswept arena, a heavy morning mist hanging low, the dusky dawn still an hour away, when my cell phone rang. In one world our song was selling 100,000 units a day while here in the black land dirt of some backwater showground the elements were challenging and the air hung heavy with the smell of cattle and horse sweat. In the US alone, we may have sold 3.5 million copies in the first week, but I was too busy peering through the grubby nylon curtains of my motel room window, checking to see if the hub caps were still on my truck.

I lived almost twenty-six years at the ranch and in that time I was single, got married, became single again, and then remarried. Jumping in for my third go around, Stephanie and I had gotten hitched at the ranch in 1994. In all honesty it could be said that our time spent before we said "I do" was the most idealistic part of our relationship and that everything that followed never managed to measure up to the magical sparks ignited in that one intimate year. I certainly have no regrets though; it was for a time far more balanced and energized than what I'd experienced in my previous marriages, this definitely due in part to my involvement with her two exceptional daughters. When their mother and I had started dating they were five and three, respectively, and my role in their lives became a stabilizing force that set me up in good stead for the future.

I took the role of stepdad seriously and became totally committed to being the best role model I could possibly be. I never once tried to usurp the role of their biological father. No one in the stepfather role ever wants to hear, "You're not my dad." So it was important I invent a uniform that was neither confrontational nor dictatorial. I simply tried to be there for them and administer ethical advice, which given my track record at times probably reverberated like a sententious echo. I'd hardly been a beacon of virtuosity, but then again, hopefully I was beginning to learn from my mistakes and could at least attempt to steer anyone who cared to listen away from doing what I had done in the more unprincipled and reckless aspects of my past.

I have an unadulterated respect for women and not always in stereotypical ways. Oh, believe me I'm not a rock. I've fallen on the sword and worshiped at the altar, but outside the obvious attributes that find favor in the eyes of men, they are so much more. I've always loved them. Not in the leering, creepy, louche way that solidifies heterosexual credentials. They have the advantage; they know us so much better than we know them, and that is their ace in the hole, their magnanimous source of power. Their innate capacity to deal with and make sense of life on a far more logical level than us men is simple in purpose but enigmatic in its execution.

I once had the distinct pleasure of spending an evening in the company of Leonard Cohen, certainly the individual whose work undoubtedly defines the mystery and intoxicating charm of women better than any of his contemporaries. It was at Cicada, my Melrose Avenue restaurant, where I discovered him alone at a corner table sipping black coffee, smoking Turkish cigarettes, and making notes in a small black journal. It didn't surprise me that he was on his own as he'd always struck me as a solitary individual, his own company possessing enough stimulation to keep his engine running between interactions with a peripheral world.

He was in his late fifties at this point, immaculately dressed, his hair cropped short, and gracious to a fault. Possessed of a serene aura he had boundless charisma and was inviting, delightful, and engaging from the get-go.

Our meeting was just prior to his stepping away from the world and retreating to the Mount Baldy Zen Center in the San Gabriel Mountains to begin his five-year meditative journey into Buddhism. I can only imagine his tranquility and monastic countenance that day could have been a preparatory psyching of the mind, steeling himself for what might prove a most arduous task.

I clearly didn't inhabit his cerebral realm, but while I was a million miles from being a solitarian, I had no problem dining solo and vacationing on my own, and I had been from day one a dyed-in-the-wool loner. The two of us fell into an easy conversation and even though everything about our musical and lyrical makeup was a creative chasm apart, there was not a condescending note in the hypnotic comfort of his mellifluous smoky baritone. On the contrary, he was highly complimentary, which was golden coming from the only recording artist who I could ever comfortably call a poet. Whatever your take might be, in my mind no matter how exceptional, the rest of us are just lyricists.

While I had always found his lyrical and poetic contemplations on women to be profoundly sexy, there was always a sense that his female protagonists had the upper hand. Even when he was pointedly carnal with his words, there was in the intimacy a heroic quality, an undeniable strength that was obvious in its admiration. His women are never cookie-cutter song fodder, they exist on multiple levels and have a literary idealism. In Leonard Cohen's world they are objects of art, not simply objects. Even when he's singing about the woman with the meter on her bed, it's in a cadence of such visual poetry that you want to applaud her for her promiscuity. Cohen had a lifetime of relationships with all manner of interesting women, and as far as I can gather drew inspiration from many of them. I believe he had a genuine respect and deep appreciation for them, an appreciation that I hope I've emulated in my own turbulent journey. Neither of us had been saints, but I'd like to believe we both shared an affinity for the tremendous attributes that women brought to our line of work.

Our conversation was easy and relaxed as it gravitated languidly from one subject to another. One minute it was poets and poetry, the next it was jazz, country, and the Great American Songbook. He spoke admiringly of e. e. cummings and Federico García Lorca while I recounted how my background was steeped in the narratives of Tennyson, Macaulay, and Stephen Vincent Benét. Hank Williams was a topic as was Duke Ellington, Ray Charles, and Joni Mitchell. Most surprisingly, though, was his appreciation of the old cowboy classic "Red River Valley" by Gene Autry, a staple of my early conversion into narrative country. He professed to his lyrical styling paling in comparison to Cole Porter and was far too humble and self-deprecating in his critical assessment of his own work. My own personal appreciation of Cohen's canon has deepened profoundly over the years, and where once I held him in high regard alongside several others of his ilk, I have recently realized that he is the master and has no lyrical equals. I've spent much more time with him of late, and on every listening I am acutely aware of how he poured over his words, editing, correcting, and embellishing until he had them crafted to perfection. He is in a league of his own, his metrical composition is sublime, his rhythmic structure intoxicating, and in all honesty, I don't believe there is anyone quite like him.

I'm unable to truly assess if his quest for enlightenment in Buddhism was successful. He was quoted as saying, "A monastery is designed to eliminate private space," and later admitted to never becoming a Buddhist at all. I can't imagine that he got too much out of it as his work makes little or no reference to Eastern religions. He seemed far more interested in wrestling with traditional Christian theology and mining the gospels of the Bible for song content. I've never been able to get a firm handle on what he believed in religious terms, although his professing "I'm ready, my Lord" on the song "You Want It Darker," from his final studio album also titled *You Want It Darker*, released nineteen days before his passing in 2016, could possibly be read as both a thank-you for the material as well as a confirmation that the subject matter set him in good stead with the Almighty.

ॐ

IT WAS OBVIOUS that the ranch life appealed to Stephanie. As an experienced rider in her own right, she had a background in hunter jumpers that helped her transition easily into the world of cutting. After all, there was a built-in no-fear factor. After thundering around all over the shop, leaping across hoary ditches and majorly intimidating obstacles on a really big thoroughbred, dancing in the dirt on a quarter horse, technically elaborate as it might be, must have been a piece of cake. She took to it like a duck to water and left me eating her dust. She excelled from day one and eventually, long after we'd called it a day, went on to win the non-pro world championship in 2008.

The collapse of my marriage to Stephanie was predictably messy, and like the demise of my previous relationships, much of the carnage wound up in my songwriting. Sometimes my impressions of romantic tension and disintegration can be blatantly in your face, and other times they're interwoven cryptically into the framework of songs that exist on different levels. Some songs are multilayered, drawing from multiple relationships, real or imagined. They wind up partly fact, partly fiction, and a conglomerate of metaphors that may at times be the reason my work is often cited as either obscure or crap, depending on your point of view.

It's not important to belabor why it fell apart, only that for a time it sent me into an emotional tailspin of disillusion and depression. I was gone when Stephanie was getting ready to go. On the road with Farm Dogs, I was in New York when I got the call that she was leaving. The equation of children in a relationship, even if they're not your own but you love them as if they were, is the most crippling aspect of divorce. The loss of the kids in my everyday life was physically debilitating. Walking into their room in the aftermath of their mother moving out took my breath away. Where once there was a cluttered warmth of excitable energy, a hollow residue of finality was omnipresent. The floor that only weeks earlier had been littered with books and the paraphernalia of juvenile preoccupation was now simply bare floorboards scattered with a discarded debris of shredded packing tape and paper. In the adjacent corners left and right, perfectly pitted dents symmetrically mocked, indicating where the legs of their beds once lived. Empty open furniture, closet doors exposing nothing but a few oscillating wire hangers, drawers, half-open like gaping mouths, an odd random sock hanging limp over the lip like a lolling tongue.

Outside the ones in my head, the memories had all but been picked clean. All that remained were two drawings desperately clinging the wall, the tape securing them having lost its anchorage. The breeze from the open window slapped them up and down till they floated to the center of the room like spectral messages. Childlike primitives, stick people and family pets, scrawling identification under each one, they depicted smaller moments of love and better times now seemingly insignificant in the big picture. Inanimate in reality, they projected something magical, a pinspot of confirmation that no matter what the current circumstances dictated, some things couldn't be erased. One drawing was titled "The Great Ranch." It was obvious I wasn't going to be forgotten anytime soon. The silence may have been deafening, but the echo of children's laughter still haunted the air.

By this point in my life I was married out and completely despondent about ever making this weird ritual work. As I saw it then, I was done and in no mood to give it a go again anytime soon. In fact, given the mindset I was currently in I was adamant in pursuing the single life indefinitely. What this whole mess of disappointment did serve up however was the one thing that has never let me down. For songwriters there is some masochistic truth in the fact that we can extract a cathartic remedy out of pain. Like unlocking a pressure cooker and releasing the steam slowly, we manage to unload some of that traumatic residue by channeling it through the only way we know how. It doesn't heal, but it helps, and out of the carnage came a beacon of redemption.

I wrote some really good material that in turn became some excellent songs on one of our best albums. In fact, my biographical testament pinpointing my mental state at the time is conceivably one of my most accomplished lyrics. "I Want Love" encapsulated my feelings completely in a way like no other song we've ever written. *Songs from the West Coast* remains one of my favorite albums in our catalog. Even though it documents some dark history, it's never morose. The songs don't wallow in self-pity; on the contrary they sound alive and angry, confident in questioning not only the fragile nature of relationships but also the cruel injustice of AIDS on the arts, and the senseless murder of gay Wyoming student Matthew Shepard. There is enough light and shade in it to counteract the romantic negativity of really good songs like "Dark Diamond" and "This Train Don't Stop There Anymore." It's one of my proudest achievements, straightforward and honest in nature, and it is, without a doubt outside *Captain Fantastic*, my most autobiographical album.

In the aftermath of all this, I was adrift like no other time in my life. It's still a blur, in fact. Although I imagine it involved a lot of irrational behavior, heavy drinking, and the odd, unenthusiastic date. Even the confines of my beloved ranch seemed to have adopted a somber tone, closing in a little and suffocating the landscape. Things seemed uglier, the irregular humpbacked hills in the evening dusk, carved through by moon-burned ochre ruts, snaked down into the darkening green thickets where the light was extinguished and the strangled cries of coyotes were carried on the wind. It was indeed a horrible time.

Then in the late afternoon of August 22, 1998, I stepped onto a bus, and my entire life changed forever.

Welcome to the Reckoning

"I will not go," answered the Cricket,
"until I have told you a great truth."

—JIMINY CRICKET
Pinocchio

Life is long and life is tough
But when you love someone
Life's not long enough

—EMMYLOU HARRIS
"Not Enough"

The suggestion was made by well-meaning friends that my perception of conjugal bliss as a myth was overly pessimistic and that time would eventually restore a more confident perspective. Not that I believed that, not for a minute. My agenda had become hollow, my outlook cynical, and my status as a confirmed bachelor etched in stone. Let's just call this a love story of old LA.

It was one of those fancy buses, the kind that touring musicians utilize to zigzag across the country rather than endure the hassles of airports. It was a warm late afternoon in August and it was parked on Crescent Drive adjacent to the luxury bungalows of the Beverly Hills Hotel. Elton was scheduled to play the Arrowhead Pond in Anaheim that evening, and someone from his management company thought it might be a fun idea for our entourage to take a bus. There were about a dozen of us making the trip, including Elton's transitional management, various assistants, and me. I'd originally considered taking a helicopter or a limo, but being leery of choppers and not wanting to be cooped up in a car, I opted for the communal charabanc. Fate, indeed, works in mysterious ways.

She was the first person I saw when I got on the bus. Standing at the top of the steps, she was impressive. Tall, brunette, and exceptionally attractive, she wore a well-tailored business suit and looked like a glamorous CEO of some Fortune 500 company. It came as a surprise then, when she welcomed me aboard and introduced herself as our hostess, Heather. With no disparagement to that profession, it's not what she looked like, but in the moment I accepted her credentials as gospel and delivered the worst opening line imaginable. Pointing at the TV above her head I blurted out, "Can you get bull riding on that thing?" Mr. Smooth, indeed, and as she, with a polite and amused smile offered me the remote, I immediately tried to rebound with something witty. It was not forthcoming, and with foot firmly planted in mouth, I skulked off to my seat like the dumbest kid in class. Honestly, I couldn't take my eyes off her, and from the moment the trip began it became apparent to several of my fellow travelers that she'd captured my attention. She really was captivating in a way that was uncharacteristic from conventional eye candy. If that's crass, I apologize, but it's the only honest way I can convey the situation. Even though she didn't appear comfortable in the role of rolling waitress, she carried herself with a dignified erectness and polished conservatism that I found unbelievably sexy. Dare I say it, but she seemed wholesome, a refreshing feature given the current egocentric climate. There was something completely different about her, a purity that I was unfamiliar with, a gracefulness in her bearing that might have been the byproduct of grooming in etiquette and social interaction. Oh yes, and she had the most stunning pair of legs I'd ever seen.

On board with us was Michael Hewitson, and Michael deserves some explaining. He had been in the employ of Elton, mainly as a valet for many years dating back to the early '70s when he had been introduced to us by drummer Nigel Olsson's then girlfriend, Jozy Pollock.

One of the most endearing and delightful individuals ever to grace the Elton John family tree, Michael had been anointed "Brenda Woodstock" by the boss for his pacifistic nature and karmic serenity. He was just a lovely man with a keen wit and a colorful backstory. A true product of swinging London, he'd started out witnessing the dark underbelly of the Kray brothers' notorious gangland empire by dating their number one enforcer, "Mad" Teddy Smith. If you've ever seen the 2015 biographical crime thriller *Legend* starring Tom Hardy in the dual role of both Reggie and Ronnie Kray, you will have seen Teddy Smith portrayed by none other than Taron Egerton, the actor who would go on to play Elton in *Rocketman*. Michael had made it out of gangland life unscathed and graduated to the slightly safer environment of the emerging beat boom, becoming a close personal friend of the drummer Dave Clark and finding employ as the road manager for his band The Dave Clark Five. Later, he had worked as a photographer and entered into a relationship with *Dr. Kildare* heartthrob Richard Chamberlain.

Michael, being Michael and fully aware of my obviously smitten state, had no compulsion about being subtle. As Heather was handing him a beverage, he looked directly at her and inquired, "Are you married?" Caught off guard, she answered yes somewhat hesitantly as if she wasn't terribly committed to the idea. Adopting a stern parental tone, he raised his eyes as if looking up over a pair of invisible spectacles and with exaggerated colonial Britishness inquired, "Happily?" I don't recall her answer if there was one at all, but I've no doubt she wondered why this picturesque limey was grilling her on her marital status.

When we got to the gig, we all piled out and headed backstage. Once the show had begun I commenced to do what I have always done. I find it impossible to stand still for any length of time, and I move constantly between the dressing rooms and the cordoned off areas at either side of the stage. In our entire time together, I have never sat in the audience for an Elton show, choosing to be free to witness it from all angles and interact with our road crew and personnel. This particular night, however, I was wondering where the lovely Heather was. I was just about to send my assistant out to reconnoiter the outer area when I saw her standing off in a corner by the curtain leading backstage.

Determined to redeem myself by attempting to make up for any lame dialogue I may have imparted earlier, I approached her and asked her if she'd care to check out the show from a better angle, inviting her to sit beside me on an anvil case at stage right, directly behind Elton. It was at this point that I wondered if she had any clue as to my position in this whole shebang. Maybe she just thought I was some nice gay guy who was simply being accommodating. If she was wondering at all, then the answer arrived as if on cue. Making a grand entrance en route to their seats, Hugh Grant, Elizabeth Hurley, and Jim Carrey paused to make nice with hugs, kisses, and handshakes. A light bulb must have gone on because five minutes later Heather leaned over and said, "So . . . how many of these songs did you write?"

It was a confidence booster, indeed, and as the evening progressed I asked her if she'd like to watch some of the show from the mixing desk in the center of the arena floor. She accepted, and we sat and watched a good portion of the second half in this location. She really was different; there was nothing remotely flighty, coy, or flirty about her, and she never lost her poise and was exquisite in a charmingly composed way. Did I mention she smelled divine?

There was absolutely no bolstered familiarity on the return trip. Any limited interaction we'd had in the time spent taking in the show was cordial at best, and while she went about her business with graceful effectiveness, I drank tequila and watched *L.A. Confidential*. What was I to do? It was a flirtation on my part that had no real possibilities. Apparently, she was married, lucky bastard whoever he was, and given my reckless tendencies of late it would be insensitive to drag such a delightful young woman onto my emotional merry-go-round. I should be encouraged with such pure happenstance, her lingering fragrance, and sophisticated charm. *Just savor the night and leave it at that*, I thought. Still, if only things were different.

A week later, I was at the ranch when the phone rang. It was Heather. Apparently they had found my apartment keys behind a cushion where I'd been sitting on the bus. I had indeed misplaced them, and no, I didn't leave them there on purpose. "I don't know if you remember me," she said. "Oh, I remember you," said I. And so it began. Well, I had an excuse, didn't I? How else was I going to get my keys back? I was convinced there was a reason this had happened, fate reaching out for one last opportunity to learn more about this beguiling beauty. Tentatively, I asked if perhaps we could meet up for a drink. She didn't jump on the offer but simply acquiesced by saying, "That sounds benign enough." *No pushover here, that's for sure*, I thought.

We met at the Beverly Hills Hotel and sat on the patio of the Polo Lounge. While I'm never self-conscious or diffident, I was for some reason nervous. This was both fascinating and confusing, having never encountered such a predicament. If either one of us was awkward, it was probably me, my attempts at adopting a relaxed and confident pose not exactly rising to the occasion. It turned out Heather was full of surprises. She was, as I had imagined, not a hostess, but the director of sales and marketing for CLS, one of LA's premier limousine services. She explained that she had simply been doing a favor for her boss due to the unavailability of anyone else. Born in Euclid, Ohio, she had grown up in and attended high school in Fort Lauderdale, Florida, before attending the University of Florida in Gainesville. Graduating from college with degrees in English and telecommunications, she had moved to California working as a conference concierge at the Ritz-Carlton in Marina del Rey. Prior to her relocation, she was signed exclusively to the Ford Modeling Agency, worked in TV, and hated it, and apparently somewhere along the way picked up a husband.

Her marriage wasn't discussed, but I had to imagine all was not well on the home front. I wasn't psychic, but she just didn't strike me as the kind of woman who'd engage in a clandestine rendezvous or anything illicit for that matter. Nothing about her indicated deceit; on the contrary, she seemed the very model of morality and intelligent resolve. I must have done something right because she agreed to see me again.

We started dating, and yes, her marriage was on the rocks and all but over. Within weeks, she left her husband and in due course moved into my old friend David Fryden's apartment building on Flores in West Hollywood. She was supersmart and funny with a wicked sense of humor. She loved music, had a really good voice, and would sing along with all the latest country hits, all of which she impressively knew the words to. She visited the ranch, was fully on board with cowboy culture, attended PBR events with me, and drove out to watch me compete when I was cutting in Paso Robles or Arroyo Grande. For my fellow competitors, she was an object of gossip and great interest. Everyone, of course, knew everyone else's business, and being that Stephanie was a leading light in the cutting game, this new arrival after the dissolution of my marriage caused a serious buzz. Cowboys and cowgirls have a wonderful way with words and phrases, many of which have been incorporated into my lyrics, like in "I Must Have Lost It on the Wind" from the *The Captain and the Kid*. The explanation of which is when you're out pushing a herd and try to communicate over the noise, the recipient will apologize for not hearing you by saying, "Sorry, I must have lost it on the wind." The first time Heather turned up at a show, she'd driven into the trailer alley at the rear of the arena in a black Porsche 911 Carrera. As the door swung open and she swung out, one of my fellow cutters, a waggish Texan woman from Dallas remarked, "Dang, that girl's legs left the car five minutes before the rest of her."

We continued to get closer, our chemistry in total compliance with each other. We'd traveled to the UK, gone to New York, and taken a weekend trip to Napa Valley. In Napa, we got up in the middle of the night to indulge in what we imagined would be an awe-inspiring balloon ride over the vineyards at dawn. It was a bust! We stood in the freezing cold for over an hour as they inflated the balloon, were shoved into the carrier like a couple of baguettes in a French bicycle basket, and then, due to zoning restrictions, remained stationary, hovering over a trailer park while the guide bragged endlessly about taking up Bobby De Niro.

In a Fort Worth hotel room, we watched an episode of *Jeopardy!* when one of the categories was "Elton John Lyrics." Out of the five questions, I only got two right. There was a lot of jumping up and down yelling, "Oh, oh, oh, I know it, I know it," which was abjectly pathetic, given they were overtly recognizable hits. We found good humor in everything, our compatibility bouncing back and forth, a winning combination of game, set, and match. Where she'd been no pushover initially and cautious with her affection, it was now plain to see that she cared deeply for me and loved me perhaps more than I'd ever been loved before. This is when I balked and bailed. It's hard to comprehend even now how irredeemably stupid I was. Not only was it callous and cruel, it was an embarrassment to my own personal identity. This complete insanity was instigated by a bout of paranoia brought on by my fear of commitment. I had temporarily forgotten my pledge to cast myself adrift of fidelity, to play the field and be the wounded warrior stumbling away from the light. It haunts my nightmares to this day that I could have lost it all, the alternatives I dare not even imagine. The fact that she continued to carry a torch after such wantonness may seem perverse on the surface, but in fact it showed an incredible depth of perception. She knew I was redeemable, that I'd been emotionally scarred, and that it was perhaps only a matter of time before I had my road to Damascus moment. There was one other notable component: Heather had God on her side.

Off the rails, I tried desperately to convince myself I was doing the right thing, even writing a mea culpa letter to her parents. That fell completely on stony ground and from then on it was me wading in muddy water and encountering ships not so much passing in the night as foundering on the rocks. I ended up in a brief relationship with a famous actress based on the fabricated illusion that it was something that might procure a distraction. It was never forthcoming and this coupling compared to the unbridled joy, intelligence, and passion that I had shared with Heather only went to prove how indebted to this lady I was for helping me realize it. Twisted perhaps, but I woke up one morning, called my actress to deliver a verbal "Dear John," and flew to Nashville.

My dear friends, Randy Bernard and my old buddy the bull rider Michael Gaffney and his wife, Robyn, were in town with the PBR. All of them loved Heather and were none too pleased with my current behavior. Still, I went to the event that night catching constant flak from everyone for my unchivalrous conduct of late. By coincidence, Heather was also in town on unrelated business, a fact that only aided and abetted my sense of consternation overload. Robyn Gaffney, who was joined at the hip with Heather, spent the best part of the event railing in my ear as to the error of my ways. Point taken, and without too much persuasion I took it upon myself to spend the rest of the night drowning my sorrows in a differential convergence of maudlin realization and sad-sackism. Simply put, I got stinking drunk, which when surrounded by hard-core cowboys young and old, all of whom are convinced they're invincible, is part protective armor, part fool's paradise. I remember it clearly, which is a contradiction in terms given my saturated state. I spent the night attached to the bar of the incredibly loud and packed Wildhorse Saloon on 2nd Avenue. Surrounded by a swirling melee of partying bull riders, I remained glued to my seat only allowing conciliatory sympathizers into my airspace until a concerned Randy decided it was time for me to go. Brushing away the dark cloud hovering above my head, he managed to wrestle me off my stool and into the night air. Back at my hotel, I made the completely inebriated decision to track Heather down. Drinking and dialing is not always a wise choice, as it can have the adverse effect of any well-intended contrition you are aiming to convey. But then everyone was not Heather, and if my memory serves me correctly she was surprisingly sympathetic, even a little amused by my slurred attempts at repentance. All that mattered is that she was booked back on the same flight to LA as me, a fact that I scrawled in crayon on the bathroom mirror lest I forget. I, then, ignobly passed out.

Seeing Heather at the departure gate that morning is the moment I fell head over heels in love for the first time. I realized everything else previously had been infatuation; love is a completely different condition and can only be compared to the ultimate euphoric high. I tried to remain composed, but my heart wanted to burst out of my chest. It was one of the best moments of my life. We were married less than a year later, and nineteen years on from that day my heart still fills with joy at the sight of her.

ULTIMATELY, AND I think Stephanie would agree, mess that it was, our divorce wound up being the best thing that could have happened for the both of us. She moved on to a better fit and I found my life's soul mate. Her daughters have remained, to this day, part of our extended family. They are happily married to wonderful young men and have beautiful children of their own. Of course, it was inevitable, and for the first time in my life, I was not only ready to join the club, but I was completely on board with Heather's propitious longing. If there was any hesitancy at all, the grumbling, selfish, set-in-his-ways old dog didn't stand a chance when Charley Indiana entered the picture. Even if it was a little later in life than normal, I had no compunction about being anything but 100 percent committed. Besides, older dads were coming into fashion, and in all honesty, I'd never felt better both physically and mentally.

I'll refrain from going overboard. I know it's standard procedure to expound effusively on the miracle of birth, and of course, what else would you expect me to say other than Charley was the most beautiful, perfect child I'd ever seen! Naturally, I said exactly the same thing when her sister, Georgey Devon, came along a couple of years later. I wasn't a complete novice, having gone through boot camp for beginners with my former stepchildren. There is a difference however, and no matter how you prioritize it, an independent dynamic comes into play when they're your own flesh and blood. They look like you, they have your characteristics, and if you're lucky, they take the most accomplished aspects of your life and run with them. This is what happened, and from day one, Charley was obsessed with horses. So much so, that she was on the back of one when she could barely walk. Admittedly, most of the time it was riding double with me, but it was easy to assess in her eyes from infancy that this was going to be way more than just giddyup-'n-go. It was the stirrings of a child very much infatuated with all aspects of ranch living. She loved animals, but horses had stolen her heart. It would eventually become an all-consuming passion.

It was obvious when Georgey came along that her interests were neither equine in nature nor Western in objective. In fact, it wasn't immediately apparent where she was leaning when it came to her enthusiasms. What was detectable was that where Charley was more hardscrabble and tough, Georgey was decidedly more genteel in her aspirations. Not to give the impression she was demure, far from it. She was a spark plug with a wicked sense of humor and skills that can only be described as performance driven. She did a spot-on Elmer Fudd in her rendition of the *Looney Tunes* classic, "The Grilled Cheese Song." She also took comfort in tradition, loving a tightly packed schedule and conducting her day-to-day routine with precision and unfailing positive energy. I was thrilled that Charley was inheriting my passion for the Western lifestyle and prayed to God that the novelty wouldn't wear off as she grew older. In Georgey, there was the real possibility that the musicality and creative drive that had dominated my life might be taking root and eventually blossom into her own brand of artistic expression.

To have them both drawing from the collective parental well was gratifying. Their young world was one of cowboys, horses, and a complete cornucopia of diversity. In the house, they existed in an environment played out to a soundtrack of mixed musical genres. The incentive was there in spades: jukebox, sound system, movie screen, and music, music, music. And in the air, the smell of stables, orange blossom, and American dirt. They have both exceeded my expectations.

MY PARENTS' MOVE to California in the '80s had benefited my father greatly; the English winters and the rigors of his ministry job certifying cattle having taken its toll on him physically. The change of climate was a healing balm, countering the damp and dreary grayness of those saturnine months. In all honesty, I'm not sure what he was expecting from suburban life in North Hollywood, but his reaction to all the storied clichés spoke volumes. They had a cozy bungalow on a leafy *Leave It to Beaver* street, a pool in the backyard, and an orange tree from which to pluck and squeeze his morning juice. Other plusses were a close proximity to markets with the emphasis on "super," abundant quantities of fresh fruit and vegetables, and an unknown phenomenon called Mexican food. For a man not known for his sense of exuberance and a steely resolve in cloistering his emotions, it could be said that he transformed slightly. His shirts got a little louder, his skin a little browner, and he would recline on the couch with a distinctly relaxed countenance. Of an evening he'd enjoy his gin and tonic, watch the sitcom *Mad About You*, and read voraciously. He consumed books on military campaigns, the World Wars, and in a decidedly unimagined turn of events, developed a crush on Julia Roberts after seeing the movie *Pretty Woman.*

It gladdened me that I was able to reciprocate for the years my parents had invested in my indecisive and hobbled dreams of youth. The fact that they no longer had any financial worries, that I didn't have to watch my father poring over receipts and bills at his small corner desk in our bungalow back in Lincolnshire, was gratifying. Another blessing was that my mother was no longer exiled in a cultural void. Galleries, theater, concerts, and movies, it was just a matter of making up for lost time. I'd take her to New York where we'd do MoMA and Broadway, eat lunch at Balthazar, and on one occasion attend a Tom Waits concert at the Beacon Theatre. They adapted well to life in the Valley, becoming completely independent, eating out, marketing, and going to the movies. Life for them was idyllic, and having them close at hand and under my protection was a balm applied to my own turbulent scars.

Another benefit to having them close at hand was that they were able to get excellent medical attention. Unfortunately, after a routine hospital visit in the early part of 1994, my father was diagnosed with bowel cancer. He dealt with this in the same manner he'd faced every other obstacle in his life, head on, no bitching, just practical resolve. Thus, we entered an interesting phase of our relationship. I had married Stephanie the year before and we were living at the ranch while still maintaining the LA house on Devlin Drive. It had been arranged for my father to begin chemotherapy sessions twice a week at a facility over the hill. This meant spending most of my time in town ferrying him back and forth to appointments. It was a little laborious as it would entail me driving over Coldwater Canyon early in the morning to pick him up, then back over at the height of rush hour. Needless to say, it took a while, a snail's pace that constituted precious time alone with his captive son. He didn't say a lot and most of what was said was small talk, but the satisfaction it obviously brought him was worth every minute of the hours I put in.

By late spring, it was apparent that these procedures weren't having the desired effect and that my father's condition was worsening. In due course, it was diagnosed that it was simply a matter of time and

that home care and his general comfort were essential. I made all the
necessary arrangements, turning my parents' bedroom into a workable
hospice and hiring a part-time nurse to assist with his welfare. As is
the way in distressing times, something emerged to put some humor into
otherwise fatalistic proceedings. What my father got was a superhero.

Her name was Susie Owens, a thirty-three-year-old, five-foot-eight-
inch, blonde bombshell. A fully registered nurse, ex-Dallas stripper,
and former Playmate of the Month, she was also the doppelgänger for
a super-sexed-up comic book hero called Flaxen. Believe me, I'm not
making this stuff up. When I walked in and met her for the first time,
I almost fell over. Dressed in a full-on starched white nurse's outfit and
smelling of night-blooming jasmine, I was convinced someone was
pulling some morbid prank. No gallows humor involved, she proved to
be the real deal. On top of the reality of her credentials she was the most
impossibly sweet, efficient, and charming young woman imaginable.
If this wasn't enough to dole out a huge degree of admiration, I later
found out that she brewed up her own blend of personal fragrance in
her garage and sold it for $100 an ounce at Fred Segal, the hip clothing
store on Melrose Avenue. There are many jokes that could be made at
this point, but I'll say in complete honesty that her personality and
effervescent spirit, coupled with her devotion to both my mother and
father, took the edge right off the severity of the situation. Once I got
used to the fact that my father's caregiver looked like every frat boy's
fantasy, I settled in to being constantly present for the real reason.

During this time, my mother went about things with stoic resign.
Most certainly made of a mettle forged during the war years, she might
have been a sparrow in design, but she was eagle hearted and as noble
as a hawk in her refusal to lapse into mawkish sorrow. She knew the
endgame and understood full well what they had shared. No tears. "A
soldier's wife never cries" was her mantra. She slept in a cot by his bed
and took his hand while the morphine patches engineered his ever-
decreasing bouts of lucidity. In his last two days of life, he referenced
a world that was once in turmoil, but in which he found a place of
comradeship and human dignity. The war years were evidently in his
fever dreams, and from them he was prompted to reminisce in short

fervent bursts. On June 23, 1994, with a slight animated motion of his head he said, "The train's coming." It was whispered but clear, followed by an exhalation of breath as he passed away. After a moment's silence, my mother got up and turned to me: "The troop trains, he was talking about the troop trains," she said.

Not long after my father passed away, my mother moved into the guest cottage at the ranch. Since I was still married to Stephanie at this point, my mother was familiar with her daughters and doted on them without the sugary patronization of a greeting card grandma. She remained an anomaly in regard to what was standard-issue aging. Her best friends were my friends, she interacted with no one of her own age, finding little in common with cliquey oldsters forming craft work-shops and playing bingo. She read voraciously, was mad about sports, watched *Seinfeld*, and loved to quote *Pulp Fiction*. In turn, young peo-ple gravitated to her; she could converse on pretty much any subject and had strong opinions but was malleable in discussion. She was the phone call made if you needed a heads-up on who won a match or a game, and she played music at a volume usually attributed to head banging teens in their bedrooms. Her tastes were eclectic: Vaughan Williams one minute, Joni Mitchell the next. She liked Julien Bream, Pentangle, and Django Reinhardt, and always wanted to be the first to hear anything new by Elton and myself. I often tried to encourage her to write a memoir, something I think she would have excelled at. She would decline demurely, always citing that she had lived her life vicar-iously through me, a compliment that touched me deeply, but hardly compared with what she could have offered in regard to her fledgling years. I did, however, make a compromise with her. I persuaded her to let me tape several hours of reminiscences. They proved provocative, to say the least. Given her forthright manner, they graduated from a genteel upbringing in polite Edwardian society to explicit tales of an avant-garde young adulthood. It was astonishingly candid, which left me impressed, perplexed, and wondering if she was actually Anaïs Nin.

I was always disappointed that Heather never got to meet my father. She would have broken down all his barriers and completely captivated him. So I'm immensely thankful that she, along with our children, had so many years of immeasurable and impassioned interaction with my mother. As a vessel to my heritage, and a fountain of learning, it was of the greatest importance to me that they got to spend so much quality time with her. To the kids she was Mimi, and characteristically, one hopes, like all grandchildren, they doted on her. It was heartwarming to see them spend so much time with her, wandering off down the hill in the late afternoon light to have her read to them, watch TV, and eat honey sandwiches.

One thing that my mother made abundantly clear on several occasions was that in the event of any physical impairment on her part she would rather go out fast than linger interminably in a state of incapacitation. In this I have always felt that I may have let her down. In 2015, she suffered a stroke and was not expected to pull through. This diagnosis proved bogus, the upshot of it being that she came out of it surprisingly well and after mild rehabilitation was soon back home. Still it was necessary to bring in assistance, which changed the dynamic of her independence and gave her cause to see the writing on the wall. Soon, so many of the pleasures that were of importance to her were impossible to indulge in, her aptitude for them slowly being shut down like doors slammed in her face. With the gratification of worldly pleasures severed, she slipped into an ignoble decline, a broken bird cruelly robbed of her heart and mind. It was abjectly painful to see her lapse into dementia as I, caught in the crosshairs of an unfulfilled obligation, paid the price by having to witness her waning days firsthand. I prayed desperately for her peaceful transition, a timely release from the withering frightened individual inhabiting her once ebullient frame. Outside of introducing hospice care, I'm at pains to concede what I could have done differently outside of pulling the plug. I know she would have wanted me to do that, but I also know that she wouldn't have wanted me to do time for doing the right thing.

If there's any audacity in talking to the shell after the soul has gone, it wasn't prominent on my mind when I conversed with her after she'd passed. I sat close to the bed and looked at her hands. There was so little of her, so much had evaporated in the twelve months since her stroke. It's as if all that invaluable knowledge had departed. Like some serene

Vesuvius, she'd metaphorically erupted. Not hissing and roaring like a jet engine, but billowing silently into the heavens. What she was composed of was carried on the wind and redistributed. No doubt, there were others in need of her wisdom.

I don't think there was anyone you could categorically describe as old at her memorial. It's a testament to her influence and lust for life that everyone there was young, part of a secret society, all feeling special, all happier for having basked in her light. It was a joyous occasion, laughter in lieu of tears and solemnity banned.

The motif for her memorial was a hummingbird. She loved them, which is hardly surprising. Delicate, small, smart, and tenacious, they zip around, a colorful inquisitor ever in search of something new. To this day, I can never see a hummingbird without thinking it's her.

THROUGH THICK AND thin and during my ups and downs, I continued to ride and compete. Part of the cowboy ethic is that if you fall off, you get right back on, and no one was going to accuse me of not filling my boots. I still worked my horses every morning I was at the ranch, and still rolled out on the road to show. The key to cowboying is dedication. It's inherent, a lifestyle that's passed down and exists where half measures aren't weighed or tolerated. It taught me a tremendous amount about moral fiber. The myth on the screen might be romantic, but the pursuit of its reality eviscerates the celluloid romance. It's the last great American tradition, and cowboys and cowgirls are America's last renegades.

After many years in the saddle, things started to break down. Not sure why since much older guys than I were competing well into their eighties. I was keenly aware that these octogenarians were tough as old boots, so for me, still only in my fifties, to be experiencing severe pain in my left shoulder was a humiliating and annoying distraction. It's obvious that it was the byproduct of extreme lateral motion, because that's when it hurt the most. I have a pretty high threshold for pain, but when my horse would dart sharply to the left or right, the flexion of my neck and shoulders felt like I was being stabbed with a hot knife.

Eventually, the problem got too debilitating to ignore, and in 2005 I had anterior cervical discectomy and fusion neck surgery. Simply put, it meant that the pain in my shoulder was coming from my neck, and that the damage had to be repaired with a stabilizing titanium plate. Although it was all very inconvenient, it worked, and in due course I was back in the saddle. As invaluable as the operation proved, I took it as a sign. The possibility of opening old wounds, doing more damage, and living my life on and off the surgeon's table was not a prospect I savored. Besides, with the children in the picture, and with a burgeoning art career proving profitable, I started to wind down on the circuit. I wasn't winning enough to justify the cost of competitive cutting, and weekends away were clearly not as romantic in the nomadic sense that they once were. For Charley's sake, I still rode at home. It was more important for me to encourage her and allow her to develop her natural ability than circumvent the same old circuit, sleeping rough and eating bad food for no great reward.

I won't say Charley was gaining confidence. The kid was born confident, and by the age of four was completely proficient at handling her own horse. We'd trail ride around the property together, and while I'd be vigilant in monitoring her progress, there was no getting away from the fact that it had taken me over forty years to achieve my Western dream, but this little girl had literally been born in the saddle. It would soon become apparent that I would do as my mother had done with me and live vicariously through my daughter.

During all this time, the pen had not been idle, and Elton and I had moved into the new millennium with renewed vigor. With *Songs from the West Coast*, we'd turned a corner. It was viewed by many as a return to form, harking back to what people loved to refer to as our "glory days." While I wholeheartedly agree that there was a new virility to our work and a maturity to the general composition of the songs, I'd always been skeptical to the reverence paid to our '70s canon. Undoubtedly, several of our (and I use the term with reticence) classics were forged in this decade, but confederating our complete output into any sort of definitive gold medal standard is completely irrational. Although each one of them contains a couple of legitimate perennials, *Caribou, Rock of the Westies*, and *Blue Moves* are not great albums. They are certainly inferior to *Too Low for Zero, Sleeping with the Past*, and *Made in England*, albums recorded in a decade when we were supposedly struggling to remain relevant in an era of shoulder pads, teased hair, and parachute pants. So to pat us on the back and tell us our work in the 2000s was an invigorating resurgence was thoughtful but hollow praise. Albums we made during this "comeback" period included *Peachtree Road*, a celebration of Elton's adopted state of Georgia. Recorded in Atlanta, it flirts with Southern influences and bears traces of spiritual resolve and the acceptance of aging. It's a good record, not the best of the bunch, but admirable. During the recording of the album, as is my want, I peeled off and drove down to Savannah for the day. Dripping with Spanish moss and antebellum charm, I was curious to see the town that (allegedly) General Sherman, in his destructive 1864 March to the Sea, deemed "too beautiful to burn." There is a haunted charm to Savannah, an antique quality free of kitsch, and it is soaked in history that makes it a complete composite of the mythical South. It also has some of the richest food on earth, and much of my short time there was spent avoiding butter and cream and sticking to fried green tomatoes and shrimp and grits. Being the beneficiary of restaurants when it comes to conceiving ideas, I did leave Savannah with a napkin full of notes. On one that I found in my pocket months later, I'd scrawled: *Heaven help the South when Sherman comes their way.* Six years later that line ended up in the lyric of "Gone to Shiloh," the best track on *The Union* album. Savannah, I thank you.

Then there was *The Captain and the Kid*, a jewel that never got the chance to shine. Written as a sequel to *Captain Fantastic and the Brown Dirt Cowboy*, it chronicles Elton's and my first trip to California in the fall of 1970. It's an interesting record. Lyrically fuller than its predecessor, Elton's melodies are immensely musical and complex. There's a lot of piano, and a lot said in a far more muted framework than the sonic tapestries of Gus Dudgeon's predecessor. They're completely different in approach, with *The Captain and the Kid* being more cinematically detailed and fatalistic in its approach to the cynicism of fate. *Captain*

Fantastic is lighter and sparkles with innocence and hope. Ultimately, they complement each other, although the darker aspects of the latter might have been tougher on the ear.

Outside of *Songs from the West Coast* and *The Union*, the best of the bunch was probably *The Diving Board*, a very grown-up record utilizing the talents of only two other players to produce the basic tracks. With Jay Bellerose on drums and Raphael Saadiq on bass, it was a minimalistic affair, allowing Elton's piano to provide the album's heartbeat. Elton's playing is inventive, subtle, and compelling. Unlike on *The Captain and the Kid* where it is strident and percussive in a jazzy sort of free form, here it was almost classical in composition. What cannot be denied is that he, through this current batch of records, had been freed up to display his extraordinary skill at the keyboard. Elton is a magnificent player, and it's unfortunate at times that his celebrity and larger-than-life persona overshadows the fact that he is one of the greats. These basic tracks were not so much built on as colored around the edges in order not to intrude on the subtlety of their organic pulse. There are atmospheric embellishments created by keyboard magician Keefus Ciancia, cryptic guitar tones by Doyle Bramhall II, Preservation Hall–styled brass arranged by Darrell Leonard, and tambourine by the legendary Jack Ashford, one of Motown's Funk Brothers and possibly the instrument's most celebrated proponent. No surprise that the songs on the album that don't deal with an obvious past have a timeless anonymity that sets them in a mysterious dreamlike setting that's part spooky old-world Europe, part gothic anecdote. Nothing is contemporary. There is no shine; the mood has a patina to it. It's brass, not silver or gold, like the dancers gliding out of the Great War in "The New Fever Waltz" or the grandiose decline of "Oscar Wilde Gets Out." It's all about melancholy and a fading yesteryear. There are heroes in "Oceans Away," the Greatest Generation slowly losing the battle with relevance. Then there's the idealist in "Home Again" and "Voyeur" looking for the past in an impossible future and the hopeless romantic of "My Quicksand" and "Can't Stay Alone Tonight," who perseveres in the properties of love. Lyrically, it's an album I'm proud of. I'm horribly critical of the things I've written and rarely ever satisfied

100 percent, but with *The Diving Board* there's an essence of literature in a lot of the work that gives me cause to reflect on it with affection. The whole record has a desaturated naturalistic tone that makes it unique in our canon.

I wrote the best part of eight albums at the ranch. My office, located on the second floor of the building, housing initially my recording studio and later my art studio, was comfortably cluttered and predisposed to an inordinate amount of books, manuscripts, archived tapes, and assorted memorabilia. It was by my standards surprisingly unorganized, cubby holes and shelves stuffed with piles of yellow legal pads and loose-leaf pages full of doodles, notations, and scrawled ideas. The walls were covered with a clashing collection of framed oddities including lobby cards for our ill-fated Broadway musical of Anne Rice's vampire gold mine *Lestat* (probably there as a reminder never to try that sort of thing again). A large poster of my old friend Leonard Nimoy as Mr. Spock signed, "To a fellow Rocket Man" and a black-and-white 8 by 10 of me and Raquel Welch sitting on a cardboard crescent moon suspended above the stage at some ancient award show. My desk was a funky pine kitchen table covered in old spurs, arrowheads, a broken bit of a meteor, and a glass dog. An ancient cassette player, my computer, and a CD boom box were positioned left, right, and center in that order while my old Ovation stood in a stand within reach to my right, ready to assist me at a moment's notice.

This is where I worked and ruminated for twenty-six years, staring out at the grand vista that folded into the distance before my desk. Wide-open spaces indeed, with an equally wide-open sky, where red-tailed hawks tumbled through the clouds and glided on the thermals. It was my very own inspiration point, a ramshackle lab where the written word was king and I was simply a vessel at the mercy of my own inventions.

ONE OF THE highlights of our post *Songs from the West Coast* era was reconnecting with Leon Russell. Elton had had an epiphany listening to a retrospective of Leon's music while on safari in South Africa. Moved by hearing these songs again, he did what Elton does best when he detects great talent has been turned out to pasture. Up in his pulpit Elton is a vociferous advocate, and very soon he had burned up the phone lines rallying the troops. There was no pushback on my part, I assure you. Leon had been such a formidable force at the time of our ascent, not just as a performer, but as a songwriter par excellence, that the idea of actually recording with him was a thrilling, if daunting, prospect. His music skipped across genres, culminating in a conglomeration of holy-roller fireworks that had inspired us in the most magical of ways. Along with his history of playing with LA's legendary Wrecking Crew (a term he once claimed to me he had never, ever heard used), he became a conduit for rock's aristocracy. Through his work with Delaney & Bonnie on their cult classic *Accept No Substitute* and his high profile slot directing the hippy caravan that became the Joe Cocker–fronted *Mad Dogs & Englishmen*, he had come to the attention of all manner of A-listers. With the release of his magnificent self-titled first album, his charisma and prodigious musical talent appealed to a star roster including George and Ringo, Mick, Keith, and Charlie, Clapton, and eventually Bob Dylan, for whom he'd produced several tracks including "Watching the River Flow" and "When I Paint My Masterpiece." His shining moment in the spotlight was when he stole the show at George Harrison's *Concert for Bangladesh*. Full of pentecostal fervor he'd torn through a medley of "Jumpin' Jack Flash," The Coasters' "Young Blood," and a snatch of George Harrison's "Beware of Darkness." Without breaking a sweat and before the crowd could catch their breath, he picked up a bass and was accompanying Bob Dylan and George Harrison in a climatic trifecta. It was one for the ages, and sadly, in many ways, his swan song of sorts.

After this, things began to slip away slowly, his last major success being *One for the Road*, a lovely hillbilly bluegrass and country record with Willie Nelson. His own output, however, began to shrink, his own albums selling in ever-diminishing numbers. Finally, the record contracts dried up and he dropped off the radar, releasing homemade recordings on his own imprint label. When Elton reached out to him, he was eking out a living touring on a secondhand bus and playing small clubs and dive bars.

It all came together quickly, so fast in fact, that it became very much a case of "Let's throw stuff at the wall and see if it sticks." After hearing Robert Plant and Alison Krauss's magical album *Raising Sand*, I called Elton suggesting we tap the innovative producer and musician T Bone Burnett about producing the next official Elton album. He'd hemmed and hawed at the suggestion, impressed by T Bone's chops, but not 100 percent sure it was the right call. When Leon came into the equation, he did a complete 180, called T Bone immediately, and stated he was the only man he wanted to helm the production.

For my part, I accompanied my good friend and Elton's then current US manager, Johnny Barbis, to Austin, Texas, for an initial meeting with Leon. It would be the first time I had seen Leon since the early 1970s, a fact that caused some minor consternation on my part. Truth be told, I always felt slightly intimidated by him, not just by his immense talent, but by his overall demeanor. He had such a powerful presence, a shamanistic and directorial aura that, along with his leonine mane and piercing eyes, had quite honestly scared the crap out of me. Before our arranged get together, Johnny and I spent the day (possibly fortifying myself) lounging in the hotel pool, getting microwaved by the Texan sun, and drinking the best part of a case of Whispering Angel rosé. By the time Leon turned up, I was the color of boiled crab, entertaining sunstroke, and significantly buzzed. Not that he would have known, for it was a completely different Leon who was wheeled in.

Yes, Leon was in a wheelchair, much older, obviously, and clearly in poor health. The eyes were still a steely blue, his hair still full and long but now snow white and totally in contrast to the salt-and-pepper locks of yesteryear. He was no longer the fearsome overlord conducting onstage traffic and wresting allegiance from the adoring masses. He was in fact a completely different animal and one who, though I was not presently aware of, would for the short time he had left become completely dear to me. It was apparent to me that night that we were doing the right thing. The reason for Austin was that Leon had a gig there, at a place that can only be described as a roadhouse. No problem with that; I love a good roadhouse. It's just that when a man you last saw mesmerizing thousands in a packed arena was now entertaining a beer-swilling, yahoo, taco crowd sitting on park benches in a parking lot was kinda depressing.

What eventually happened in LA in the studio is there to hear in the record we cut and in the documentary that director Cameron Crowe made of the process. I chose not to be filmed for the latter. I didn't do this for any contrarian value; I just thought the work would be better served by honing in on Elton's dedication to revitalizing Leon's career and the high regard in which he held him. There was a whole new generation that was ignorant of Leon's contribution to a certain style of cosmic rock, and I felt too many talking heads making the same point was unnecessary. Of course, I was gratified to be part of the process, and while Leon's voice had lost some of its clarity, there was a world-worn dignity in it that added a discernible gravitas to the lyrics. His voice brought a sense of lived-in history to the songs that benefited from it most, like "Jimmie Rodgers' Dream" and "Gone to Shiloh," two numbers that dealt with an earlier America. The musical equivalents of a sepia-soaked tintype, they were to my way of thinking a bridge back to where we'd all originally come from. The fact that Leon could perform was a miracle in itself, because he had undergone almost six hours of major surgery a week before we started recording. He would get tired, that's for sure, but it didn't stop him from bringing his A-game, his dry wit, and a healthy appetite.

What became a ritual with Leon, Johnny, and me was dinner. Leon loved food, and discovering a dish he was unfamiliar with was on par with unearthing an old gospel song he'd never heard before. The highlight of his day was the prospect of an early supper. This is not to say he didn't love what he was doing in the studio, but then again that just came so naturally to him that the revelation of culinary discovery was an intriguing alternative. At times, he was in a little bit too much of a hurry to wrap up his commitments and stick a bib under his collar, leaving me to occasionally run interference. Our go-to place was my old Le Dome pal Eddie Kerkhofs's restaurant, Il Piccolino, on Robertson between Beverly Boulevard and Melrose Avenue. The fare was bistro style, vast, and varied. It was also hearty, delicious, and, given advance warning, Eddie would pretty much accommodate you with anything you wanted. Leon loved it. He didn't want to go anywhere else and liked to eat at what we referred to as "old people's hour," which was sometime before 6 p.m. I came to realize that although he had an uneducated palate, he was by no means squeamish. On the contrary, he would scan the menu and pepper me with questions. "Duck confit, would I like it?" "Beef bourguignon, how's that done?" "Cassoulet, what's in that?" It was completely endearing, and I loved every minute of being a part of it. It was an area where I knew my salt, and seeing that big wrinkled smile that had never been prevalent in the early years break out on his face gave me a feeling that I was contributing something worthwhile other than lyrical munitions. In many ways, looking back he possibly knew his days were numbered and was intent on savoring the good life rather than suffer the humiliation of Jell-O and chicken broth.

Invariably, people of a certain age group, which was common at Il Piccolino, would stop by to pay their respects. He dispensed benediction like some Okie Buddha, thanking everyone kindly, as his mane, a corona in the evening light, recaptured the spotlight and momentarily returned some flickering semblance of the old "master of space and time." I imagine after years in the wilderness, his eminence being acknowledged was gratifying. He had long since quit circulating in the realm of his peers, so to see so many of them reconnect with him over the course of our collaboration was a bonus point en route to our objective.

We were sitting alone in the control room one day shooting the breeze about one thing or another when the subject of Elvis came up. Leon remarked that supposedly he'd played on *Viva Las Vegas* but didn't recall doing so. Grabbing my computer, I hunted around and confirmed that not only had he played on it, he also arranged it. It was also reported that Presley was a bit of a fan and had at one time considered putting "Delta Lady" in his act. This information didn't seem to stimulate Leon's recall, but it did pry a pretty good story from his collected memories. Sometime during his session work in the late '60s, Leon encountered an unchaperoned Elvis in the corridor of RCA studios in Hollywood. He claimed that the King was looking a little lost and appeared dazed and confused due to who knows what. Leon, his confidence bolstered by his intake of several joints, said, "Hi," and inquired of Elvis, "Hey man, how come you keep making all those shitty movies?" Apparently undeterred by this direct inquisition, the bleary-eyed icon simply shrugged and said, "Agh, dunno man, last thing I remember I wuz drivin' a truck."

Leon never could pronounce my name, and with his Tulsa drawl I was always "Barney." Never having cared for Bernie, it was an improvement. As the little guy on the steps in *Rocketman* says, "Not very rock 'n roll." I always thought I sounded like an accountant, which given my mathematical skills is laughable. Like Bono, Edge, Iggy, and Ozzy, I should have thought ahead and in 1967 gone with something indelible. So Barney was cool, and so was Leon. I'm happy we got to make *The Union* before his frailty incapacitated him. I got to write a pretty good song with him, which he wrote from a lyric of mine in about five minutes. There's a reason he looked like a biblical character, the Good Book was in his genes. I used to imagine him in a tent down South extolling his own brand of Pentecostal fireworks, part Jimmy Swaggart, part Little Richard, 100 percent Leon Russell.

ART HAD ALWAYS been a priority waiting in the wings. Not figurative, not inanimate still life, and certainly not sitting on the side of the road painting mountains and cows. To put it simply, polite art didn't interest me. I have always been drawn to the abstract movement, the risk takers, those who didn't compartmentalize, didn't sew things up neatly, but left jagged edges on large oblongs and squares of graphic color. Those who attacked the canvas with visceral energy and made statements that caused consternation through vague simplicity or multimediums and found objects.

The first painter to awake my interest in the same way that narrative poets infused my games was J. M. W. Turner. Turner was the granddaddy of abstract art, not in the traditional sense, but certainly in his execution. His landscapes were more than photographic-like reproductions of pastoral scenes; they were introspective and experimental, the light and scale in them removing any discussion as to the genteel nature of formulaic scenic art. It's no wonder he unsettled and angered his peers, his critics condemning his work as "blots." To me they were magical. The best representation of nature I had ever seen, it was as if he had harnessed the elements and found some unfathomable way to execute them on canvas.

I first saw Turner's work in a large ratty coffee-table book belonging to my mother. From an early age, I would sit on her knee, flipping through the pages and consuming the images. The landscapes were one thing, but even these were minimized with my discovery of his fiery images of sea warfare and maritime despair. They were riveting, and I was completely intoxicated by their fervor. Better than any comic book, they were *The Boy's Own Paper* on steroids. *The Battle of Trafalgar*, *The Fighting Temeraire*, and *The Slave Ship*, the latter remains to this day one of the most unsettling and inspiring paintings I've ever seen, were violent testaments to the power and autonomy of the sea. In my youthful capacity it was impossible to formulate how one man could create anything this good. In years to come, when I learned of his life and techniques, his unapologetic eccentricity and reclusive nature, I was doubly fascinated. He was the quintessential angst-driven artist, shabby and grumpy, successful yet preferring to live in squalor, never marrying, yet fathering two children with his housekeeper and living with his father for thirty years. He spat on his canvases to combine colors, traveled extensively alone, and somehow managed to purvey the beauty he was incapable of finding in himself into works of shimmering magnificence.

From then on it was a journey, a voyage that invested in me an exploratory desire. For decades I remained simply a fan with a growing appreciation for analytic and explosive styles. Although, looking back, I'm sure it was just an infected youthful pretension that fueled me, but I was confused by what I perceived to be London's conservatism, gallery-wise, during my formative years. I found it all a bit musty and boring, museums full of suits of armor and galleries heavy on the old masters and fat naked ladies. It's obvious I didn't know where to look, and at an age when I was not proficient enough in my geography to embark on serious investigation, I simply thought I could locate Mark Rothko in the Natural History Museum.

This all changed once I hit New York for the first time and discovered the Museum of Modern Art at 11 West Fifty-Third. The lights
came on, and the gray cobwebby antiquity of Agincourt and the dark
brooding of Rembrandt gave way to a bright new world, a world
of virile vitality and uncompromising ideas. As an impressionable
twenty-year-old in the embrace of an inflexible winter, MoMA was
a sanctuary, a watershed of cultural awakening in a fever dream of
burgeoning rock and roll ethos. New names adorned the walls, making me embarrassingly aware of how little I knew. Sure, along with
Rothko I was hip to Jackson Pollock and Willem de Kooning, while
I'd have to have been living under a rock not to know the work of pop
avatar Andy Warhol, but here was so much more, manna from heaven
in every sense of the phrase. This is where the yearning began, and
the discoveries that rained down were all nudges in one direction. Oh
for sure, it would take several decades for the spark to ignite, but that
was because my life was transient and the real possibilities were out of
reach for so long. The catalysts were innumerable, but the magnetism
of a mere handful were enough to generate in me a palpable desire
to create. It began with Franz Kline, his large white canvases slashed
with haphazard confident black motifs painted randomly, using
cheap commercial house paint. Towering pieces by the German artist
and sculptor Anselm Kiefer, whose themes on his nation's history and
the horrors of the Holocaust were created into Battle of Somme–
like panoramas out of clay, lead, straw, shellac, and ash. Finally, there
was Hans Hofmann, again German, again groundbreaking. His scattered fields of disjointed shapes, irregular boxes, and daubed random
diagonals all butting together in some mad traffic jam of Cubism
and painted in bold primary colors was again audacious, unfettered,
and simply irresistible. It would be Hofmann, and Kline to a lesser
extent, who would be my first motivational inspirations when I took
up brushes at the dawn of the new millennium. For now, my odyssey
with art would continue through pilgrimages of self-education and
an ever-increasing desire to ultimately express myself. It didn't come
without its learning curves, but then again sometimes the best results
come from a rough ride.

In the ensuing years, I visited some illuminating installations, beautiful museums, and extraordinary exhibitions, none more moving than "The Art of Paul Gauguin" at the National Gallery of Art in Washington, DC, in 1988. The most comprehensive exhibition of Gauguin's work ever mounted, it is one of the most beautiful and emotional events I have ever witnessed. The primitive aspect of his work, especially in later years when he had succumbed to the siren call of French Polynesia, was so overwhelmingly incandescent that by the time I reached the actual portals from his last house in the Marquesas I had tears running down my cheeks. The homely bureaucracy he gave up so as to devote his life to raw independency and abject poverty was so poignantly conveyed in the curation that it was hard not to be moved.

In our early touring days, the opportunity to tap into museums both international and within the US was a luxury I didn't take lightly. It wasn't lost on me that our gradual climb up the ladder of success offered me the opportunity to indulge in my other passion. How lucky was I? I got to see, hear, and make music with the best gang in the world while peeling off at any given time for a hard-core fix of artwork by the century's other rock stars. To get lost in these palaces of wonder was not only euphoric in the most carefree of times, it was also a healing balm in times of great upheaval and consternation.

In Paris, although the Louvre is iconic, my preference had always been for the Impressionism and Postimpressionism housed in the beautiful old converted train station Musée d'Orsay. The Tate Modern in London (opened in 2000) was redemption for my early days of looking for contemporary work in cobwebbed alcoves. In Chicago, it was the Art Institute, the Van Gogh Museum in Amsterdam, and in Philadelphia the amazing one of a kind Barnes Foundation, last visited when we kicked off Elton's Farewell Yellow Brick Road Tour in 2018.

WHEN I PURCHASED the ranch back in 1992, it was with the strict intention to go full-on cowboy. At the same time, now that it looked like I was free of restrictions, putting down solid roots, and blessed with expansive possibilities, it was only a matter of time before I realized another dream. For the time being, my priority was the Western way.

Getting into the game was a rigorous task and it demanded all my time and concentration. This isn't to say the wheels weren't in motion, and while I was honing my chops down in the dirt, a flickering ember was sputtering into life somewhere at the back of my head. Before it burst into flame fully formed, I got sidetracked by Farm Dogs. I was fully entrenched in the world of non-pro cutting by this point, and writing and recording with the band filled in the gaps between traveling for competition. My dance card was full, but I would often consider the space where we recorded and imagined how it might be utilized in the inevitable aftermath of the band. By 1998, after conquering the world and selling millions of records in our dreams, Farm Dogs was euthanized by monetary overload and national apathy. What I was left with was a lot of equipment, a control room, and a large empty racquetball court. All that was left in this space was a drum room and vocal booth built into the corner, perfect for storing canvas and sundry items to begin my next phase of creativity. *Let's give it a go*, I thought.

The room was an appealing space, the perfect environment to hurl paint and move around with freedom. It was standard racquetball court dimensions: twenty feet wide, twenty feet high, and forty feet long. For quite some time leading up to this, I'd kept notebooks, sketching motifs and ideas that might serve me well as initial forays into my take on abstract expressionism, and this room seemed to be the consummate setting to execute these ideas. I wanted to get my hands dirty, stalk the canvas, and get as primal as possible in creating something that didn't just lay lifeless but moved, that seemed like it was shifting to find a voice. It came easily. I'd even say it came naturally. The very first things I did weren't bad. In fact, some of the larger 60-by-48-inch pieces were invested with techniques that showed a sense of individuality. I was completely aware that, as with all things creative, we are prone to start out by imitating the originators. While it's a compliment to them, it is ultimately a derivative of someone else and, while not exactly plagiarism, is hardly satisfying.

If I was a little too close to anyone in some of my preliminary pieces it would have to be Hans Hofmann. Much of my work had the same blocky configurations and standard colors associated with the great master, although I did my best to utilize some elements that took a detour from outright piracy. One tactic I'd discovered was using paint rollers to create a different texture than brushes. Rollers also had a completely different way of combining color and distributing oil and acrylic, resulting in a far more compelling blend.

One morning in Los Angeles, Heather was having breakfast at Le Pain Quotidien on Melrose Avenue when she heard my name mentioned in a conversation at a table nearby. The discussion was centered on art, and when one of the three men happened to bring up that they'd heard good reports of my work, Heather was all ears. It became apparent that he was interested in representation, and that the motive was to get in touch and get a look at the goods. Her interest piqued, my wife said, "Excuse me, but I believe you're talking about my husband." And with that, doors opened and a whole new era dawned.

The man in question was Daniel Crosby, a veteran of the '80s art scene in New York who had worked his way up through the ranks to become the youngest president of Martin Lawrence Galleries, the premier gallery chain in the United States. Along the way, Daniel had represented and published some of the world's most recognizable artists; from Andy Warhol and Keith Haring to Hiro Yamagata, Mark Kostabi, and Jean-Michel Basquiat.

From our very first meeting, I knew this guy was the genuine article. He not only "got" my work, he understood my concerns and was encouraging as well as knowledgeable in all areas pertaining to marketing and sales. He was also a gregarious, fun guy who had a story for every occasion and a seemingly inexhaustible arsenal of anecdotes. He was wonderful company and very soon became one of my handful of best friends. In time we would travel together regularly and extensively, not only on business to gallery shows and art fairs, but simply for the enjoyment of each other's company. He was also a big, broad, strong guy who excelled in mixed martial arts, an attribute that would prove invaluable when gallery shows were crowded and folks became a little overenthusiastic. Daniel, just standing beside me, gave off a protective vibe rather than a representative one, which at times could be most comforting.

On a business level, he interacted perfectly with Heather, which laid the groundwork for a great team. Off the bat, while somewhat mercenary in its objective, we hooked up with a company that created pop-up shows across the US. These shows, while not up to the level of respectability I was striving for, proved to be remarkably successful. We sold a lot of paintings and created a buzz that in time would create a ripple of interest, eventually leading to a more credible regard.

My breakthrough came with *Plain Brown Wrapper*, a 60-by-48-inch piece I created in 2015. While there had been works previously that I liked and felt had merit, this was the first time that I had created something that was wholly original and unadorned by outside influence. It was stark: a canvas wallpapered in newsprint, wood stained and varnished, the whole thing strung in a latticework of conventional twine and sprayed in a spider webbing of aerosol glue. The effect was intriguing and played on the mystery of illicit commercialism and unknown entities. I liked it, it was liberating, and it sold the minute it was exhibited. It appeared I had found what I was looking for.

I called my new style "webbing & weaving" and began to play into variations on its genus. I all but gave up on brushes and paint in favor of power tools, found objects, and industrial components. I shopped at the hardware store and the lumberyard for art supplies, and joked that my workspace looked like a chop shop rather than a studio. I loved the physicality that came into play with the new work. I was no longer a painter; that terminology would never again be used to describe my work. It seemed like I'd established my signature component.

Sleeping Beauty was in the "webbing & weaving" style. Again it was 60 by 48, an American flag bound in twine and frosted in synthetic cobwebbing. Somehow it struck a nerve, perhaps through the title that intimates a simple interpretation. In his essay "Bernie Taupin's Visual Anthem," the arts writer and filmmaker Richard Bailey, MA, writes:

> In the folk tale, Sleeping Beauty dreams and waits until she can be awakened with a kiss. A kiss is a deeply romantic gesture and in mythology may also symbolize a promise or prayerful intercession.

It's no secret that the piece was done at the dawn of the Trump era, which led many (depending on your political leanings) to believe that no matter how bad things get, America always gets back on its feet. I'd like to believe that it was more broad ranging than that, more historical and braver than governmental nitpicking. Up to date, I have created fifteen singular versions of *Sleeping Beauty*, each one slightly different, each one bound in contrasting lattice-like configurations of string, twine, and twisted fabric. In 2020, I built a 25-by-12-foot wall consisting of twenty connecting and numbered versions of *Sleeping Beauty* as an installation for my retrospective at the Museum of Biblical Art in Dallas, Texas. In some ways, it was my last word on that particular title, although the medium has been reinvented into a fresh series of pyrotechnical work.

By 2015, I was creating in a prodigious frenzy and the flag was everywhere. I buried it in a scorched torn canvas and encased it in a Lucite sarcophagus. I layered ravaged sheets of burnt cardboard over it and scrawled the Preamble to the United States Constitution on it in primitive text. I affixed a dozen or so flags of varying sizes to a large oblong canvas, burnt holes all over it, sowed the gashes up crudely with twine, and poured heavy wax resin into the apertures. My most vigorous and involved piece was a sculpture entitled *American Burka*, a mummified mannequin stained into antiquity and wrapped in yards of rusted barbed wire and malleable metallic diversity, including padlocks, chicken wire, and a halo brace-like crown.

The next step was a whole other form of expression. While still favoring the technique of decomposing materials in destructive ways, I turned my attention to incorporating American roots music into the mix while maintaining the flag as a blooming motif among the debris. Preserving the heritage of consequential Americana had always been of the greatest importance to me. Not only had it served me well as an inspirational arsenal, it had quite simply been the music I'd always fallen back on when contemporary sounds began to chafe. It's why I developed, hosted, and produced a two-year run of my own show on SiriusXM. *American Roots Radio* had been a labor of love. I did the show gratis, recorded it at the ranch, programmed it from my personal library, and in one hundred episodes never played the same track twice. I talked extensively about obscure artists, shared (hopefully) incisive stories, and played every genre imaginable including Hawaiian slack-key guitar, Native American rock, and Hasidic comedy. It was an enjoyable period but, no matter how gratifying it proved, incredibly time-consuming. What I was doing now was a visual version of what the show set out to communicate.

There was a lot of fire involved and many instruments demolished. As the studio boom box blared out its usual eclectic mix, I would set to executing my intentions. Rows of guitars would be hung by their necks and blasted into blackened hulks by a welding torch before being dismembered by electric saws and hammers. Remnants large and small would be bolted and screwed into large three-quarter-inch panels that would then, depending on the artist or genre featured, be elaborated on with associated relics. This could be anything from faded portraits, fragments of vinyl, empty bottles, and, in the case of my 2019 piece *Clear Lake '59,* a pair of melted horn-rimmed glasses. In the course of time, I incorporated not just guitars both acoustic and electric but fiddles, banjos, mandolins, and even keyboards. And in the case of my 2019 piece *Pops* (a tip of the hat to Louis Armstrong), a rusting trumpet. Most, but not all, had the flag incorporated, a symbol of their ties to the nation that birthed their identity, my personal impression tying them to one unified force.

The first behemoth I assembled was a 48-by-72-by-8-inch piece called *I Do Not Play No Rock N Roll.* Based on Mississippi Fred McDowell's edgy 1969 album of the same name, it consists of eight deconstructed acoustic guitars, chicken wire, assorted ephemera, and coagulations of ash and wax. With the title of the piece graffitied in giant letters as a backdrop, it weighs about fifty-five pounds and looks like Fred McDowell's house fell down. For a short time it covered a wall on the second floor of the Bobby, a hotel in Nashville, until we reacquired it and sent it to be exhibited in different locations through-out the country. Between 2016 to 2020, I created over twenty-five of these homages, celebrating among others Link Wray, Jimmy Martin, Chuck Berry, Merle Haggard, Dick Dale, Lightnin' Hopkins, Cliff

Gallup, the Louvin Brothers, Maybelle Carter, Robert Johnson, and the Everly Brothers. In 2019, my justification for creating these pieces was acknowledged in the most perfect way possible when the Earl Scruggs Center in Shelby, North Carolina, acquired my 2018 work *He Will Set Your Fields on Fire*. The complex assemblage, including fiddle, banjo, and mandolin, salutes not only Lester Flatt and Earl Scruggs but the bluegrass genre in general. It is featured in a specially created permanent installation and remains one of my proudest artistic contributions.

Along with creating the giant wall of *Sleeping Beauty(s)* for the Dallas museum show, I was asked if I would consider doing a large original freestanding piece to be used as a focal point for the center of the museum's main floor. Realizing I had perhaps come to the end of my tenure with what I was now referring to as "musical archeology," I acceded, feeling that this might be the opportunity to retreat from this style with a big bang. It turned out that the "big bang" was all the inspiration I needed. The "big bang" in question being the Bristol Sessions that took place in Bristol, Tennessee, in 1927. Often considered by some as the moment in musical history when country music was born, it involved the field recording of various hopefuls looking for a break. They were conducted by the eminent music producer Ralph Peer and introduced to the world two of country's fabled architects: the great Jimmie Rodgers and the equally prodigious Carter Family. What I created was *Excavating State Street, Bristol Tennessee*, a 48-by-40-by-42-inch assemblage described by Richard Bailey, MA, as:

> The sculpture *Excavating State Street, Bristol Tennessee* is like an altar in a fabled ruin. Bristol has been called the "Big Bang" of country music, and indeed the sculpture looks as if a bomb recently went off. Several hurt guitars are piled up. There is one that stands upright, scorched but resilient. It is the designated mourner, a tower of hope and remembrance. In 1998, Congress declared Bristol the birthplace of country music. Perhaps that congressional act is signaled by the U.S. flags that poke through the broken places of the guitars like strange fluorescence. The sculpture's scorched state and partial flags suggest the Alfred P. Murrah Federal Building and the World Trade Center. The guitars in

Excavating State Street have lost their strings and are silent. But they are still recognizable as guitars; their curves remain the embodiment of song. The funerary sense of this sculpture is given a national scale for the appearance of the flag. That the flags seem to be blooming in wounded places suggest the possibility of enrichment after loss. The viewer might abhor what happened to the guitars, but might also feel some sense of purpose in the flags.

The methodology of dead guitars and the prominence of flags in my work most likely ended with *Excavating State Street*. The flag, however, will more than likely continue to remain prominent, since it is a friend I'm not ready to part ways with anytime soon. In fact, I expounded on my connection with it at length in an essay. I composed it for the accompanying catalog for an exhibition I did at the Callanwolde Fine Arts Center in Atlanta, Georgia. I wanted something that was my definitive statement on the subject. Before this book shut me down temporarily, I was already experimenting in the polar opposite of the muted textures of my "musical archaeology" by reinstating paint, making psychedelic formations created with highly fluid liquid colors onto stacked configurations of found objects.

From as early as 2013, my work was and would be shown at art fairs and galleries nationwide. There were annual fairs in New York, Miami, Aspen, Palm Springs, and San Francisco along with featured exhibitions at Waterhouse & Dodd on Madison Avenue, the Bill Lowe Gallery in Atlanta, Galerie Michael on Rodeo Drive, Chase Contemporary in Chelsea, and Mark Borghi Fine Art in Bridgehampton, New York. Much of this is thanks to my curator, Dana Yarger, who Daniel brought on board to run things on an everyday basis, communicating directly with Heather and Daniel, overseeing installations, briefing sales staff, and writing delightfully rambling emails. Coming out of an education in environmental science and engineering, Dana started collecting art and operating galleries in California in the 1980s. Dedicated to representing artists and curating and producing exhibitions, his work had taken him worldwide not only through the United States but to Europe, Asia, and the Middle East. One of the most endearing things about Dana is that he is completely nescient in regard to music. I was sold on him immediately when I realized he had no idea that I was established in the music world and that he was drawn to my visual art for its merit alone.

The elephant in this room, of course, will always be the stigma of "celebrity art." It is a term I loathe; it's demeaning, obtuse, and asinine, and simply invites knives to be drawn. It brings up the whole issue of legitimacy and fuels critics and elitists with dismissive venom. Personally, I got over it long ago, although surprisingly enough I've never suffered from any negativity, having hopefully conducted the diversity of my expressions with a degree of ethical respect. I once said somewhere that "Music and art is an inevitable collision. I've always maintained that music is sonic art for the ears and that artwork for the eyes, it's ridiculous to assume that the two can't exist in the same vortex."

Visual art, not unlike rock and roll, is undoubtedly the most over-analyzed, not to say overintellectualized, creative medium. If Turner was the godfather of Abstract Expressionism, then Vasily Kandinsky is his punk equivalent. He was the first person to really go the whole nine yards and set the wheels in motion. He was magnificent and, along with Anselm Kiefer and Richard Rauschenberg, remains heroic in the realm of my cherished provocateurs. Kandinsky also saw the correlation between music and art saying, "Music is the ultimate teacher. Painting is 'visual music' with colors being like sounds." I'll take my lead from Kandinsky over some bilious critic and leave it at that.

AM I A Christian? Yes, I am, although born again is not a term I'm comfortable with. It always sounded cultish, and too much like some fad from the '80s. Besides, I was never not a believer, I just drifted away from the denomination I'd been raised in. There was no vitality in the Catholic church I attended as a child. It was drab and stuffy, overly pious, and centered on a droning, unenthusiastic sermon conducted by a charisma-free priest. The nuns weren't too likable either, my earliest schooldays populated by starchy, unpleasant sisters picking you up by your sideburns and whacking you on the back of the head with a ruler.

In fact, the only pleasant memory I have of Catholicism was a ruddy-faced old Irish priest who'd stop by the house every couple of weeks to share a smoke from a pack of Woodbines and a glass of whisky. Big and jovial, he seemed the only one of his kind I was familiar with who saw Jesus as someone more approachable than his dour brethren would have me believe. Even in my preteen years, and with my limited grasp on theology, the emphasis on wrath and retribution far outweighed the presence of a benevolent God. As I grew older, I grew away, confused and disillusioned by the grandiose religiosity of the Roman Catholic Church.

Let me emphasize that I am deeply in love with a great cathedral and awed by their architecture, but back in my formative years the Vatican City looked like El Dorado. So much gold and ostentatious pomp and circumstance that I wasn't sure how it related to a guy who lived his life in abject poverty. One candlestick could feed a third world country, and if the meek were indeed going to inherit the earth, then how was that going to pan out for the papal gang?

Religion. This single word, which on the human highway and in social circles of indiscriminate numbers, has taken on the mantle of averted eyes, raised hackles, and much wringing of hands. I was always more than a little perplexed. I was never intentionally in the closet about my beliefs. I guess no one ever thought to ask. I never had a St. Peter moment and denied my views; I just didn't have a church and regarded myself for many years as an unconventional Christian. Of course, this theology is a complete cop-out, and in due course, on my road to a better understanding, realized people either are or are not, and there is no middle ground. I began to take a stand, and in my darkest moments I'd find myself taking solace in, not traditional prayer, but a befriending of whatever celestial comfort I could find between lucidity and depravation, and it was, undoubtedly, a conversation worth having. Falling back on the Holy Spirit was better than any other alternative.

I was irritated by ignorance, especially the ineptitude that came along with the easy ennui associated with superficial omniscience. It just seemed so easy to malign something that the perpetrators knew would not be contradicted in their dogmatic circles. Segregated from any critical blowback, they felt imperviously immune. In this way, I witnessed much that, to my mind, was as illogical as most of the detractors' observations.

One of Heather's finest attributes was her faith. It wasn't just admirable, it was attractive and completely captivating. It wasn't blind faith; on the contrary, it came with none of the baggage associated with caricature. It was unswerving and knowledgeable, devoid of predictability and never remotely paradoxical in nature. I wanted what she had, that sort of compassion and understanding, free of pious inequality and liberating in ethical diversity. Bob Marley sang, *There ain't no hiding place from the Father of Creation*, and while I'd never been hiding out, I'd always been searching. Heather, with no strong-arm tactics on her part, simply let me observe and enter into things of my own accord. It was rehab for the soul, and Presbyterianism was the answer. A far cry from my childhood and the grim opulence and rigid veneration of 1950s Catholicism, this had a simplicity and joy I could relate to. Here was a God with a sense of humor (witness the giraffe and Kenny G), one who I could talk to without being engulfed in brimstone. I owed the Lord my life, and besides through the past decades my muse had frequently led me to the well of the Scriptures.

If we're going to delve into semantics, the Bible is the lyricist's best crib sheet. Leonard Cohen's catalog was the Good Book in itself, and lest we forget, Bob Dylan, arguably rock's greatest magpie, has plundered it mercilessly. Witness my career in writing. It's completely littered with religious references, many of them dealing with conflicted protagonists wrestling with non-secular issues. "Where to Now St. Peter?," "Levon," "All the Girls Love Alice," and "Ticking" are examples of this while "Salvation," "Grey Seal," "Religion," "Cry to Heaven," and "Answer in the Sky" dwell on more positive aspects. Being an equal opportunity lyricist, I wasn't without internalized corruption and even gave the devil five and half minutes in "Chasing the Crown."

"Imagine no religion" and aside from wiping out an enormous amount of the world's greatest paintings, historical architecture, and classical music, we'd be seriously short a few rock staples. For example, no

"Sympathy for the Devil," "Highway 61 Revisited," and "Hallelujah." No "God Only Knows," "Turn! Turn! Turn!," "Exodus," and a lot of U2. Great movies like Pasolini's *The Gospel According to St Matthew*, Dreyer's *The Passion of Joan of Arc*, and Powell and Pressburger's *Black Narcissus*, all the way down to cool creepy stuff like *The Exorcist* and *The Omen*. Oh, and sorry kids, no Christmas and Easter, and one less way to protect yourself against vampires! Sermon over.

WITH THE INTRODUCTION of partners who transcended a multitude of brief interludes and extended excursions, both Elton and I found our anchors. In 1993, Elton met Canadian filmmaker and former advertising executive, David Furnish. Entering into a civil partnership in 2005, they eventually married when same-sex marriage became legal in 2014. They have fathered two sons through surrogacy, Zachary in 2010 and Elijah in 2013, and have, as I write this, been devoted to each other for over thirty years.

The parallels between us are uncanny: Elton, finding happiness after innumerable years in a wilderness of addiction and unfulfilled relationships, and me doing the same. While I'd describe my journey as more of a learning curve, we each have in our own way struck compatibility gold.

The beneficiaries of gracious good fortune, we had seen our relationships follow similar paths. He had two sons, I had two daughters. He had a bright, savvy, and personable husband in David, and I had a bright, savvy, and personable wife in Heather. It was inevitable, as our corresponding relationships developed, that David and Heather would take on considerably more active roles in the day-to-day running of our ongoing careers. What this did was create a family collective, a protective in-house consortium void of overzealous percentage takers. It also weeded out the deadwood and, certainly in my case, dispensed with certain elements who were happy to take advantage or, who in some areas, were just plain incompetent. With David managing all aspects of Elton's career, as well as serving as co-chief of Rocket Pictures, and Heather functioning as the sole representative for all facets of mine, we finally reached a place where in-house fighting and peripheral egos were a thing of the past.

OK, THIS IS the happily ever after bit, which in actuality is pretty much the truth. The ranch had served its purpose after almost twenty-five years, and with my retirement from riding and competition its expansive acreage and spacious equine facilities seemed like a completely unnecessary financial burden. I'd gaze down on the panorama of the entire property devoid of horses and ranch personnel and fret over the abundant emptiness. It would be tragic to let it fall into disrepair and it was insane to maintain it when no one was utilizing it. It made no sense to keep it all ticking along for Charley, who was not even stabling her horse there but down the road at an alternate training facility. She had alleviated me of any fears that she might lose interest in the culture that I had so aspired to, and was, if anything, more determined to become a competitor in her own right.

The property was beginning to feel like a monkey on my back, and as I was getting older I yearned for something simpler and easier to maintain. I wanted manageability and yearned to downsize. No matter my financial capabilities, I was never the kind of guy who either needed or desired multiple properties and palatial homes. Not that I looked down my nose on that way of living, on the contrary I was immensely impressed by anyone who could orchestrate such a thing. Part of me enjoyed afforded leisure and the perks success brings, but deep down when it came to hearth and home, I was still a small-town country boy.

We sold the ranch in 2018 and moved into a small magical house tucked into a cul-de-sac in a quaint neighborhood. Only fifteen minutes from the ranch, it was a stress-free dream. With moderate renovation we turned it into an oasis of light and airiness, the generous French doors leading onto a congenial patio perfumed by orange blossoms and fronted by a delightful old-fashioned garden full of bay leaf and olive trees, rosemary bushes, and diverse wild flowers. Fruit trees bearing peaches, pomegranates, plums, figs, grapefruit, and tangerines were dotted over a compact acre while herbs, tomatoes, and rhubarb thrived in tidy irradiant spots.

The kids were coming completely into their own and evolving into the personalities they had shown inklings of from day one. Charley, as noted, had become not just proficient in her horsemanship but had surpassed me in every element of knowledgeability and aptitude. She was a 100 percent dyed-in-the-wool cowgirl and, once she turned sixteen and obtained her driver's license, was hauling a three-horse trailer and living quarters. Her rate of maturity was phenomenal, and her expertise in her chosen events of barrel racing and pole bending was impressive, not only in her triumphs but in her gutsy overall attitude. It was a satisfying alternative, whereas I had had to divide my time between three different worlds, Charley inhabited just one 24/7. "Hey, Charley, ya wanna go to Paris for a week?"

"No, thanks, I've got a rodeo in Chowchilla."

That about sums it up.

If Charley had embraced one of these worlds, Georgey was no less proficient in the one that might well be deemed my day job. While my art career was on the rise, no one was ever going to concede to the fact that songwriting wasn't what had afforded me all the other opportunities. She wasn't writing songs, but she was full-on into entertainment in varying degrees of capability. Petite and assured, she had started flamenco dancing at the age of five and by ten years old became the Junior Spirit of Santa Barbara's Old Spanish Days Fiesta. Locally, this is a tremendous honor and entails hours of precision training and dedication in order to simply make the grade. Flamenco is classic in its choreography and passionate in its execution. Georgey was a natural, dancing with sophisticated fire and flawless traditionalism. Witnessing her win this coveted accolade, and then dance on the mission steps before five thousand cheering locals, was a tear-inducing night to remember. Georgey is simply stunning, not only in her beauty but in her overall attitude and comportment. She is a perfectionist, meticulous, punctual, and socially exquisite in all areas of design and skill. She plays piano, is active in local theater productions, has her own home-baked cookie company, does a little ballet on the side to keep her chops in, and is only fourteen (at the time of writing). Homeschooled since they began their education, they are scholastically advanced (COVID-19 never derailing them for a second) and are my pride and joy. I don't like to stop and think how lucky I am lest by chance it's all a dream and I'll wake up as someone else.

The Santa Ynez Valley is still quintessentially small-town America. I've lived here for over thirty years and have undoubtedly earned my gold watch as an established resident. They still wash your windows and pump your gas at the local Chevron, the coffee shop knows what I want without asking, and I know everyone on a first-name basis at the local market. I'm indebted to it and its inhabitants for giving me a stable and concurrently ordinary life. Everyone knows who I am, yet no one panders or fawns. I might garner a little extra attention, but in every other way I'm just another neighbor. They're hardworking, good-natured people intrinsically patriotic in their respect for American tradition. Horses and wine are king, and LA is a foreign country whose incoming consumers are viewed suspiciously. Gentrification is not a word they use, but forsaking the one they might use it's a better alternative.

It isn't heavy on celebrity, but they're here. Mostly actors, musicians, and kings of industry. There are those who were here before me and those who have passed away. Several were a delight. They include the dapper John Forsythe, who played patriarch Blake Carrington in *Dynasty* and Charles Townsend in *Charlie's Angels*; disk jockey, concert promoter, and game show host Bob Eubanks, whose credits include *The Beatles at the Hollywood Bowl* and *The Newlywed Game*; and prolific independent film producer Ray Stark. Back in the '90s, Ray, who incidentally had a staggering art collection including works by Picasso and Kandinsky, would invite me over to drink vodka with Kirk Douglas. For some reason, Kirk took a shine to me and once he realized I was a Grey Goose man decided I was his designated drinking buddy. He was gregarious company and told wonderful stories, or least I think he did.

The other area I lucked into after leaving the ranch was a studio in which to construct my art work. What I got gratis, care of my contractor, was warehouse space in an abandoned mill and lumberyard five minutes from the house. It was absolutely perfect, accessible, funky, and big enough to work on several pieces simultaneously. The surrounding buildings were a wrecked and dilapidated group of skeletal structures composed of wonderfully inspirational materials. Roofs of naturally patinaed tin and collapsed sidings of moss-stained and corroded wood panels, all tailor made for the kind of deconstructed and distressed wall sculptures I was producing.

Representing indestructible age and defiance, the completed pieces were a testament to music's long historic road. Unwilling to go gentle into the good night, they push back against the inviting earth, ravaged and scarred by flame and antiquity, the very mirror image of what it means to really live.

I consider myself lucky. Fifty-five years ago I was incinerating decomposing chickens and breaking into condom machines for loose change. Life has afforded me many opportunities. It has also thrown up roadblocks, warning signs, and scary monsters. I have taken detours into venturesome territory and tasted bitter fruit. I'd like to say I wouldn't change a thing, and for the most part that's true. At the same time, I consider it all one long life lesson, a sort of *The Pilgrim's Progress* without the allegory and in name only. If there is any similarity at all, it's in the individuals I've encountered on my journey. Some are celebrated, many aren't. Those who aren't are equally interesting, and at times more so than their storied counterparts. Clearly though, in this travelogue, one character stands out. He's the most colorful, constant, and omnipresent. He's been a staff to lean on, a most excellent musical conduit, and comes replete with massive benevolence. He is also in absentia for much of this narrative. We may be two sides of the same coin, but the minute we were flipped into orbit, the trajectory of our ascent, while remaining integrated, split the yin and yang. There are several aphorisms for what we are, but alike we are not, and that is our magic. Still, he is an eternal love and perhaps the reason I got to write this book.

Epilogue

He crests the ridge and hunkers low, hands crossed on the pommel. The lathered horse snorts and shudders, throwing its head, the saddle heaves, the tack rattles and slaps, he squints into the horizon. He's ridden hard and far, the terrain behind him littered with brittle bones and carrion, poisonous creek beds and dead towns full of tumbleweeds and dust evaporating into the prairie like the lost fortunes of foolish men. He has heard the night song of coyotes, the thunderous roar of moving cattle and seen the howling ghosts of gunfighters in his dreams. Unapologetic in his recklessness, the ramifications of hard drinking are at play in the lines of his sand-ravaged face. He has ridden out of Purgatory and has been delivered. In the distance is a calmer, greener nature, a small town, and a trickling river. There is a bridge, a simple stone crossing. On the far side a small boy wields a stick fashioned into a sword. He does battle with the air, vanquishing an invisible foe. It is how he once saw himself as a child. The cowboy smiles, tips his hat, and turns away.

Acknowledgments

I am indebted to a small group of individuals for aiding and assisting me in my rusty chronological deficiency. They are as follows:

Robert Appere, Randy Bernard, Shaun Cassidy, Sheryl and Alice Cooper, Daniel Crosby, Jacqueline Dixon, Bob Ezrin, Shaun Gleason, Shep Gordon, Stephanie Haymes Roven, Michael Hewitson, James Newton Howard, Davey Johnstone, Eddie Kerkhofs, David Larkham, Mark Paladino, Loree Rodkin, Tony Taupin, and Dana Yarger.

Many thanks to Gina Vaisey for her invaluable assistance and to Ben Schafer and Jake Lingwood for their suggestions and editing skills.

Last but by no means least, I'm indebted to my literary agent, Zoe Sandler, who has a place in this book and a place in my heart.

Song Credits

"The Whores of Paris"
Bernard J.P. Taupin, (Dennis Tufano)
Universal PolyGram Int. Publishing, Inc. on behalf of Little Mole Music
©Tufano Tunes

"One Love"
Bob Marley
Irish Town Songs on behalf of Fifty Six Hope Road Music Ltd. and Primary Wave/Blue Mountain

"Carolyn"
© 1981 Sony Music Publishing (US) LLC.
All rights administered by Sony Music Publishing (US) LLC, 424 Church Street Suite 1200, Nashville, TN 37219.
All rights reserved. Used by permission.

Elton John/Bernie Taupin songs
"Mona Lisas and Mad Hatters"
"Blues Never Fade Away"
"The Bridge"
"Sorry Seems to Be the Hardest Word"
"Madman Across the Water"
"Sacrifice"

"Two Rooms at the End of the World"
"Simple Life"
"Gone to Shiloh"
Elton John, Bernard J.P. Taupin
Universal Songs of PolyGram Int., Inc., on behalf of Universal/Dick James Music Ltd.